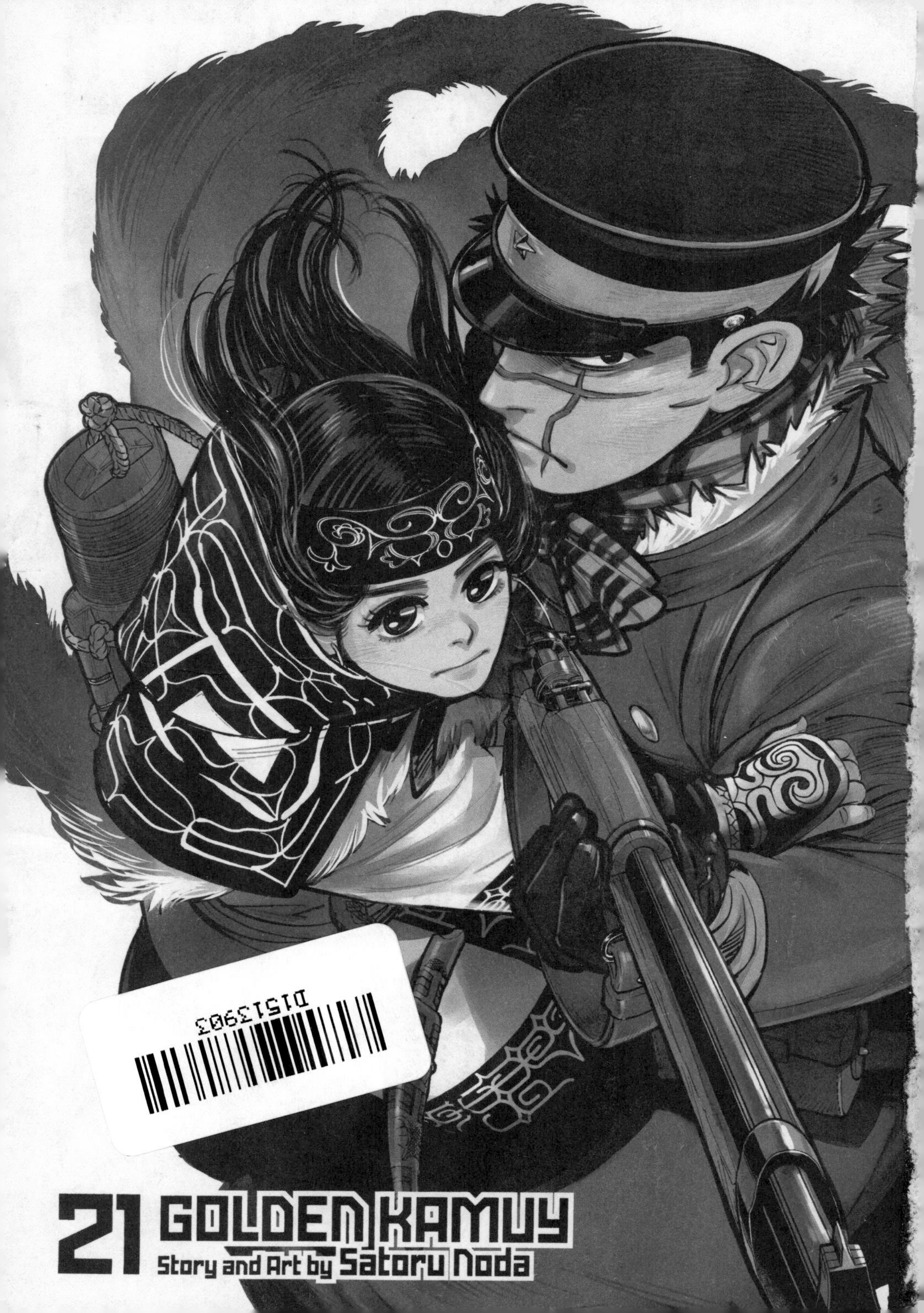

21 GOLDEN KAMUY

Story and Art by Satoru Noda

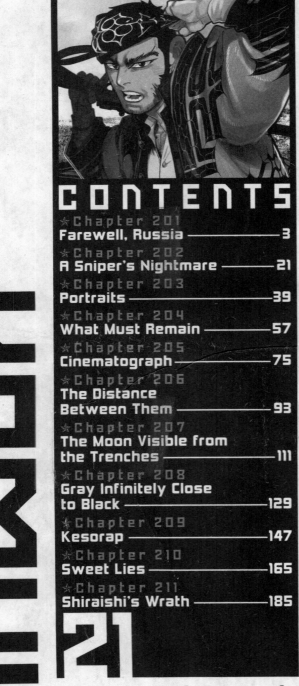

CONTENTS

★Chapter 201
Farewell, Russia —————— 3

★Chapter 202
A Sniper's Nightmare —————— 21

★Chapter 203
Portraits —————— 39

★Chapter 204
What Must Remain —————— 57

★Chapter 205
Cinematograph —————— 75

★Chapter 206
**The Distance
Between Them** —————— 93

★Chapter 207
**The Moon Visible from
the Trenches** —————— 111

★Chapter 208
**Gray Infinitely Close
to Black** —————— 129

★Chapter 209
Kesorap —————— 147

★Chapter 210
Sweet Lies —————— 165

★Chapter 211
Shiraishi's Wrath —————— 185

GOLDEN KAMUY

21

Story and Art by **Satoru Noda**

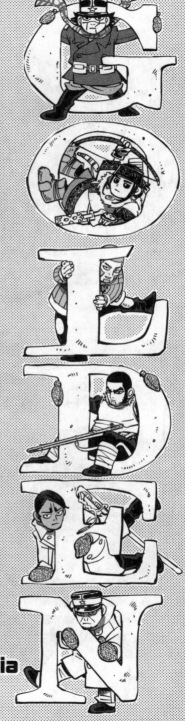

Chapter 201: Farewell, Russia

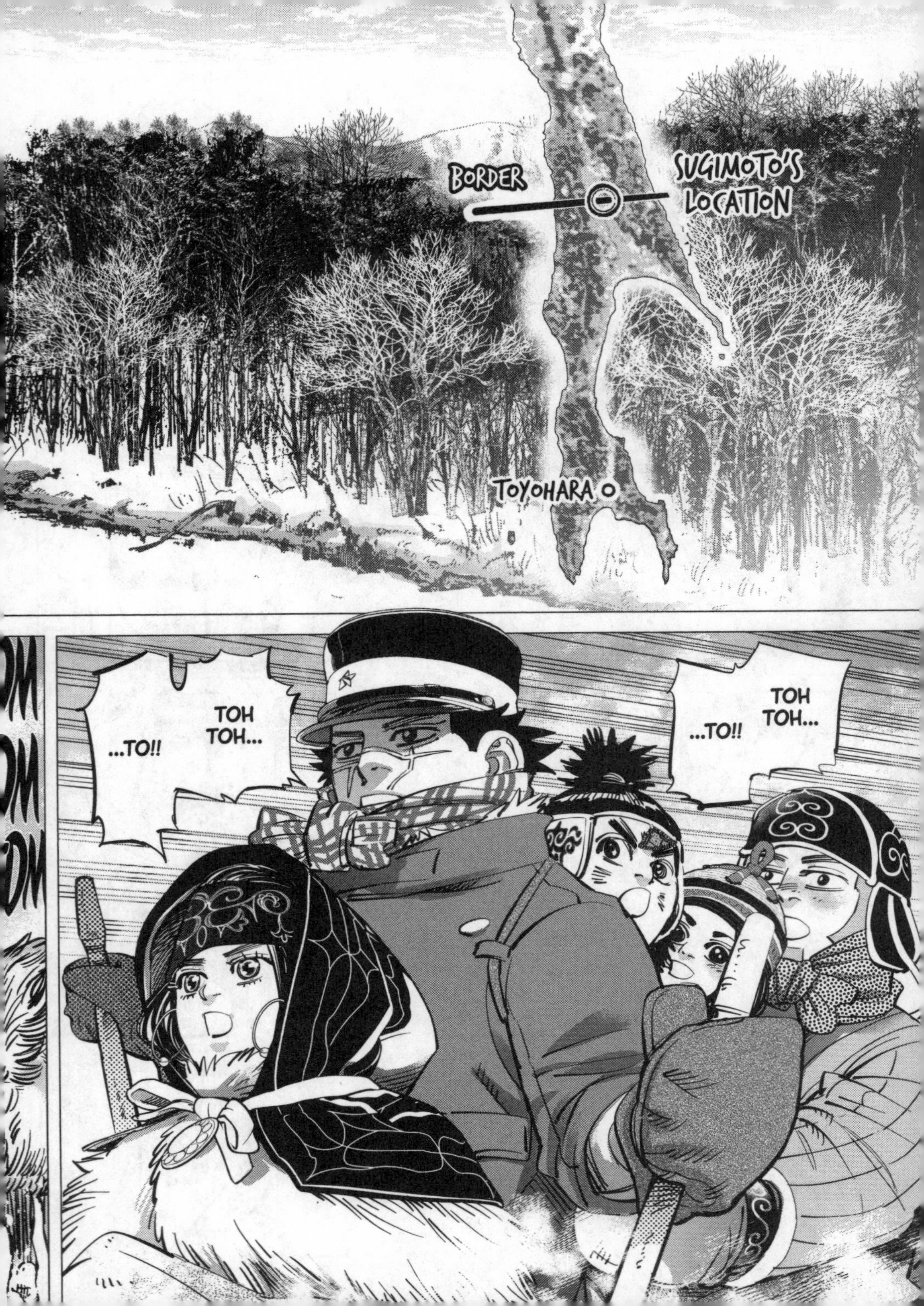

SUGIMOTO'S LOCATION
BORDER
TOYOHARA
TOH TOH... ...TO!!
TOH TOH... ...TO!!

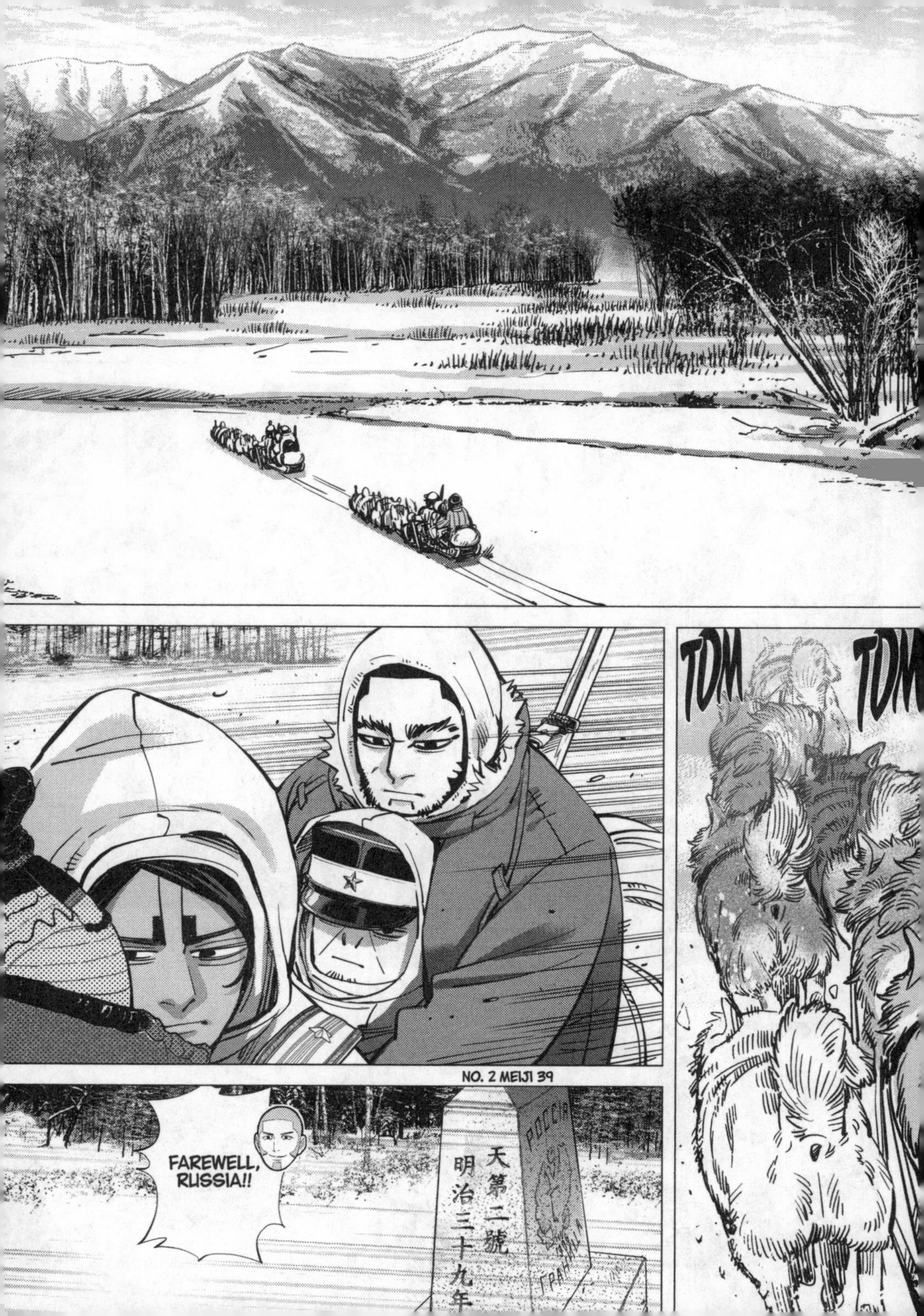
TOM
TOM
NO. 2 MEIJI 39
天第二號
明治三十九年
FAREWELL, RUSSIA!!

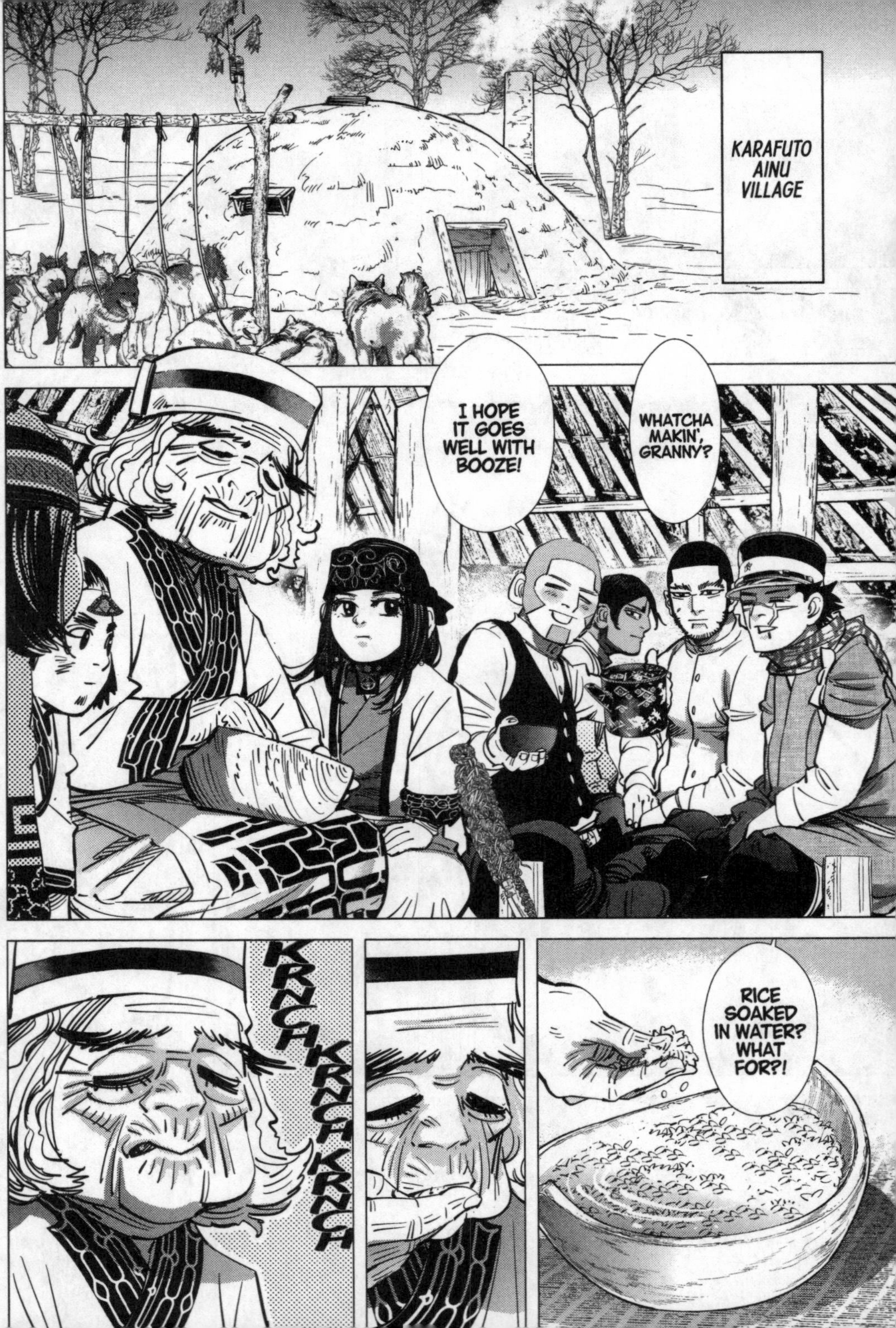
KARAFUTO AINU VILLAGE
WHATCHA MAKIN', GRANNY?
I HOPE IT GOES WELL WITH BOOZE!
RICE SOAKED IN WATER? WHAT FOR?!
KRNCH KRNCH KRNCH

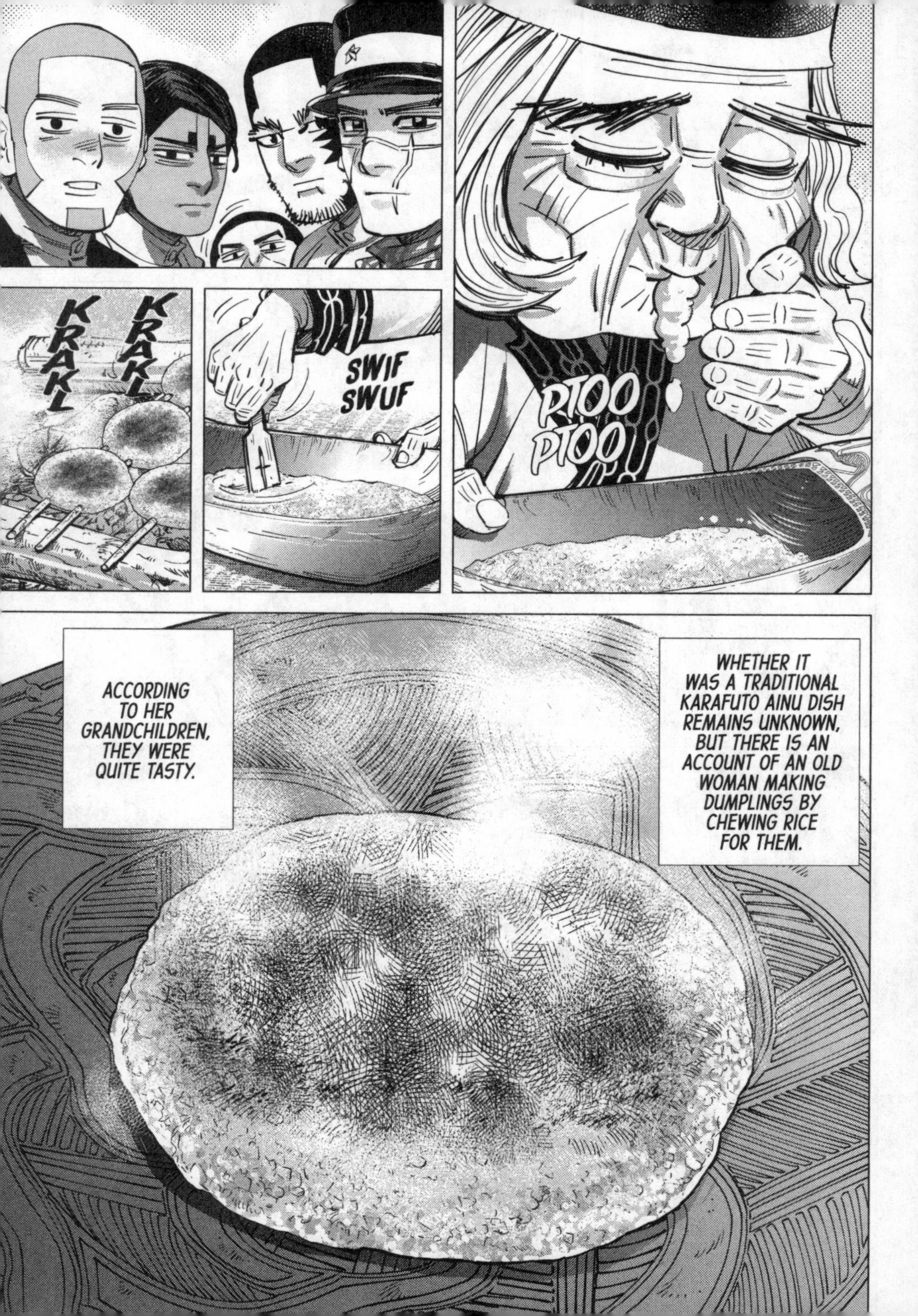
PTOO
PTOO
SWIF
SWUF
KRAKL
KRAKL
WHETHER IT WAS A TRADITIONAL KARAFUTO AINU DISH REMAINS UNKNOWN, BUT THERE IS AN ACCOUNT OF AN OLD WOMAN MAKING DUMPLINGS BY CHEWING RICE FOR THEM.
ACCORDING TO HER GRANDCHILDREN, THEY WERE QUITE TASTY.

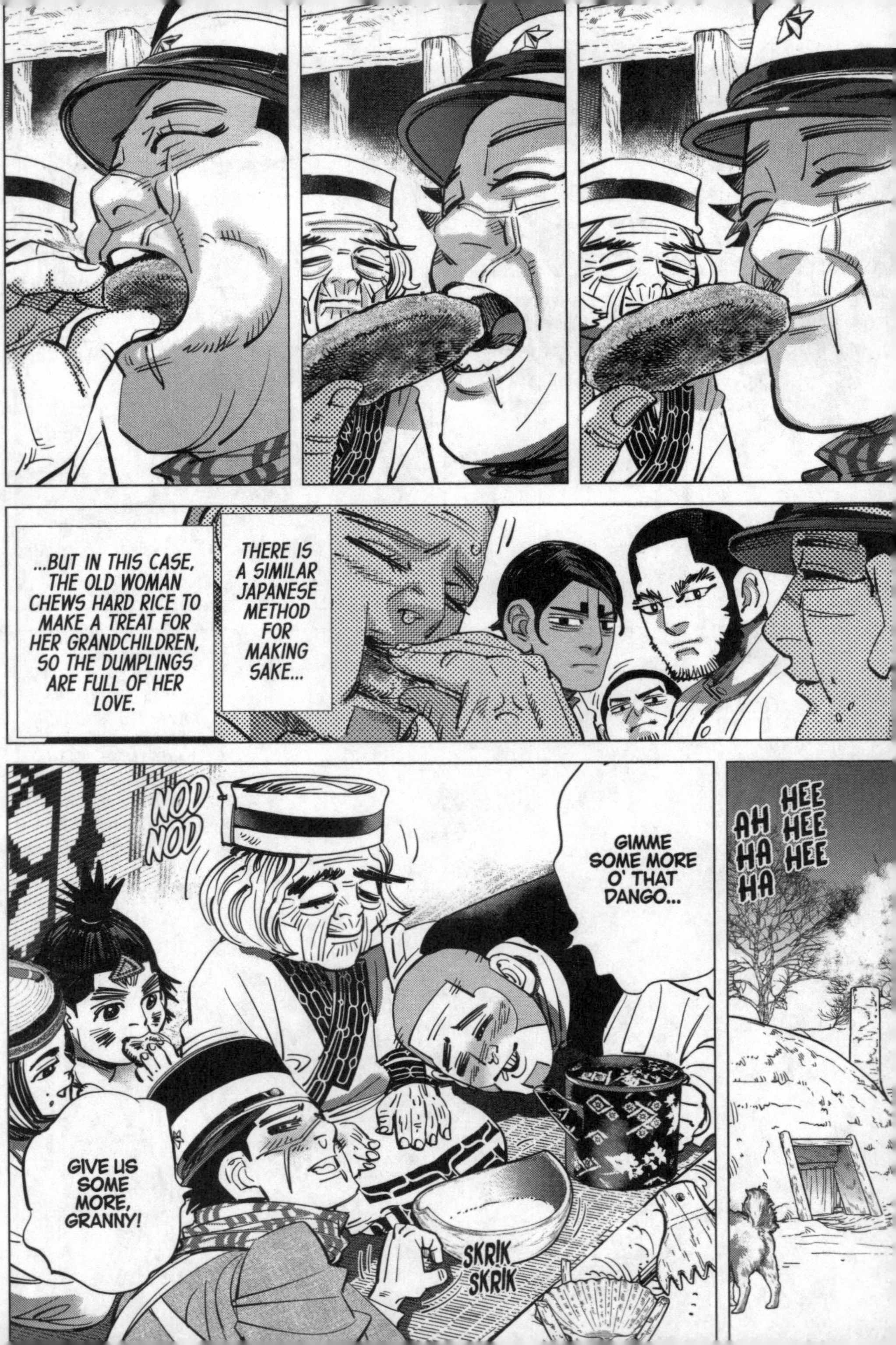
THERE IS A SIMILAR JAPANESE METHOD FOR MAKING SAKE...
...BUT IN THIS CASE, THE OLD WOMAN CHEWS HARD RICE TO MAKE A TREAT FOR HER GRANDCHILDREN, SO THE DUMPLINGS ARE FULL OF HER LOVE.
HEE HEE HEE
AH HA HA HA
GIMME SOME MORE O' THAT DANGO...
NOD NOD
GIVE US SOME MORE, GRANNY!
SKRIK SKRIK

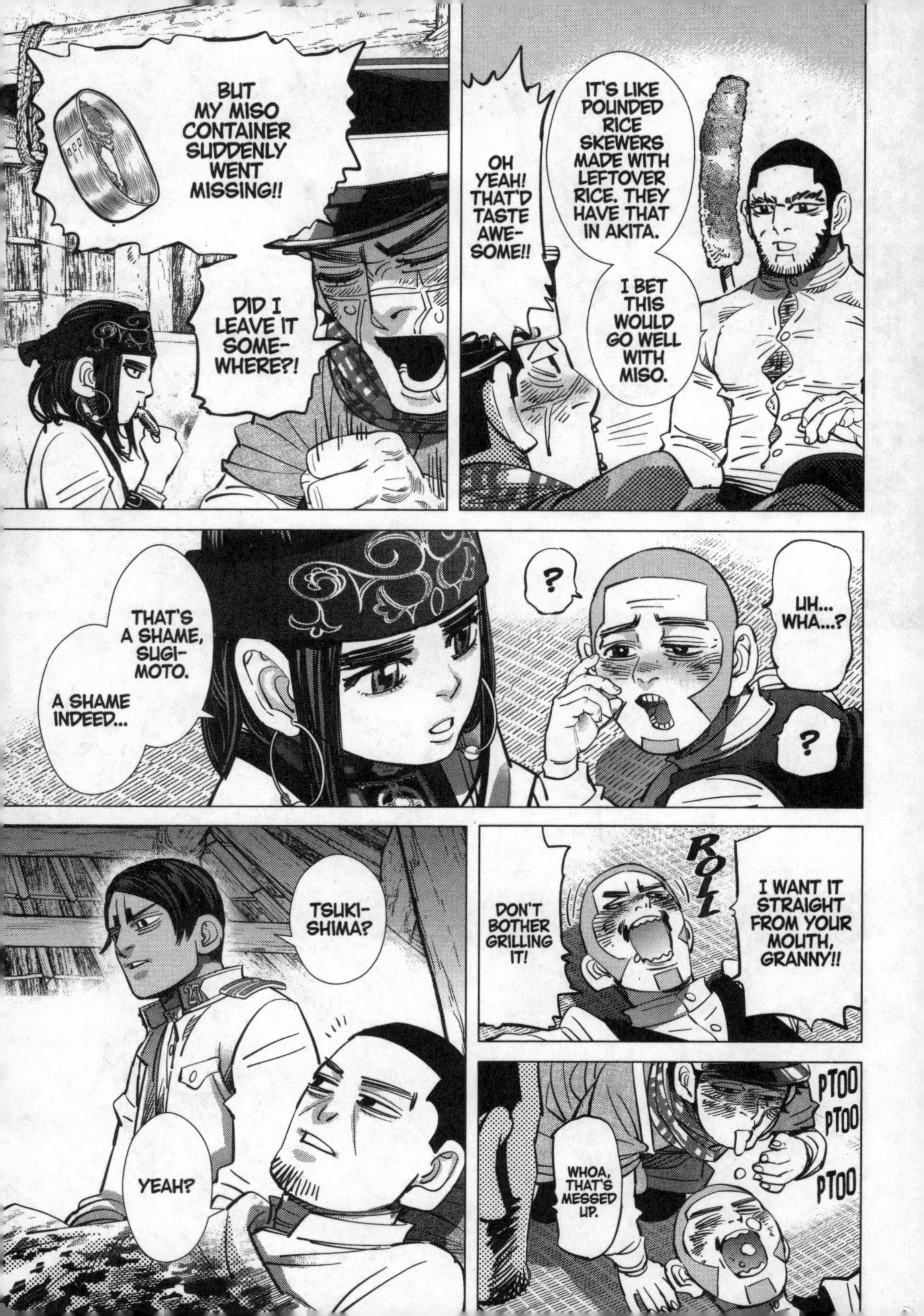
IT'S LIKE POUNDED RICE SKEWERS MADE WITH LEFTOVER RICE. THEY HAVE THAT IN AKITA.
OH YEAH! THAT'D TASTE AWE-SOME!!
I BET THIS WOULD GO WELL WITH MISO.
BUT MY MISO CONTAINER SUDDENLY WENT MISSING!!
DID I LEAVE IT SOME-WHERE?!
UH... WHA...?
?
?
THAT'S A SHAME, SUGI-MOTO.
A SHAME INDEED...
I WANT IT STRAIGHT FROM YOUR MOUTH, GRANNY!!
ROLL
DON'T BOTHER GRILLING IT!
PTOO
PTOO
PTOO
WHOA, THAT'S MESSED UP.
TSUKI-SHIMA?
YEAH?

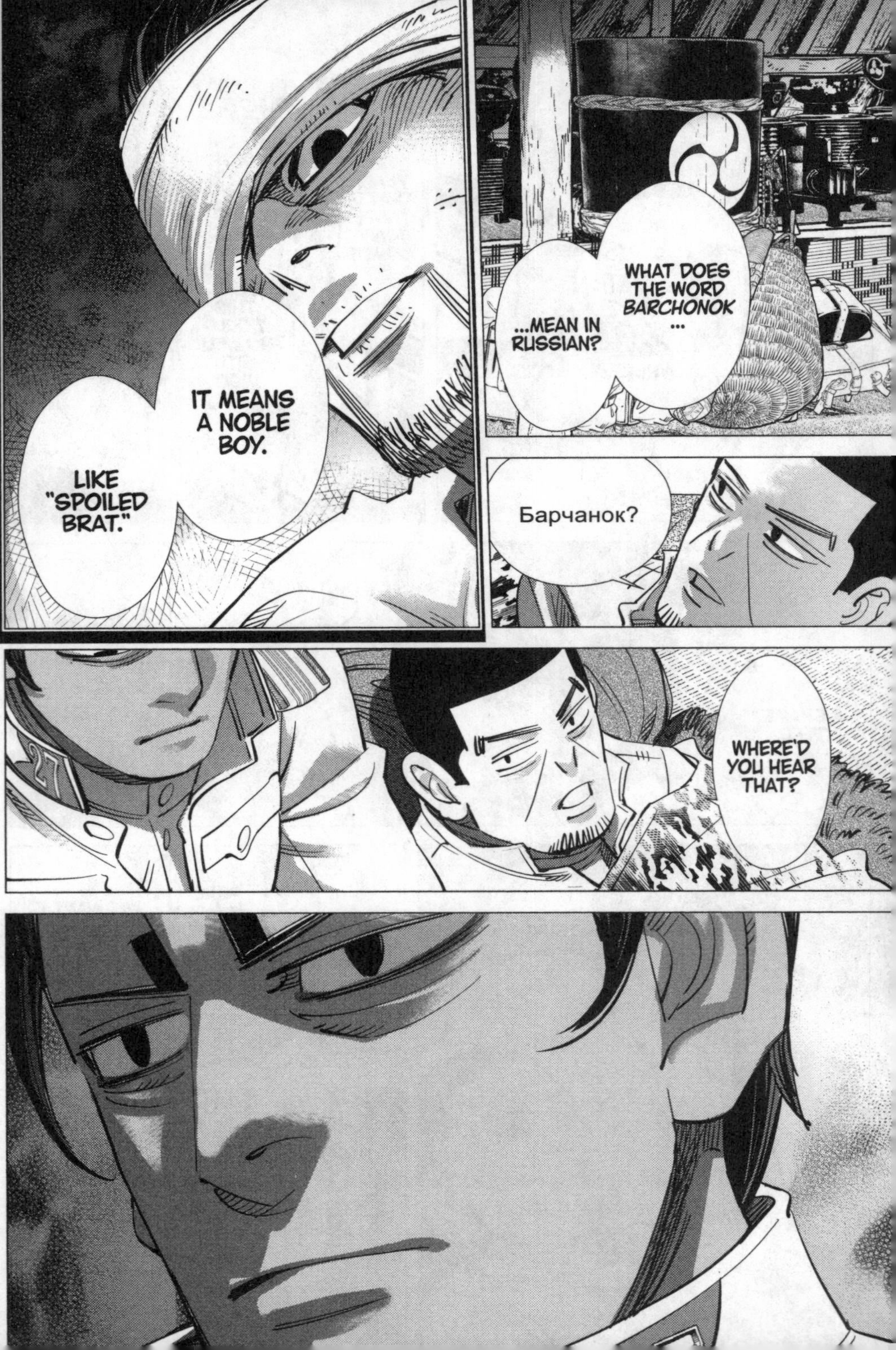
WHAT DOES THE WORD BARCHONOK ...
...MEAN IN RUSSIAN?
Барчанок?
IT MEANS A NOBLE BOY.
LIKE "SPOILED BRAT."
WHERE'D YOU HEAR THAT?

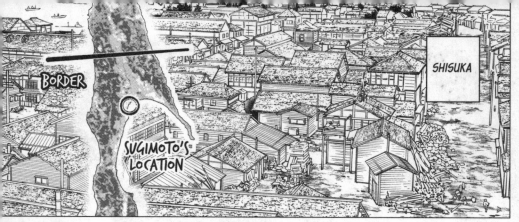

BORDER

SUGIMOTO'S
LOCATION

SHISUKA

BUYING
NECESSITIES

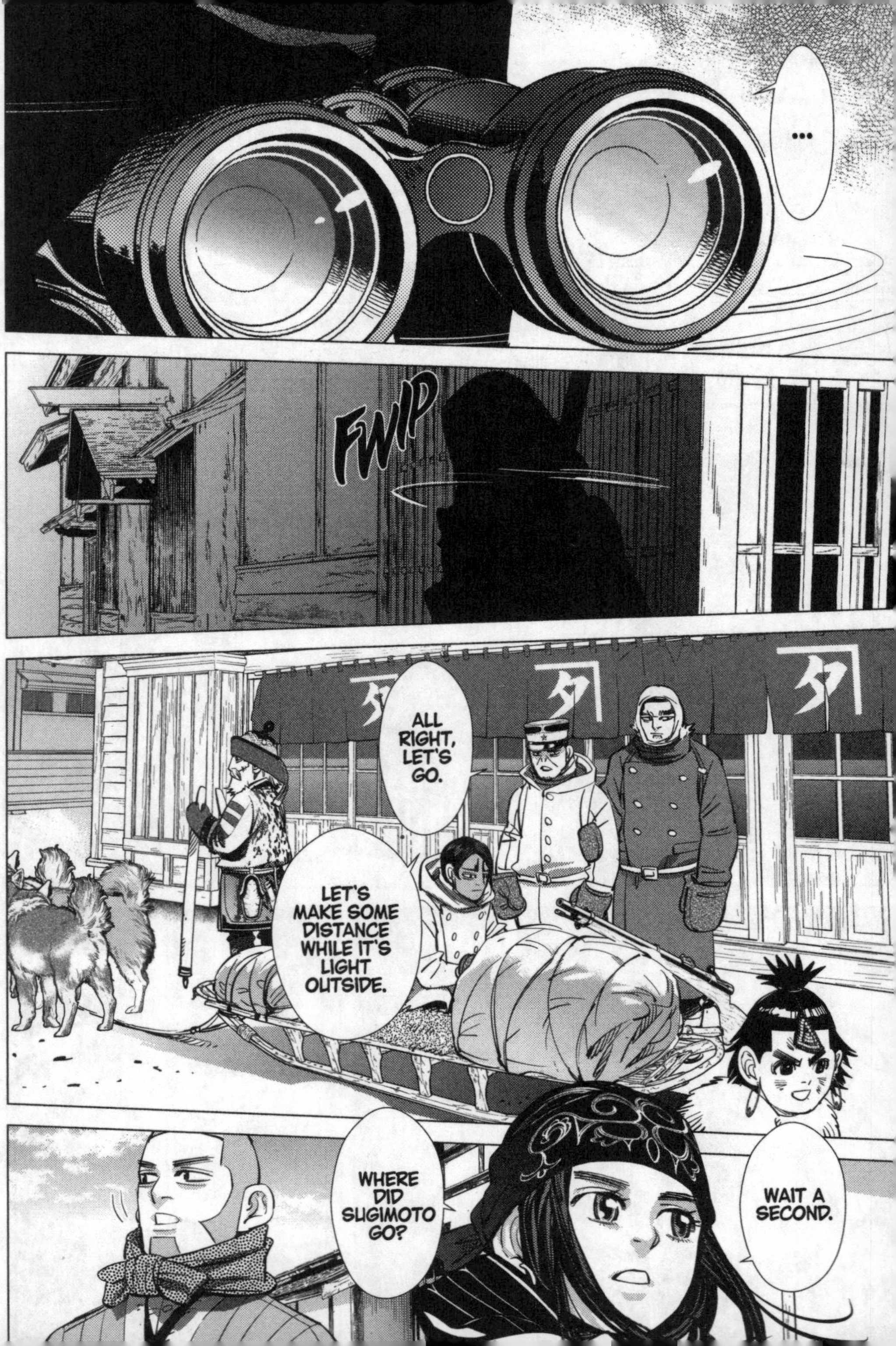
...
FWIP
ALL RIGHT, LET'S GO.
LET'S MAKE SOME DISTANCE WHILE IT'S LIGHT OUTSIDE.
WAIT A SECOND.
WHERE DID SUGIMOTO GO?

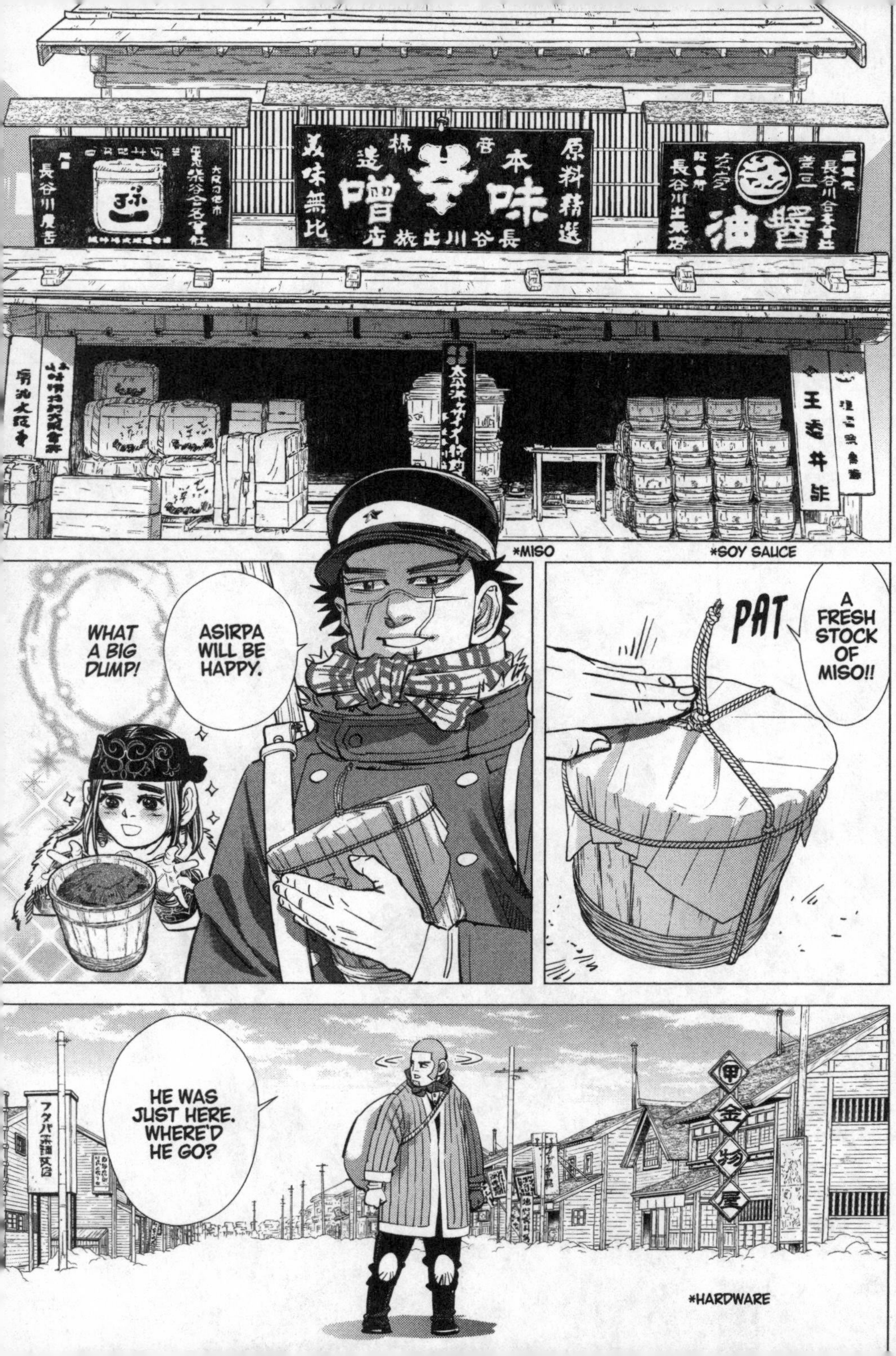

醤油
*SOY SAUCE
味噌
*MISO
PAT
A FRESH STOCK OF MISO!!
ASIRPA WILL BE HAPPY.
WHAT A BIG DUMP!
金物屋
*HARDWARE
HE WAS JUST HERE. WHERE'D HE GO?

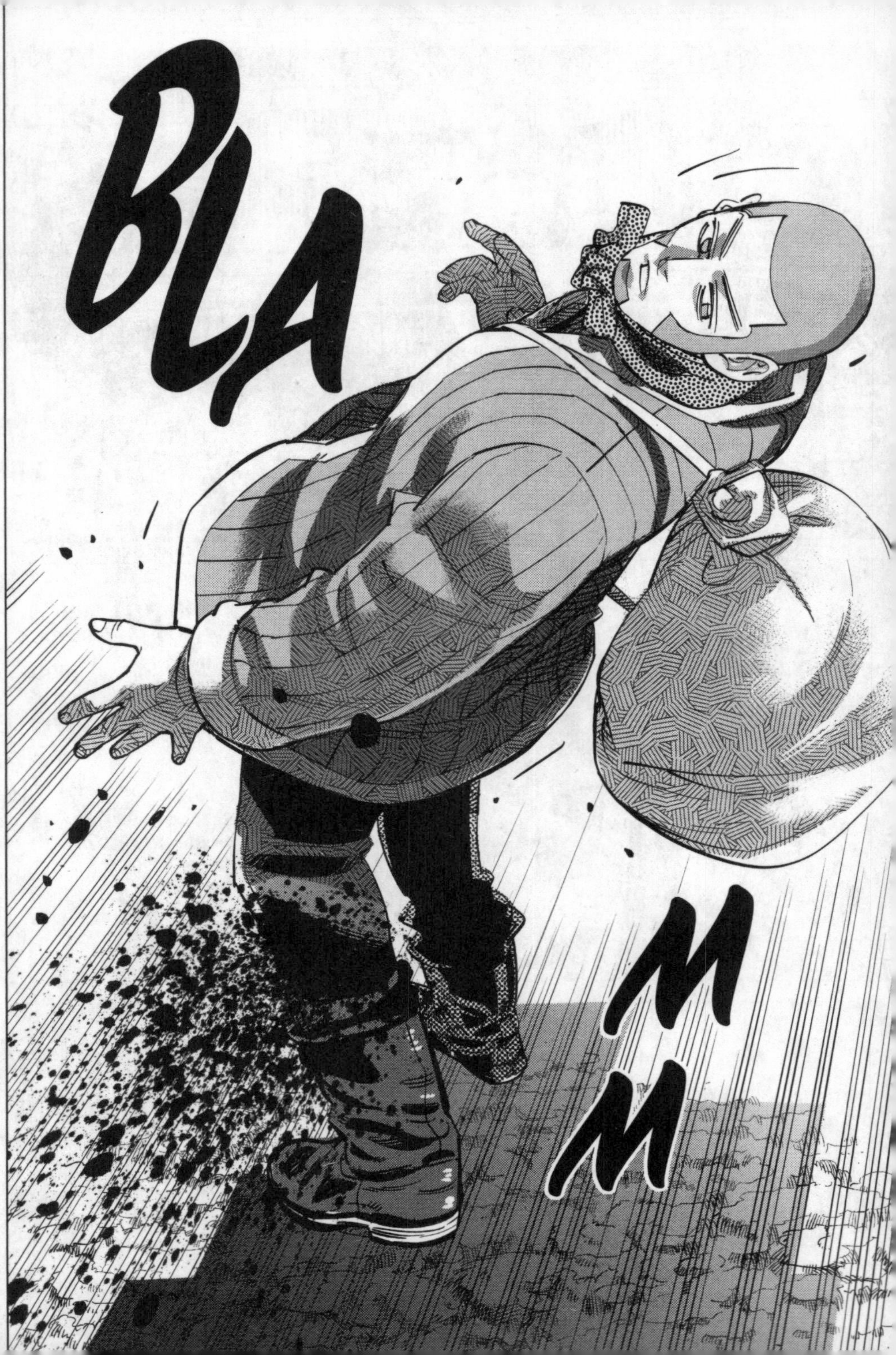
BLAMMM

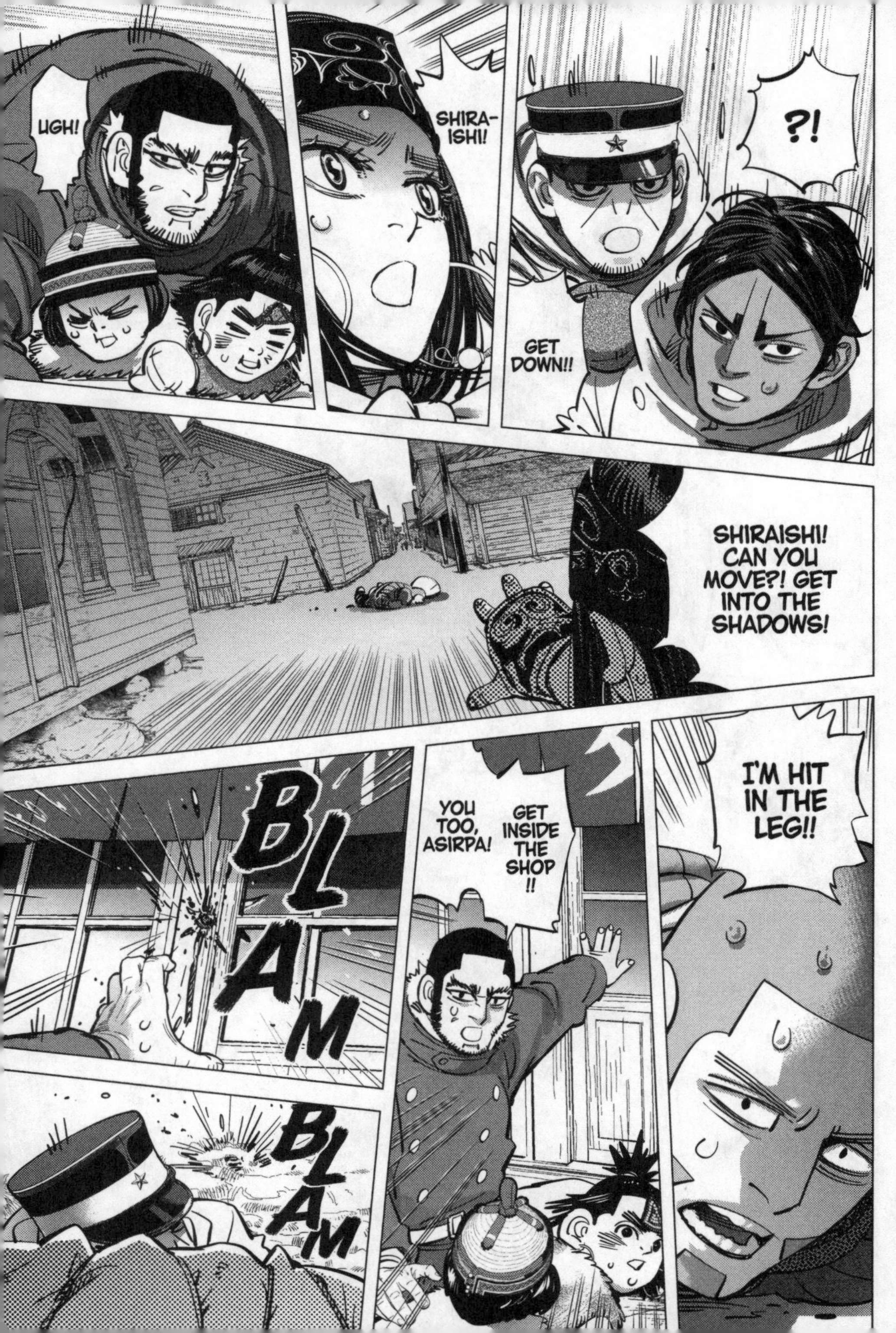
?!
GET DOWN!!
SHIRA-ISHI!
UGH!
SHIRAISHI! CAN YOU MOVE?! GET INTO THE SHADOWS!
I'M HIT IN THE LEG!!
GET INSIDE THE SHOP!!
YOU TOO, ASIRPA!
BLAM
BLAM

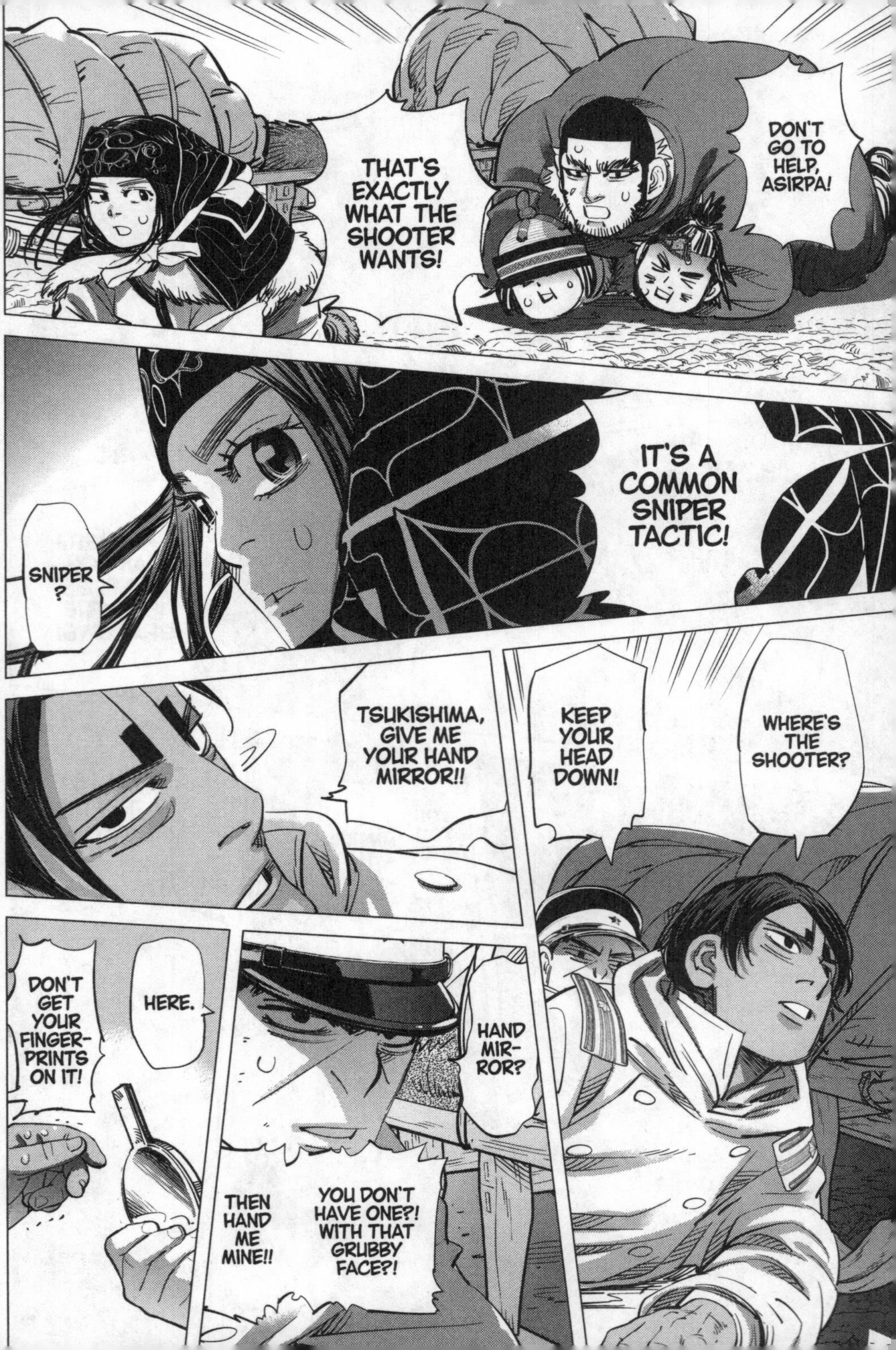
DON'T GO TO HELP, ASIRPA!
THAT'S EXACTLY WHAT THE SHOOTER WANTS!
IT'S A COMMON SNIPER TACTIC!
SNIPER?
WHERE'S THE SHOOTER?
KEEP YOUR HEAD DOWN!
TSUKISHIMA, GIVE ME YOUR HAND MIRROR!!
HAND MIR-ROR?
YOU DON'T HAVE ONE?! WITH THAT GRUBBY FACE?!
THEN HAND ME MINE!!
HERE.
DON'T GET YOUR FINGER-PRINTS ON IT!

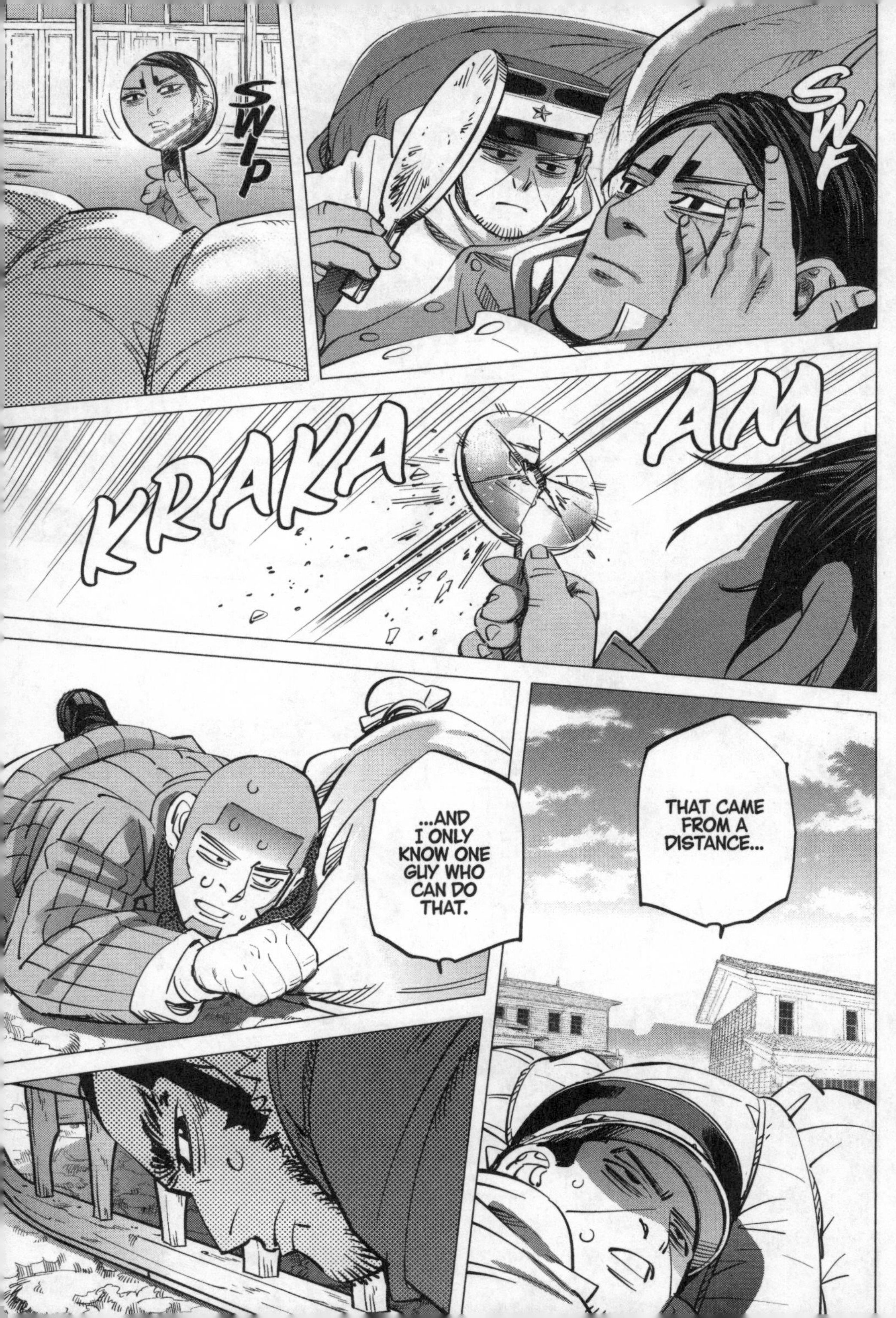
SWF
SWIP
KRAKA AM
THAT CAME FROM A DISTANCE...
...AND I ONLY KNOW ONE GUY WHO CAN DO THAT.

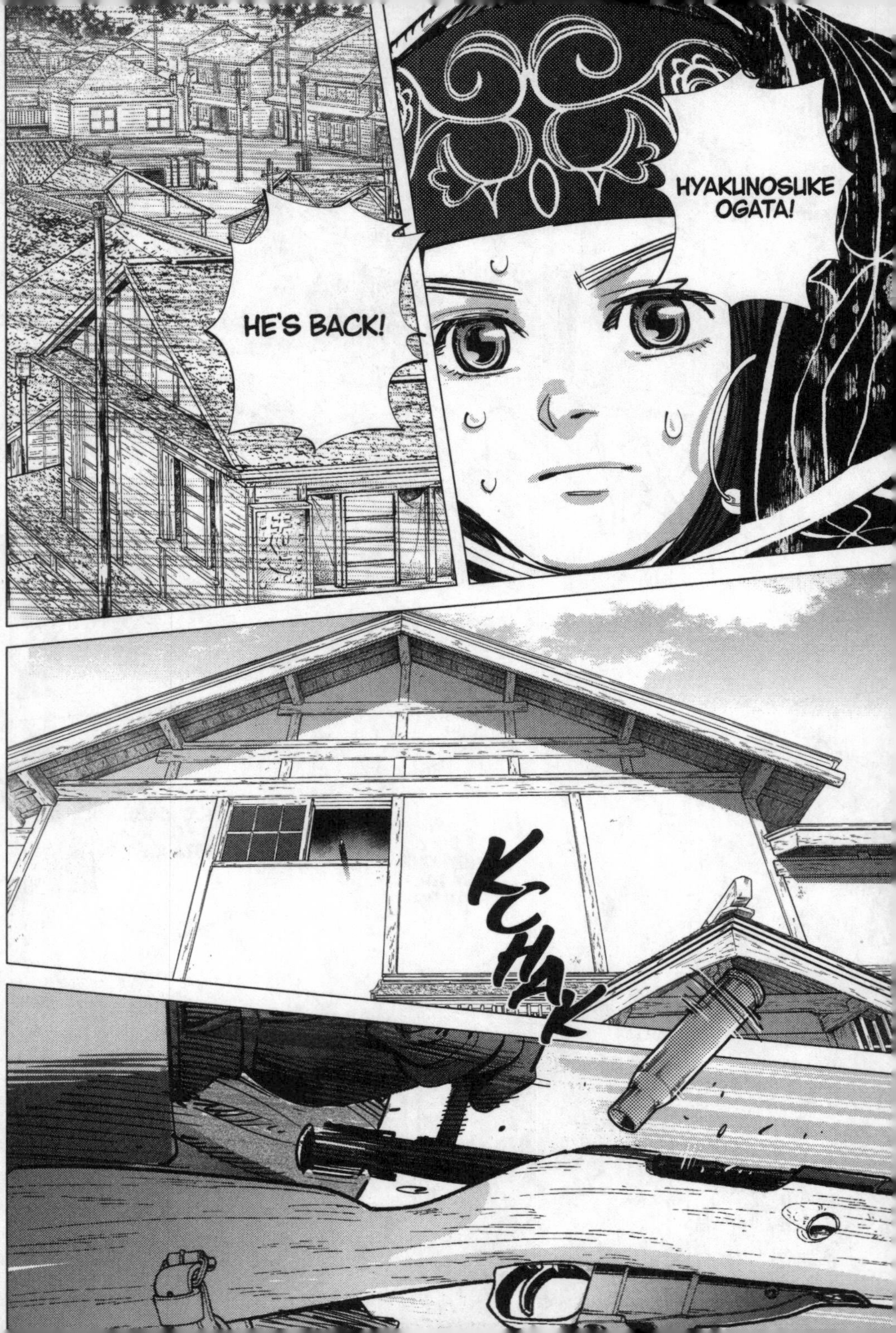
HYAKUNOSUKE OGATA!
HE'S BACK!
KCHAK

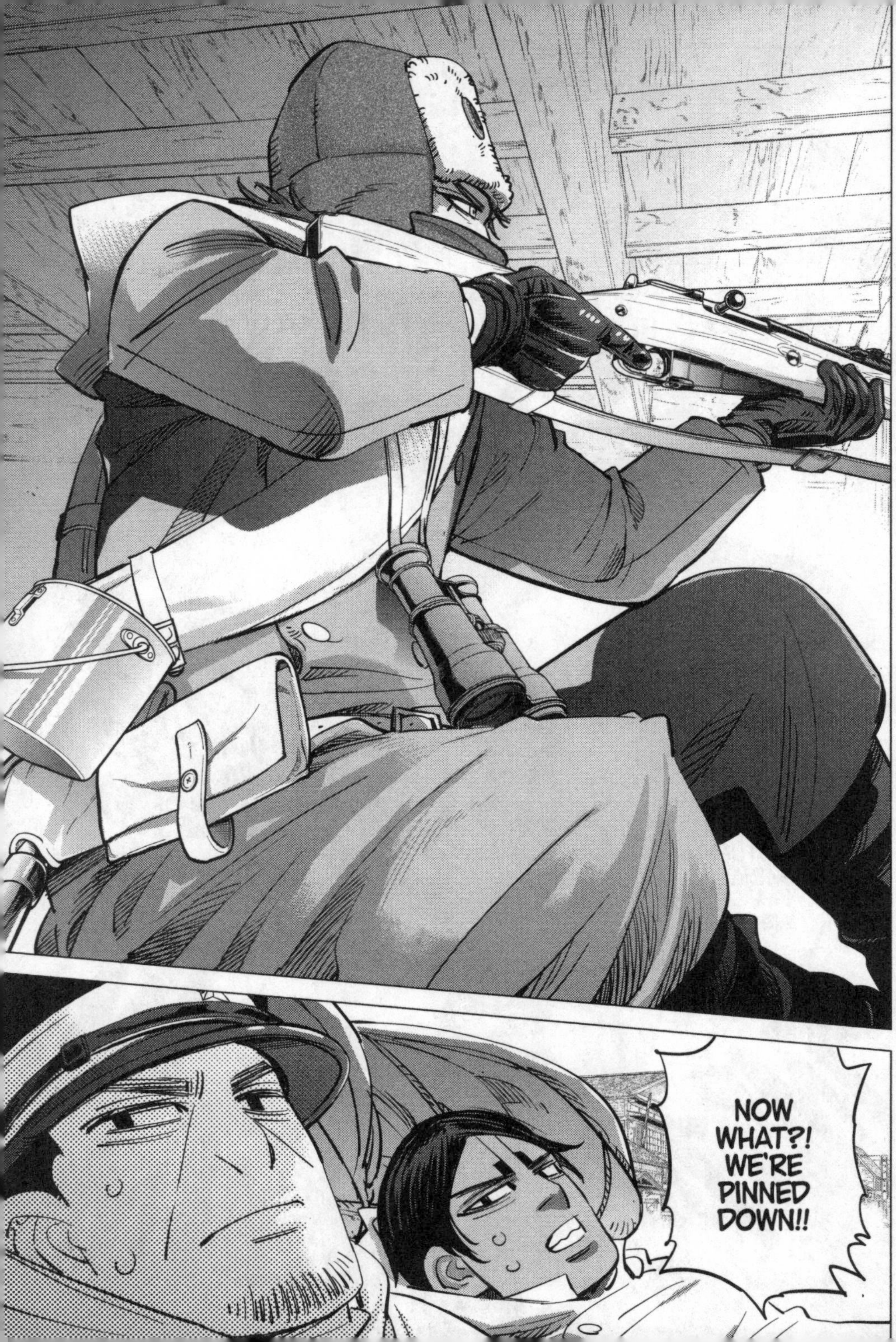
NOW WHAT?! WE'RE PINNED DOWN!!

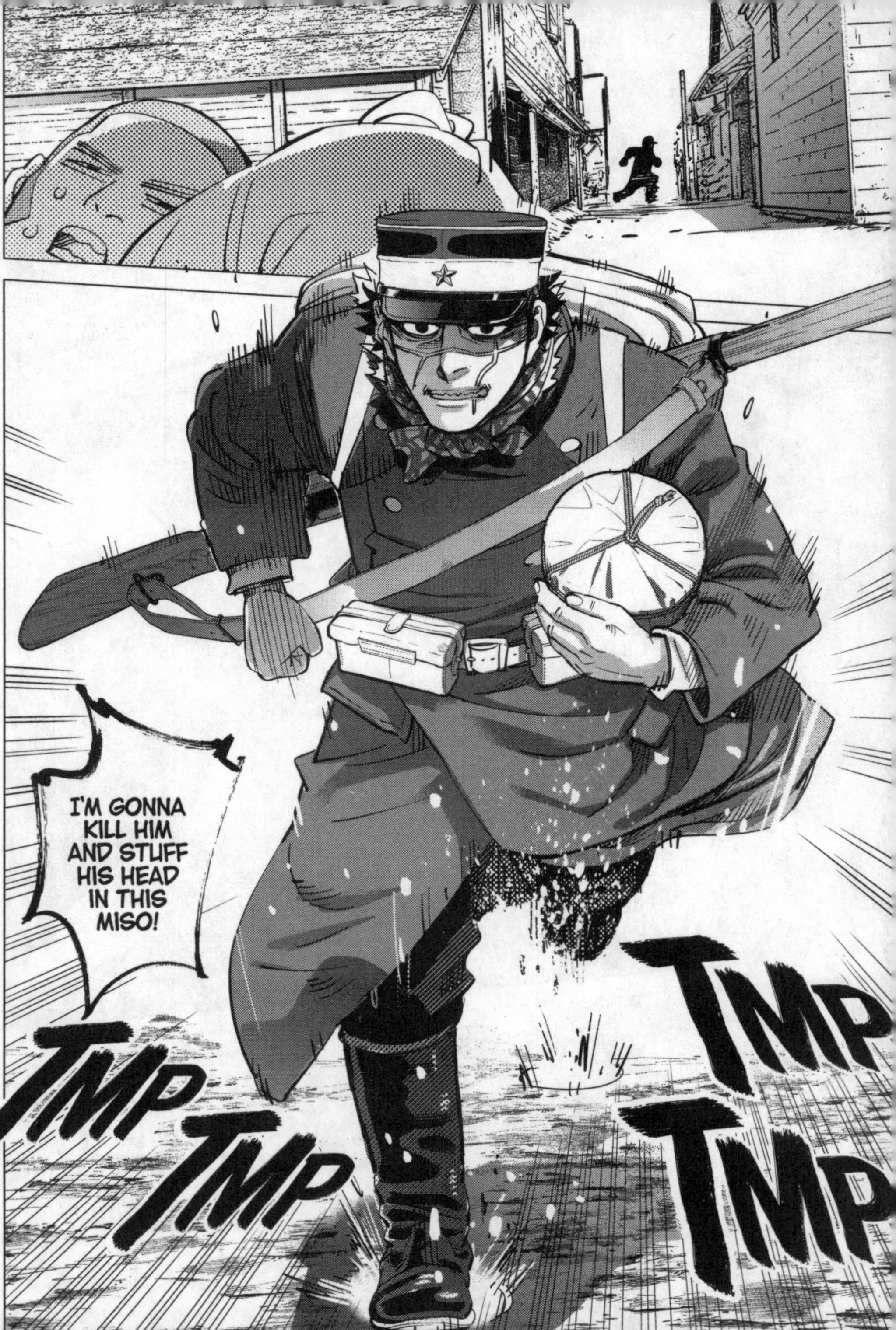
I'M GONNA KILL HIM AND STUFF HIS HEAD IN THIS MISO!
TMP TMP
TMP TMP

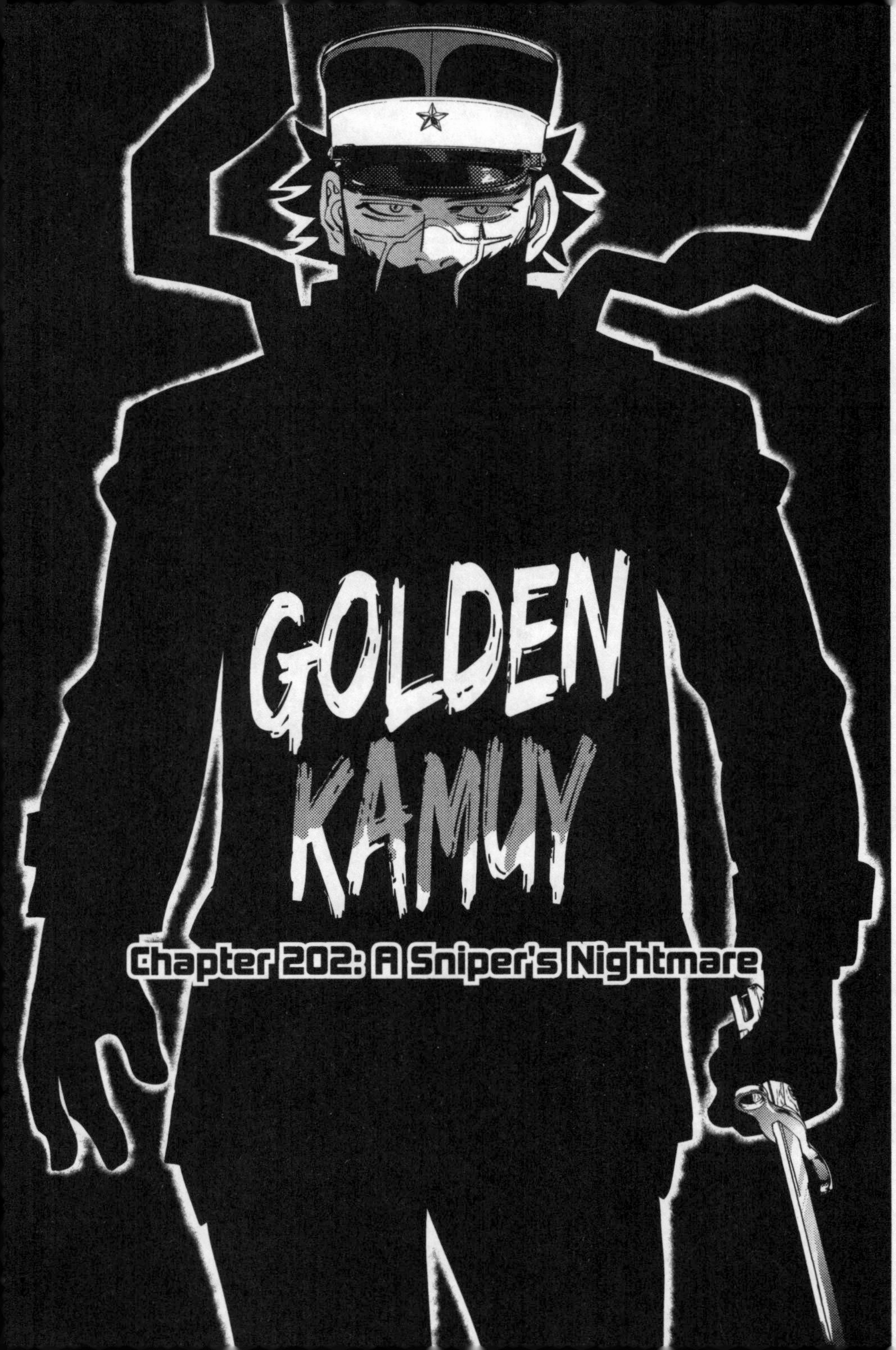
GOLDEN KAMUY
Chapter 202: A Sniper's Nightmare

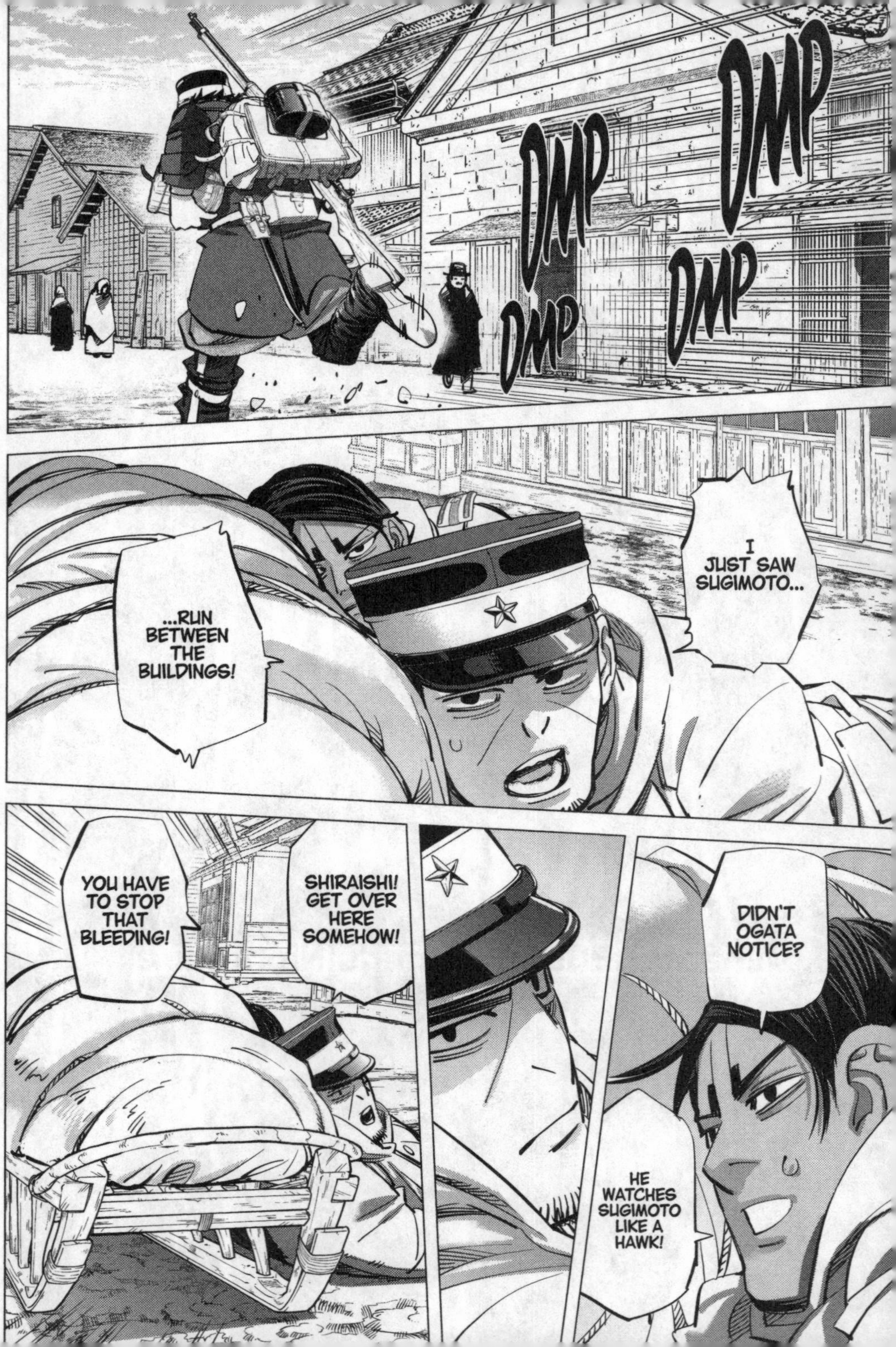
DMP
DMP
DMP
DMP
I JUST SAW SUGIMOTO...
...RUN BETWEEN THE BUILDINGS!
DIDN'T OGATA NOTICE?
HE WATCHES SUGIMOTO LIKE A HAWK!
SHIRAISHI! GET OVER HERE SOMEHOW!
YOU HAVE TO STOP THAT BLEEDING!

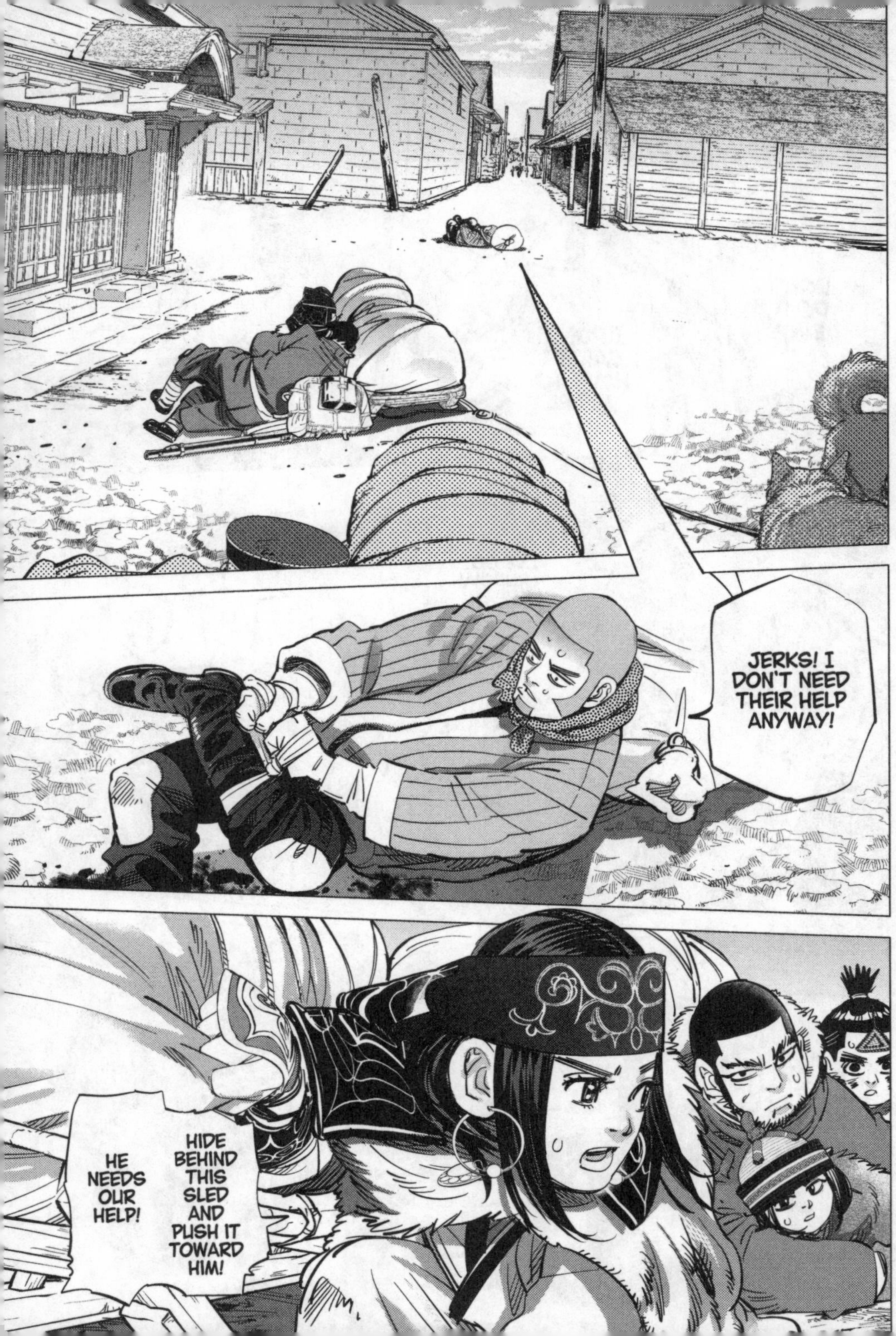
JERKS! I DON'T NEED THEIR HELP ANYWAY!
HIDE BEHIND THIS SLED AND PUSH IT TOWARD HIM!
HE NEEDS OUR HELP!

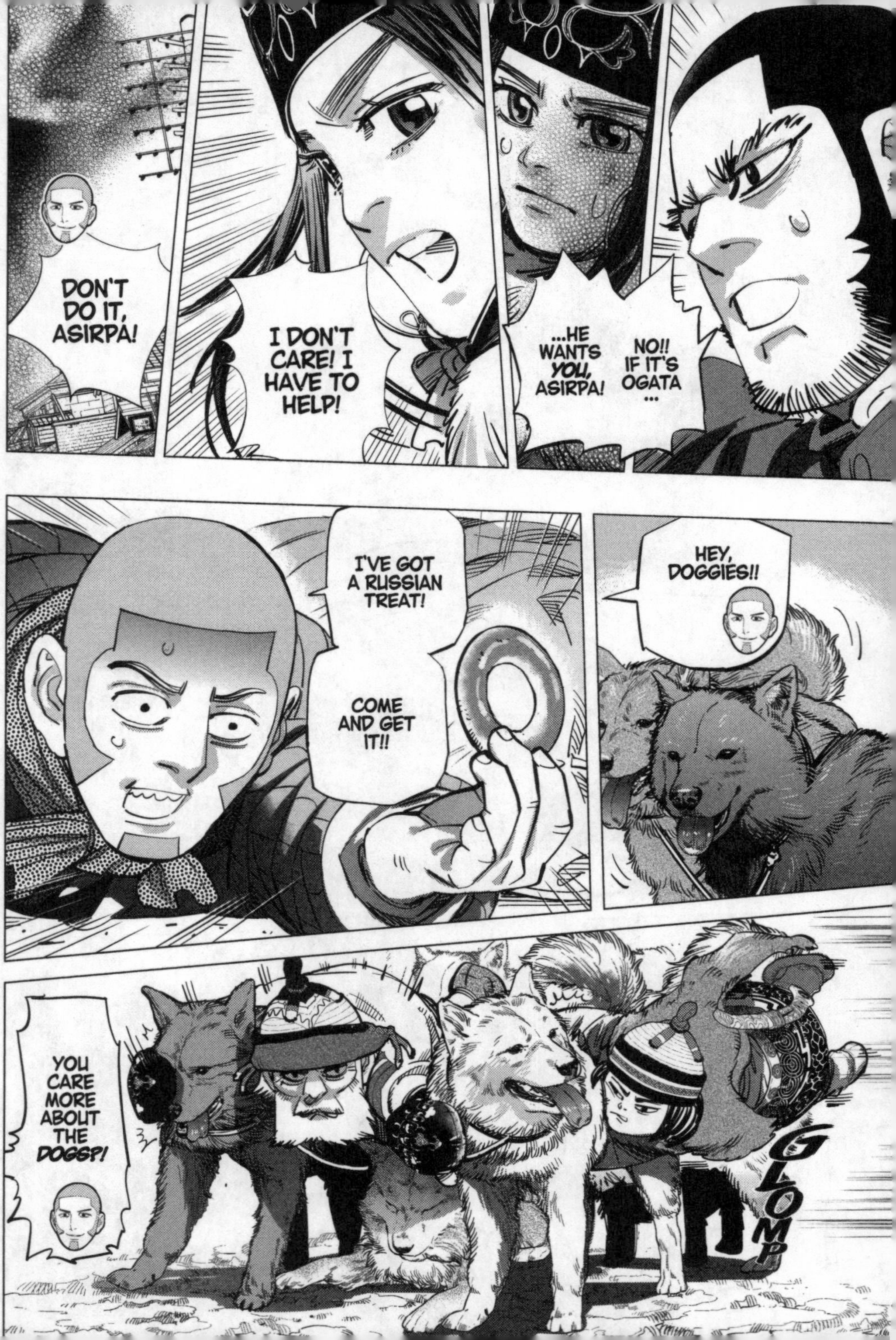
NO!! IF IT'S OGATA ...
...HE WANTS YOU, ASIRPA!
I DON'T CARE! I HAVE TO HELP!
DON'T DO IT, ASIRPA!
HEY, DOGGIES!!
I'VE GOT A RUSSIAN TREAT!
COME AND GET IT!!
GLOMP
YOU CARE MORE ABOUT THE DOGS?!

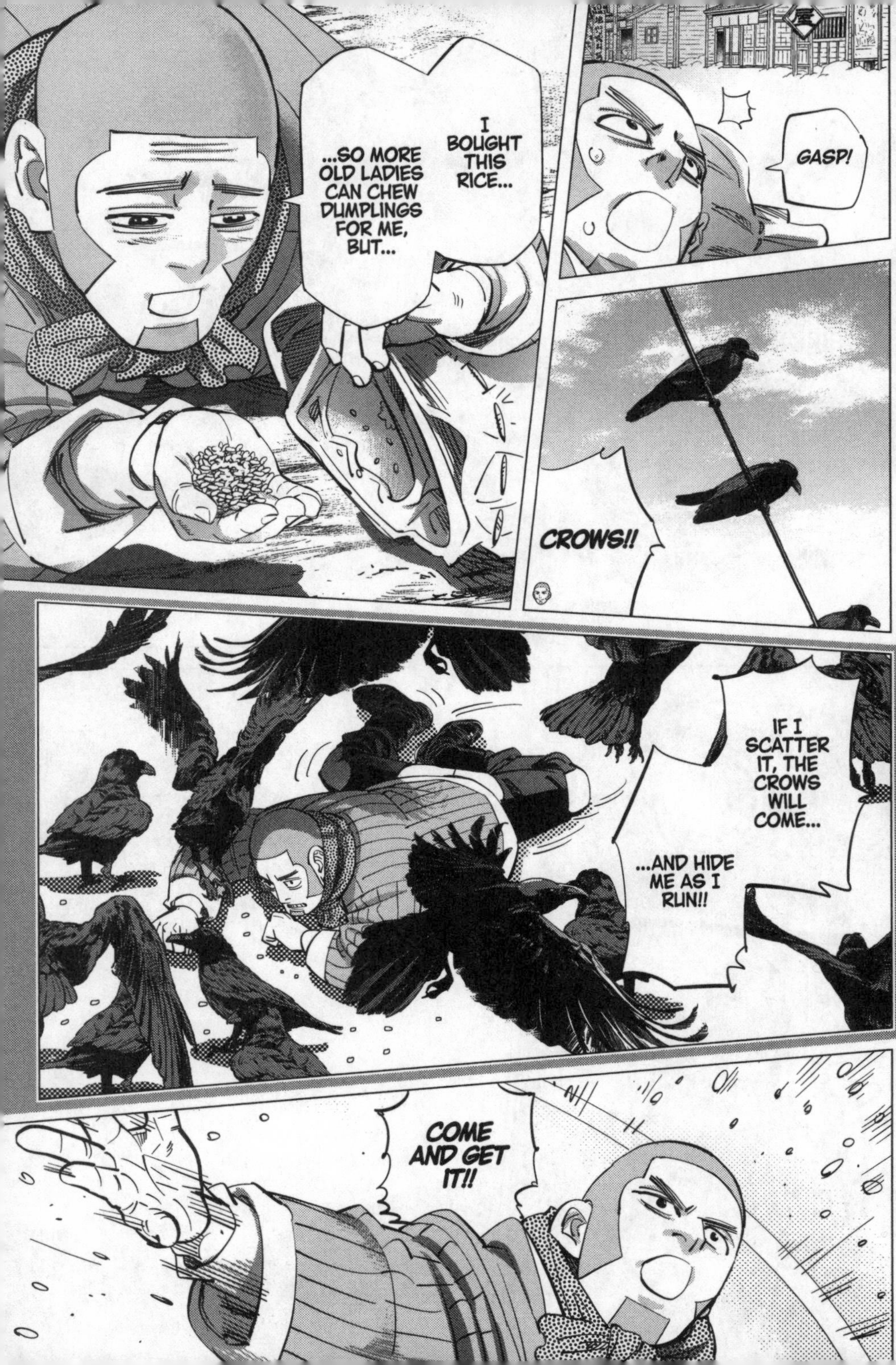
屋
GASP!
CROWS!!
I BOUGHT THIS RICE...
...SO MORE OLD LADIES CAN CHEW DUMPLINGS FOR ME, BUT...
IF I SCATTER IT, THE CROWS WILL COME...
...AND HIDE ME AS I RUN!!
COME AND GET IT!!

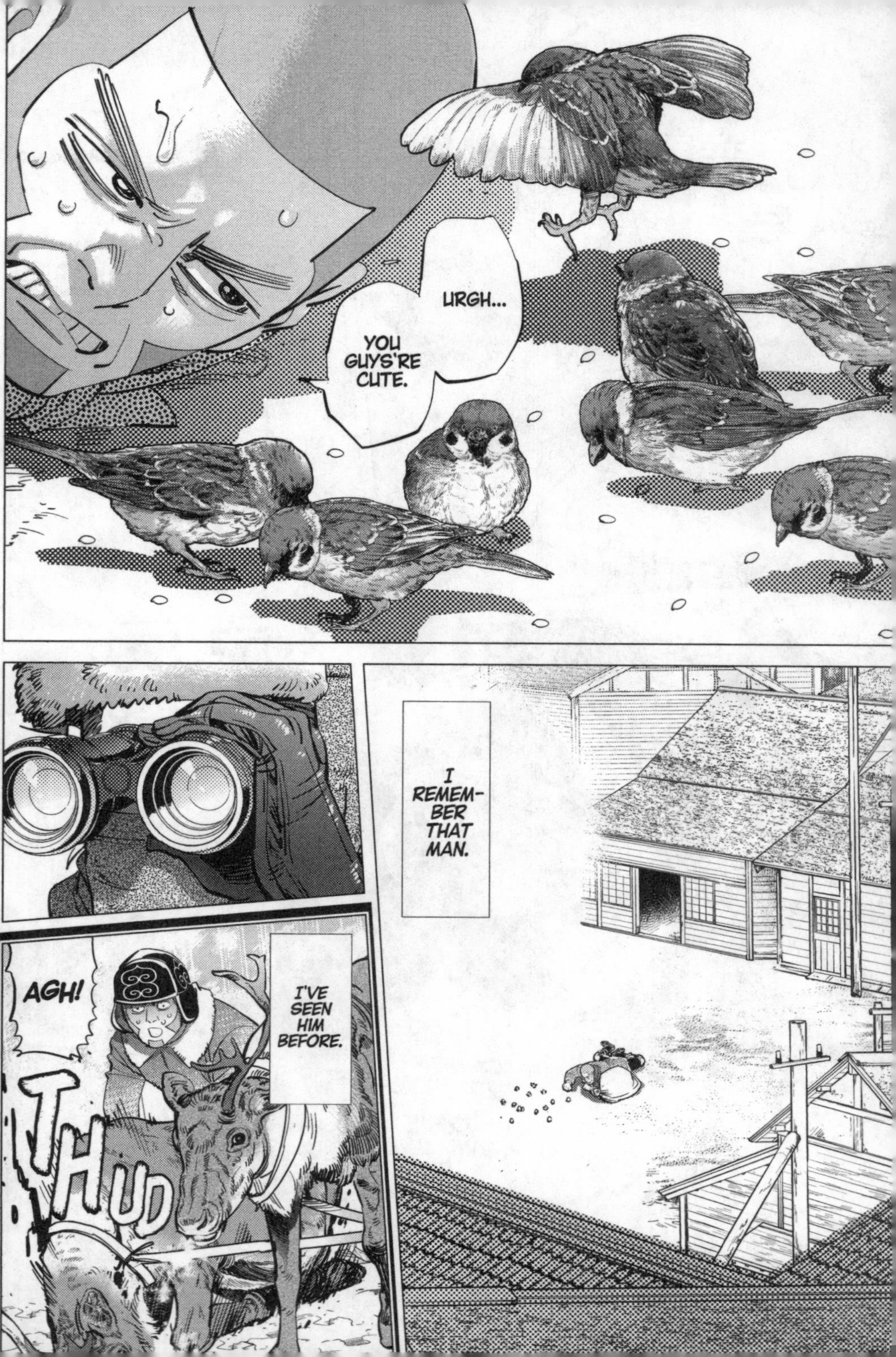
URGH...
YOU GUYS'RE CUTE.
I REMEMBER THAT MAN.
I'VE SEEN HIM BEFORE.
AGH!
THUD

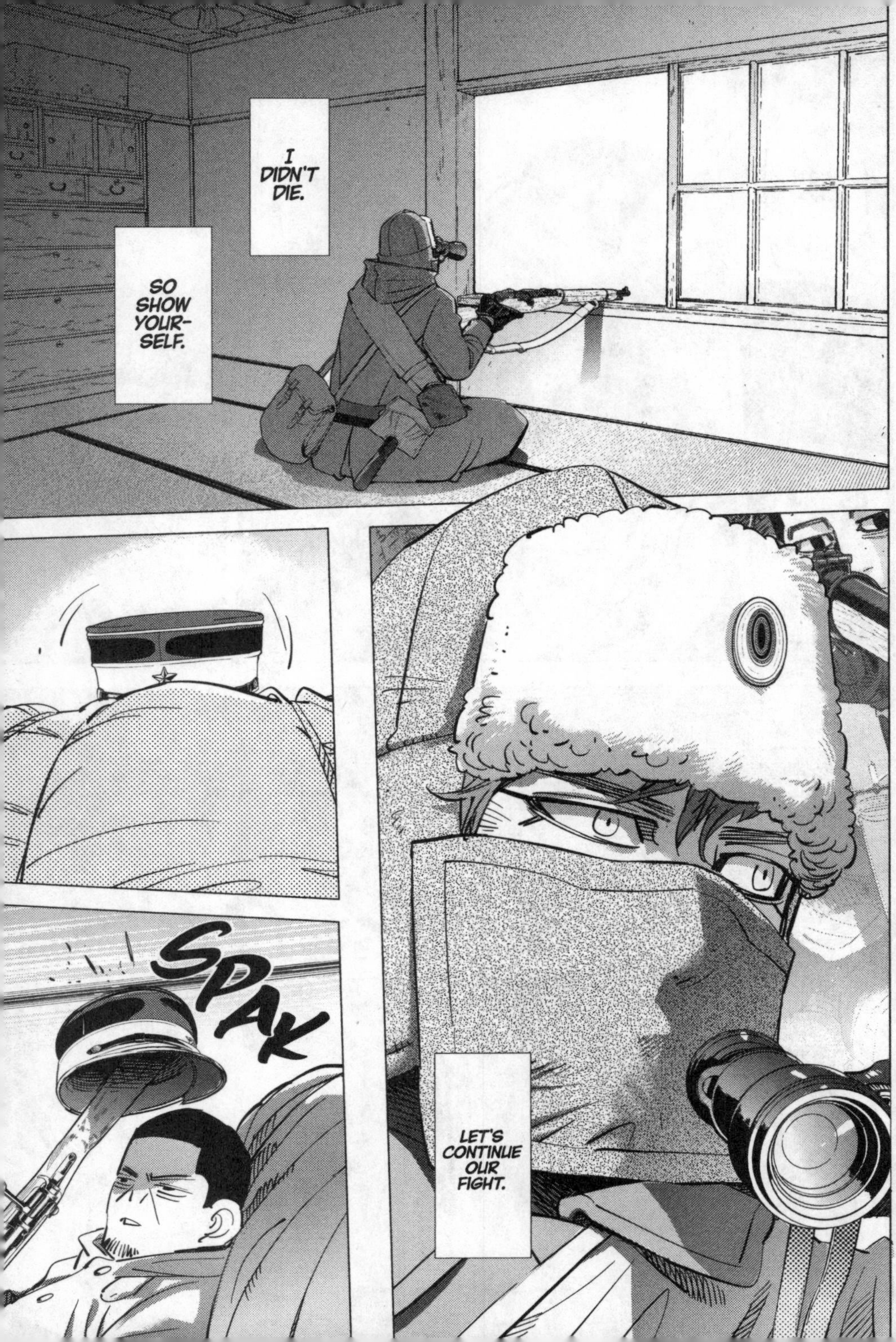
I DIDN'T DIE.
SO SHOW YOUR-SELF.
LET'S CONTINUE OUR FIGHT.
SPAK

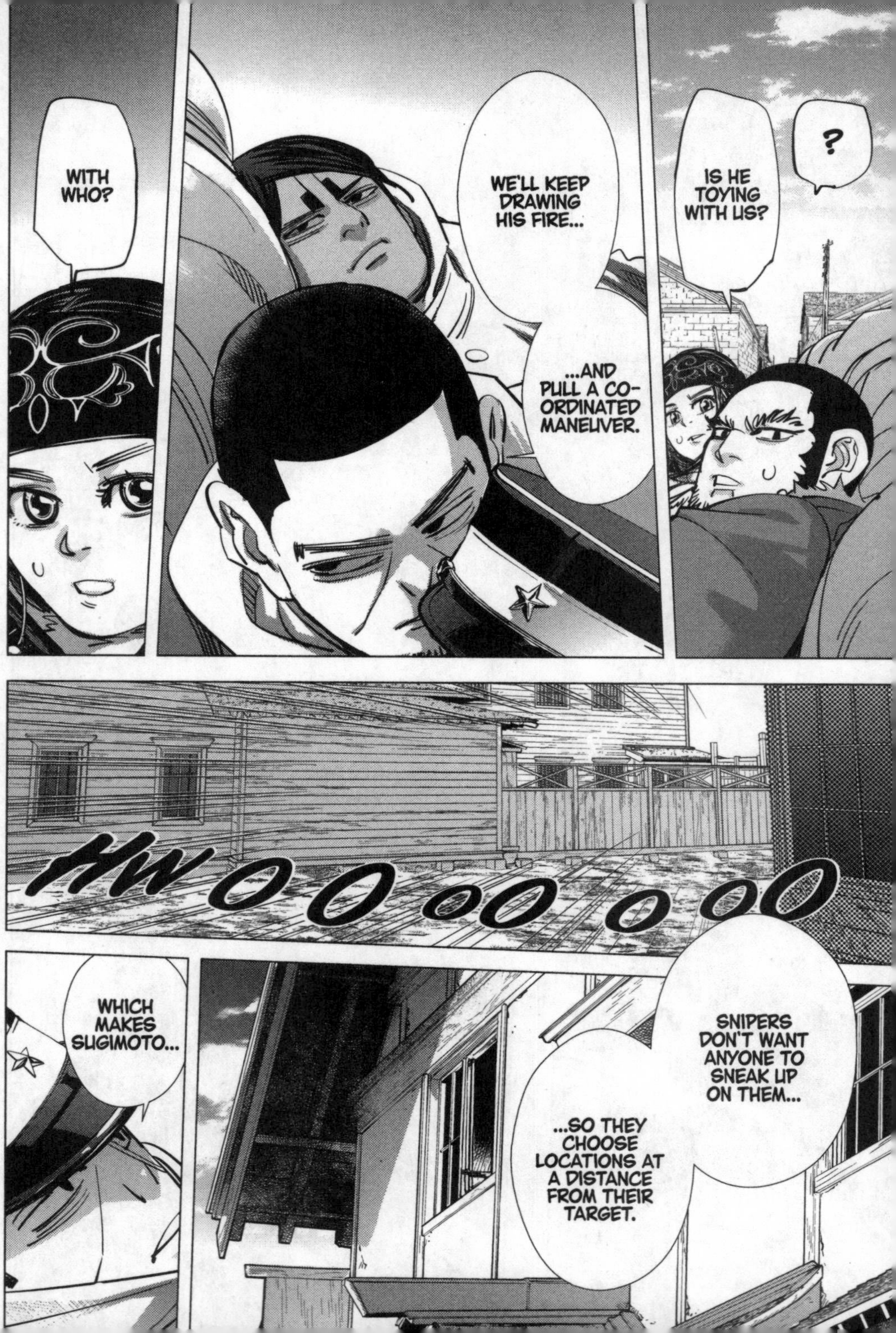
?
IS HE TOYING WITH US?
WE'LL KEEP DRAWING HIS FIRE...
...AND PULL A CO-ORDINATED MANEUVER.
WITH WHO?
HWOOOOOOO
SNIPERS DON'T WANT ANYONE TO SNEAK UP ON THEM...
...SO THEY CHOOSE LOCATIONS AT A DISTANCE FROM THEIR TARGET.
WHICH MAKES SUGIMOTO...

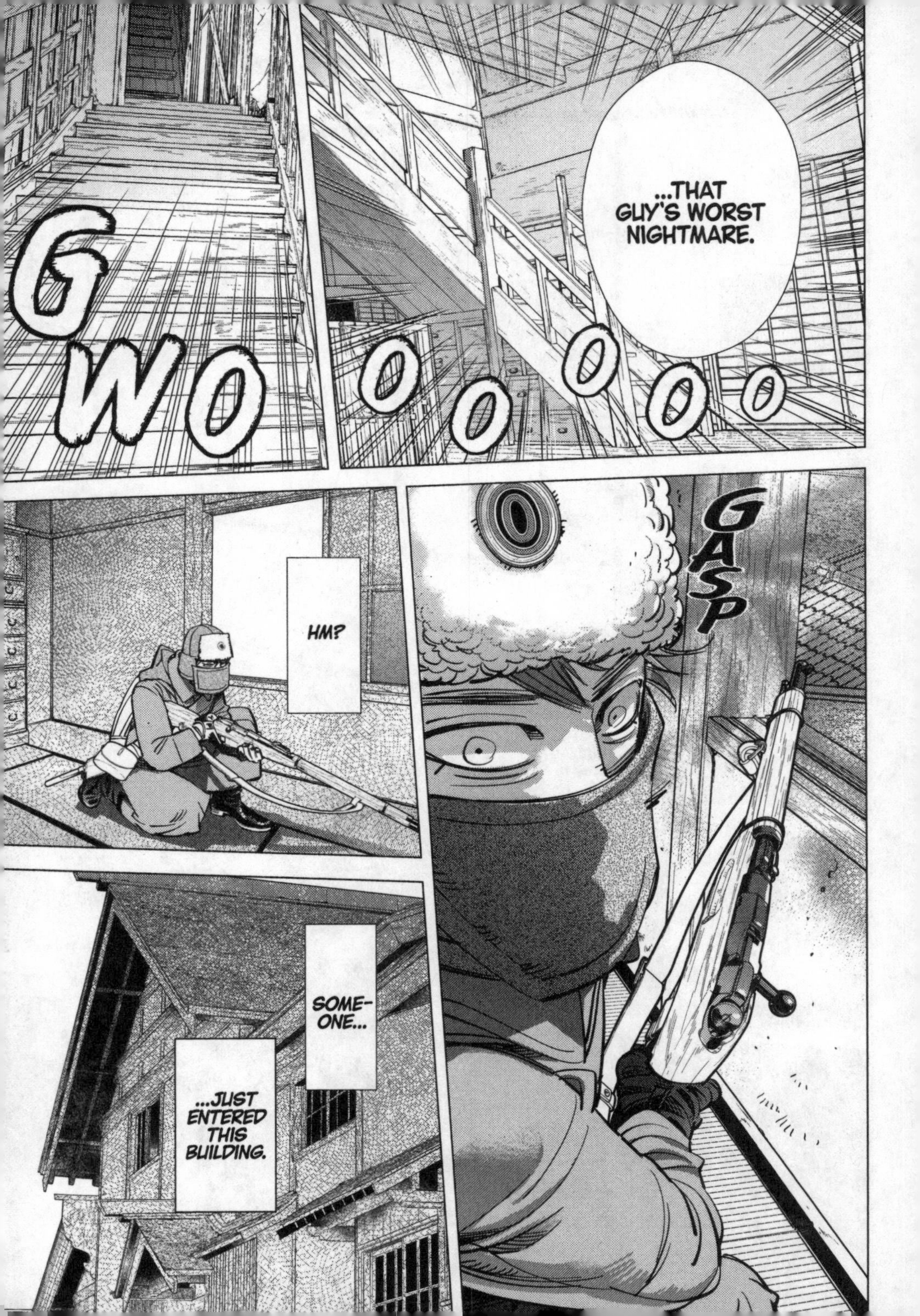
...THAT GUY'S WORST NIGHTMARE.
GWOOOOOO
GASP
HM?
SOME-ONE...
...JUST ENTERED THIS BUILDING.

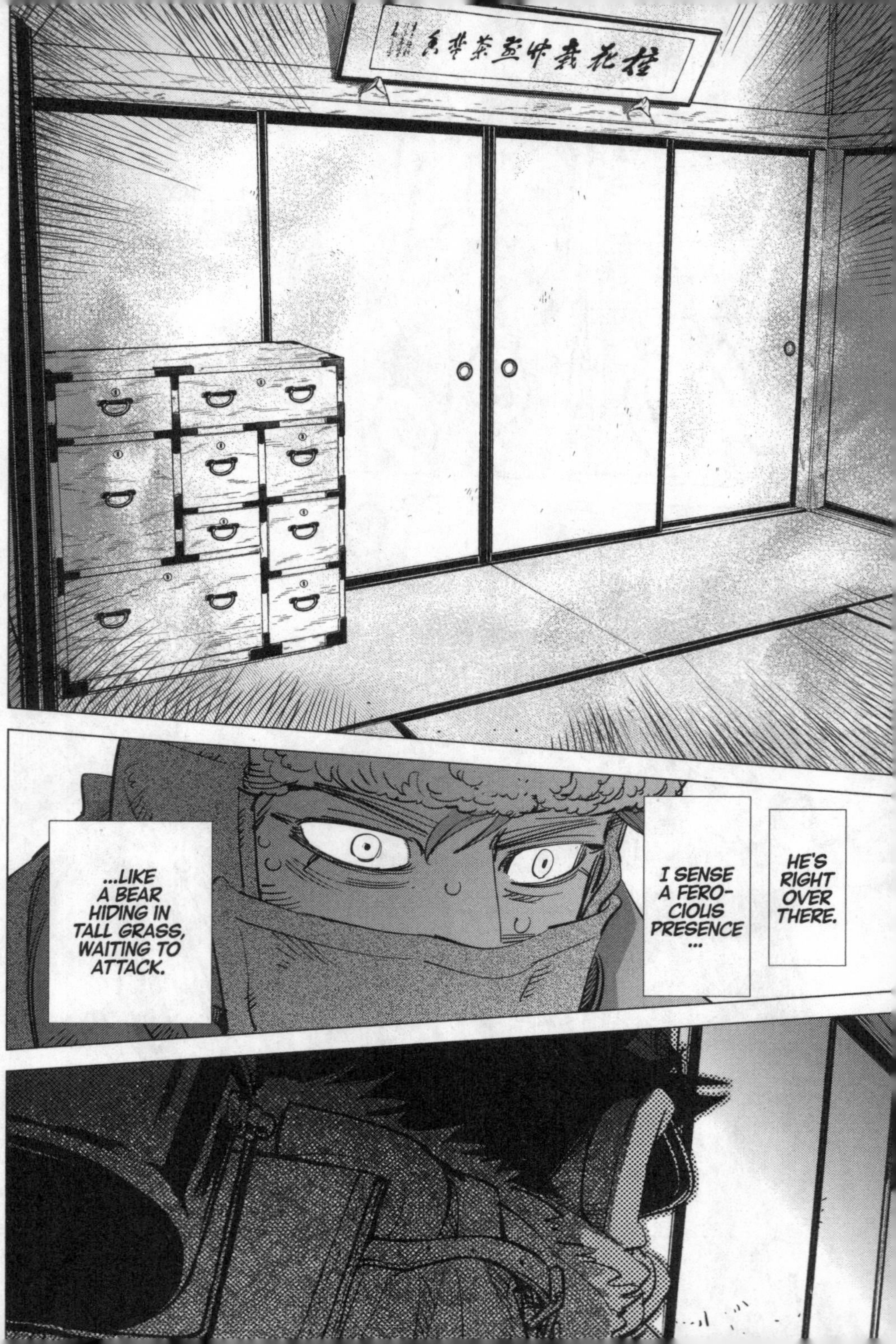
HE'S RIGHT OVER THERE.
I SENSE A FERO-CIOUS PRESENCE...
...LIKE A BEAR HIDING IN TALL GRASS, WAITING TO ATTACK.

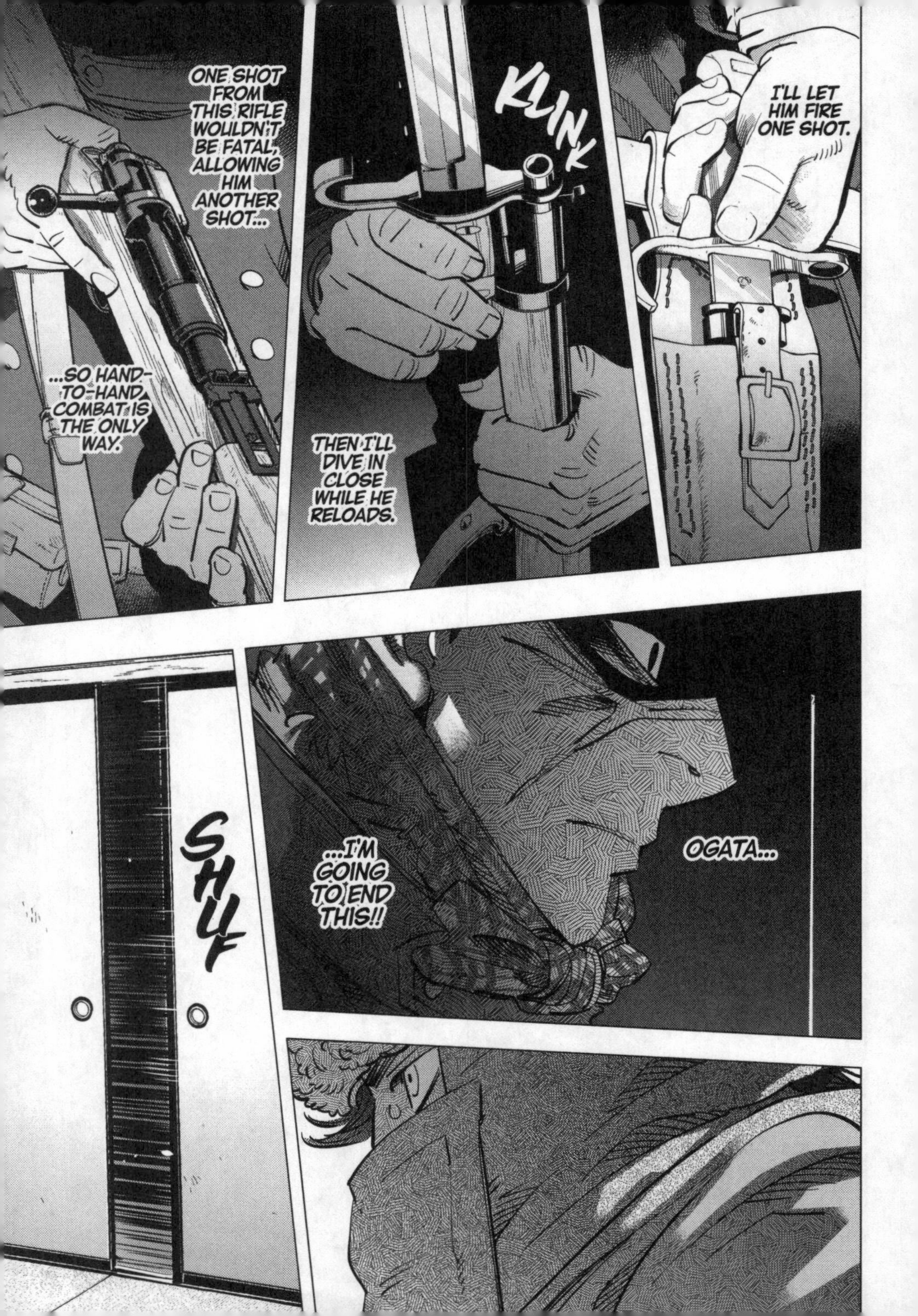
I'LL LET HIM FIRE ONE SHOT.
KLINK
THEN I'LL DIVE IN CLOSE WHILE HE RELOADS.
ONE SHOT FROM THIS RIFLE WOULDN'T BE FATAL, ALLOWING HIM ANOTHER SHOT...
...SO HAND-TO-HAND COMBAT IS THE ONLY WAY.
OGATA...
...I'M GOING TO END THIS!!
SHUF

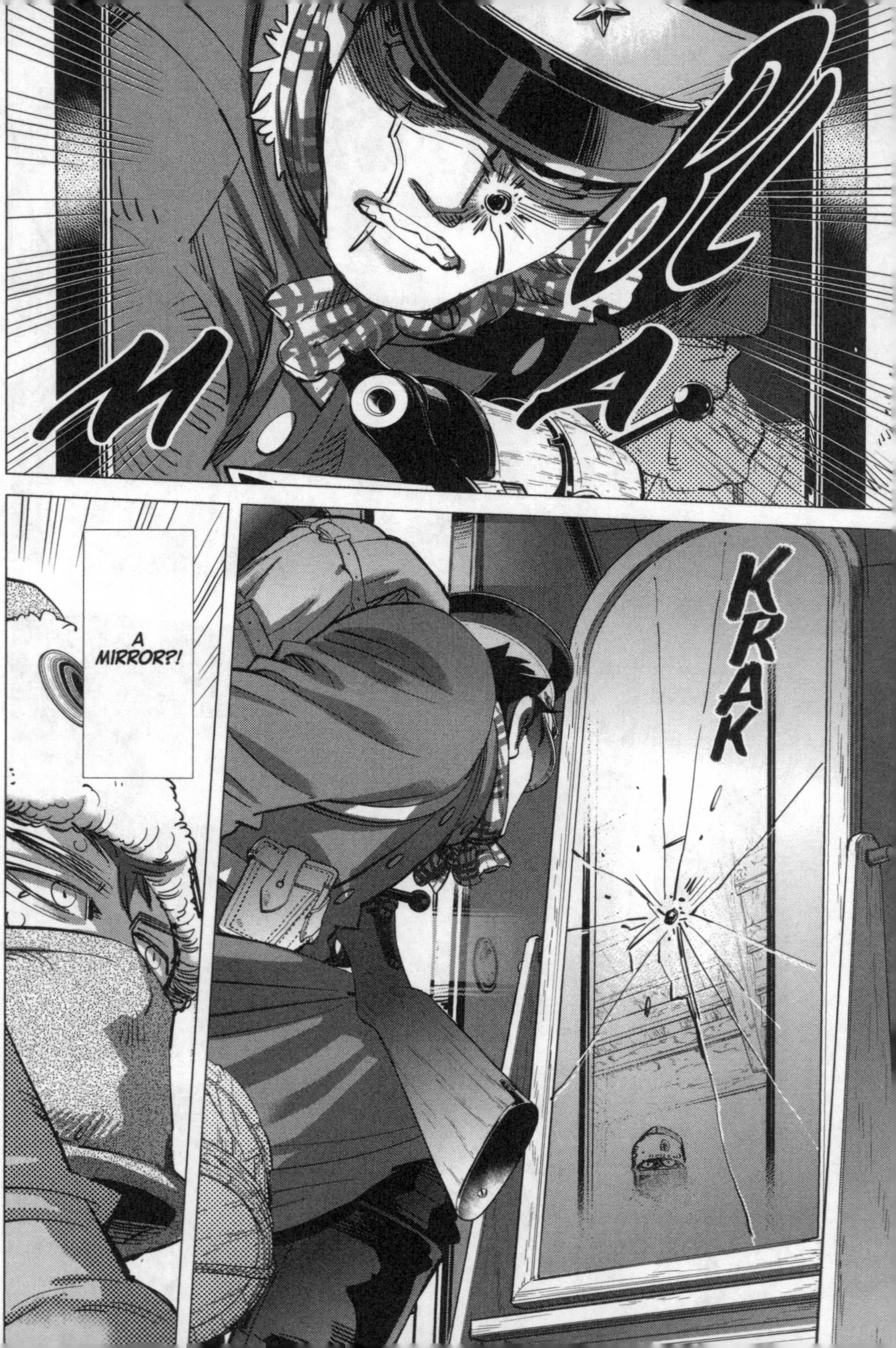
KRAK
A MIRROR?!

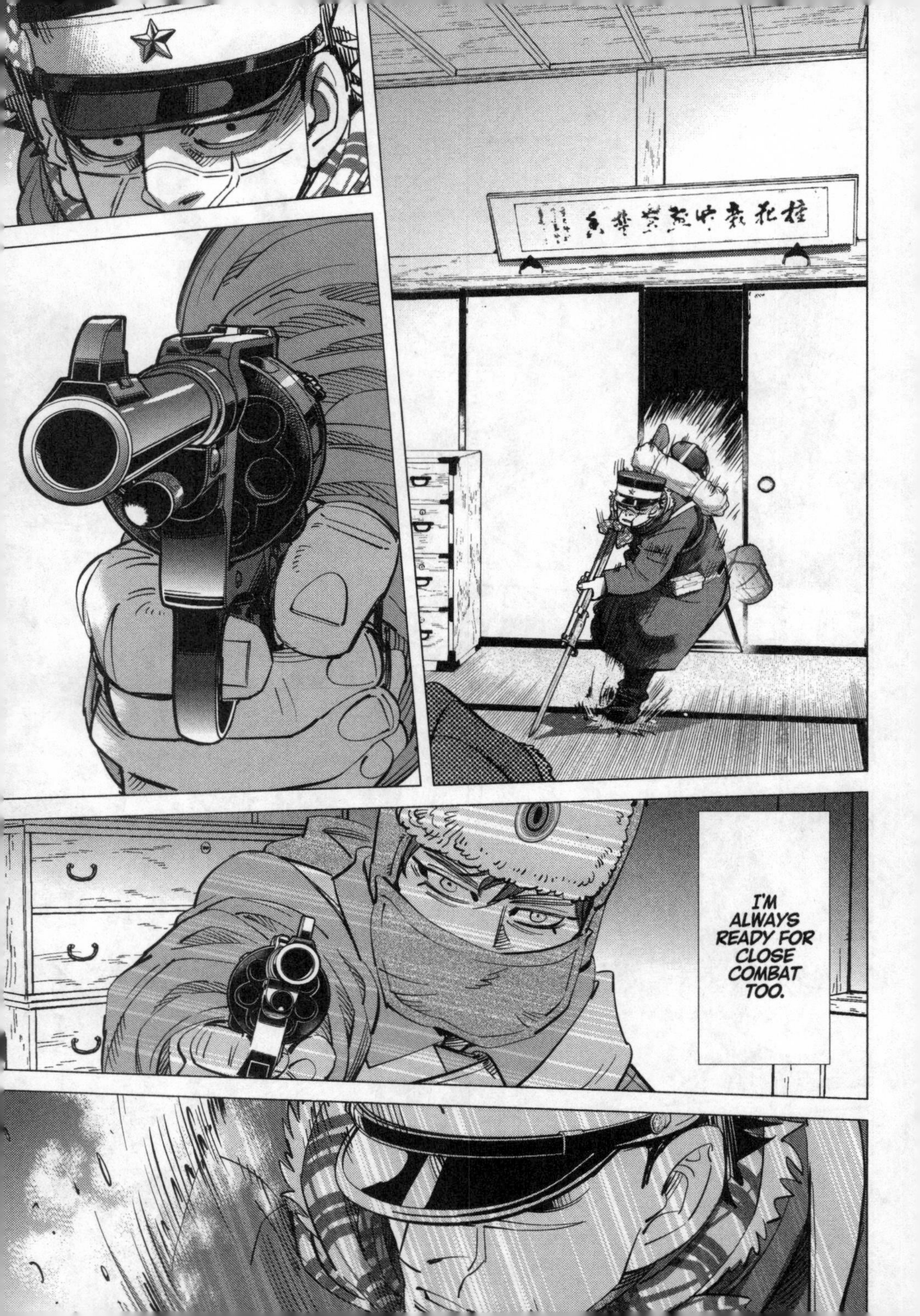
I'M ALWAYS READY FOR CLOSE COMBAT TOO.

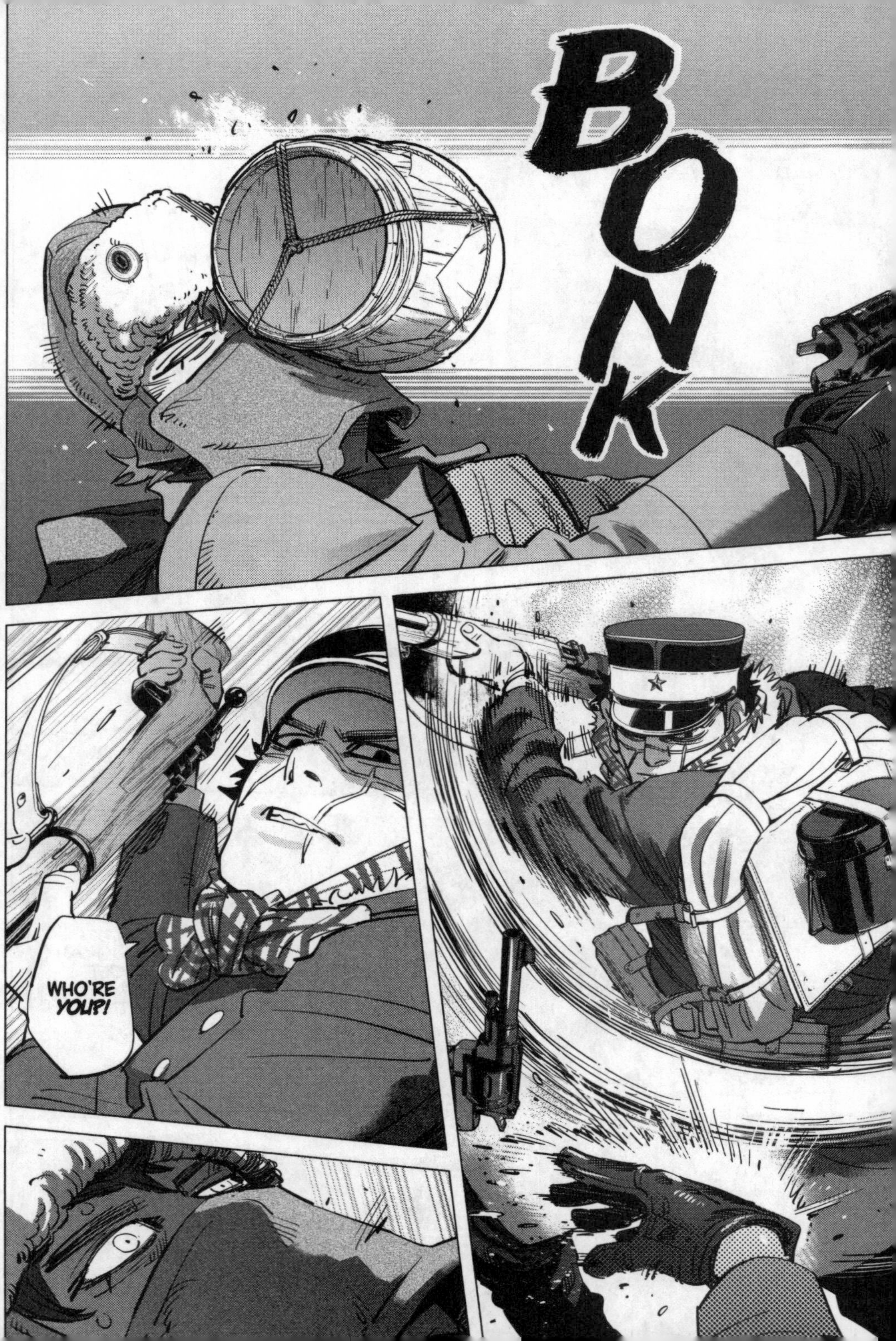
BONK
WHO'RE YOU?!

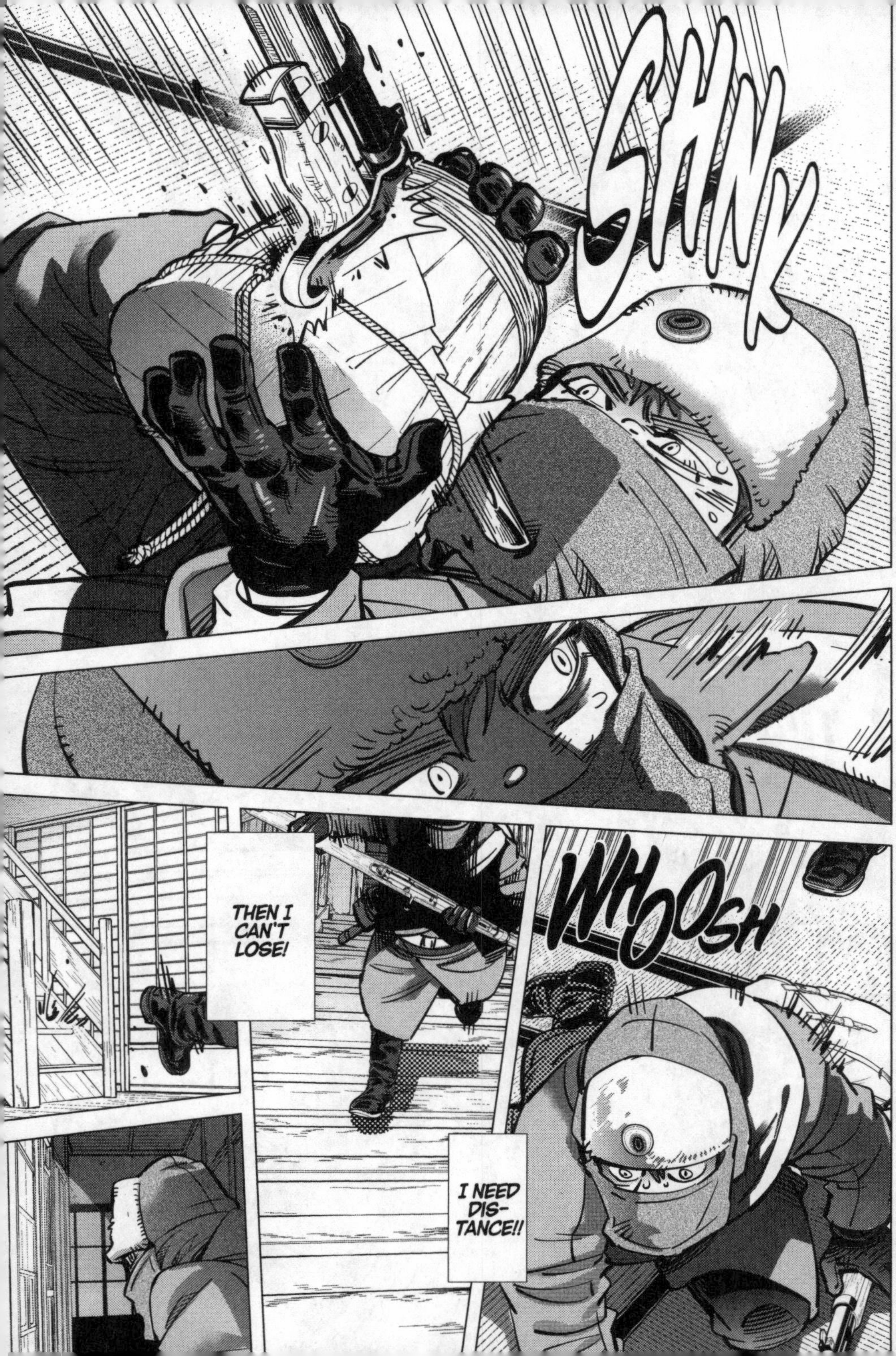
SHINK
WHOOSH
I NEED DIS- TANCE!!
THEN I CAN'T LOSE!

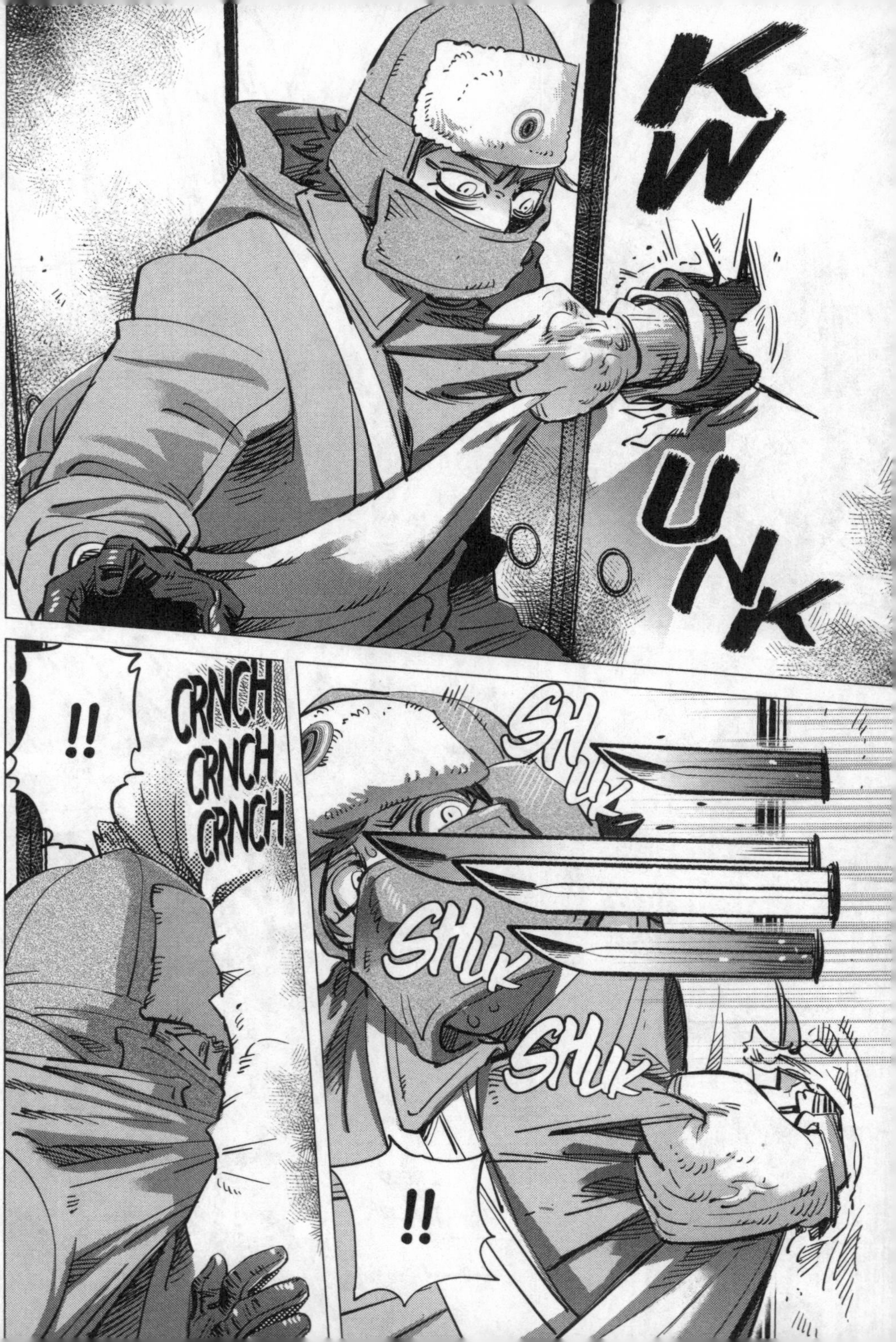
KWUNK
SHUK
SHUK
SHUK
!!
CRNCH
CRNCH
CRNCH
!!

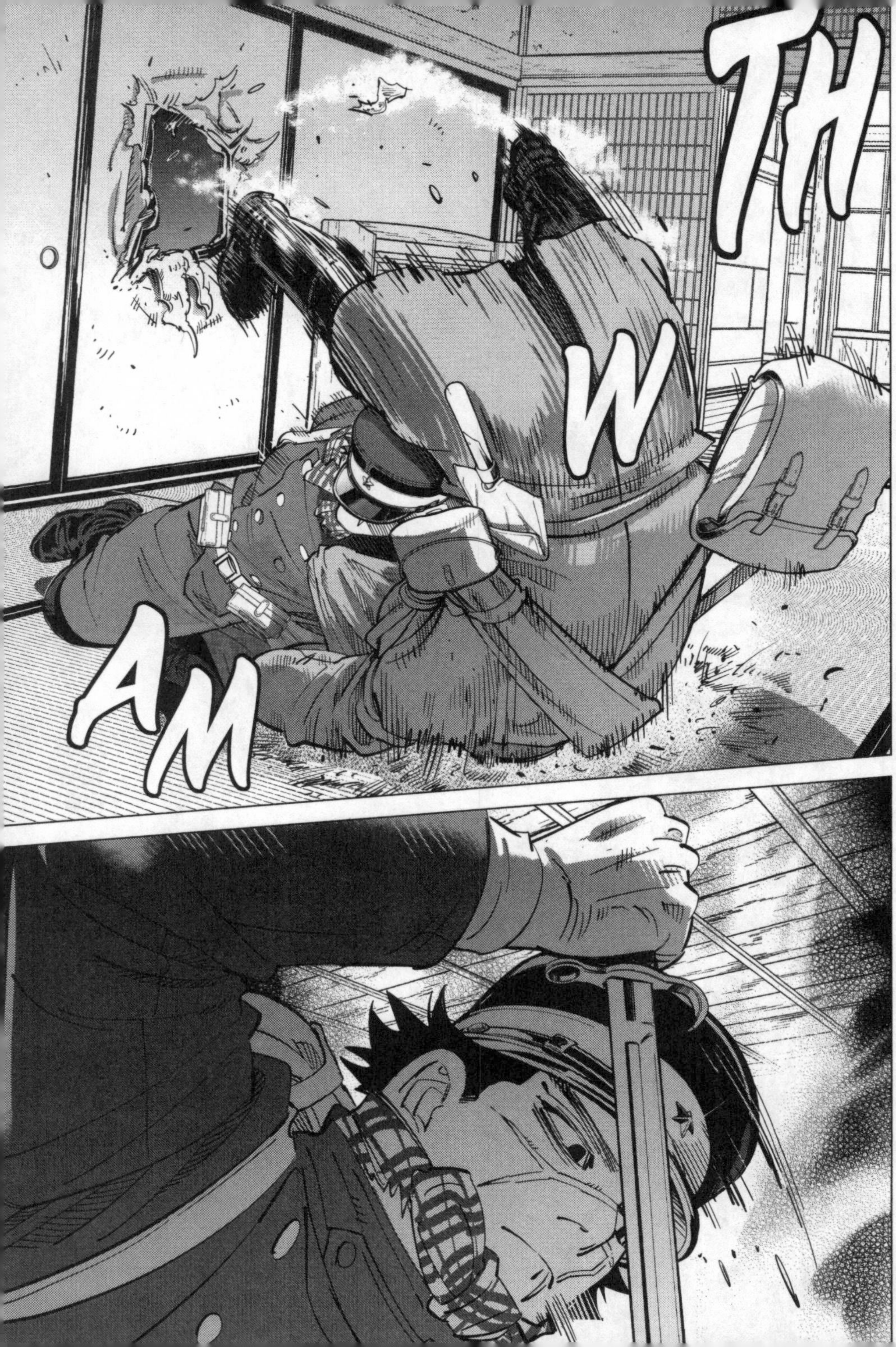
TH
W
AM

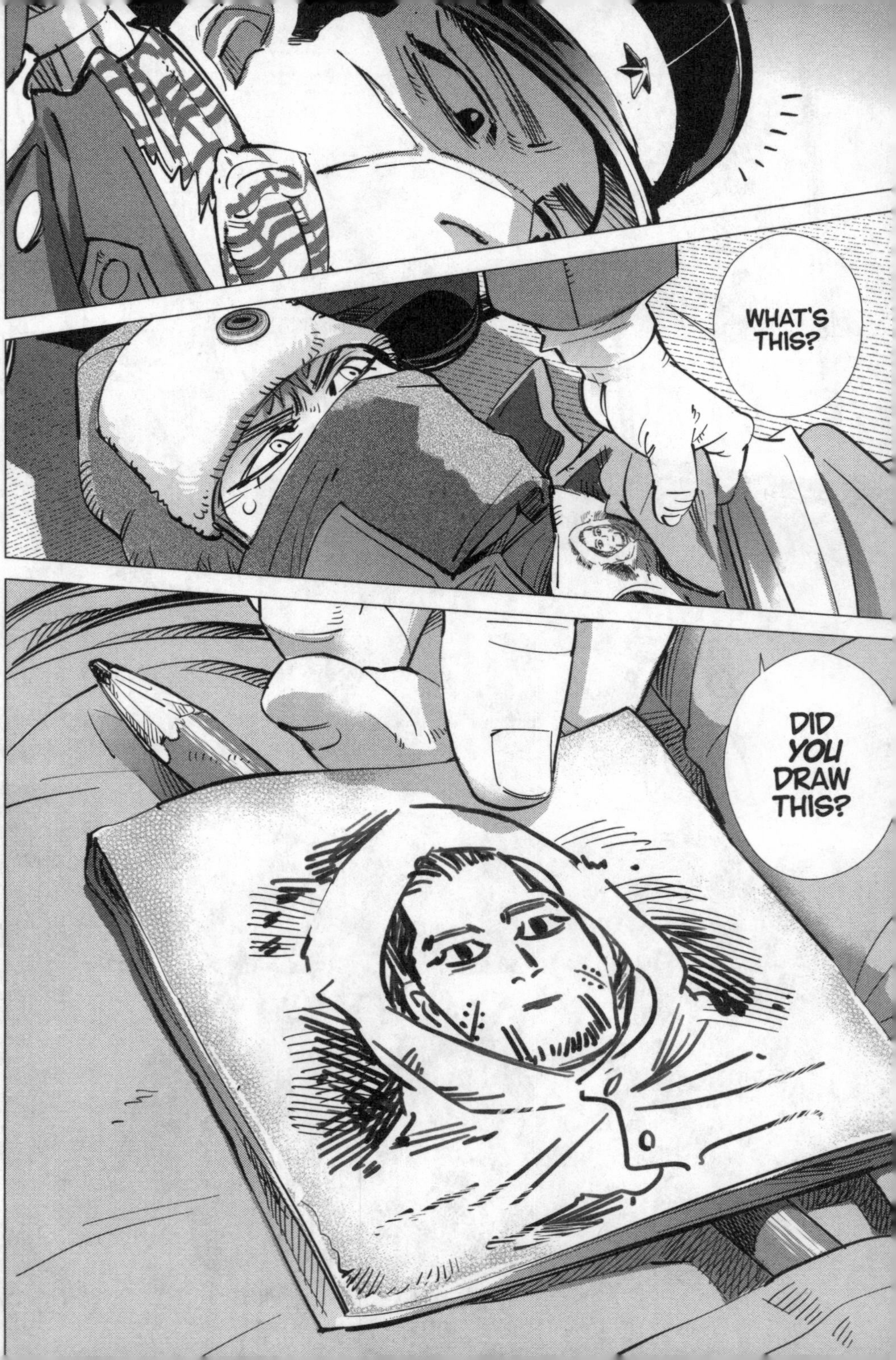
WHAT'S THIS?
DID *YOU* DRAW THIS?

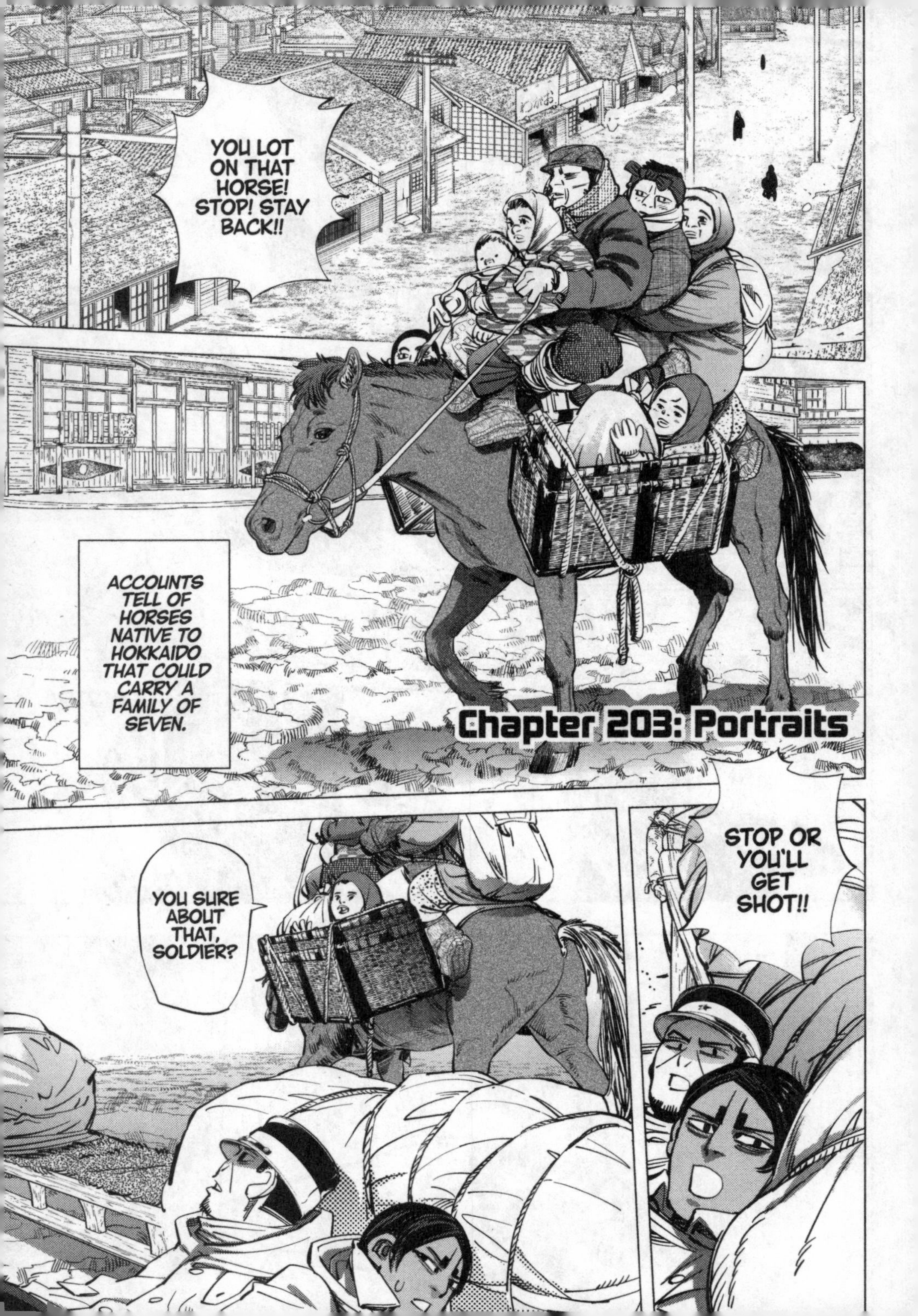
YOU LOT ON THAT HORSE! STOP! STAY BACK!!
ACCOUNTS TELL OF HORSES NATIVE TO HOKKAIDO THAT COULD CARRY A FAMILY OF SEVEN.
Chapter 203: Portraits
STOP OR YOU'LL GET SHOT!!
YOU SURE ABOUT THAT, SOLDIER?

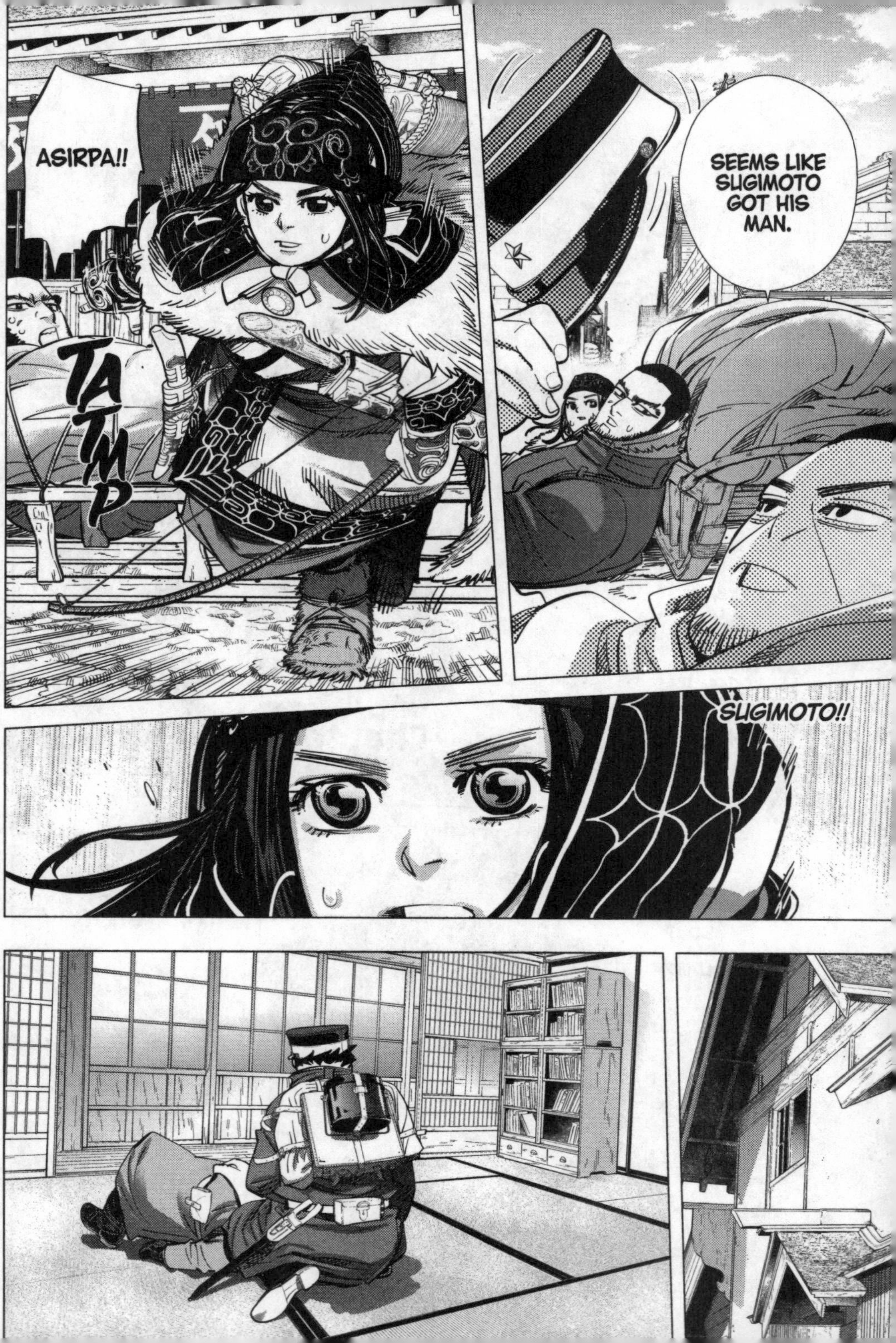
SEEMS LIKE SUGIMOTO GOT HIS MAN.
ASIRPA!!
TATMP
SUGIMOTO!!

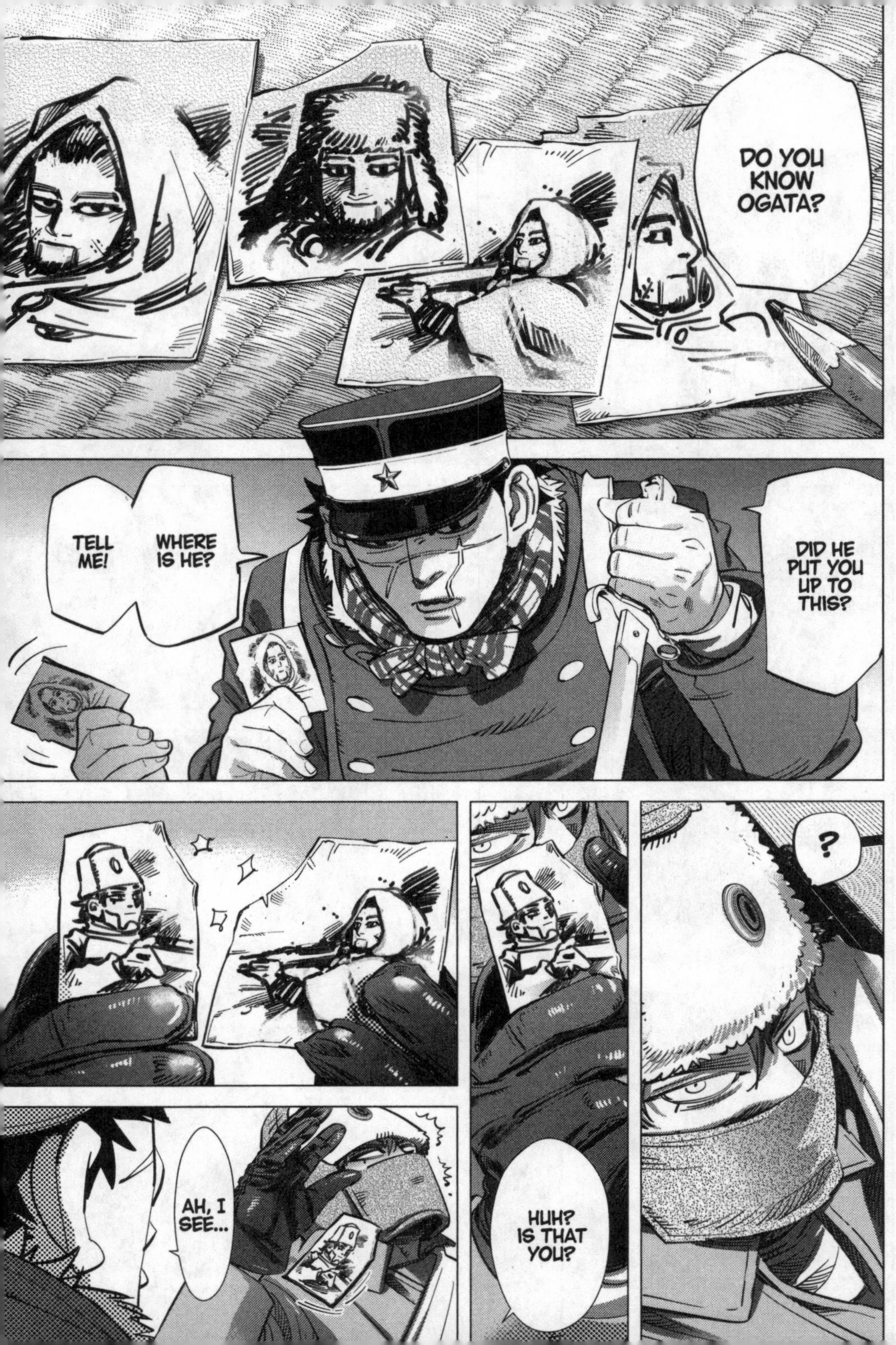
DO YOU KNOW OGATA?
DID HE PUT YOU UP TO THIS?
WHERE IS HE?
TELL ME!
?
HUH? IS THAT YOU?
AH, I SEE...

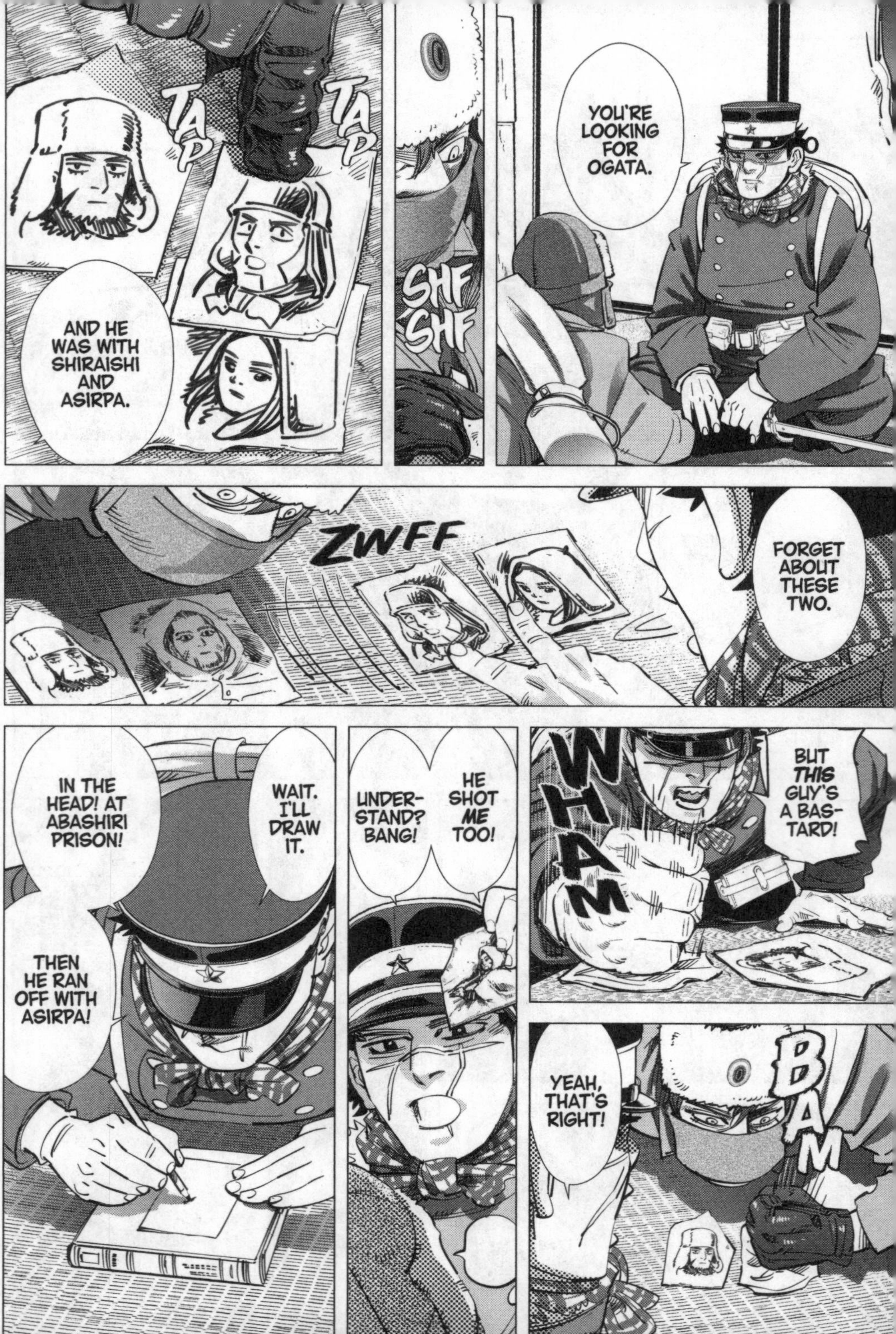
YOU'RE LOOKING FOR OGATA.
SHF SHF
TAP TAP
AND HE WAS WITH SHIRAISHI AND ASIRPA.
FORGET ABOUT THESE TWO.
ZWFF
BUT *THIS* GUY'S A BAS-TARD!
WHAM
BAM
YEAH, THAT'S RIGHT!
HE SHOT *ME* TOO!
UNDER-STAND? BANG!
WAIT. I'LL DRAW IT.
IN THE HEAD! AT ABASHIRI PRISON!
THEN HE RAN OFF WITH ASIRPA!

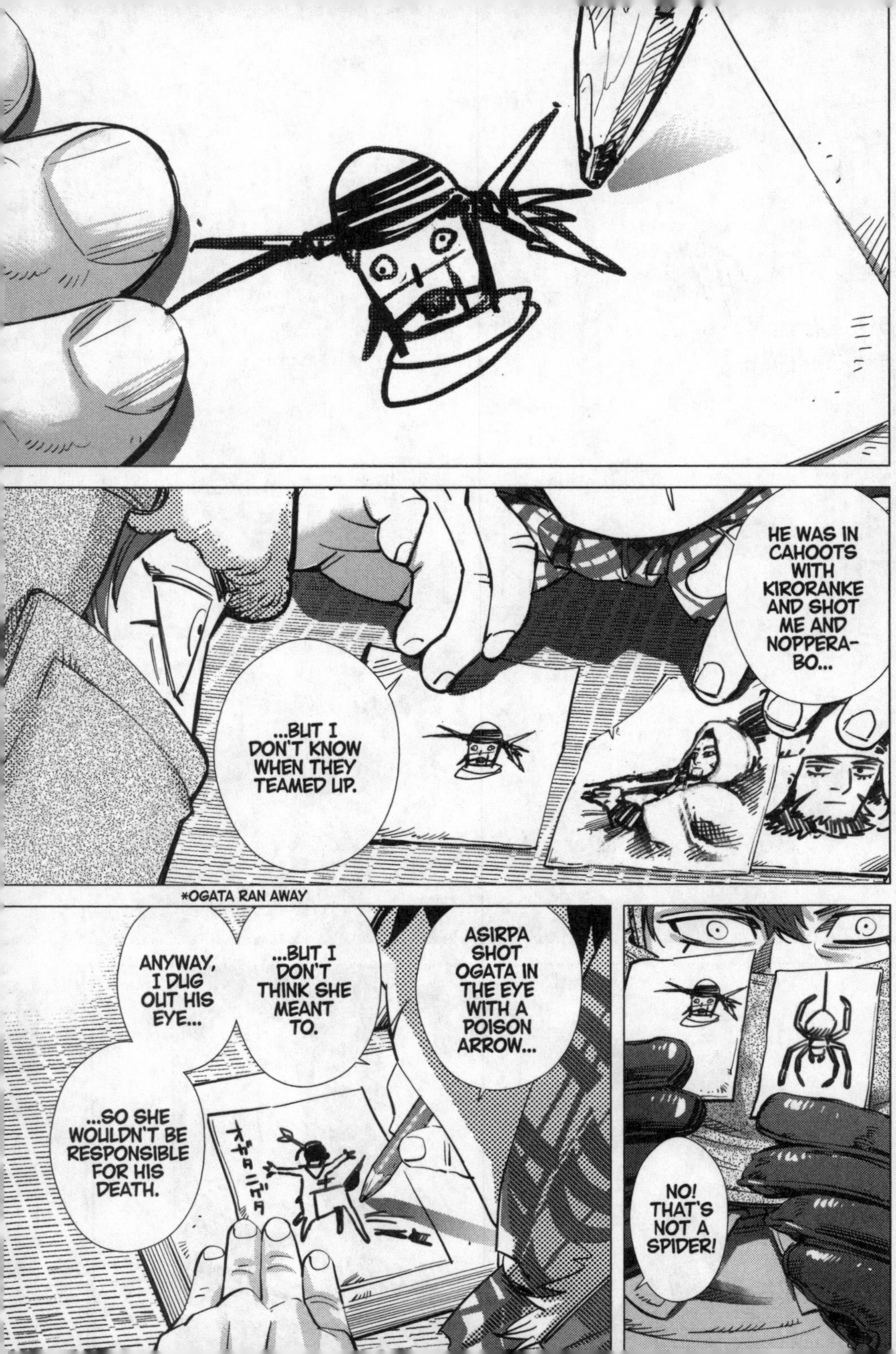
HE WAS IN CAHOOTS WITH KIRORANKE AND SHOT ME AND NOPPERA-BO...
...BUT I DON'T KNOW WHEN THEY TEAMED UP.
*OGATA RAN AWAY
NO! THAT'S NOT A SPIDER!
ASIRPA SHOT OGATA IN THE EYE WITH A POISON ARROW...
...BUT I DON'T THINK SHE MEANT TO.
ANYWAY, I DUG OUT HIS EYE...
...SO SHE WOULDN'T BE RESPONSIBLE FOR HIS DEATH.
オガタニゲタ

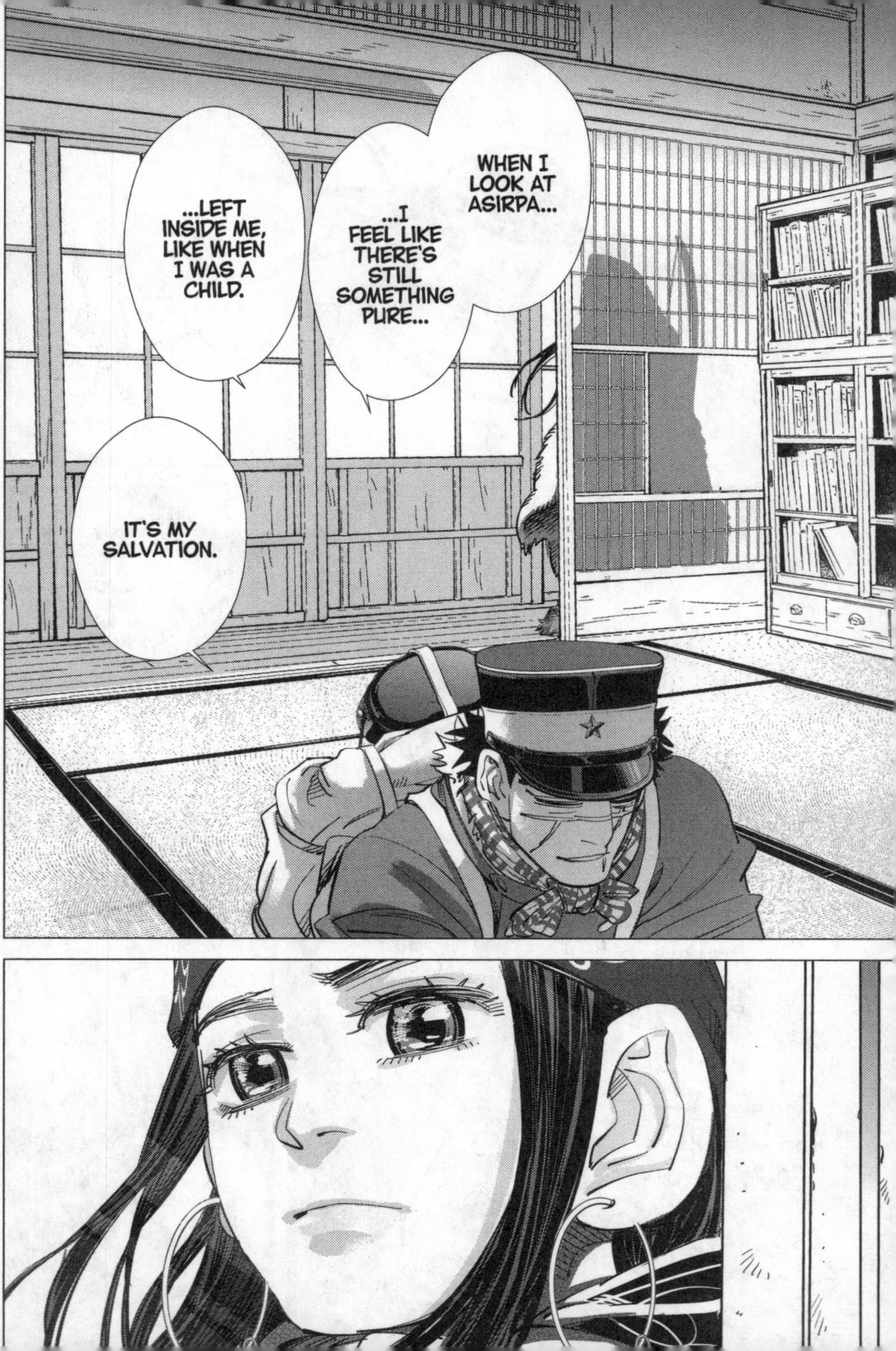
WHEN I LOOK AT ASIRPA...
...I FEEL LIKE THERE'S STILL SOMETHING PURE...
...LEFT INSIDE ME, LIKE WHEN I WAS A CHILD.
IT'S MY SALVATION.

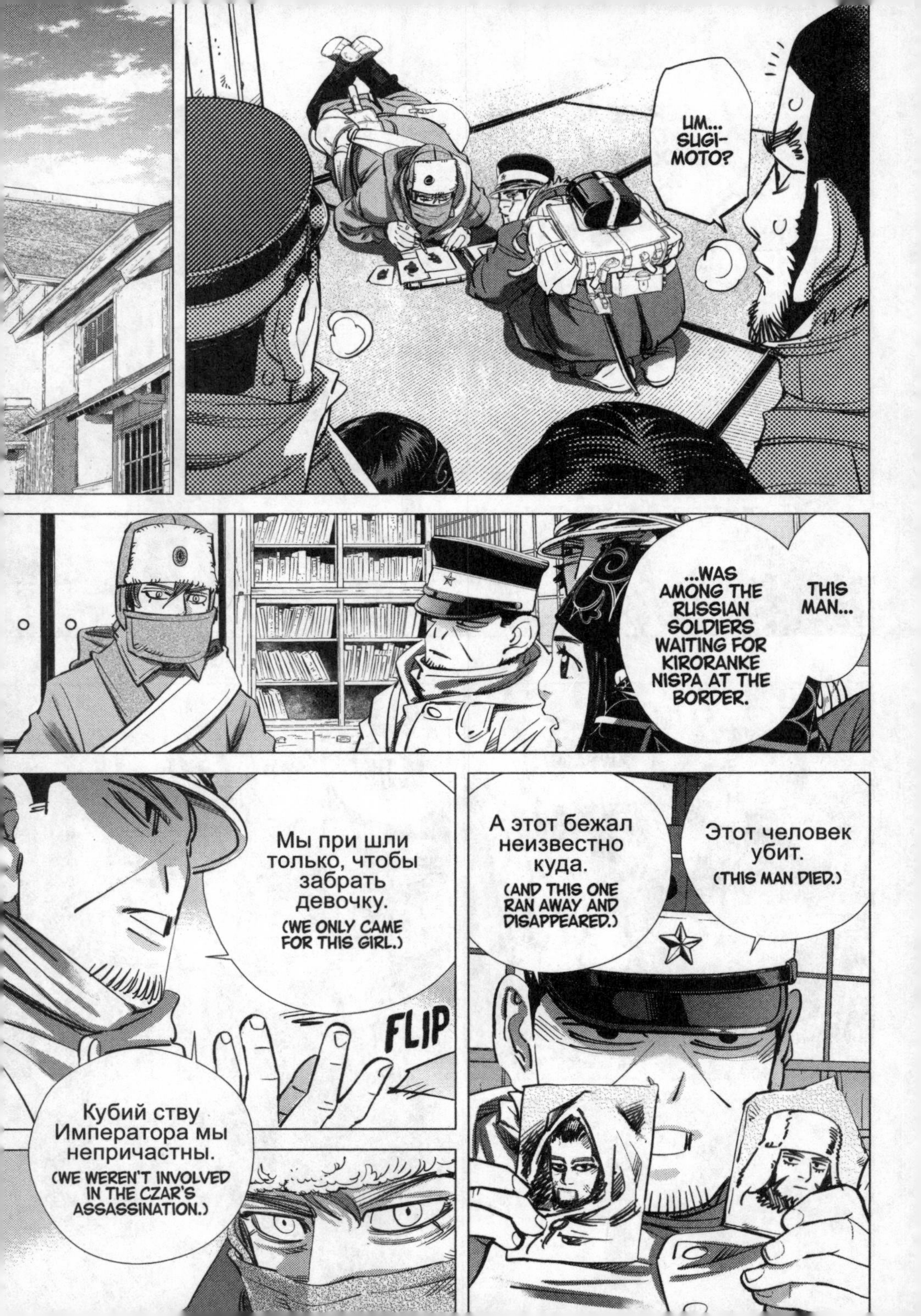
UM... SUGI-MOTO?
THIS MAN...
...WAS AMONG THE RUSSIAN SOLDIERS WAITING FOR KIRORANKE NISPA AT THE BORDER.
Этот человек убит.
(THIS MAN DIED.)
А этот бежал неизвестно куда.
(AND THIS ONE RAN AWAY AND DISAPPEARED.)
Мы при шли только, чтобы забрать девочку.
(WE ONLY CAME FOR THIS GIRL.)
FLIP
Кубий ству Императора мы непричастны.
(WE WEREN'T INVOLVED IN THE CZAR'S ASSASSINATION.)

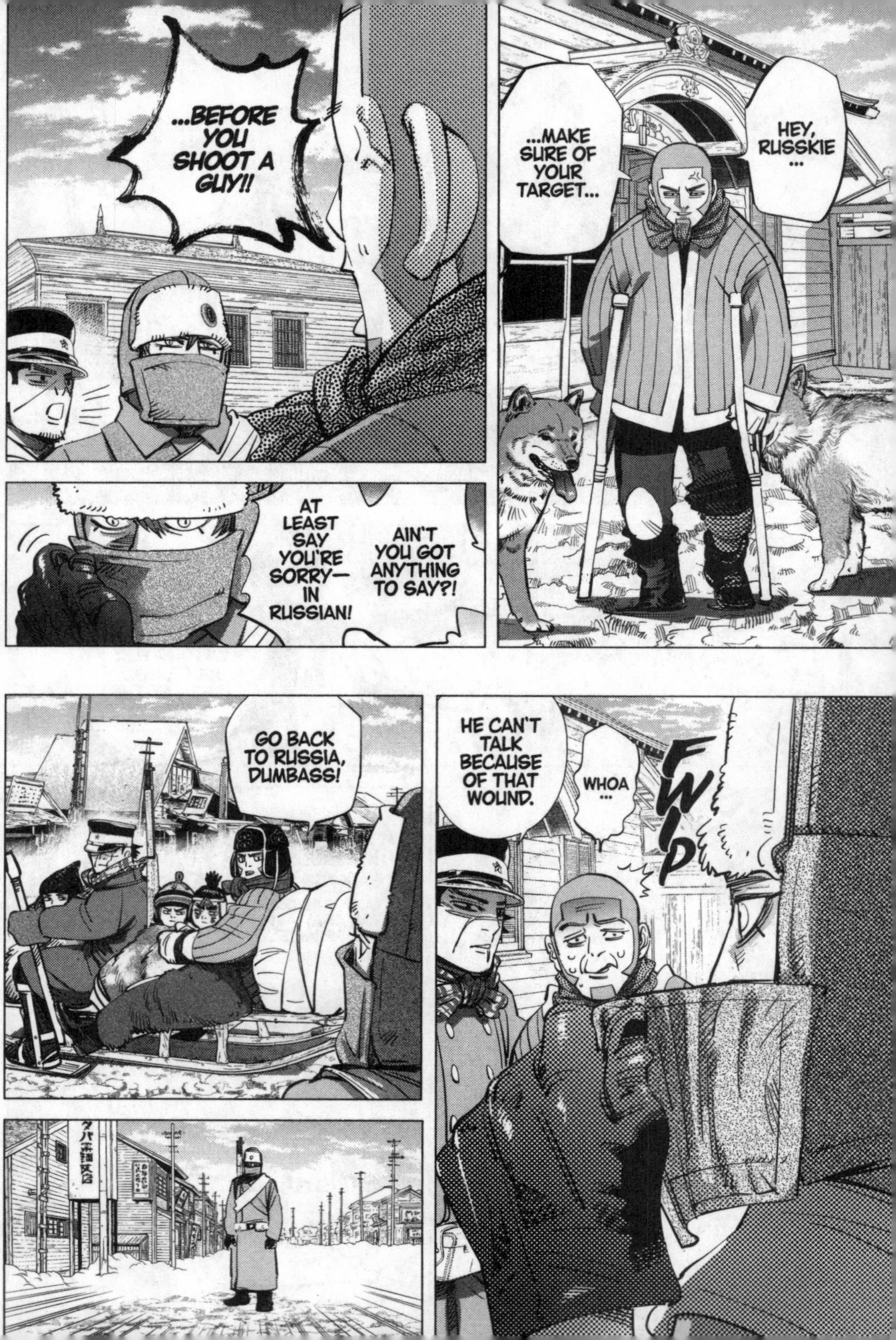
HEY, RUSSKIE...
...MAKE SURE OF YOUR TARGET...
...BEFORE YOU SHOOT A GUY!!
AIN'T YOU GOT ANYTHING TO SAY?!
AT LEAST SAY YOU'RE SORRY— IN RUSSIAN!
FWIP
WHOA...
HE CAN'T TALK BECAUSE OF THAT WOUND.
GO BACK TO RUSSIA, DUMBASS!

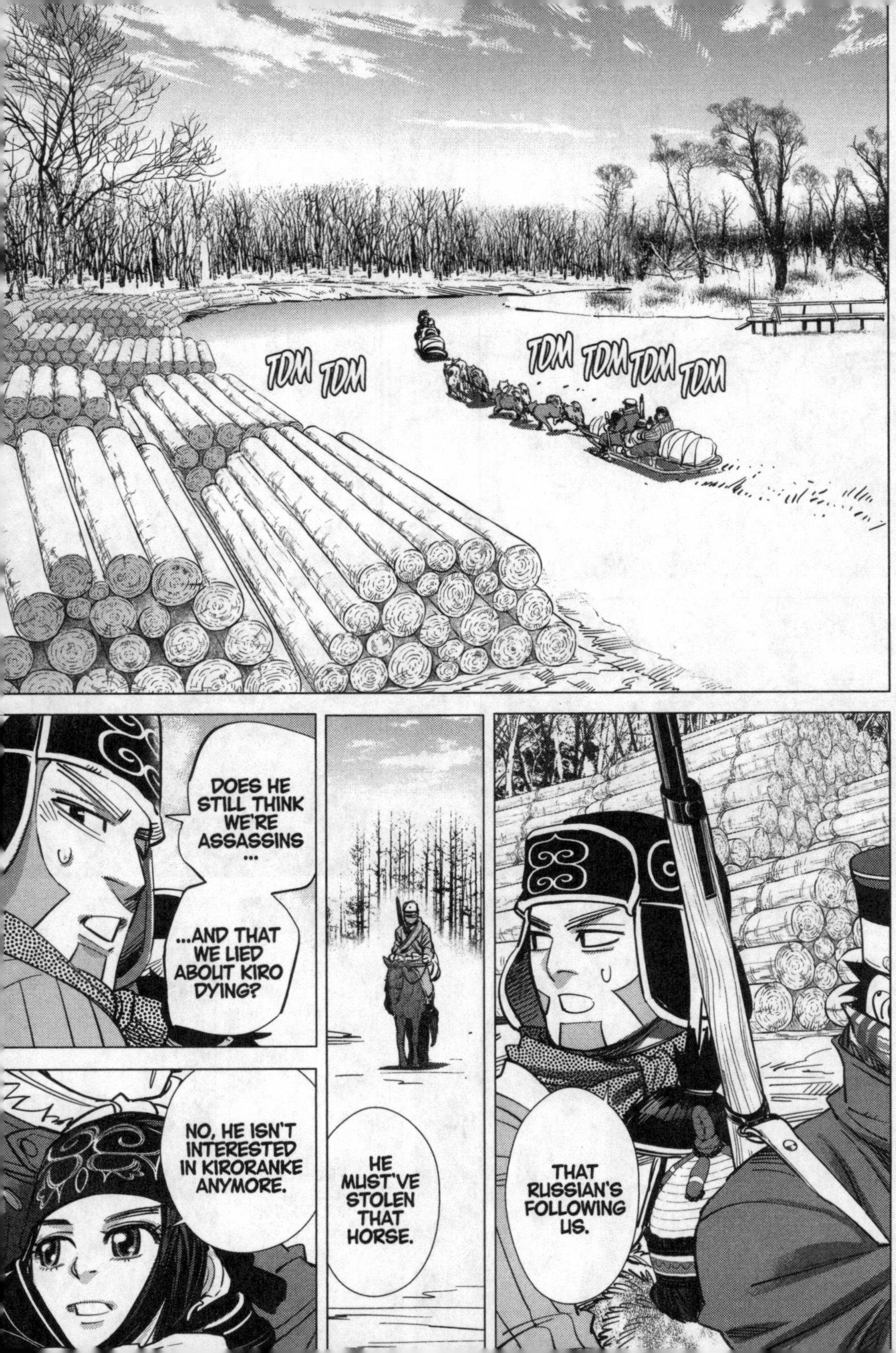
TDM TDM TDM TDM
TDM TDM
THAT RUSSIAN'S FOLLOWING US.
HE MUST'VE STOLEN THAT HORSE.
DOES HE STILL THINK WE'RE ASSASSINS ...
...AND THAT WE LIED ABOUT KIRO DYING?
NO, HE ISN'T INTERESTED IN KIRORANKE ANYMORE.

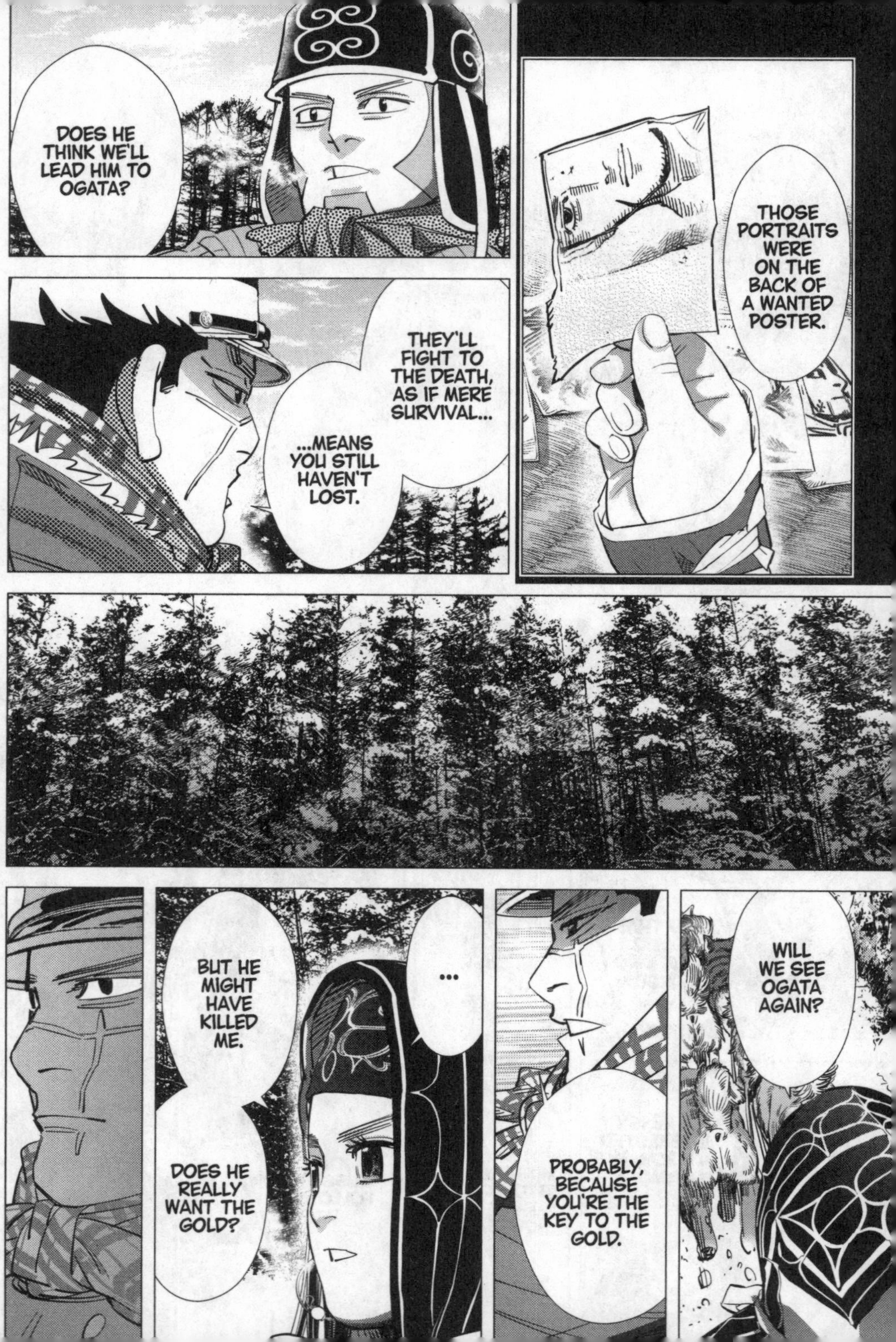
THOSE PORTRAITS WERE ON THE BACK OF A WANTED POSTER.
DOES HE THINK WE'LL LEAD HIM TO OGATA?
THEY'LL FIGHT TO THE DEATH, AS IF MERE SURVIVAL...
...MEANS YOU STILL HAVEN'T LOST.
WILL WE SEE OGATA AGAIN?
PROBABLY, BECAUSE YOU'RE THE KEY TO THE GOLD.
...
BUT HE MIGHT HAVE KILLED ME.
DOES HE REALLY WANT THE GOLD?

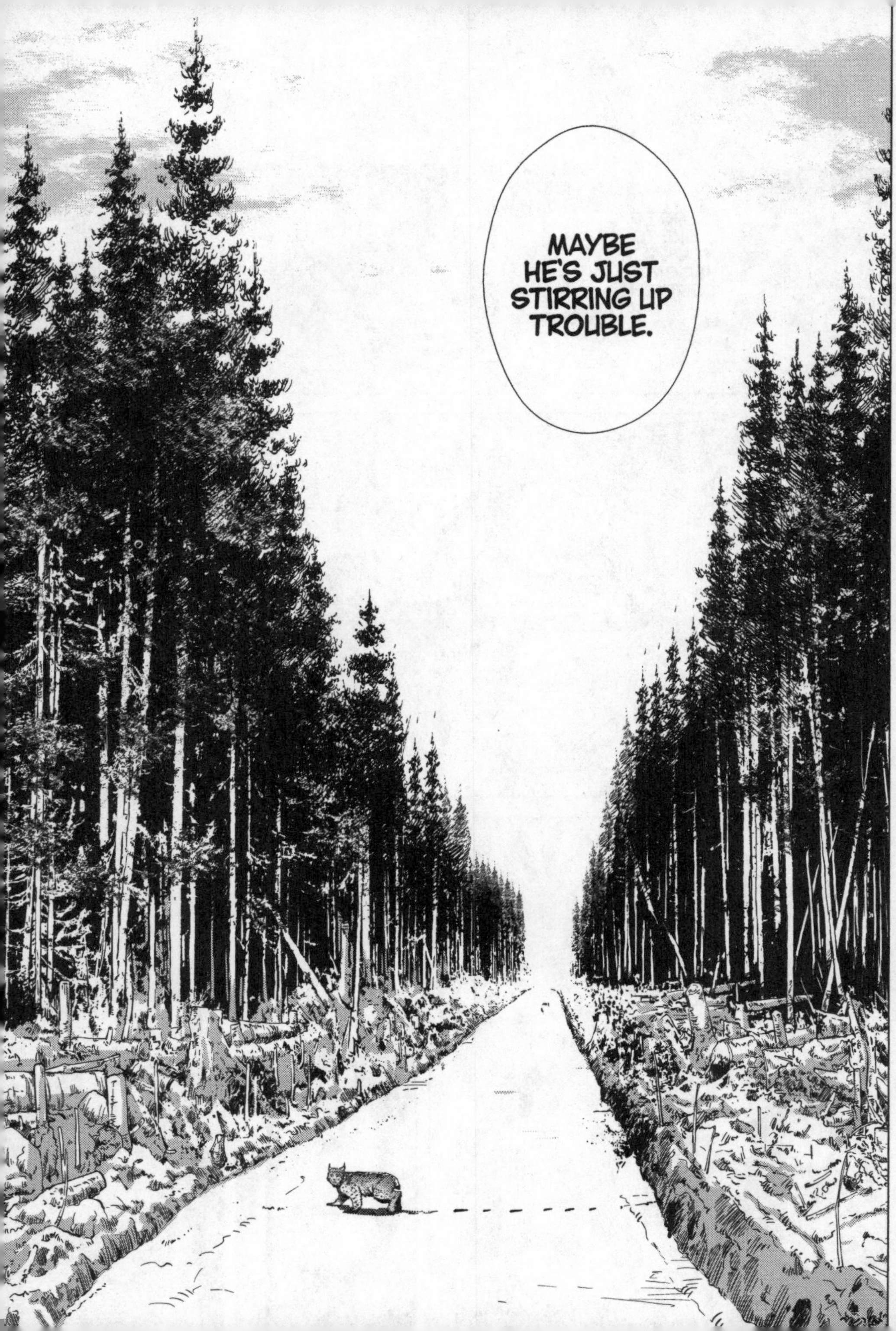
MAYBE HE'S JUST STIRRING UP TROUBLE.

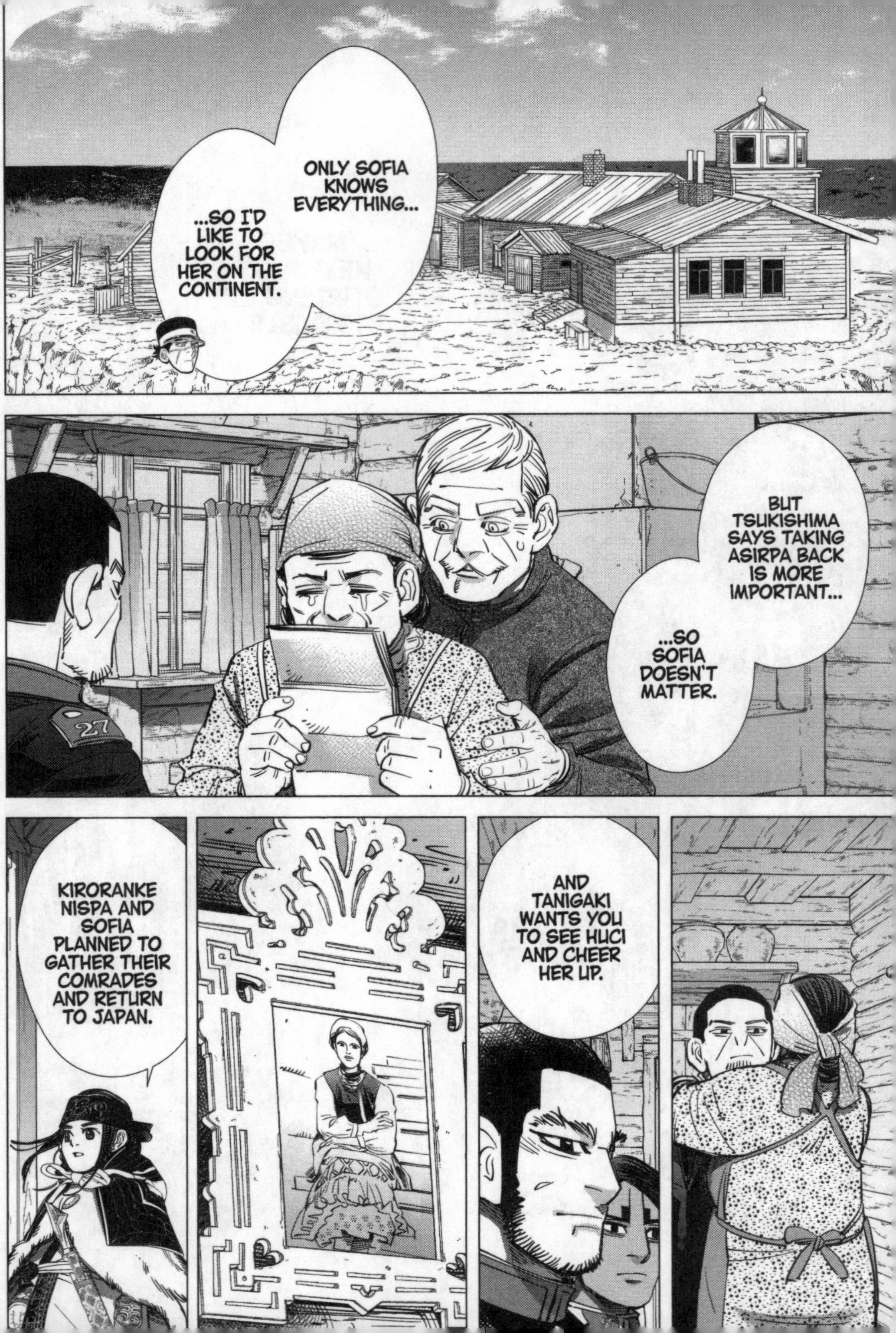
ONLY SOFIA KNOWS EVERYTHING...
...SO I'D LIKE TO LOOK FOR HER ON THE CONTINENT.
BUT TSUKISHIMA SAYS TAKING ASIRPA BACK IS MORE IMPORTANT...
...SO SOFIA DOESN'T MATTER.
AND TANIGAKI WANTS YOU TO SEE HUCI AND CHEER HER UP.
KIRORANKE NISPA AND SOFIA PLANNED TO GATHER THEIR COMRADES AND RETURN TO JAPAN.

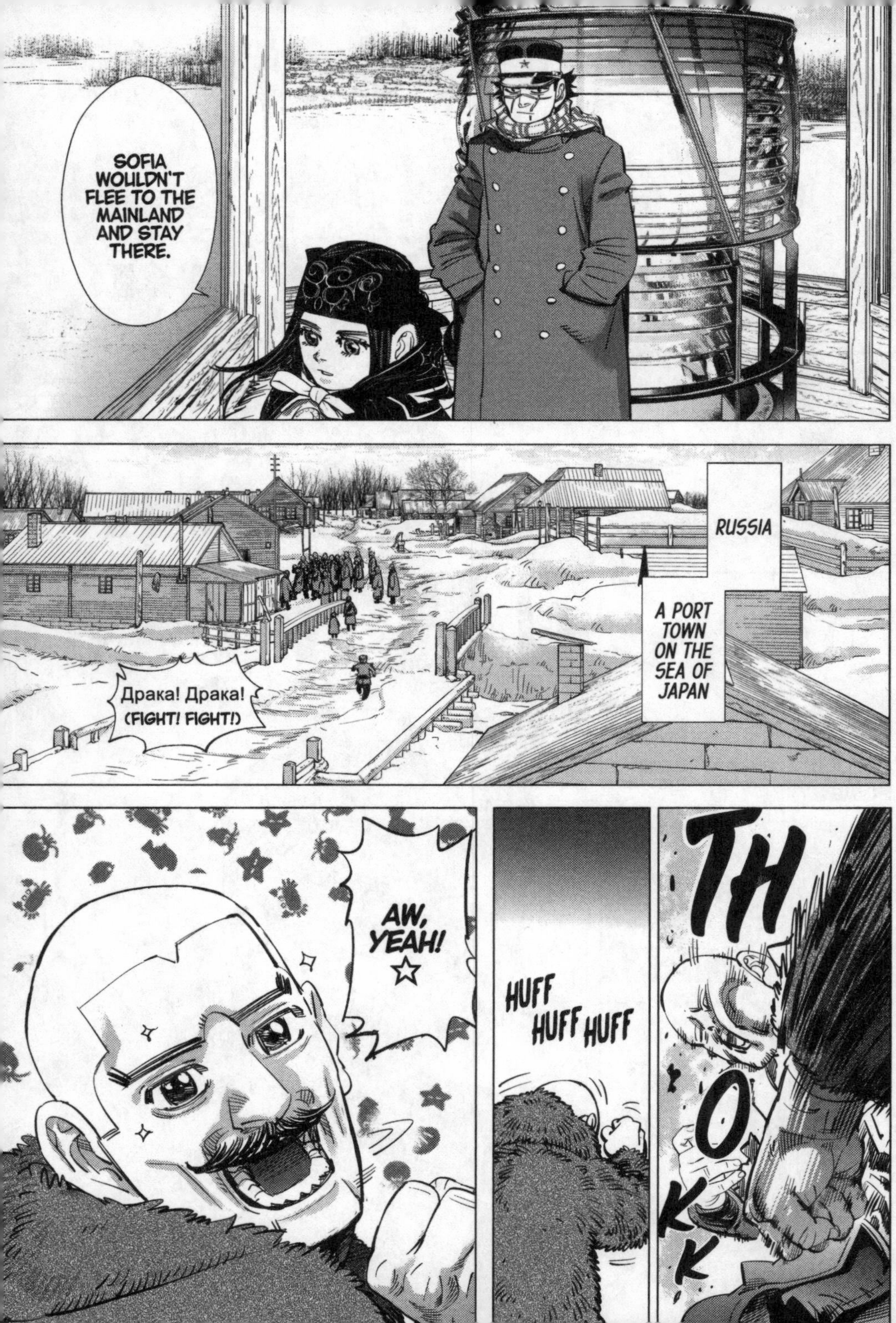
SOFIA WOULDN'T FLEE TO THE MAINLAND AND STAY THERE.
RUSSIA
A PORT TOWN ON THE SEA OF JAPAN
Драка! Драка!
(FIGHT! FIGHT!)
THOKK
HUFF HUFF HUFF
AW, YEAH! ☆

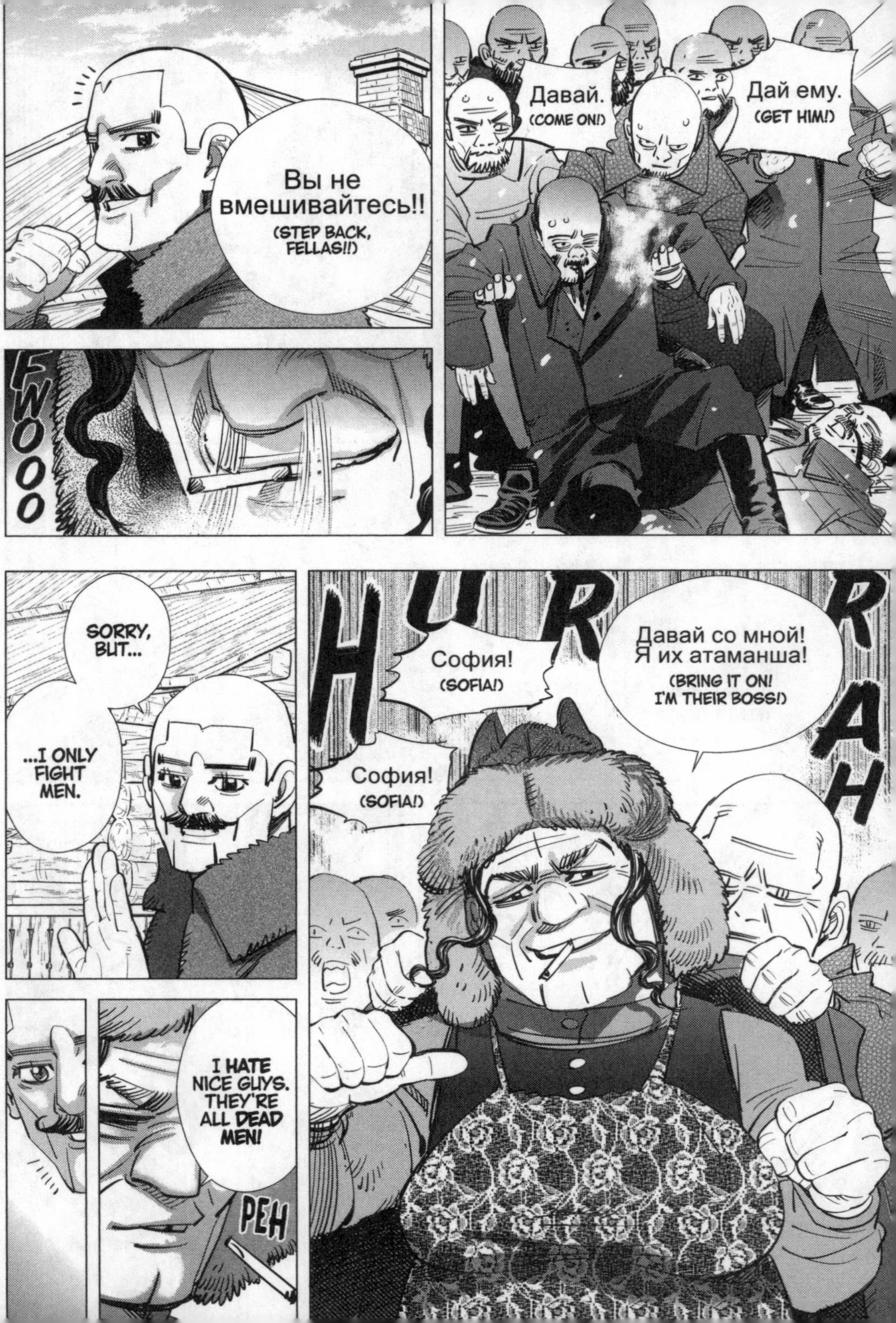
Дай ему.
(GET HIM!)
Давай.
(COME ON!)
Вы не вмешивайтесь!!
(STEP BACK, FELLAS!!)
FWOOOO
HURRAH
Давай со мной! Я их атаманша!
(BRING IT ON! I'M THEIR BOSS!)
София!
(SOFIA!)
София!
(SOFIA!)
SORRY, BUT...
...I ONLY FIGHT MEN.
I HATE NICE GUYS. THEY'RE ALL DEAD MEN!
PEH

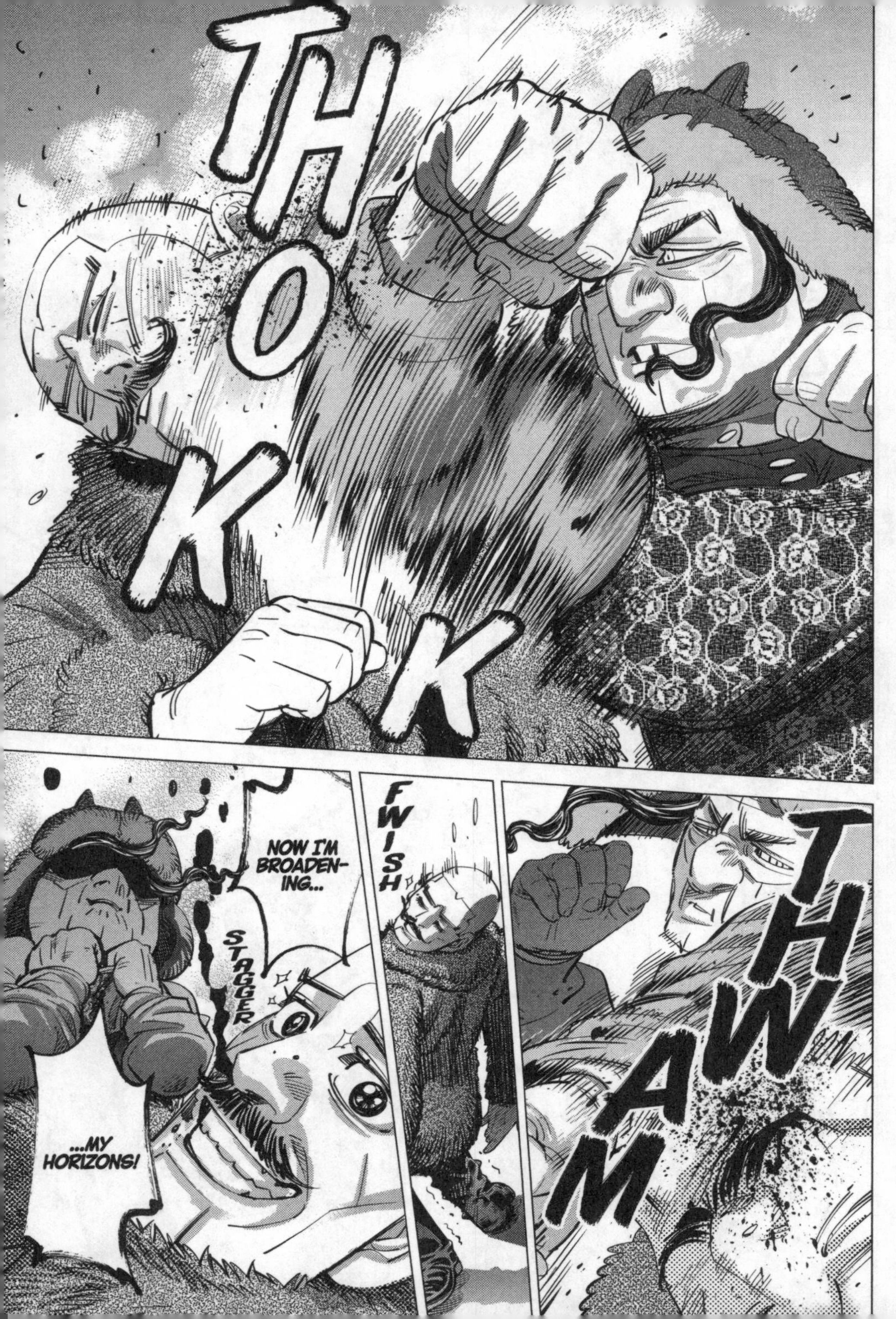
THOKK
THWAM
FWISH
NOW I'M BROADEN-ING...
STAGGER
...MY HORIZONS!

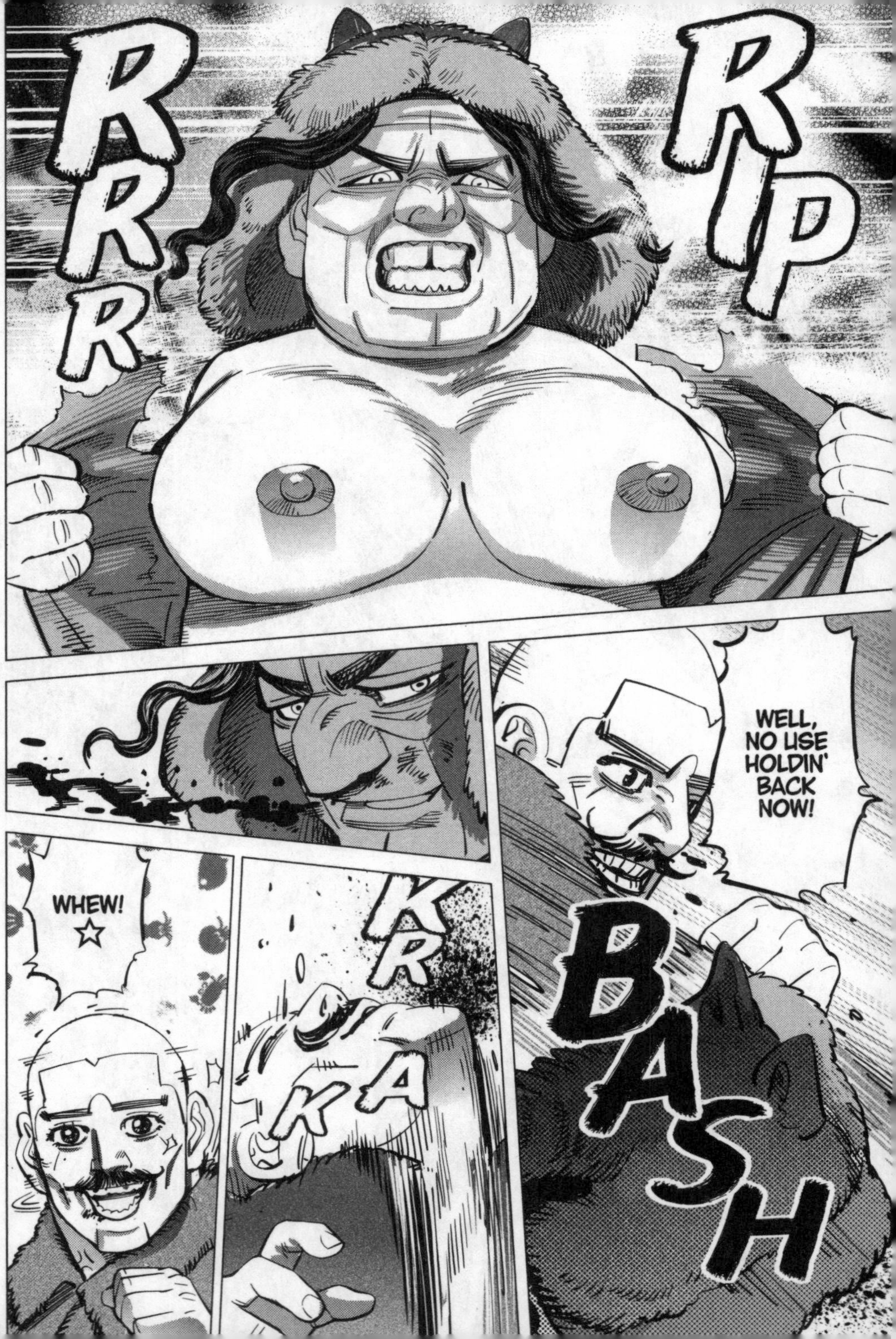
RRR
RIP
WELL, NO USE HOLDIN' BACK NOW!
BASH
KRAKA
WHEW! ☆

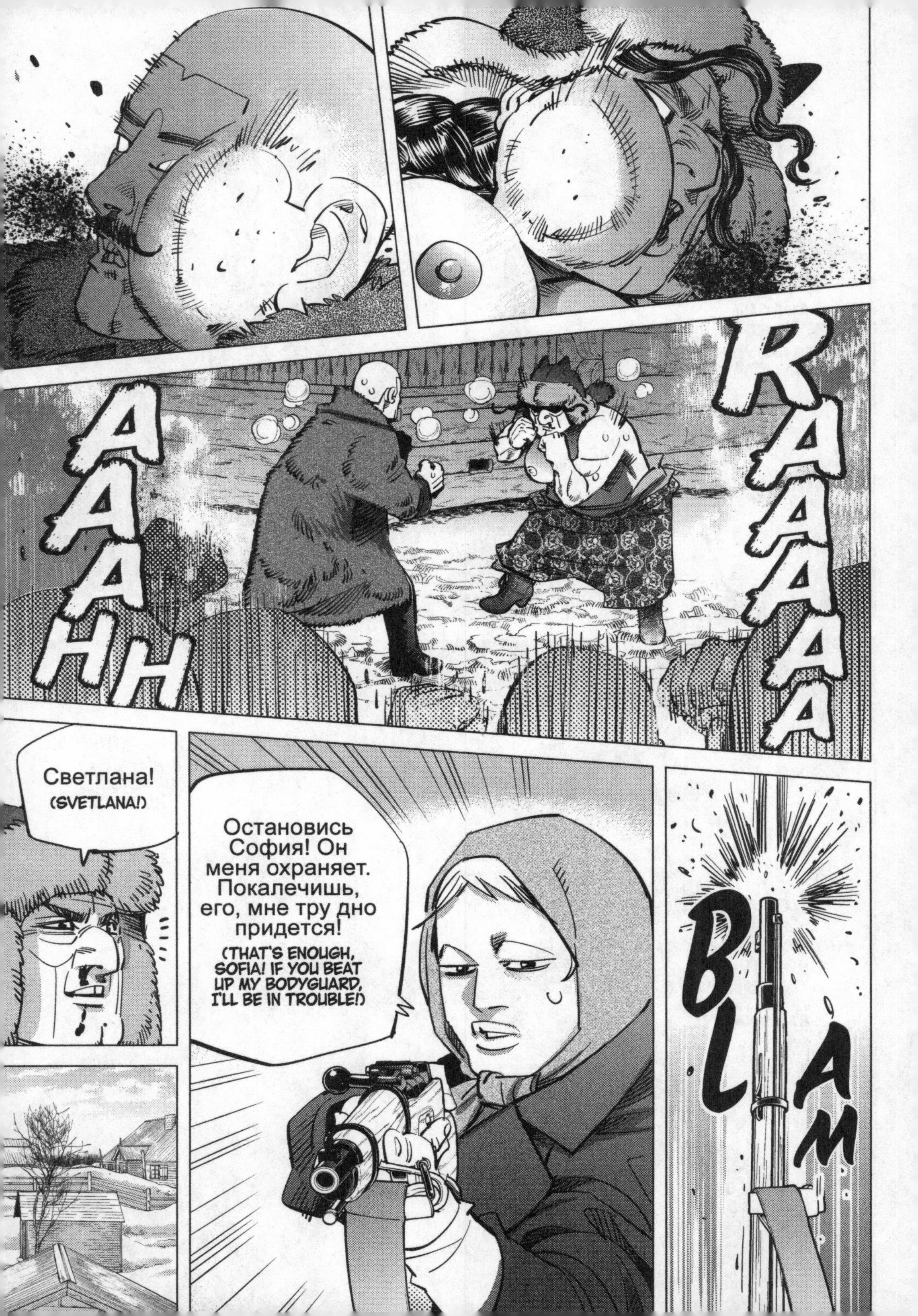
RAAAAAA
AAAHH
BLAM
Остановись София! Он меня охраняет. Покалечишь, его, мне тру дно придется!
(THAT'S ENOUGH, SOFIA! IF YOU BEAT UP MY BODYGUARD, I'LL BE IN TROUBLE!)
Светлана!
(SVETLANA!)

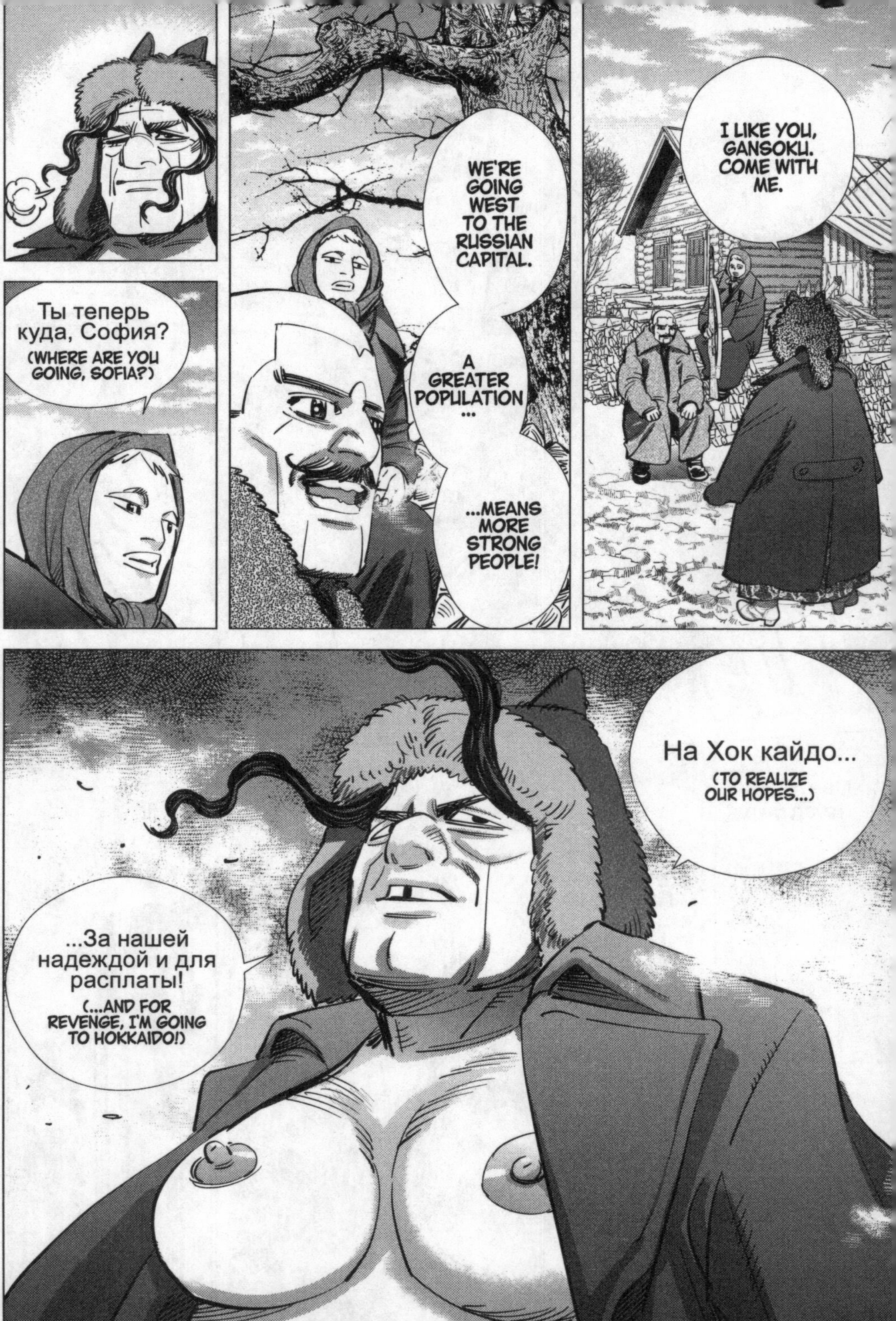
I LIKE YOU, GANSOKU. COME WITH ME.
WE'RE GOING WEST TO THE RUSSIAN CAPITAL.
A GREATER POPULATION...
...MEANS MORE STRONG PEOPLE!
Ты теперь куда, София?
(WHERE ARE YOU GOING, SOFIA?)
На Хок кайдо...
(TO REALIZE OUR HOPES...)
...За нашей надеждой и для расплаты!
(...AND FOR REVENGE, I'M GOING TO HOKKAIDO!)

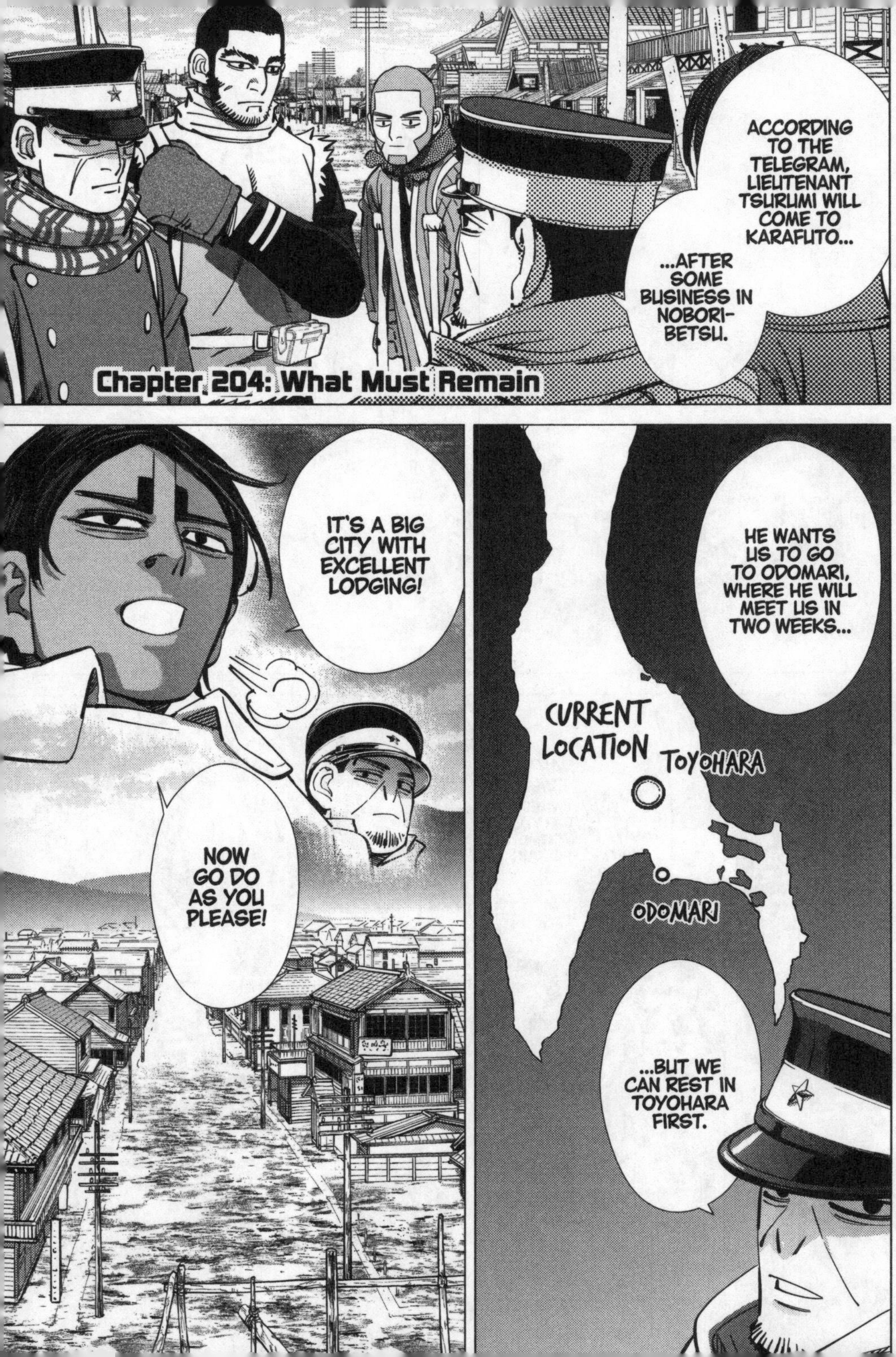
Chapter 204: What Must Remain
ACCORDING TO THE TELEGRAM, LIEUTENANT TSURUMI WILL COME TO KARAFUTO...
...AFTER SOME BUSINESS IN NOBORI-BETSU.
HE WANTS US TO GO TO ODOMARI, WHERE HE WILL MEET US IN TWO WEEKS...
CURRENT LOCATION
TOYOHARA
ODOMARI
...BUT WE CAN REST IN TOYOHARA FIRST.
IT'S A BIG CITY WITH EXCELLENT LODGING!
NOW GO DO AS YOU PLEASE!

Chapter 204: What Must Remain

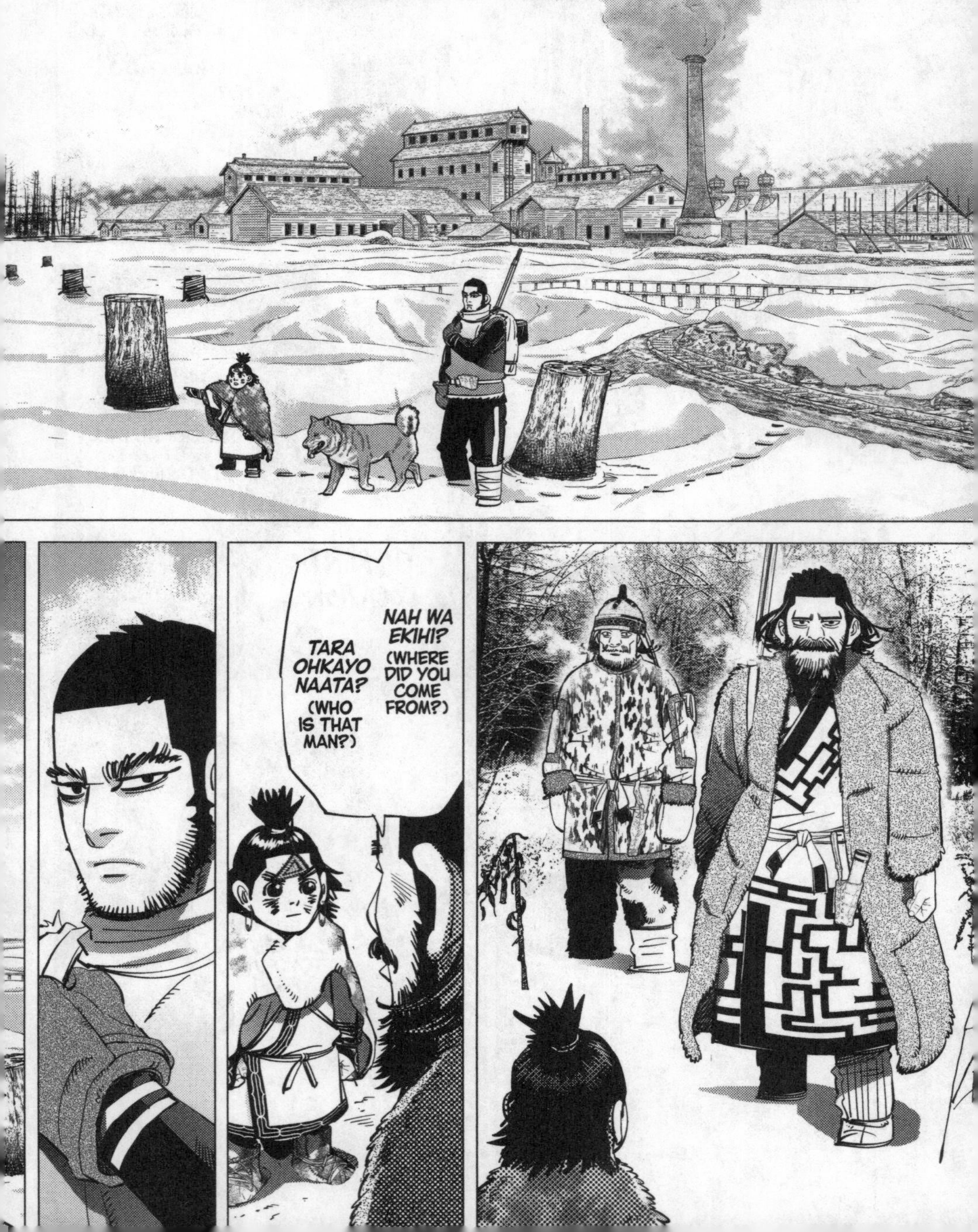
NAH WA EKIHI? (WHERE DID YOU COME FROM?)
TARA OHKAYO NAATA? (WHO IS THAT MAN?)

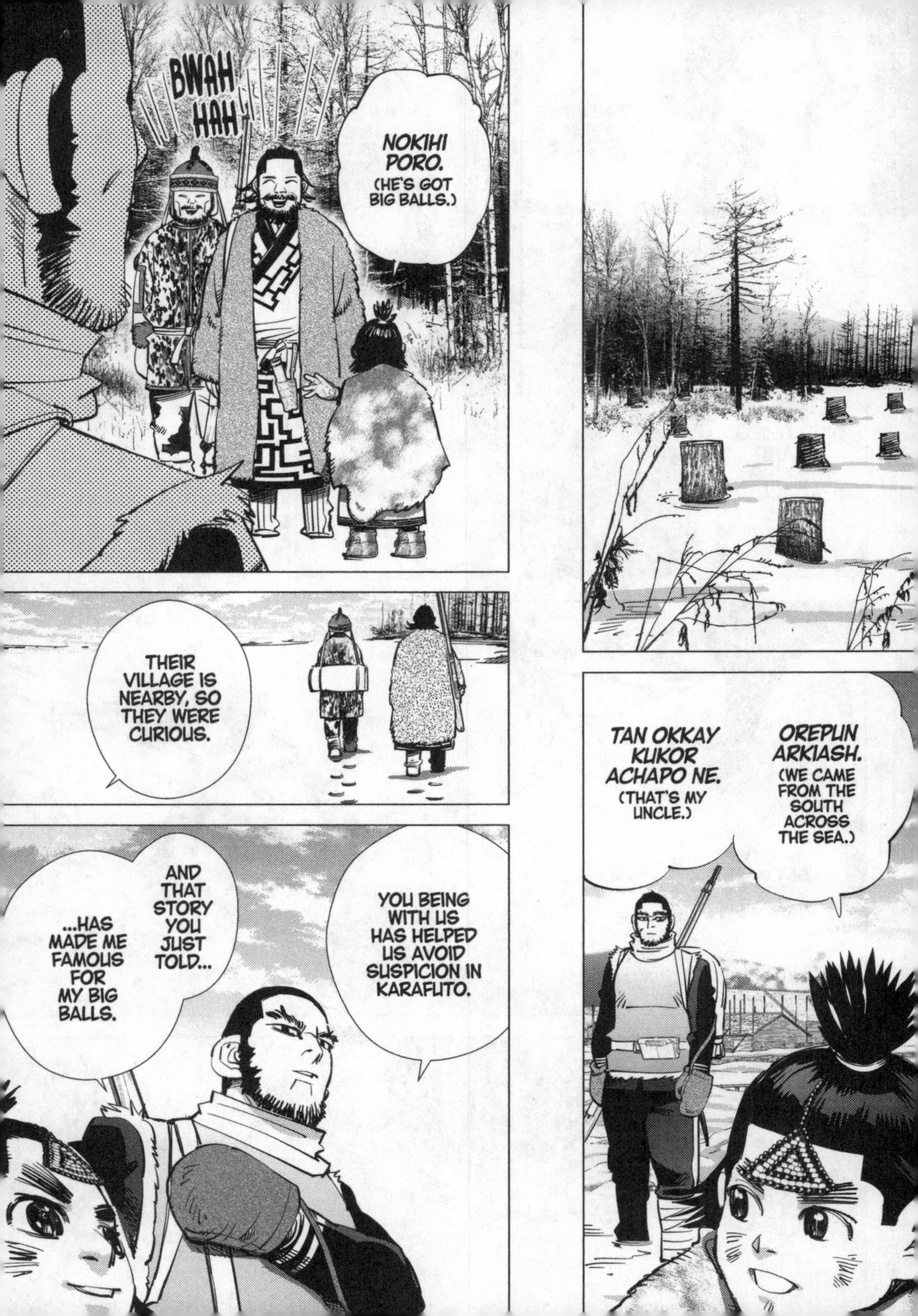

OREPUN ARKIASH.
(WE CAME FROM THE SOUTH ACROSS THE SEA.)
TAN OKKAY KUKOR ACHAPO NE.
(THAT'S MY UNCLE.)
BWAH HAH
NOKIHI PORO.
(HE'S GOT BIG BALLS.)
THEIR VILLAGE IS NEARBY, SO THEY WERE CURIOUS.
YOU BEING WITH US HAS HELPED US AVOID SUSPICION IN KARAFUTO.
AND THAT STORY YOU JUST TOLD...
...HAS MADE ME FAMOUS FOR MY BIG BALLS.

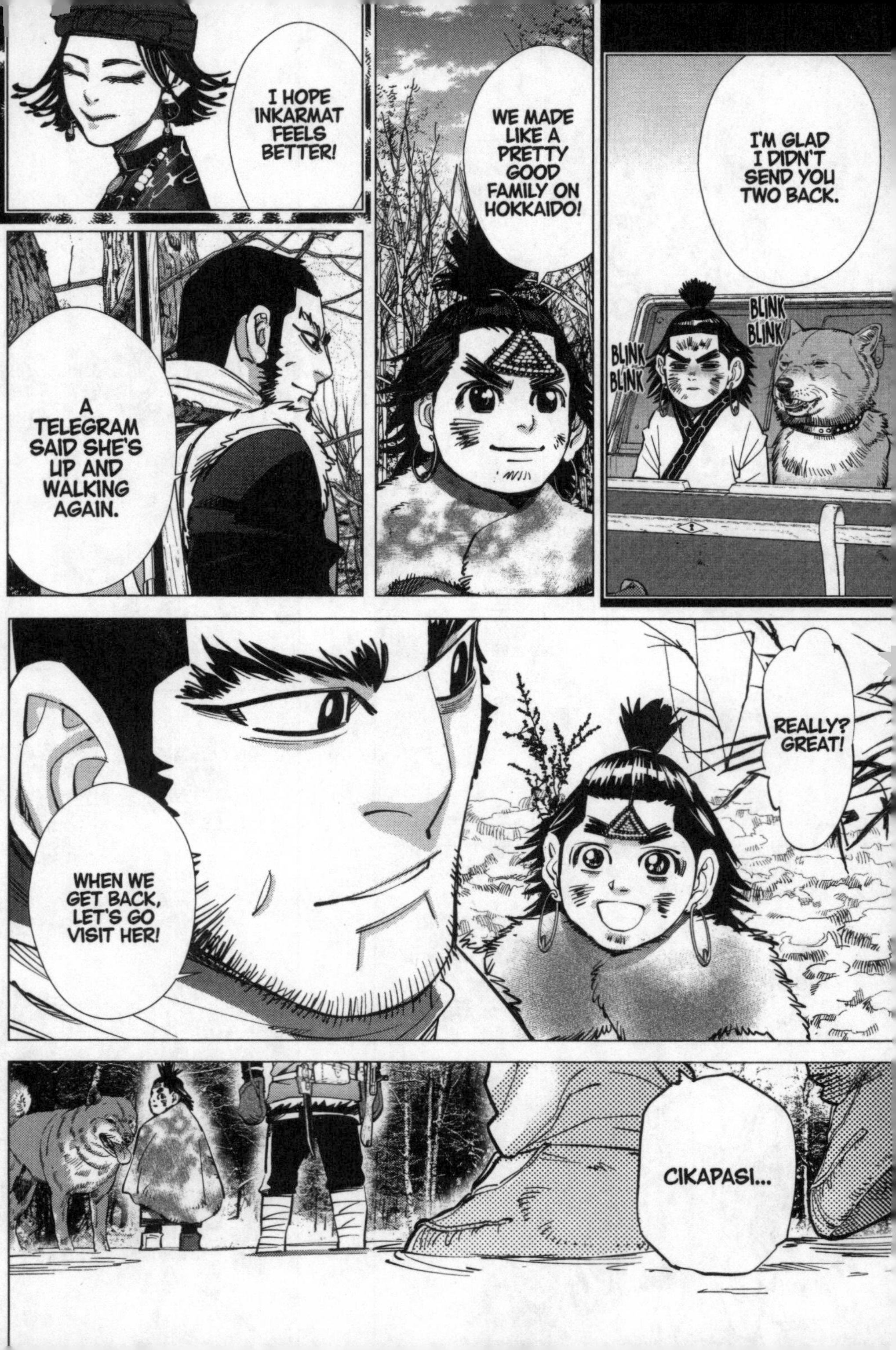
I'M GLAD I DIDN'T SEND YOU TWO BACK.
BLINK BLINK
BLINK BLINK
WE MADE LIKE A PRETTY GOOD FAMILY ON HOKKAIDO!
I HOPE INKARMAT FEELS BETTER!
A TELEGRAM SAID SHE'S UP AND WALKING AGAIN.
REALLY? GREAT!
WHEN WE GET BACK, LET'S GO VISIT HER!
CIKAPASI...

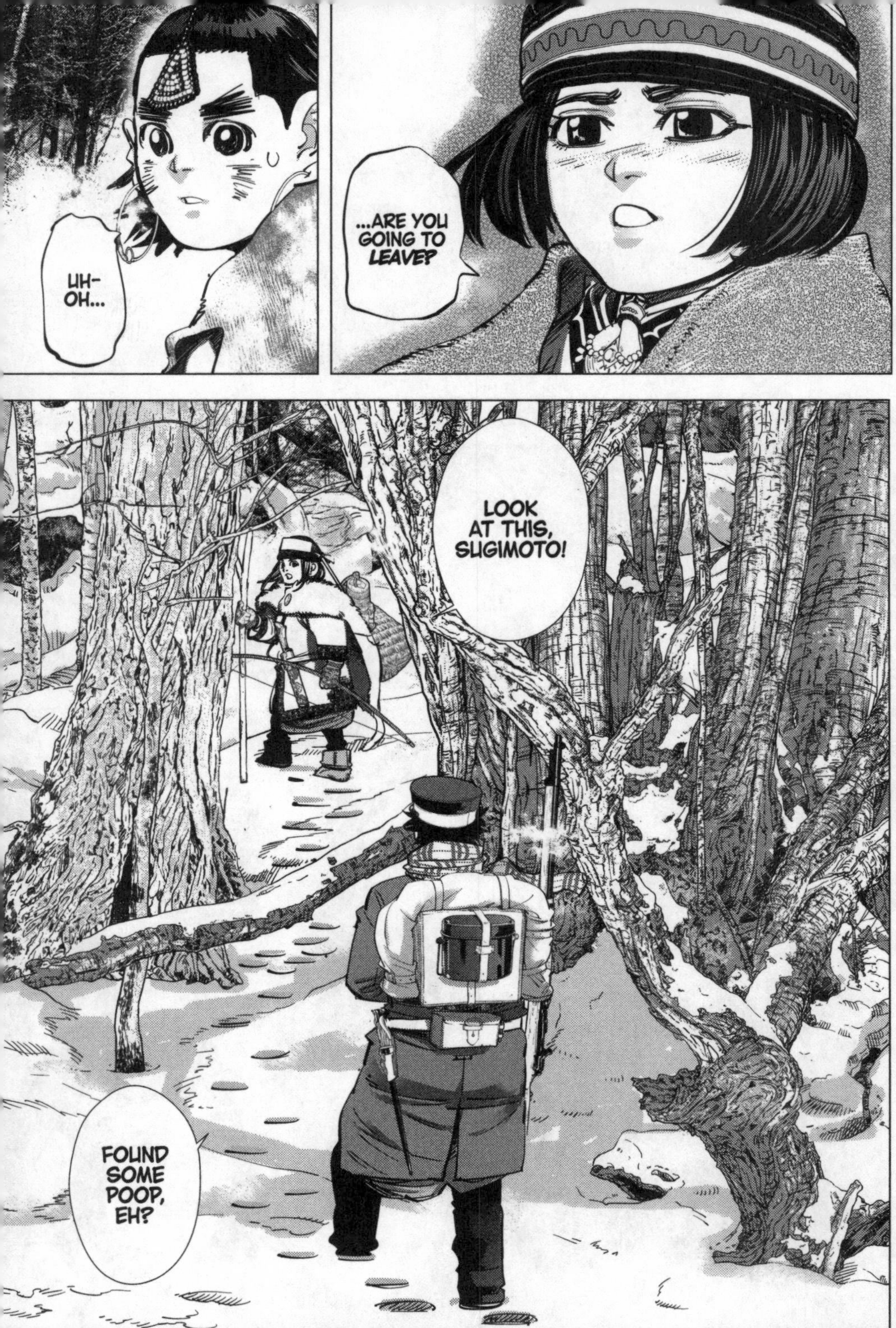
...ARE YOU GOING TO LEAVE?
UH-OH...
LOOK AT THIS, SUGIMOTO!
FOUND SOME POOP, EH?

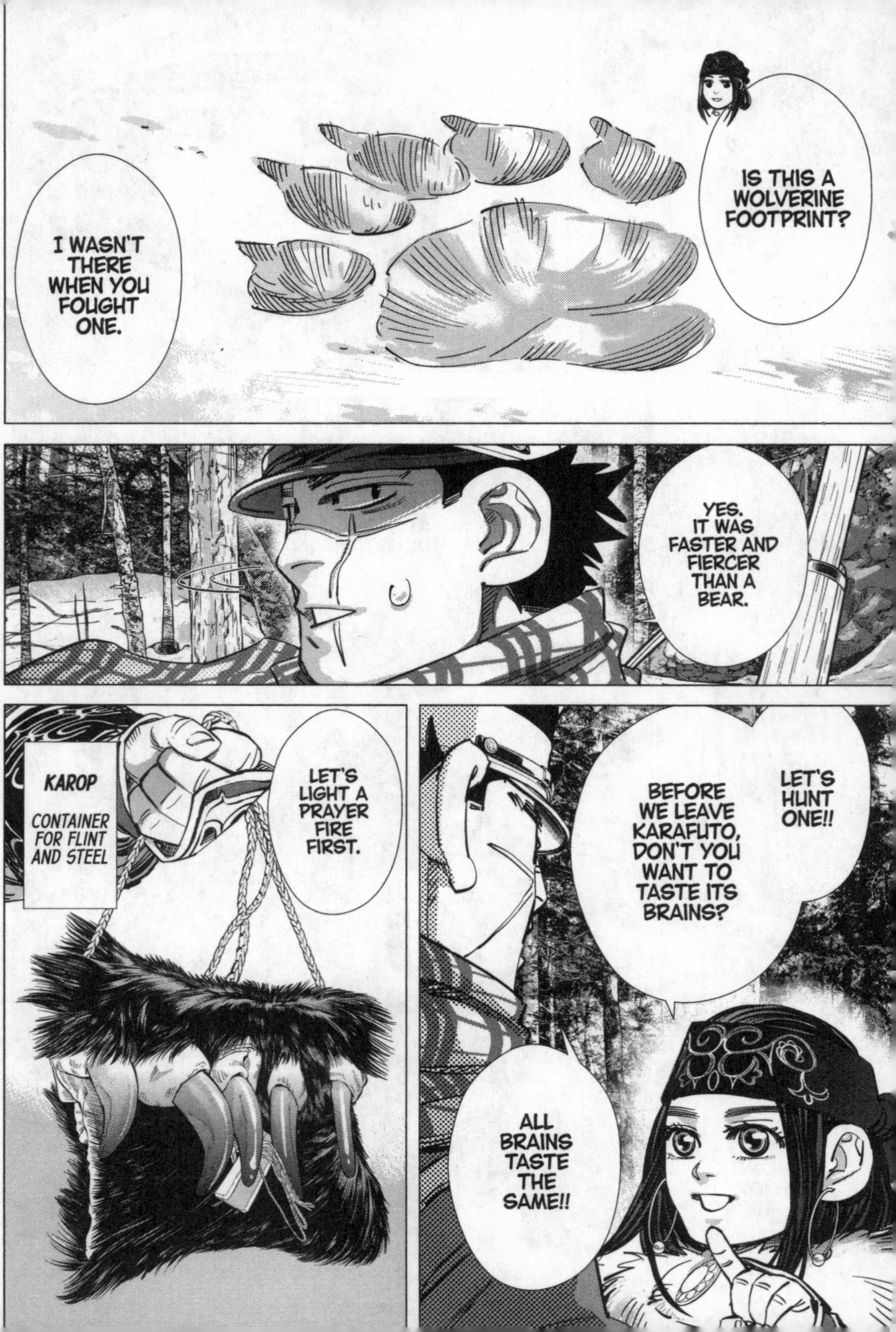
IS THIS A WOLVERINE FOOTPRINT?
I WASN'T THERE WHEN YOU FOUGHT ONE.
YES. IT WAS FASTER AND FIERCER THAN A BEAR.
LET'S HUNT ONE!!
BEFORE WE LEAVE KARAFUTO, DON'T YOU WANT TO TASTE ITS BRAINS?
ALL BRAINS TASTE THE SAME!!
KAROP
CONTAINER FOR FLINT AND STEEL
LET'S LIGHT A PRAYER FIRE FIRST.

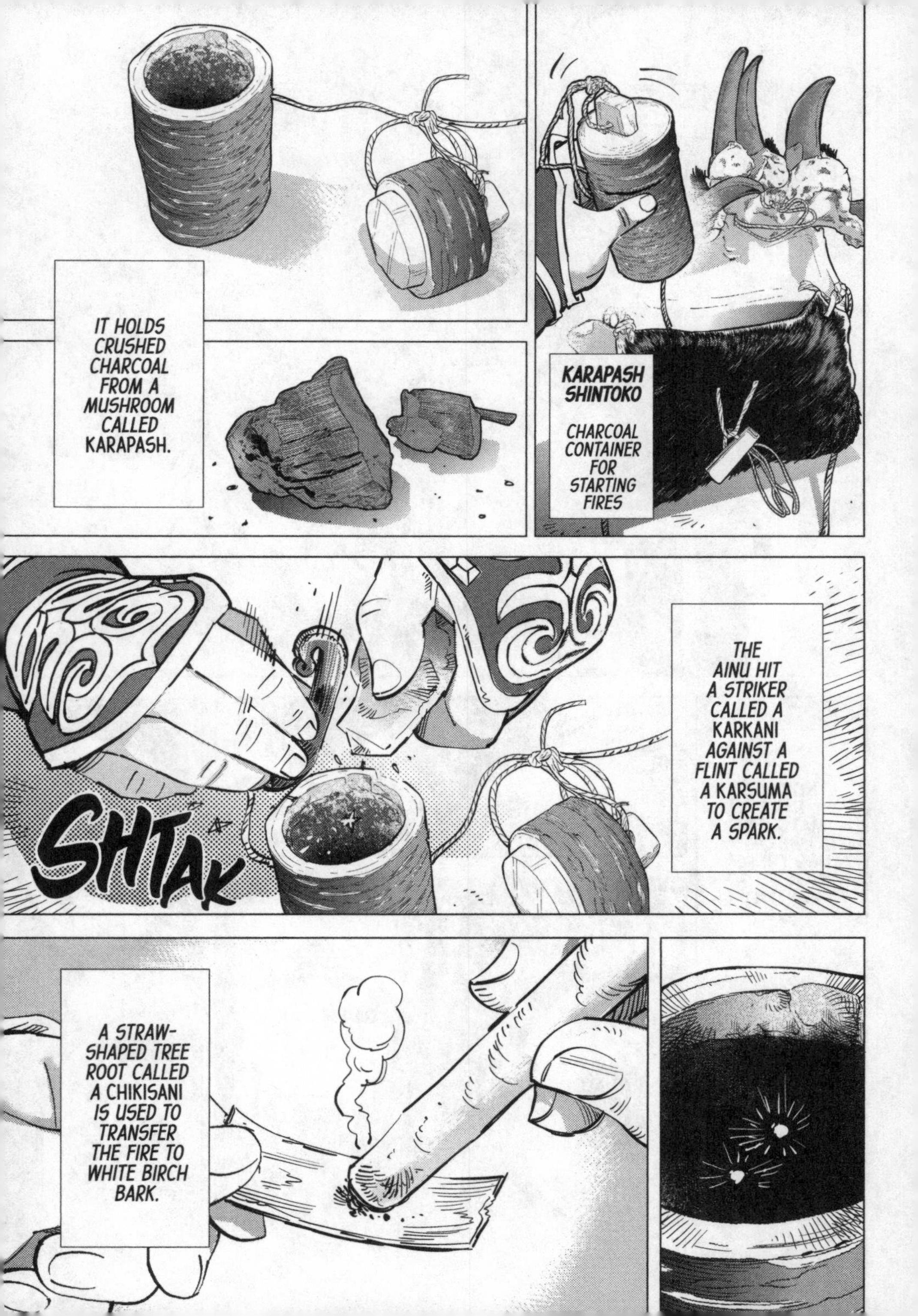
KARAPASH SHINTOKO
CHARCOAL CONTAINER FOR STARTING FIRES
IT HOLDS CRUSHED CHARCOAL FROM A MUSHROOM CALLED KARAPASH.
THE AINU HIT A STRIKER CALLED A KARKANI AGAINST A FLINT CALLED A KARSUMA TO CREATE A SPARK.
SHTAK
A STRAW-SHAPED TREE ROOT CALLED A CHIKISANI IS USED TO TRANSFER THE FIRE TO WHITE BIRCH BARK.

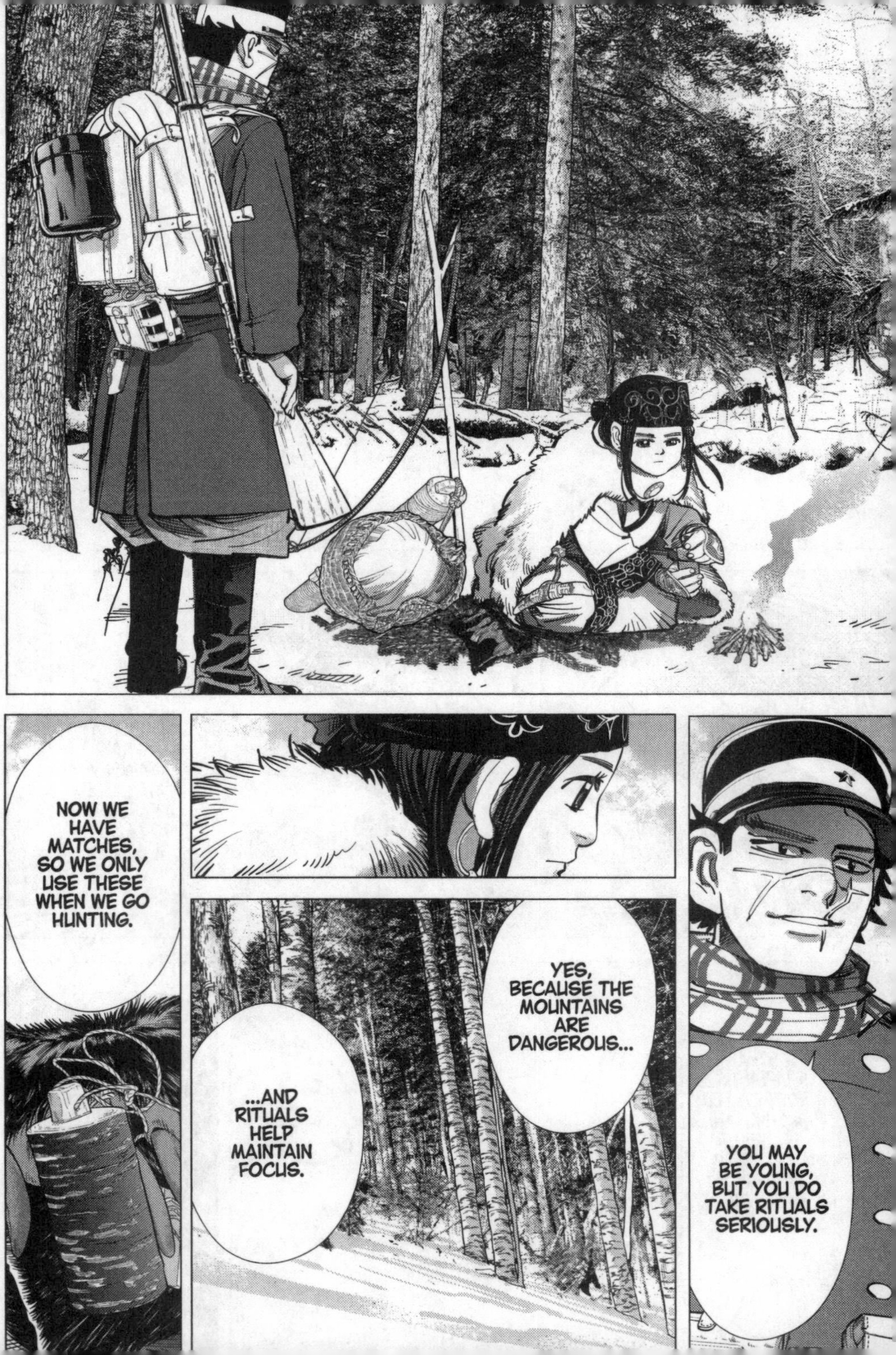
YOU MAY BE YOUNG, BUT YOU DO TAKE RITUALS SERIOUSLY.
YES, BECAUSE THE MOUNTAINS ARE DANGEROUS...
...AND RITUALS HELP MAINTAIN FOCUS.
NOW WE HAVE MATCHES, SO WE ONLY USE THESE WHEN WE GO HUNTING.

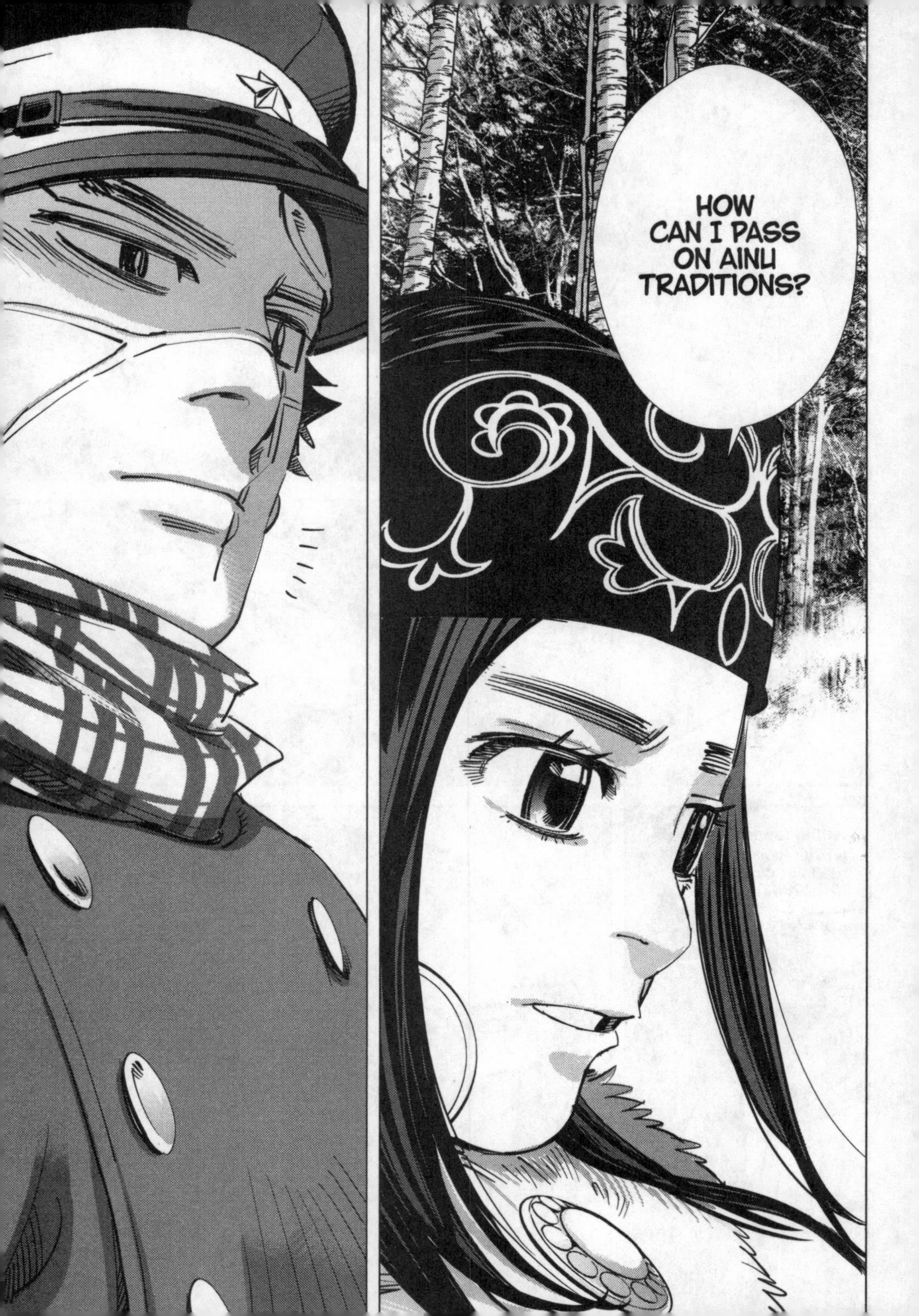
HOW CAN I PASS ON AINU TRADITIONS?

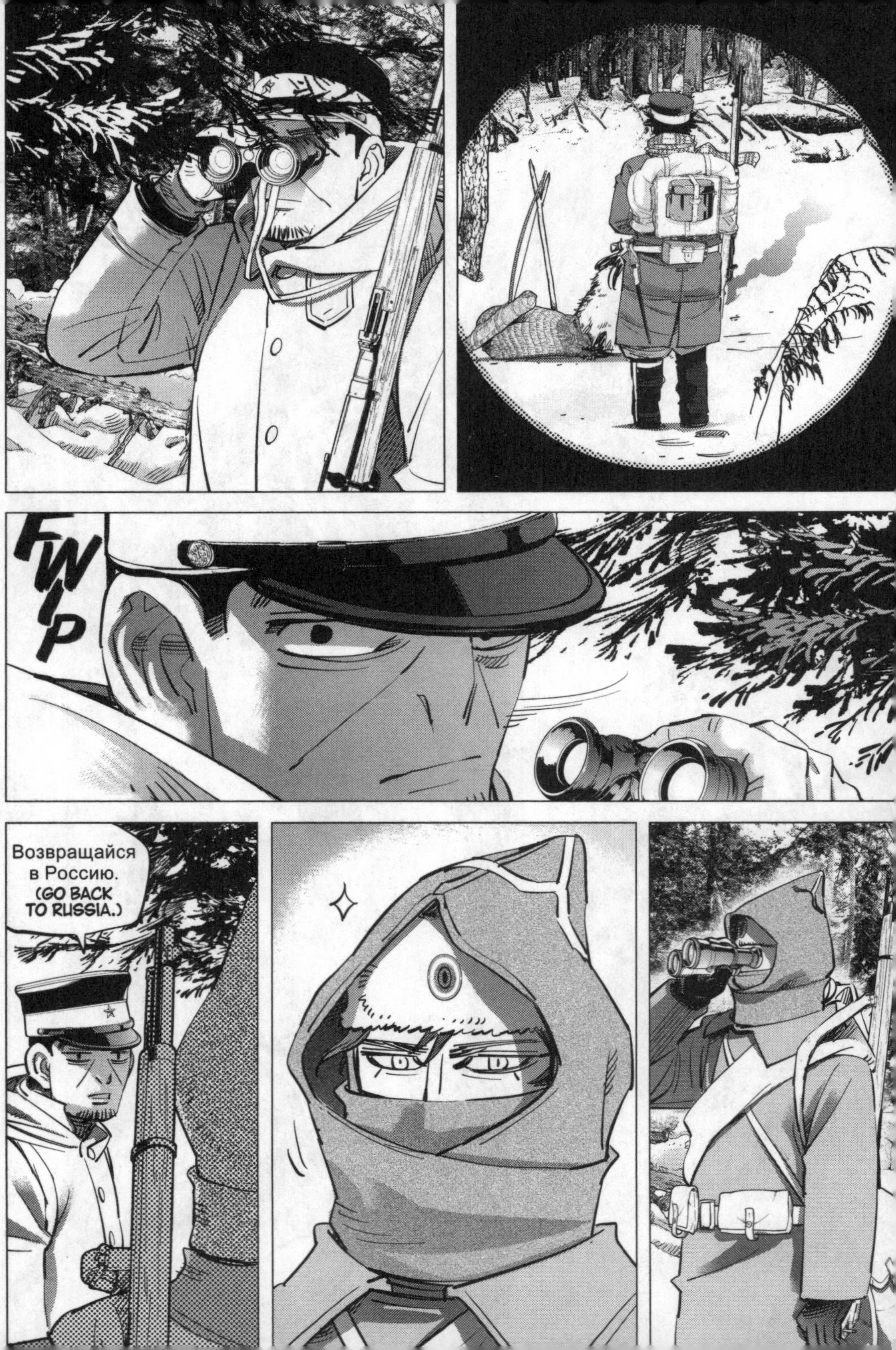
FWIP
Возвращайся в Россию. (GO BACK TO RUSSIA.)

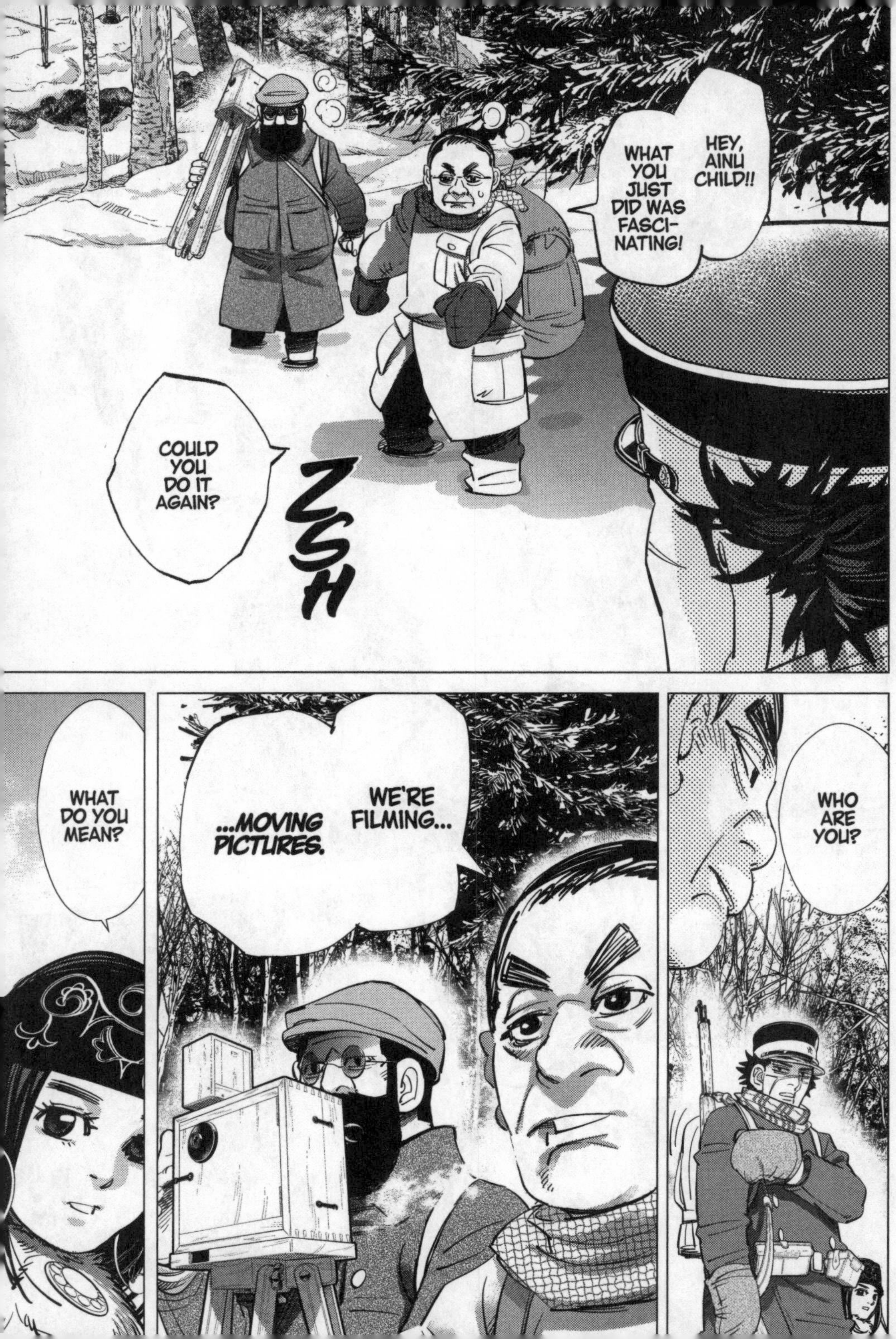
HEY, AINU CHILD!!
WHAT YOU JUST DID WAS FASCI-NATING!
COULD YOU DO IT AGAIN?
ZSH
WHO ARE YOU?
WE'RE FILMING...
...MOVING PICTURES.
WHAT DO YOU MEAN?

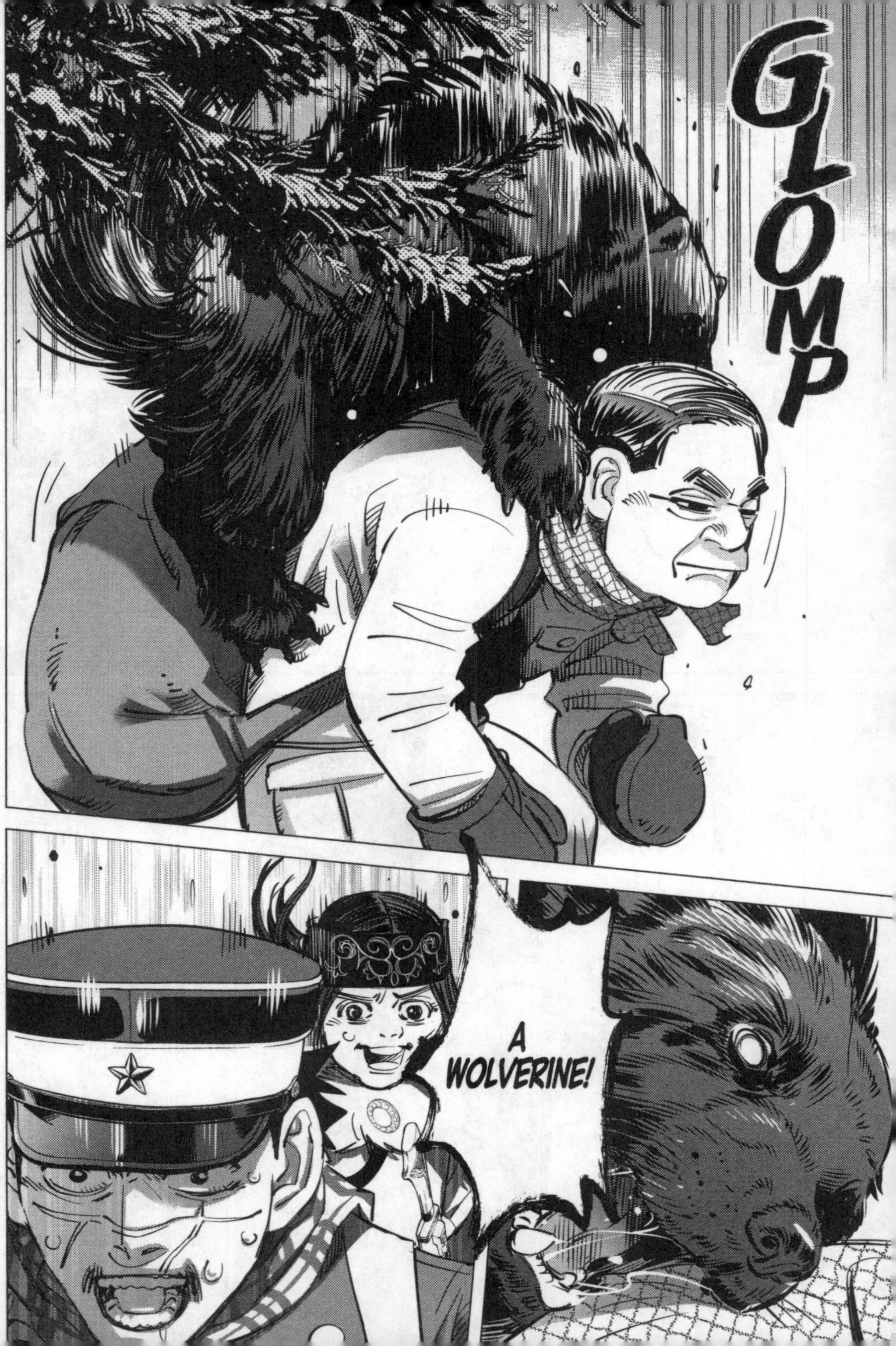
GLOMP
A WOLVERINE!

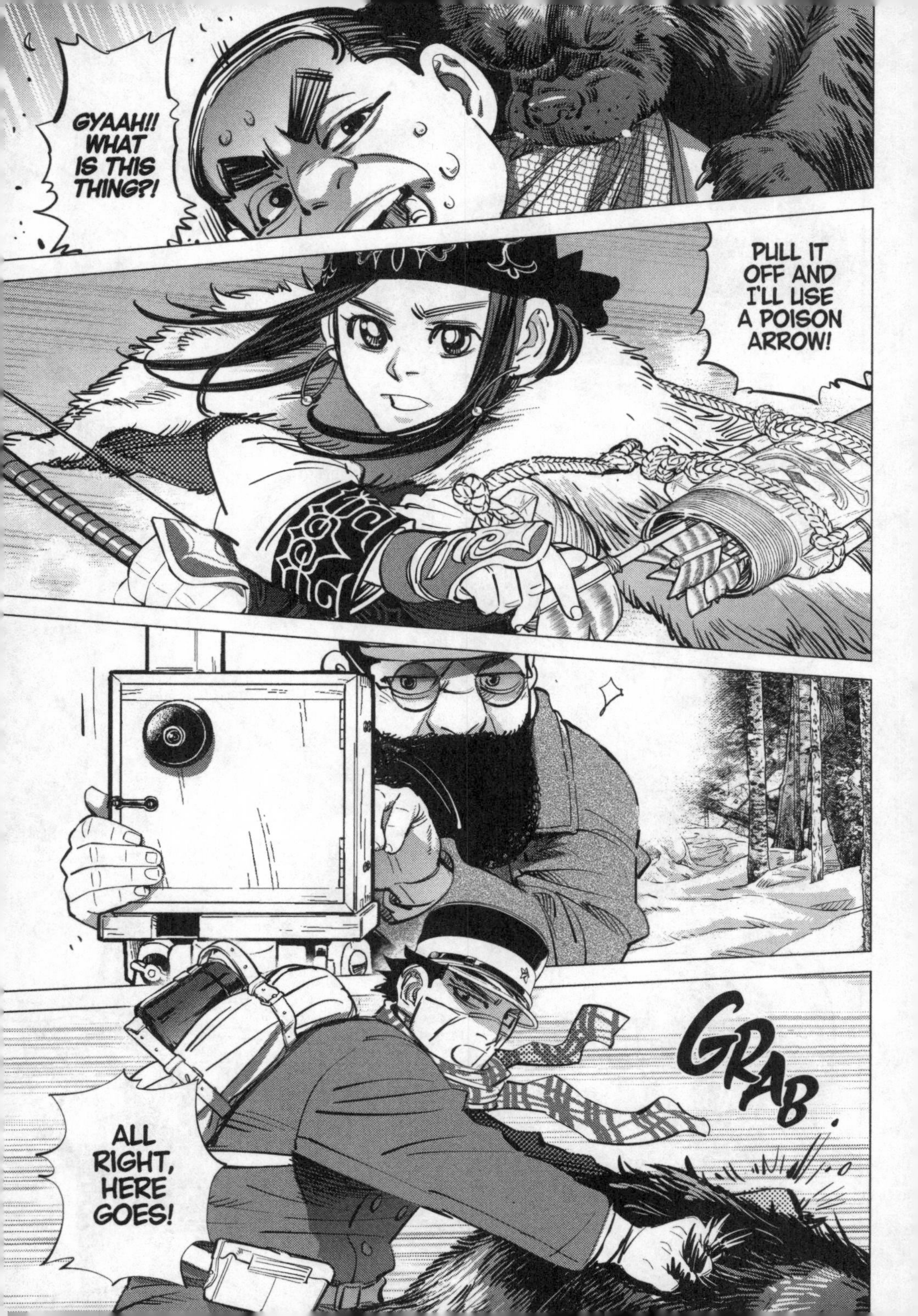
GYAAH!! WHAT IS THIS THING?!
PULL IT OFF AND I'LL USE A POISON ARROW!
GRAB
ALL RIGHT, HERE GOES!

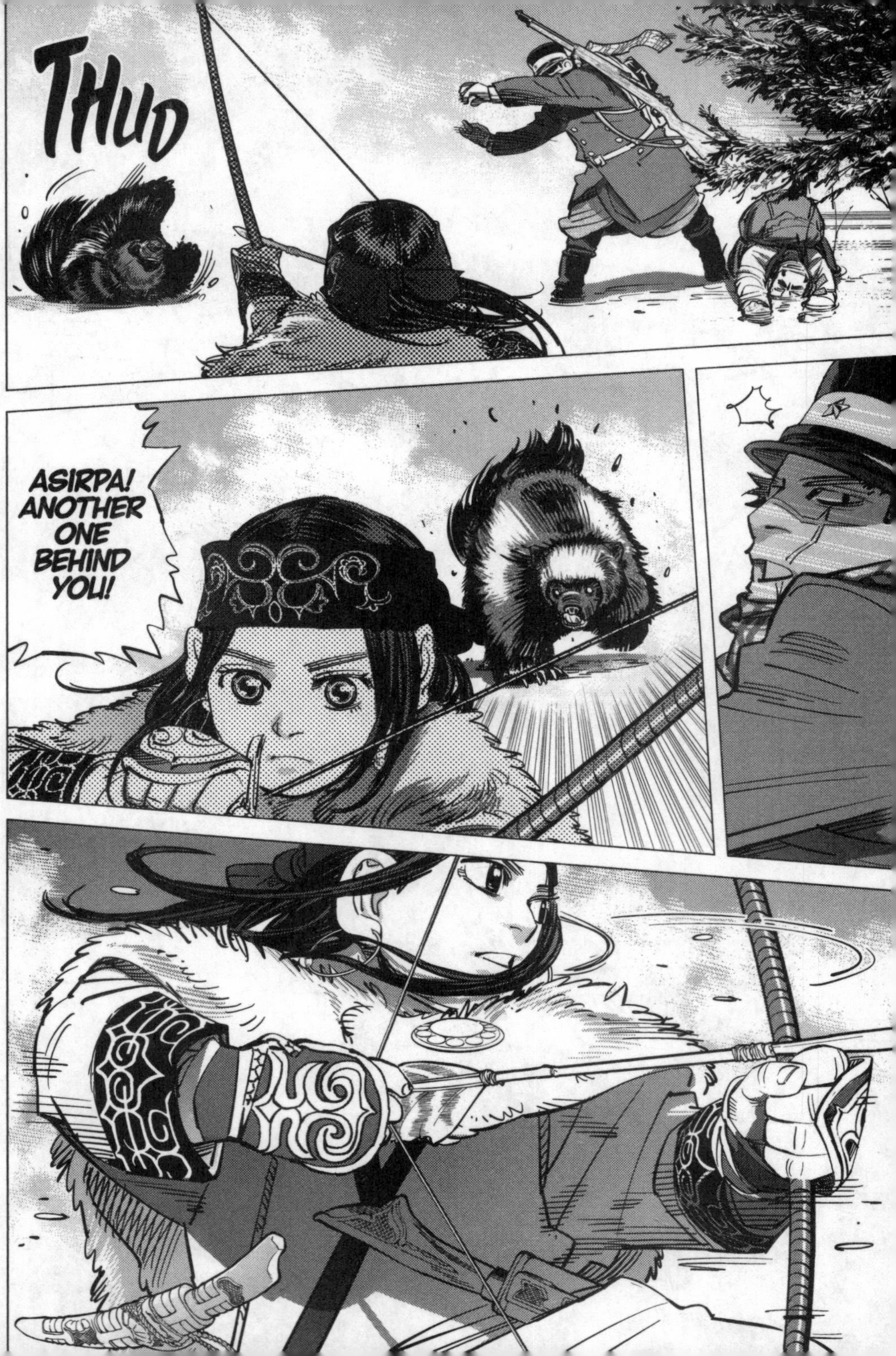
THUD
ASIRPA! ANOTHER ONE BEHIND YOU!

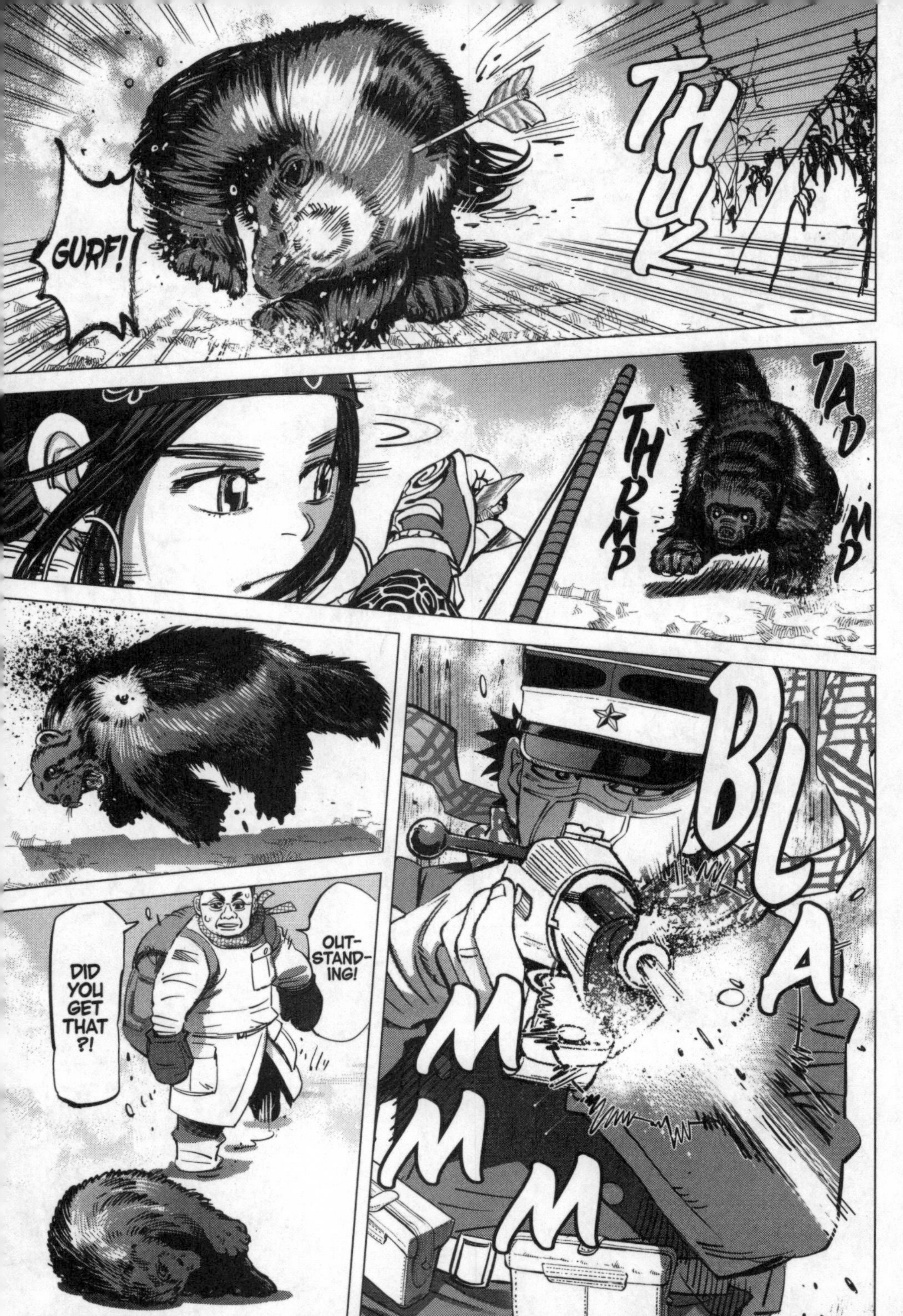
THUNK
GURF!
TAD
MP
THRMP
BLAMMMM
OUT-STANDING!
DID YOU GET THAT?!

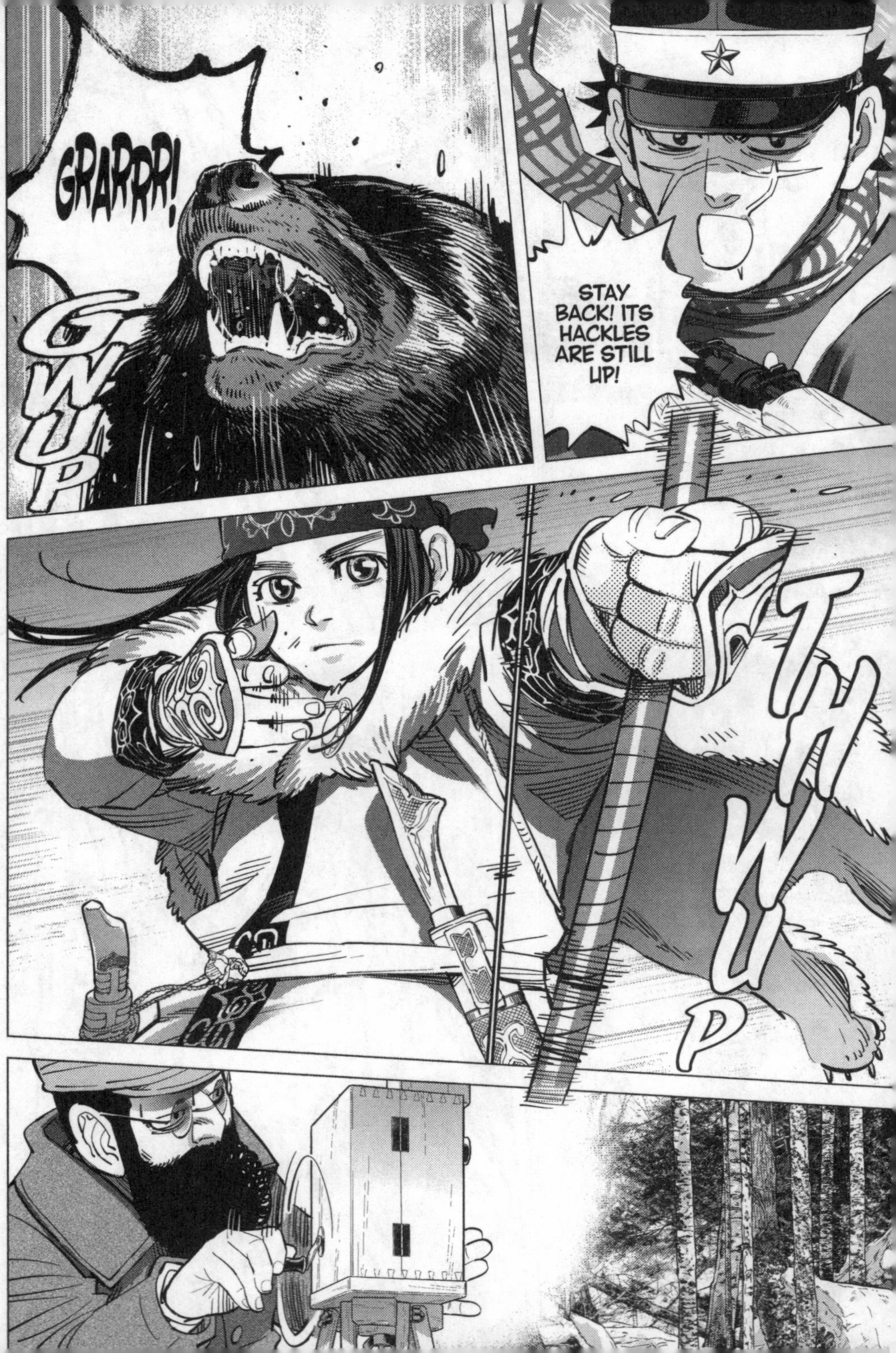
STAY BACK! ITS HACKLES ARE STILL UP!
GRARRR!
GWUP
THWUP

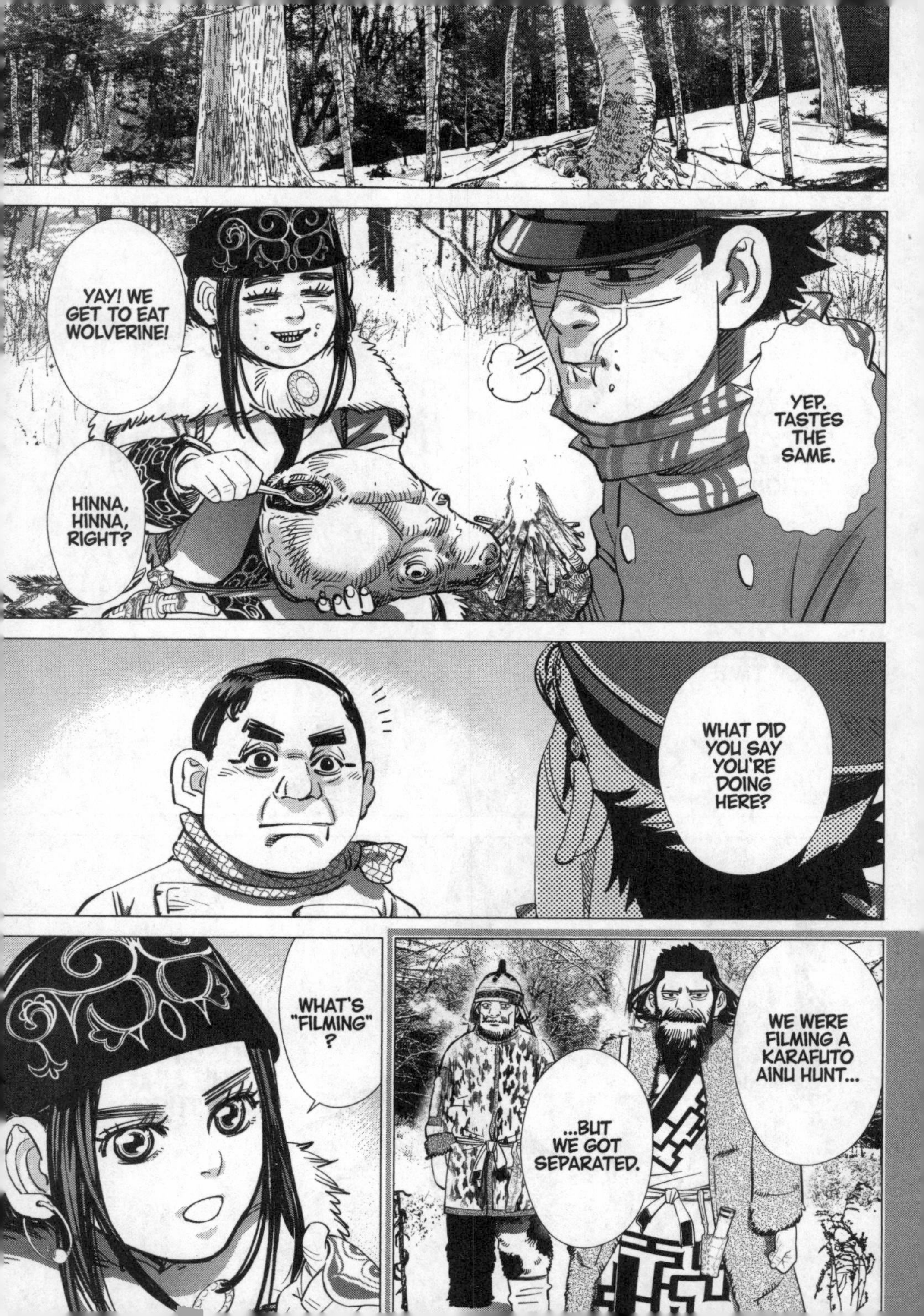
YAY! WE GET TO EAT WOLVERINE!
HINNA, HINNA, RIGHT?
YEP. TASTES THE SAME.
WHAT DID YOU SAY YOU'RE DOING HERE?
WE WERE FILMING A KARAFUTO AINU HUNT...
...BUT WE GOT SEPARATED.
WHAT'S "FILMING"?

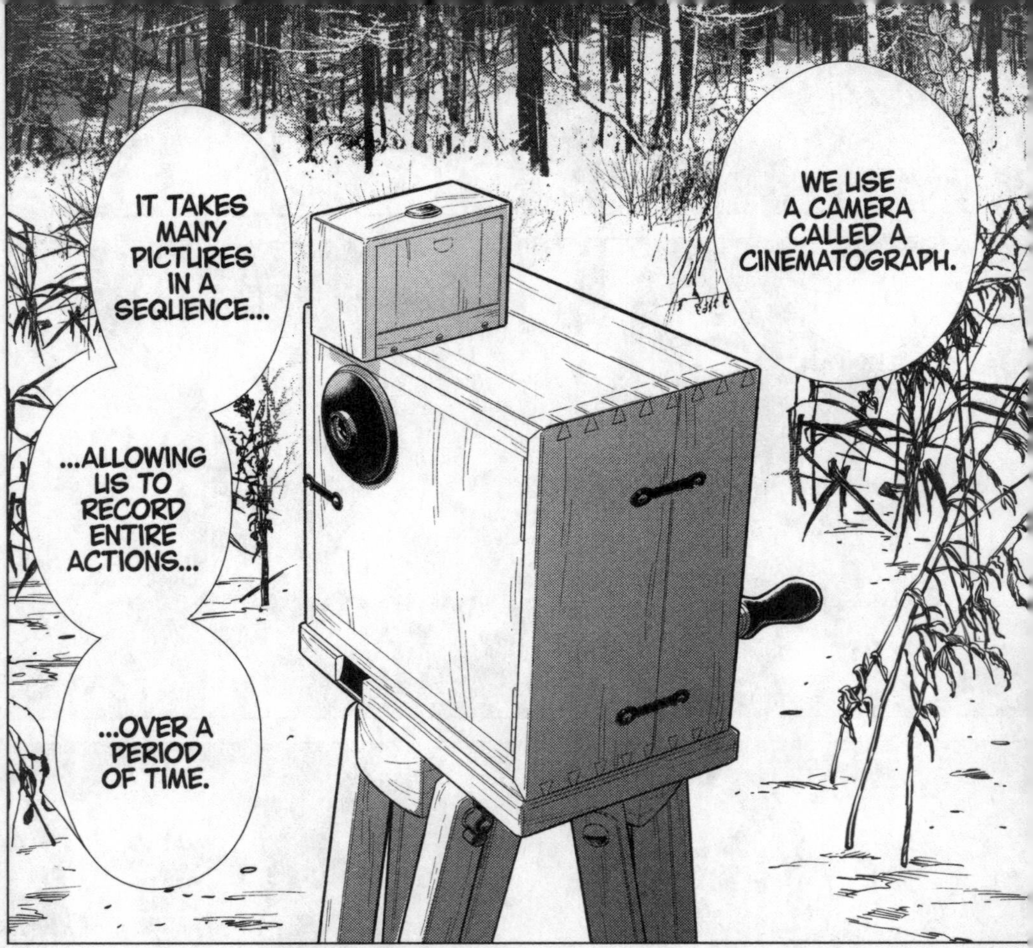
WE USE A CAMERA CALLED A CINEMATOGRAPH.
IT TAKES MANY PICTURES IN A SEQUENCE...
...ALLOWING US TO RECORD ENTIRE ACTIONS...
...OVER A PERIOD OF TIME.

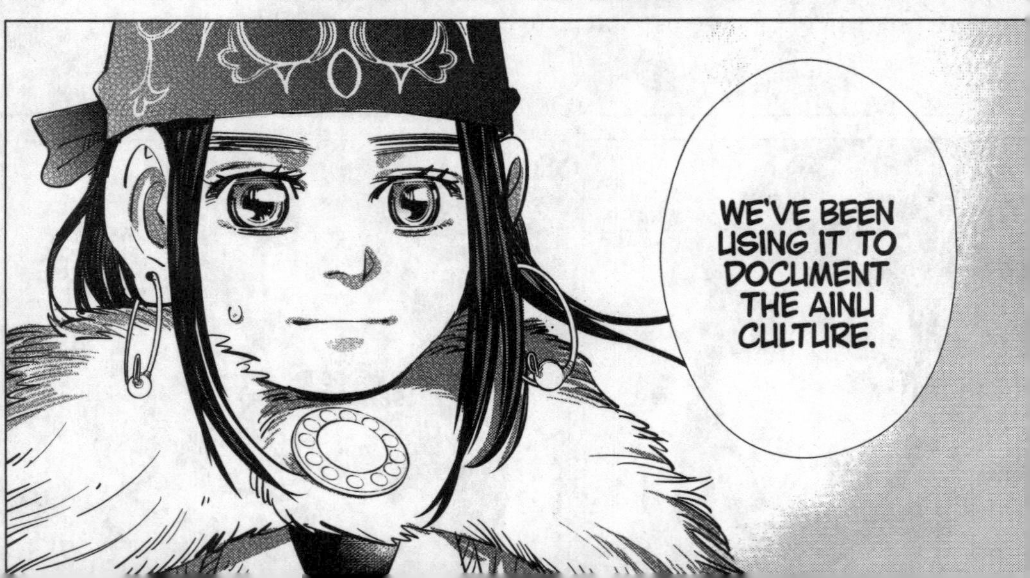
WE'VE BEEN USING IT TO DOCUMENT THE AINU CULTURE.

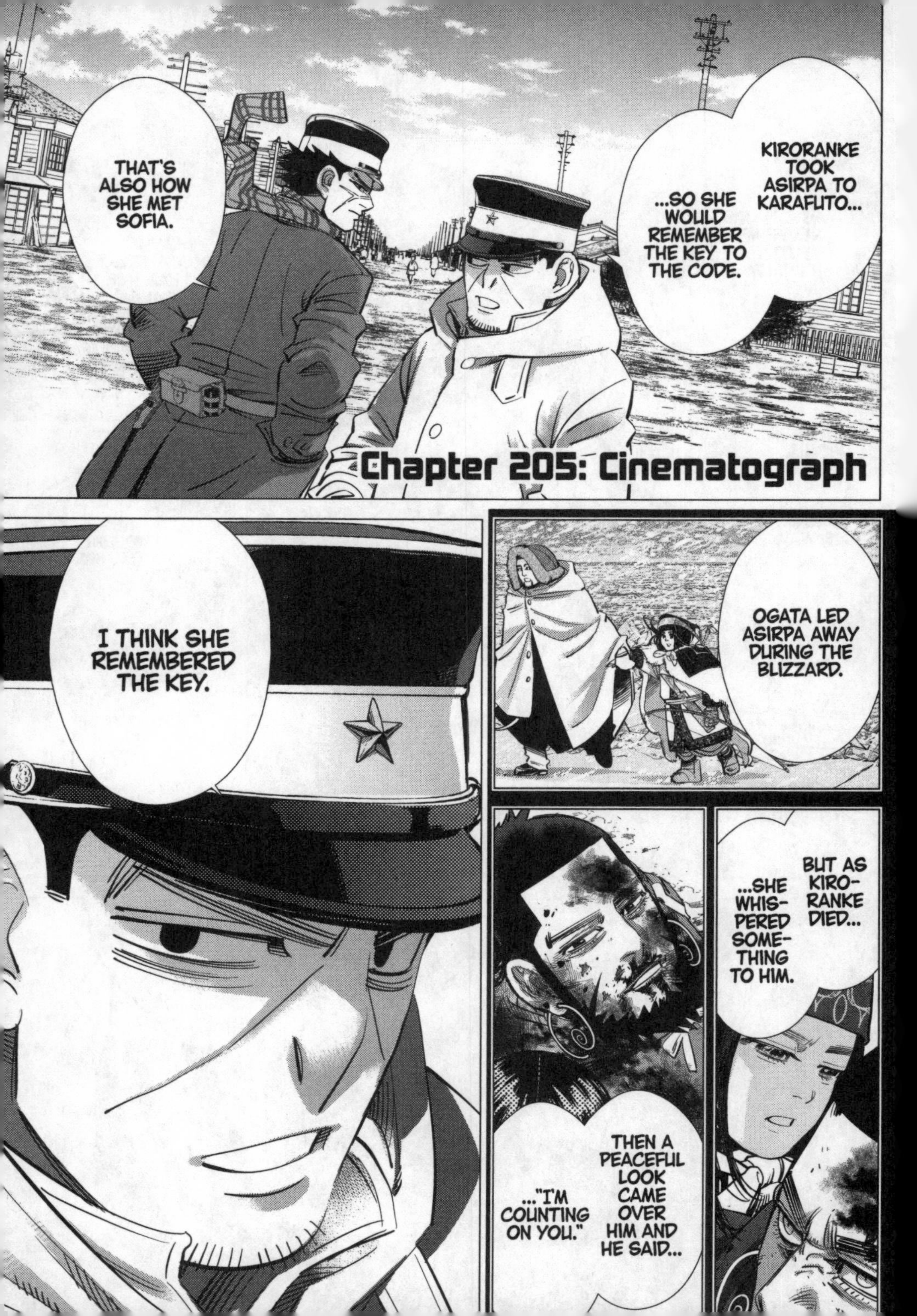
KIRORANKE TOOK ASIRPA TO KARAFUTO...
...SO SHE WOULD REMEMBER THE KEY TO THE CODE.
THAT'S ALSO HOW SHE MET SOFIA.
Chapter 205: Cinematograph
OGATA LED ASIRPA AWAY DURING THE BLIZZARD.
BUT AS KIRO-RANKE DIED...
...SHE WHIS-PERED SOME-THING TO HIM.
THEN A PEACEFUL LOOK CAME OVER HIM AND HE SAID...
..."I'M COUNTING ON YOU."
I THINK SHE REMEMBERED THE KEY.

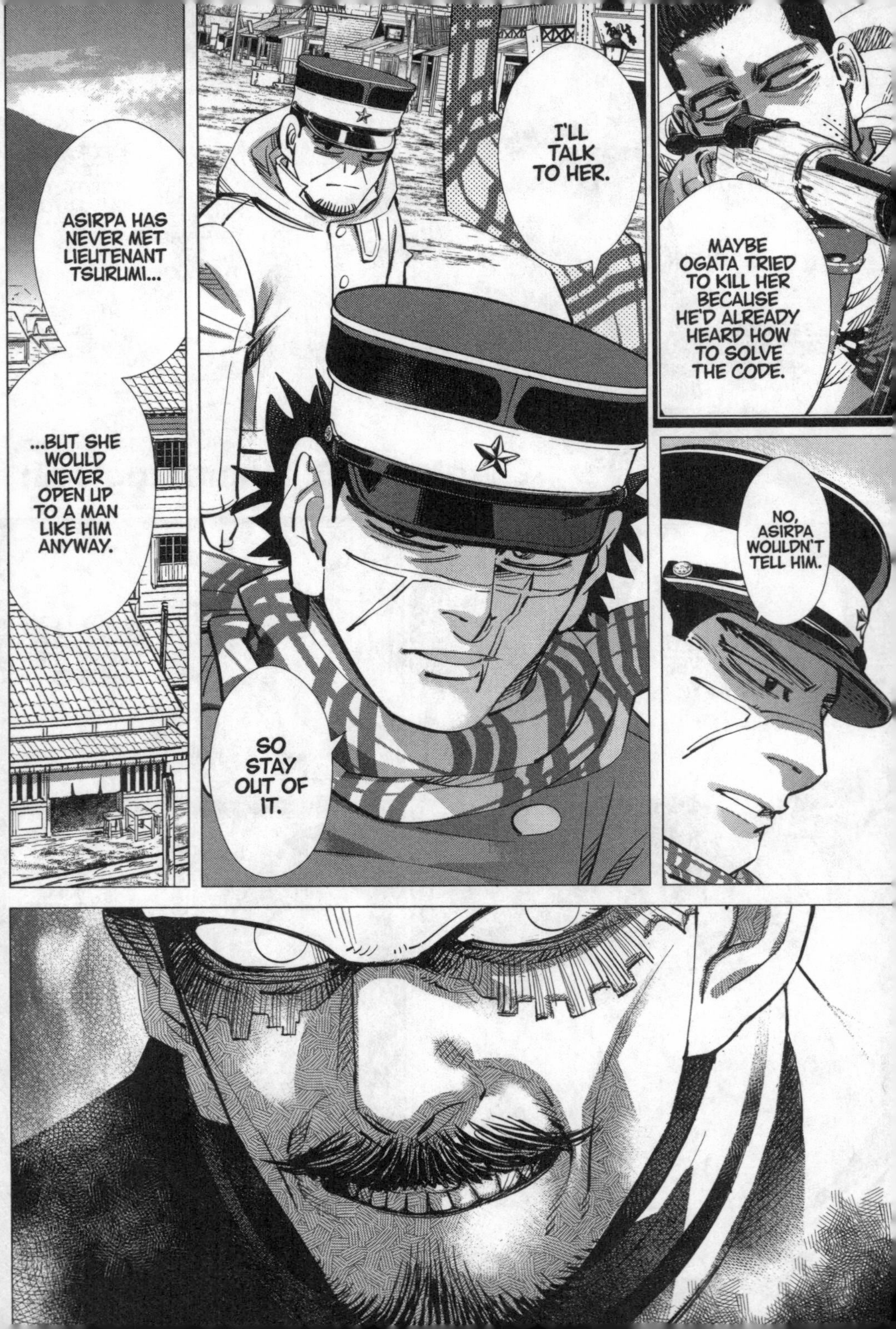
MAYBE OGATA TRIED TO KILL HER BECAUSE HE'D ALREADY HEARD HOW TO SOLVE THE CODE.
NO, ASIRPA WOULDN'T TELL HIM.
I'LL TALK TO HER.
SO STAY OUT OF IT.
ASIRPA HAS NEVER MET LIEUTENANT TSURUMI...
...BUT SHE WOULD NEVER OPEN UP TO A MAN LIKE HIM ANYWAY.

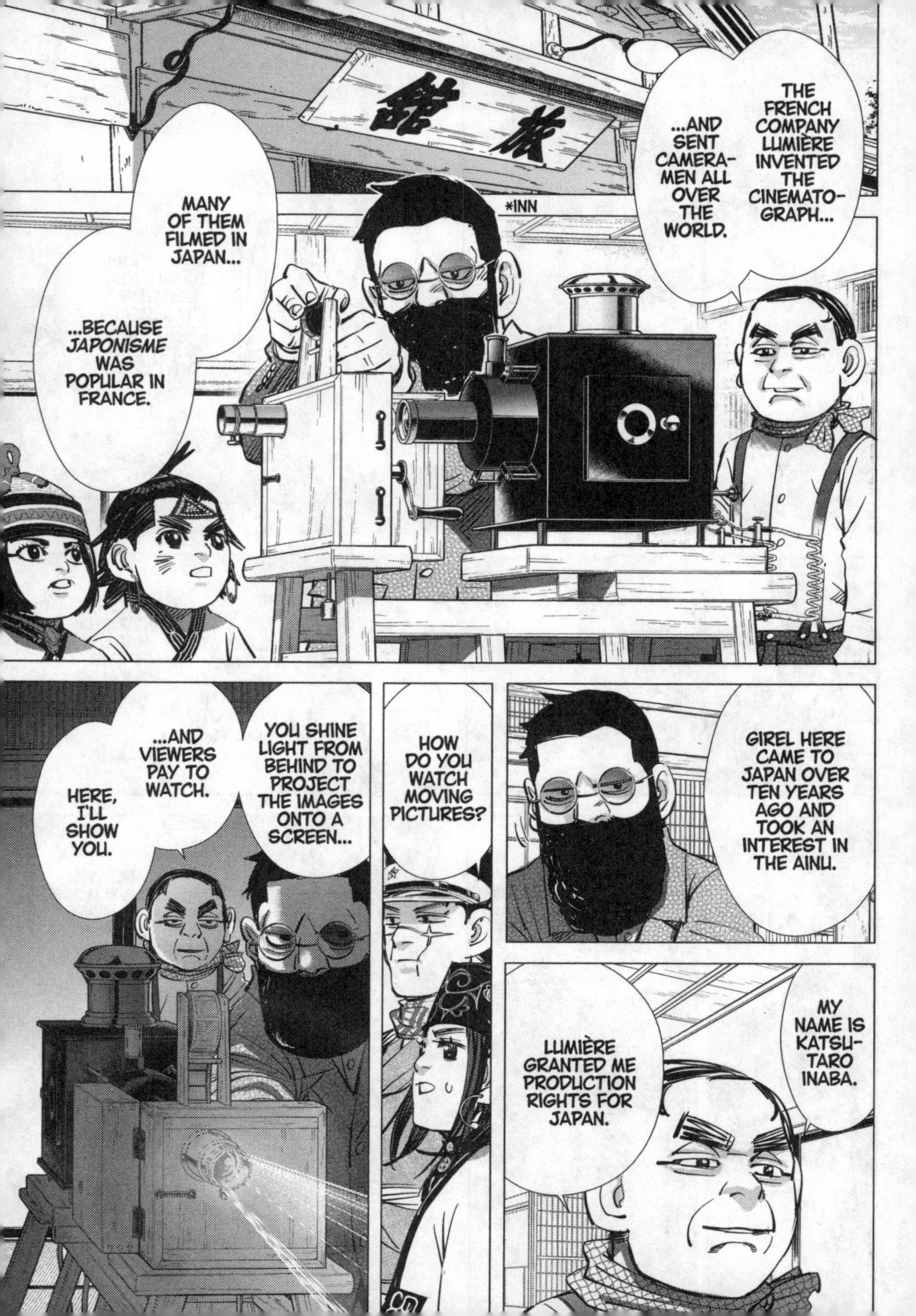
THE FRENCH COMPANY LUMIÈRE INVENTED THE CINEMATOGRAPH...
...AND SENT CAMERAMEN ALL OVER THE WORLD.
旅館
*INN
MANY OF THEM FILMED IN JAPAN...
...BECAUSE JAPONISME WAS POPULAR IN FRANCE.
GIREL HERE CAME TO JAPAN OVER TEN YEARS AGO AND TOOK AN INTEREST IN THE AINU.
MY NAME IS KATSUTARO INABA.
LUMIÈRE GRANTED ME PRODUCTION RIGHTS FOR JAPAN.
HOW DO YOU WATCH MOVING PICTURES?
YOU SHINE LIGHT FROM BEHIND TO PROJECT THE IMAGES ONTO A SCREEN...
...AND VIEWERS PAY TO WATCH.
HERE, I'LL SHOW YOU.

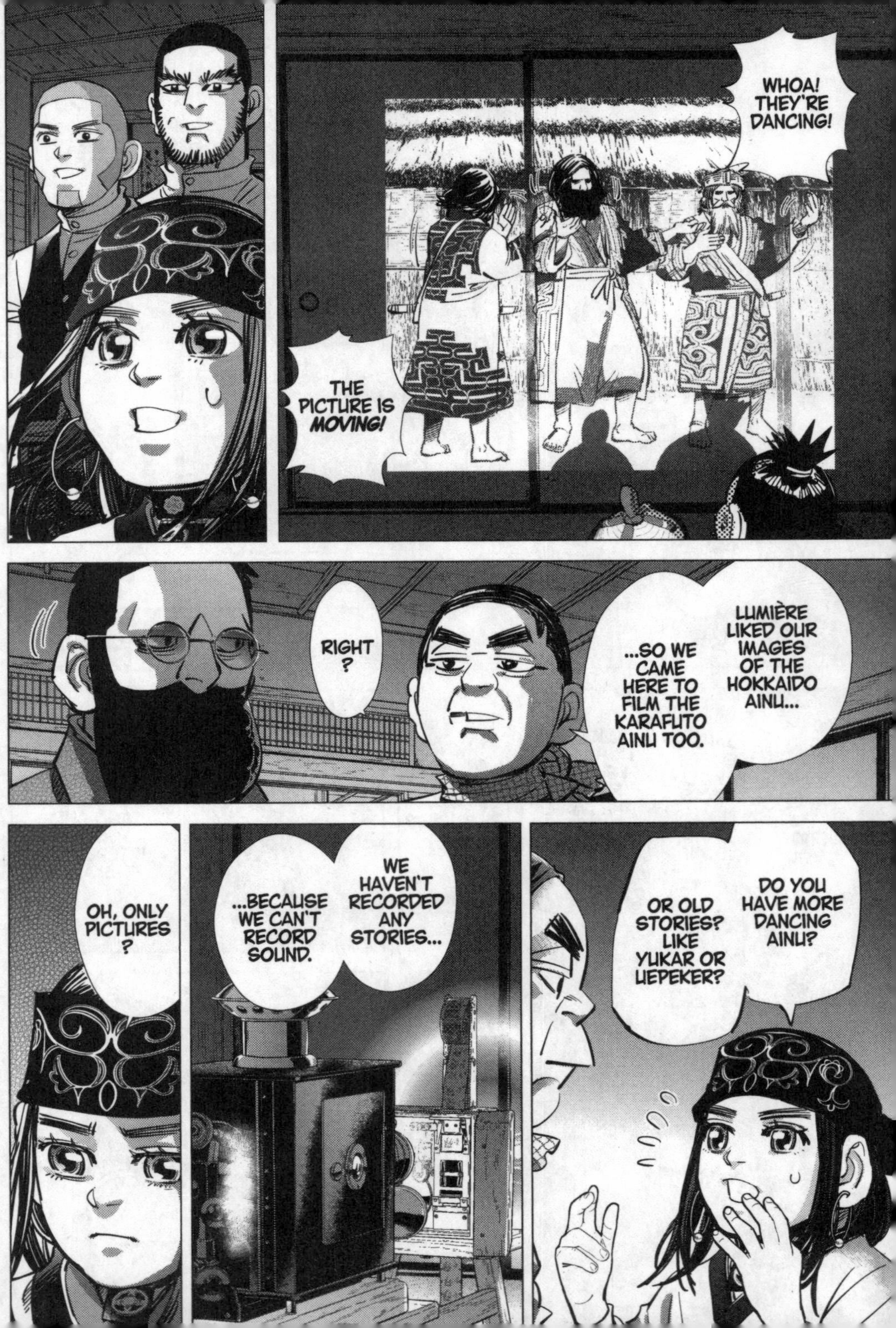
WHOA! THEY'RE DANCING!
THE PICTURE IS *MOVING!*
LUMIÈRE LIKED OUR IMAGES OF THE HOKKAIDO AINU...
...SO WE CAME HERE TO FILM THE KARAFUTO AINU TOO.
RIGHT?
DO YOU HAVE MORE DANCING AINU?
OR OLD STORIES? LIKE YUKAR OR UEPEKER?
WE HAVEN'T RECORDED ANY STORIES...
...BECAUSE WE CAN'T RECORD SOUND.
OH, ONLY PICTURES?

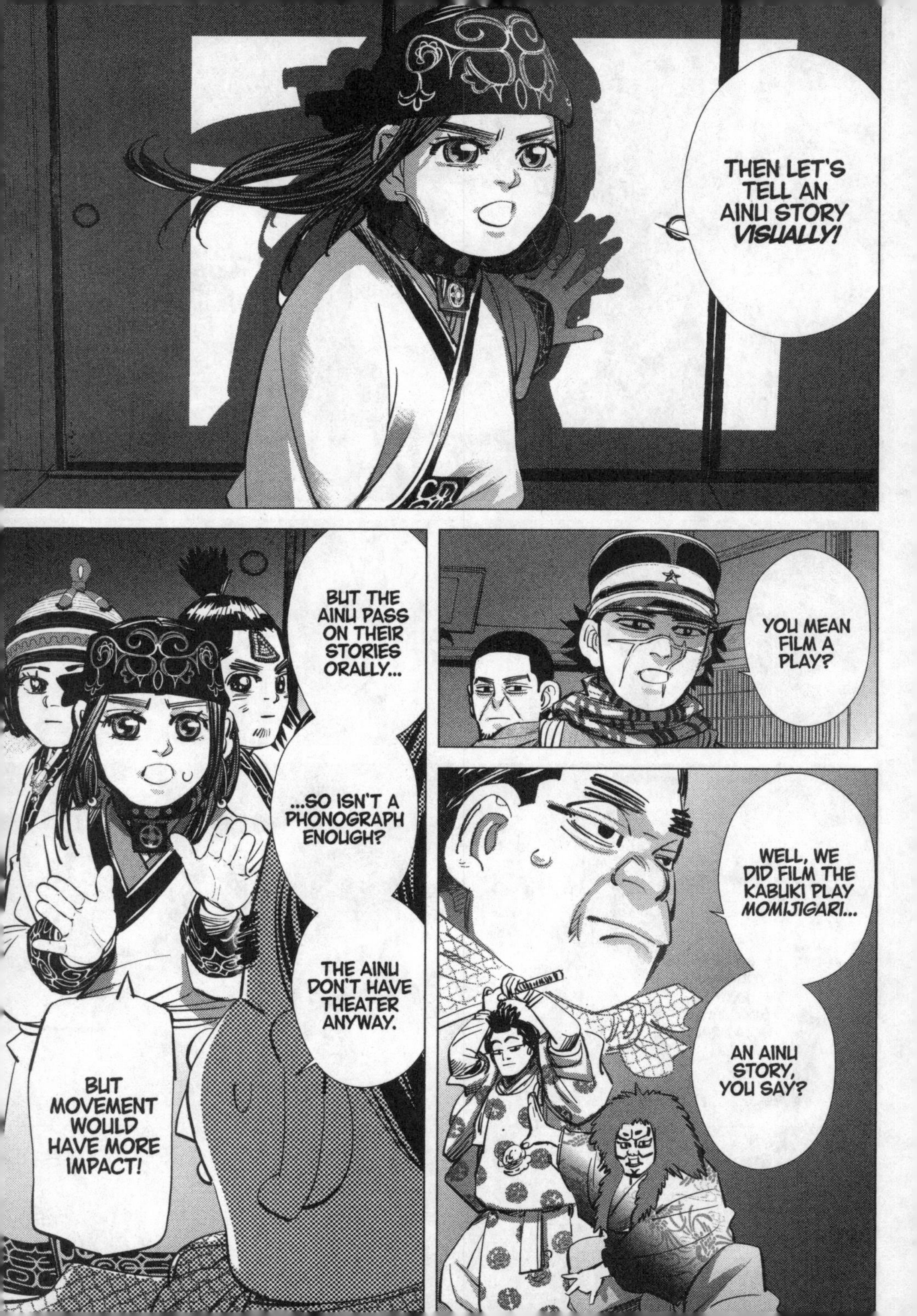
THEN LET'S TELL AN AINU STORY *VISUALLY!*
YOU MEAN FILM A PLAY?
WELL, WE DID FILM THE KABUKI PLAY *MOMIJIGARI*...
AN AINU STORY, YOU SAY?
BUT THE AINU PASS ON THEIR STORIES ORALLY...
...SO ISN'T A PHONOGRAPH ENOUGH?
THE AINU DON'T HAVE THEATER ANYWAY.
BUT MOVEMENT WOULD HAVE MORE IMPACT!

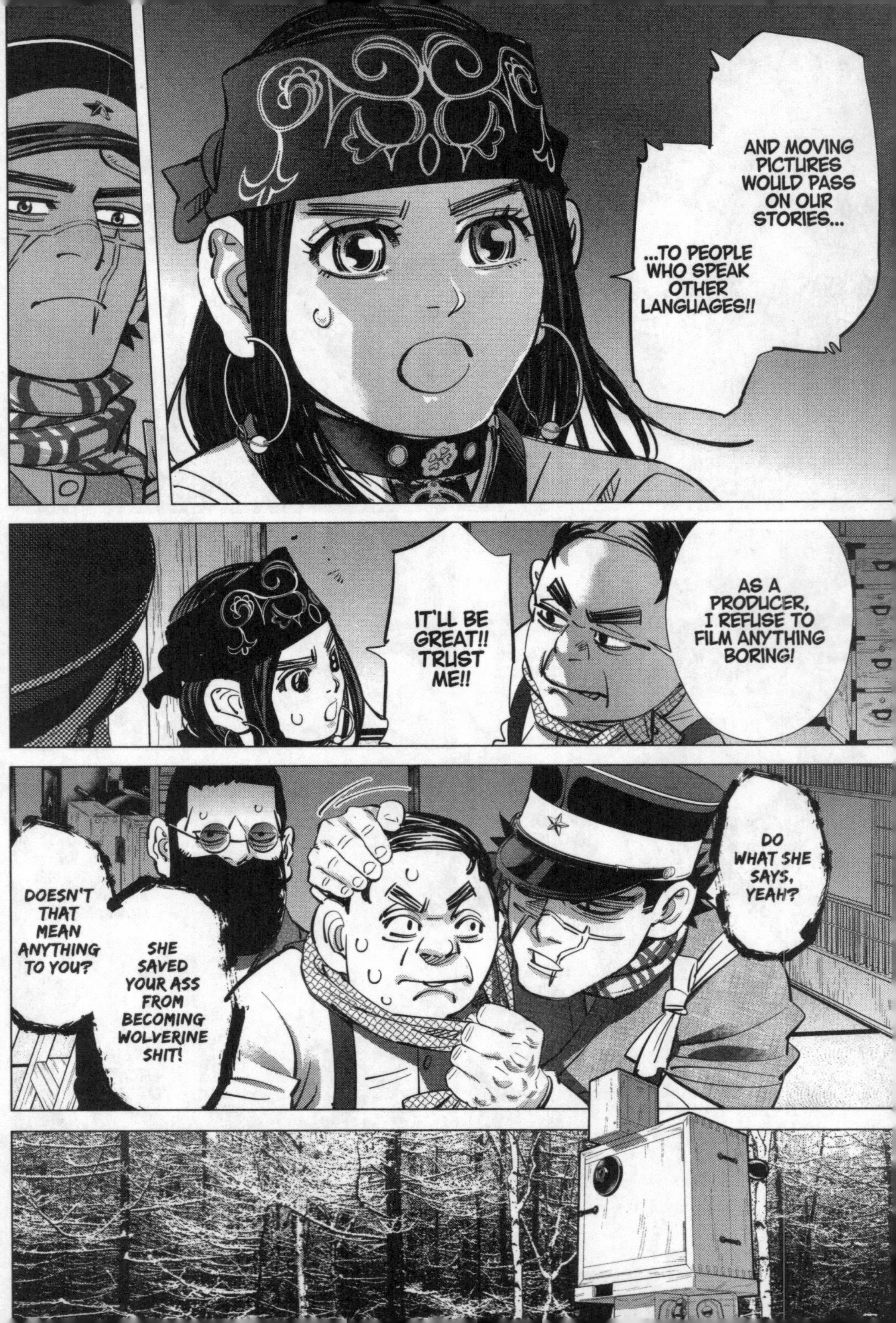
AND MOVING PICTURES WOULD PASS ON OUR STORIES...
...TO PEOPLE WHO SPEAK OTHER LANGUAGES!!
AS A PRODUCER, I REFUSE TO FILM ANYTHING BORING!
IT'LL BE GREAT!! TRUST ME!!
DO WHAT SHE SAYS, YEAH?
SHE SAVED YOUR ASS FROM BECOMING WOLVERINE SHIT!
DOESN'T THAT MEAN ANYTHING TO YOU?

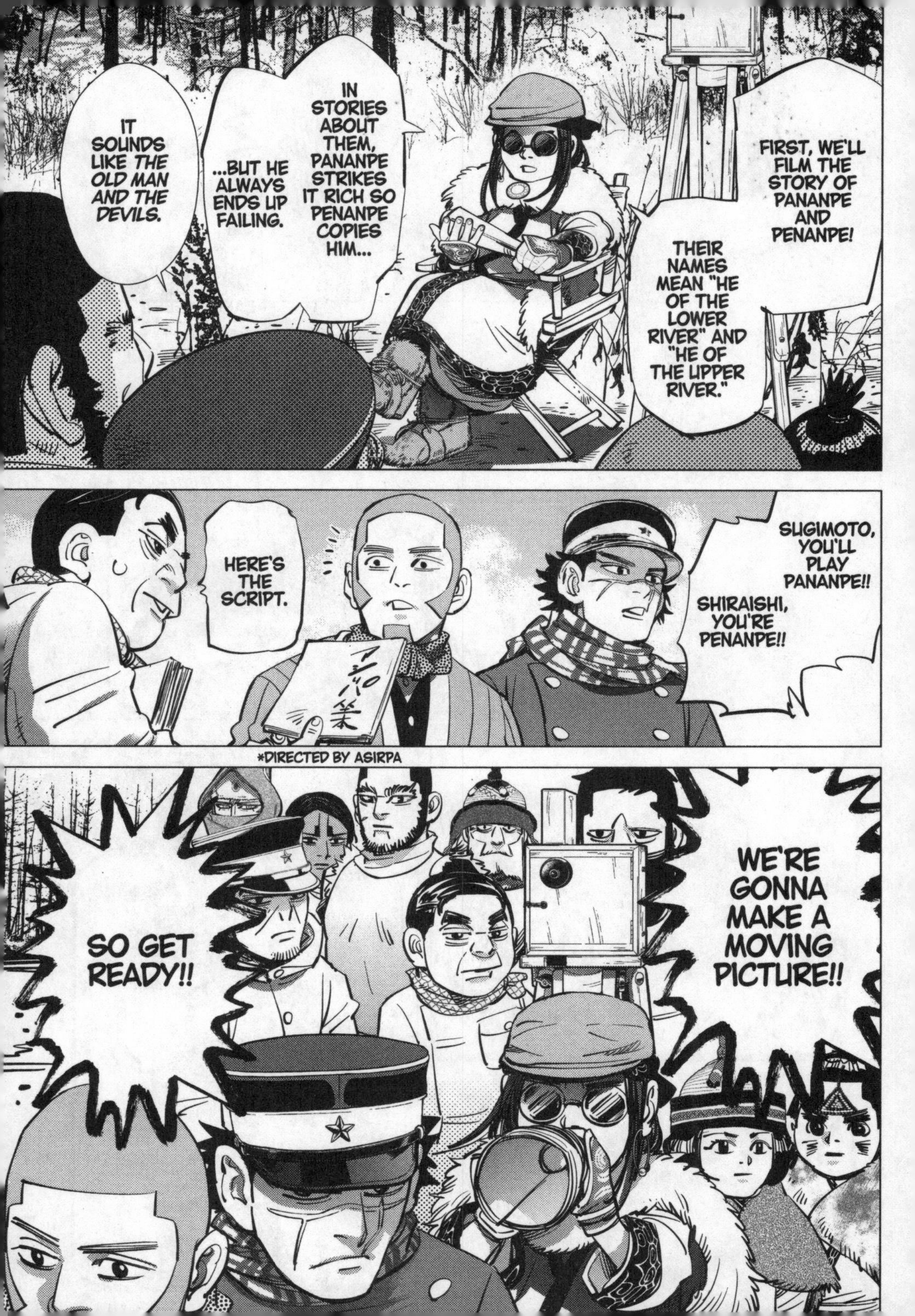
FIRST, WE'LL FILM THE STORY OF PANANPE AND PENANPE!
THEIR NAMES MEAN "HE OF THE LOWER RIVER" AND "HE OF THE UPPER RIVER."
IN STORIES ABOUT THEM, PANANPE STRIKES IT RICH SO PENANPE COPIES HIM...
...BUT HE ALWAYS ENDS UP FAILING.
IT SOUNDS LIKE *THE OLD MAN AND THE DEVILS.*
SUGIMOTO, YOU'LL PLAY PANANPE!!
SHIRAISHI, YOU'RE PENANPE!!
HERE'S THE SCRIPT.
*DIRECTED BY ASIRPA
WE'RE GONNA MAKE A MOVING PICTURE!!
SO GET READY!!

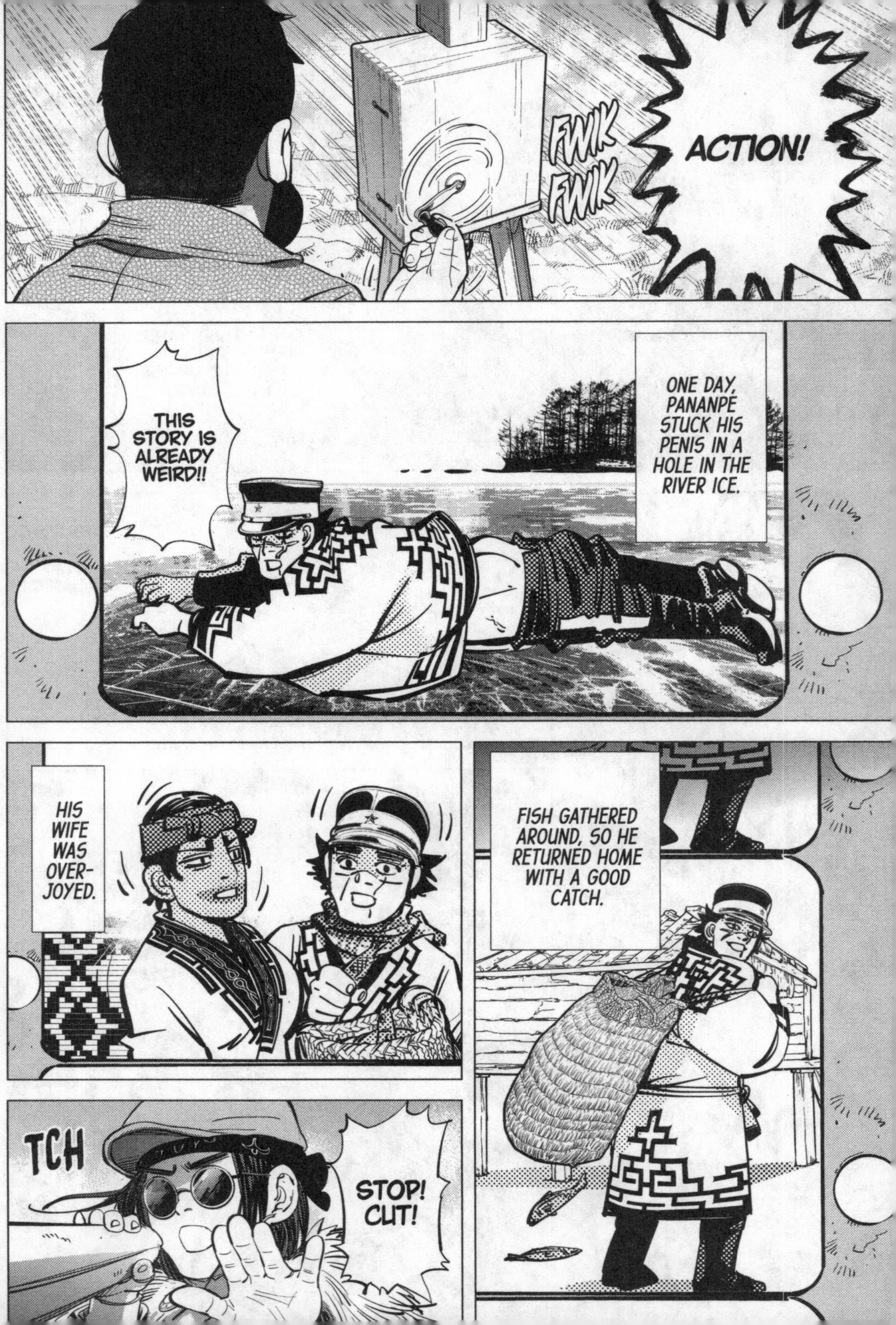
ACTION!
FWIK FWIK
ONE DAY, PANANPE STUCK HIS PENIS IN A HOLE IN THE RIVER ICE.
THIS STORY IS ALREADY WEIRD!!
FISH GATHERED AROUND, SO HE RETURNED HOME WITH A GOOD CATCH.
HIS WIFE WAS OVER-JOYED.
TCH
STOP! CUT!

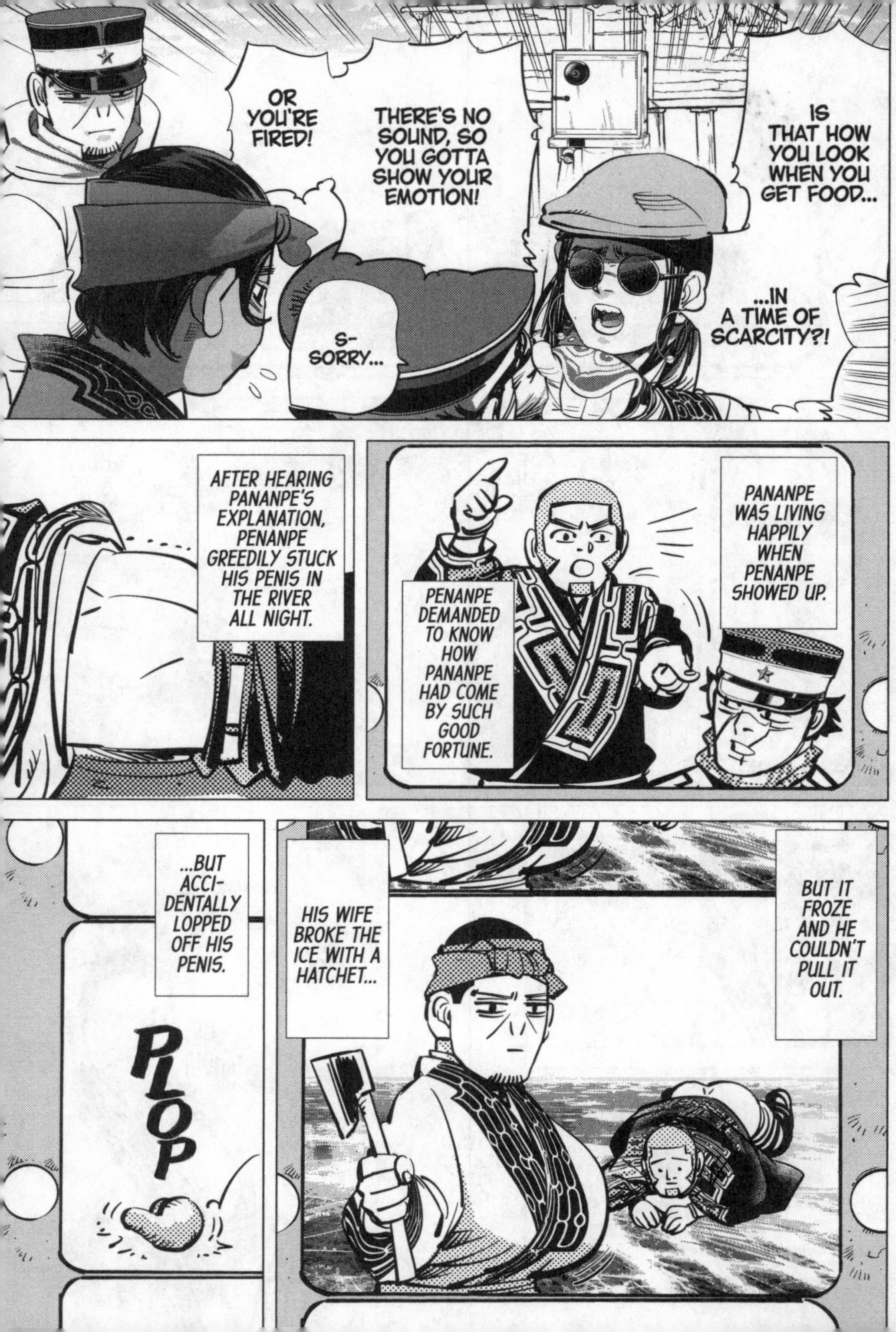
IS THAT HOW YOU LOOK WHEN YOU GET FOOD...
...IN A TIME OF SCARCITY?!
THERE'S NO SOUND, SO YOU GOTTA SHOW YOUR EMOTION!
OR YOU'RE FIRED!
S-SORRY...
PANANPE WAS LIVING HAPPILY WHEN PENANPE SHOWED UP.
PENANPE DEMANDED TO KNOW HOW PANANPE HAD COME BY SUCH GOOD FORTUNE.
AFTER HEARING PANANPE'S EXPLANATION, PENANPE GREEDILY STUCK HIS PENIS IN THE RIVER ALL NIGHT.
BUT IT FROZE AND HE COULDN'T PULL IT OUT.
HIS WIFE BROKE THE ICE WITH A HATCHET...
...BUT ACCI-DENTALLY LOPPED OFF HIS PENIS.
PLOP

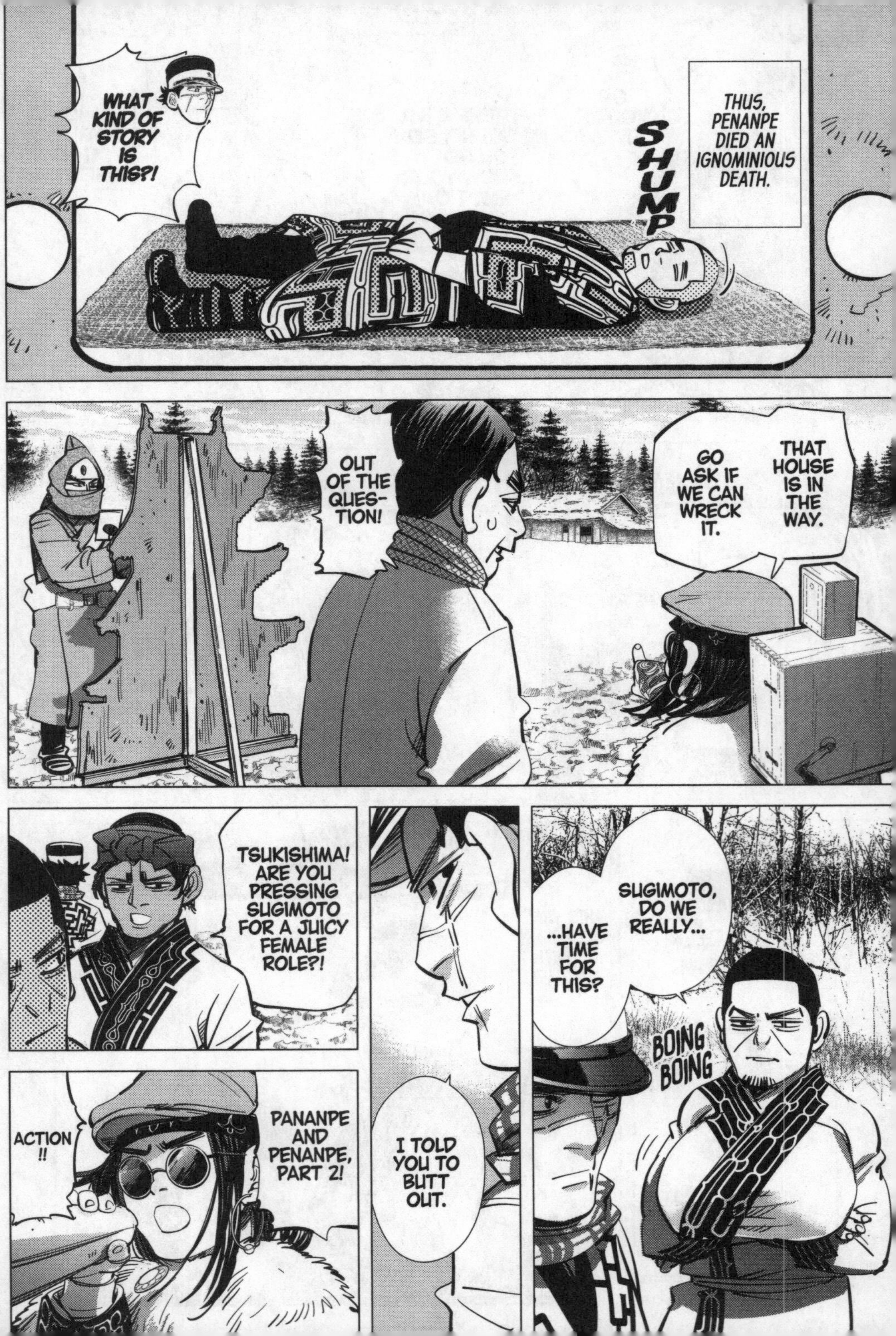
THUS, PENANPE DIED AN IGNOMINIOUS DEATH.
SHUMP
WHAT KIND OF STORY IS THIS?!
THAT HOUSE IS IN THE WAY.
GO ASK IF WE CAN WRECK IT.
OUT OF THE QUES-TION!
SUGIMOTO, DO WE REALLY...
...HAVE TIME FOR THIS?
BOING BOING
I TOLD YOU TO BUTT OUT.
TSUKISHIMA! ARE YOU PRESSING SUGIMOTO FOR A JUICY FEMALE ROLE?!
PANANPE AND PENANPE, PART 2!
ACTION !!

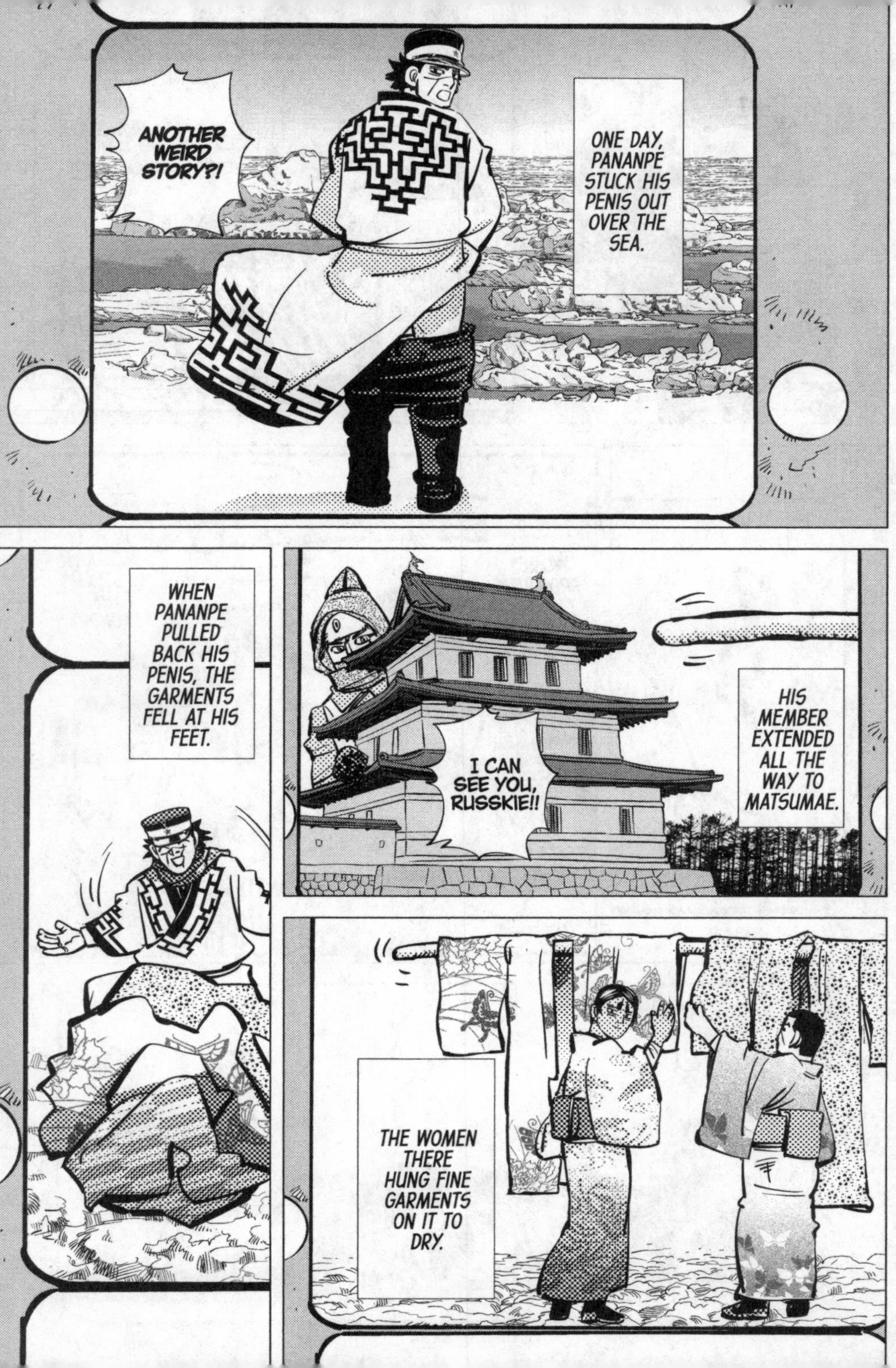
ONE DAY, PANANPE STUCK HIS PENIS OUT OVER THE SEA.
ANOTHER WEIRD STORY?!
HIS MEMBER EXTENDED ALL THE WAY TO MATSUMAE.
I CAN SEE YOU, RUSSKIE!!
THE WOMEN THERE HUNG FINE GARMENTS ON IT TO DRY.
WHEN PANANPE PULLED BACK HIS PENIS, THE GARMENTS FELL AT HIS FEET.

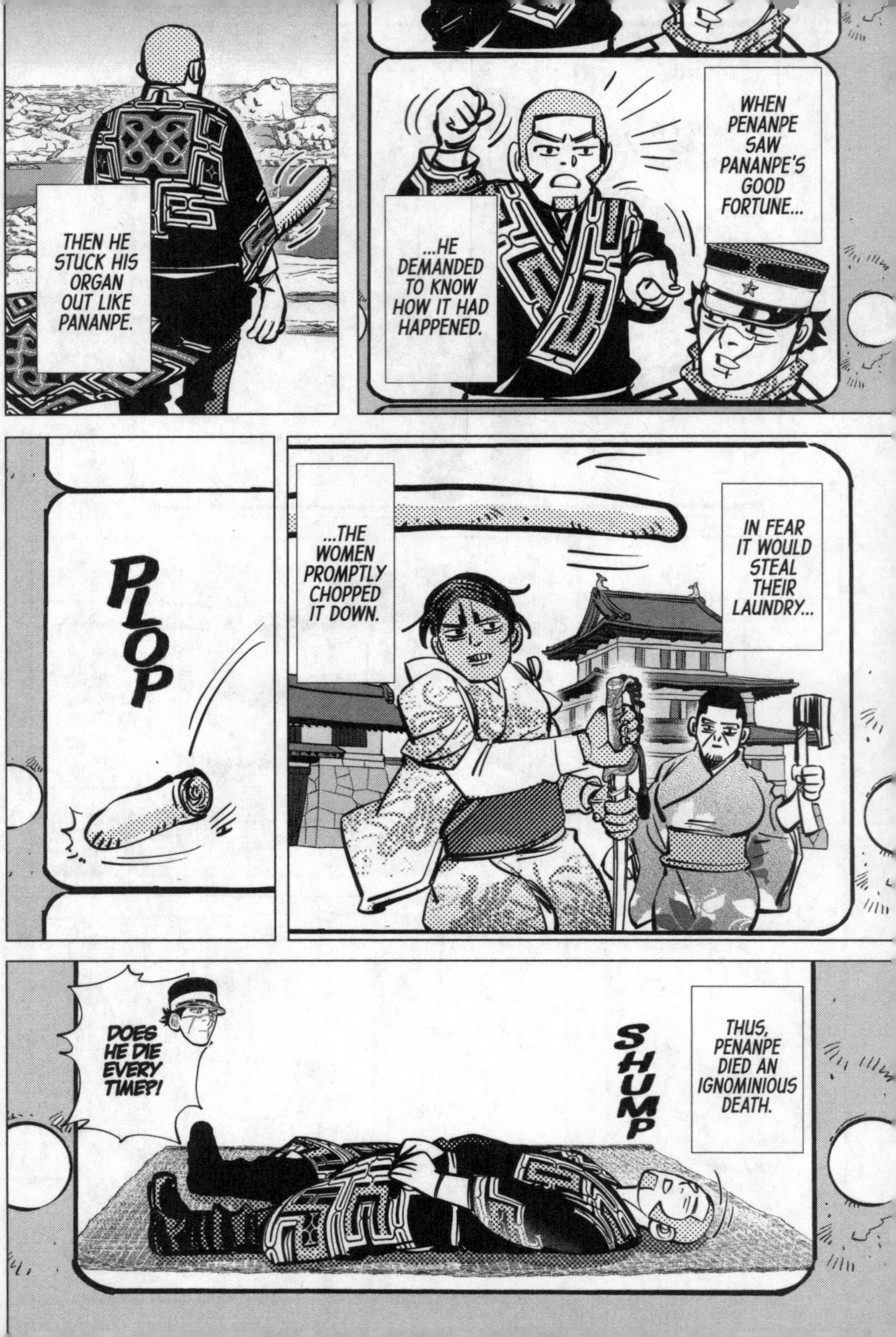
WHEN PENANPE SAW PANANPE'S GOOD FORTUNE...
...HE DEMANDED TO KNOW HOW IT HAD HAPPENED.
THEN HE STUCK HIS ORGAN OUT LIKE PANANPE.
IN FEAR IT WOULD STEAL THEIR LAUNDRY...
...THE WOMEN PROMPTLY CHOPPED IT DOWN.
PLOP
THUS, PENANPE DIED AN IGNOMINIOUS DEATH.
SHUMP
DOES HE DIE EVERY TIME?!

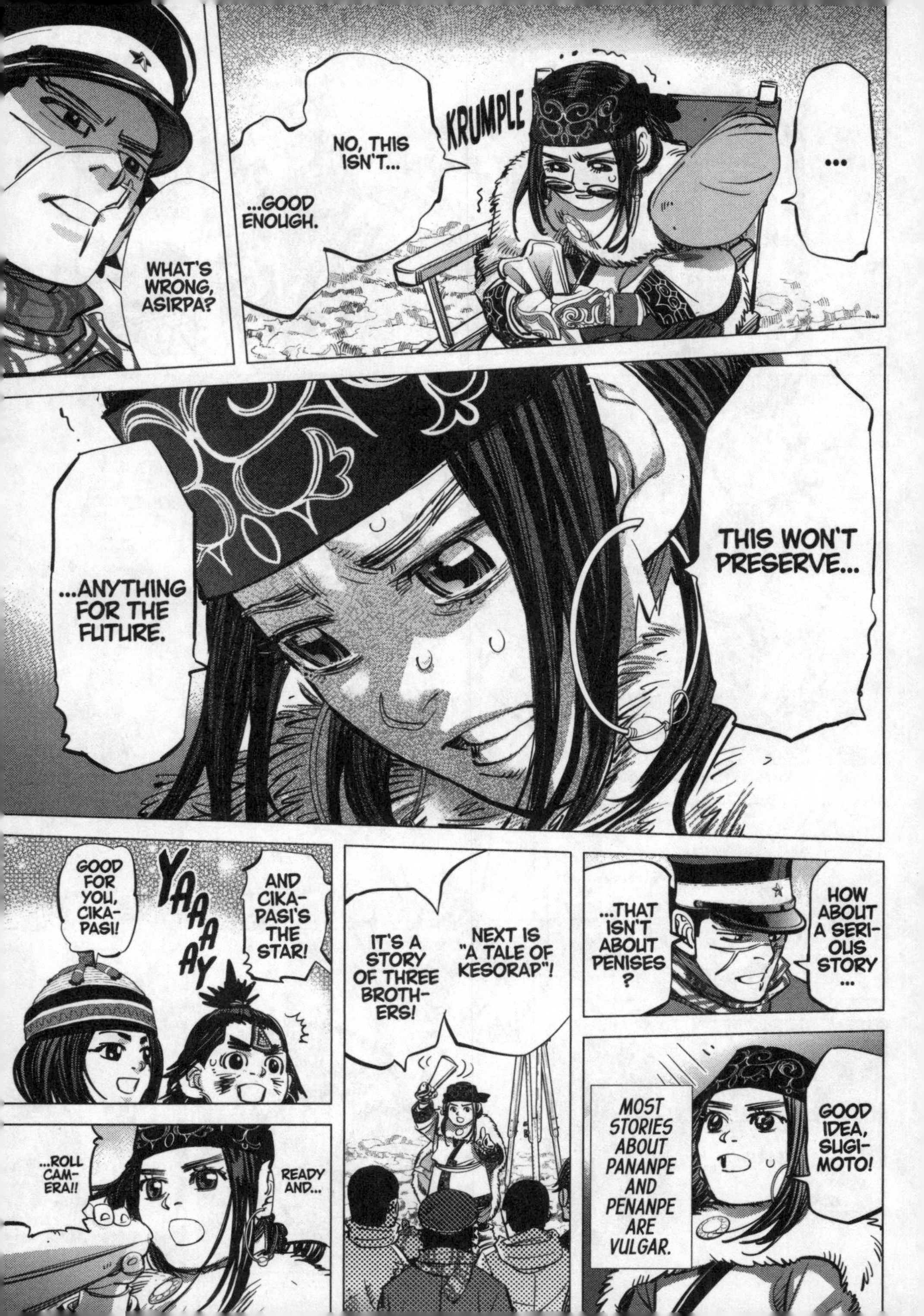
...
KRUMPLE
NO, THIS ISN'T...
...GOOD ENOUGH.
WHAT'S WRONG, ASIRPA?
THIS WON'T PRESERVE...
...ANYTHING FOR THE FUTURE.
HOW ABOUT A SERIOUS STORY...
...THAT ISN'T ABOUT PENISES?
GOOD IDEA, SUGIMOTO!
MOST STORIES ABOUT PANANPE AND PENANPE ARE VULGAR.
NEXT IS "A TALE OF KESORAP"!
IT'S A STORY OF THREE BROTHERS!
AND CIKAPASI'S THE STAR!
YAAAAAY
GOOD FOR YOU, CIKAPASI!
READY AND...
...ROLL CAMERA!!

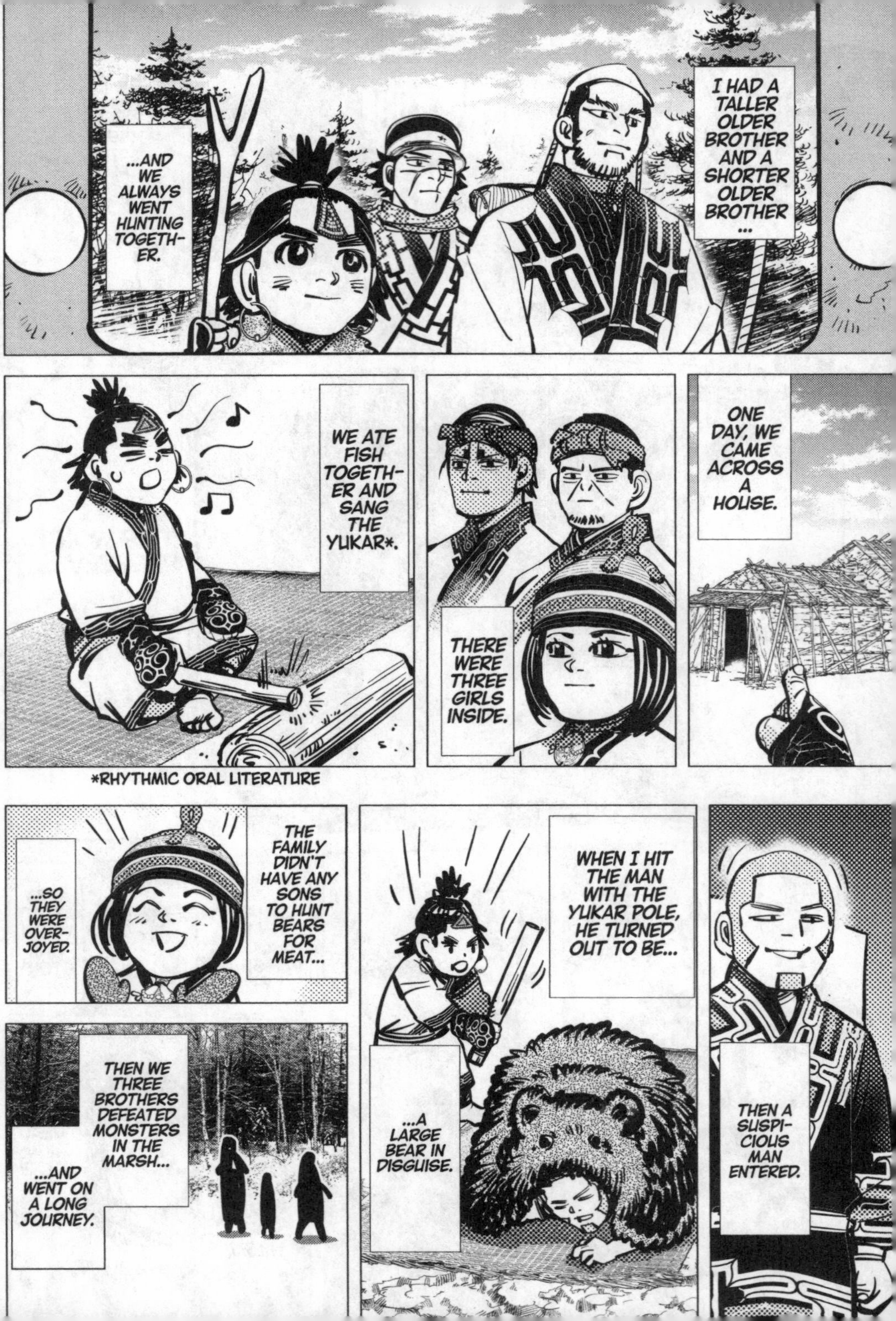
I HAD A TALLER OLDER BROTHER AND A SHORTER OLDER BROTHER...
...AND WE ALWAYS WENT HUNTING TOGETH-ER.
ONE DAY, WE CAME ACROSS A HOUSE.
THERE WERE THREE GIRLS INSIDE.
WE ATE FISH TOGETH-ER AND SANG THE YUKAR*.
*RHYTHMIC ORAL LITERATURE
THEN A SUSPI-CIOUS MAN ENTERED.
WHEN I HIT THE MAN WITH THE YUKAR POLE, HE TURNED OUT TO BE...
...A LARGE BEAR IN DISGUISE.
THE FAMILY DIDN'T HAVE ANY SONS TO HUNT BEARS FOR MEAT...
...SO THEY WERE OVER-JOYED.
THEN WE THREE BROTHERS DEFEATED MONSTERS IN THE MARSH...
...AND WENT ON A LONG JOURNEY.

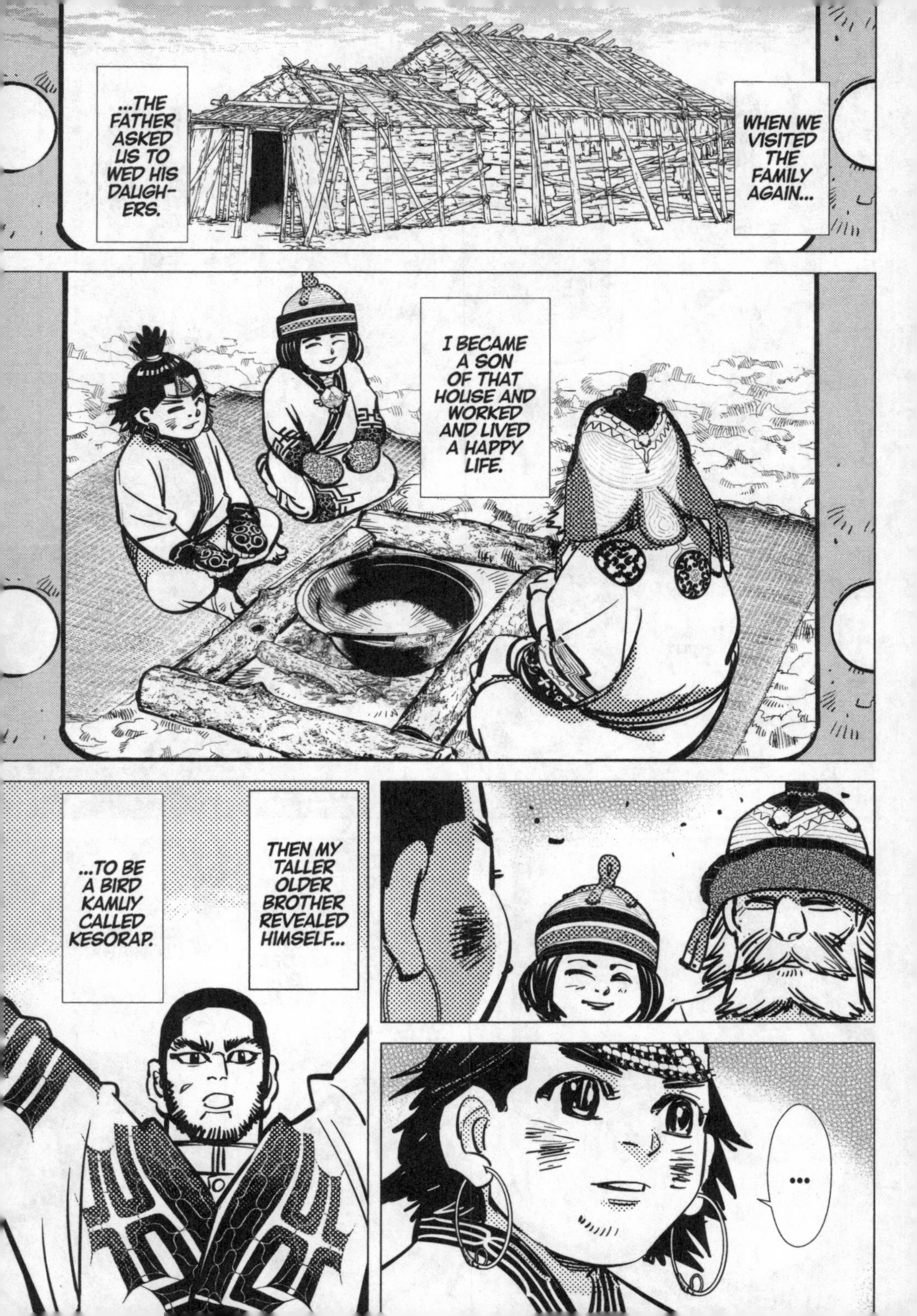
WHEN WE VISITED THE FAMILY AGAIN...
...THE FATHER ASKED US TO WED HIS DAUGHTERS.
I BECAME A SON OF THAT HOUSE AND WORKED AND LIVED A HAPPY LIFE.
...
THEN MY TALLER OLDER BROTHER REVEALED HIMSELF...
...TO BE A BIRD KAMUY CALLED KESORAP.

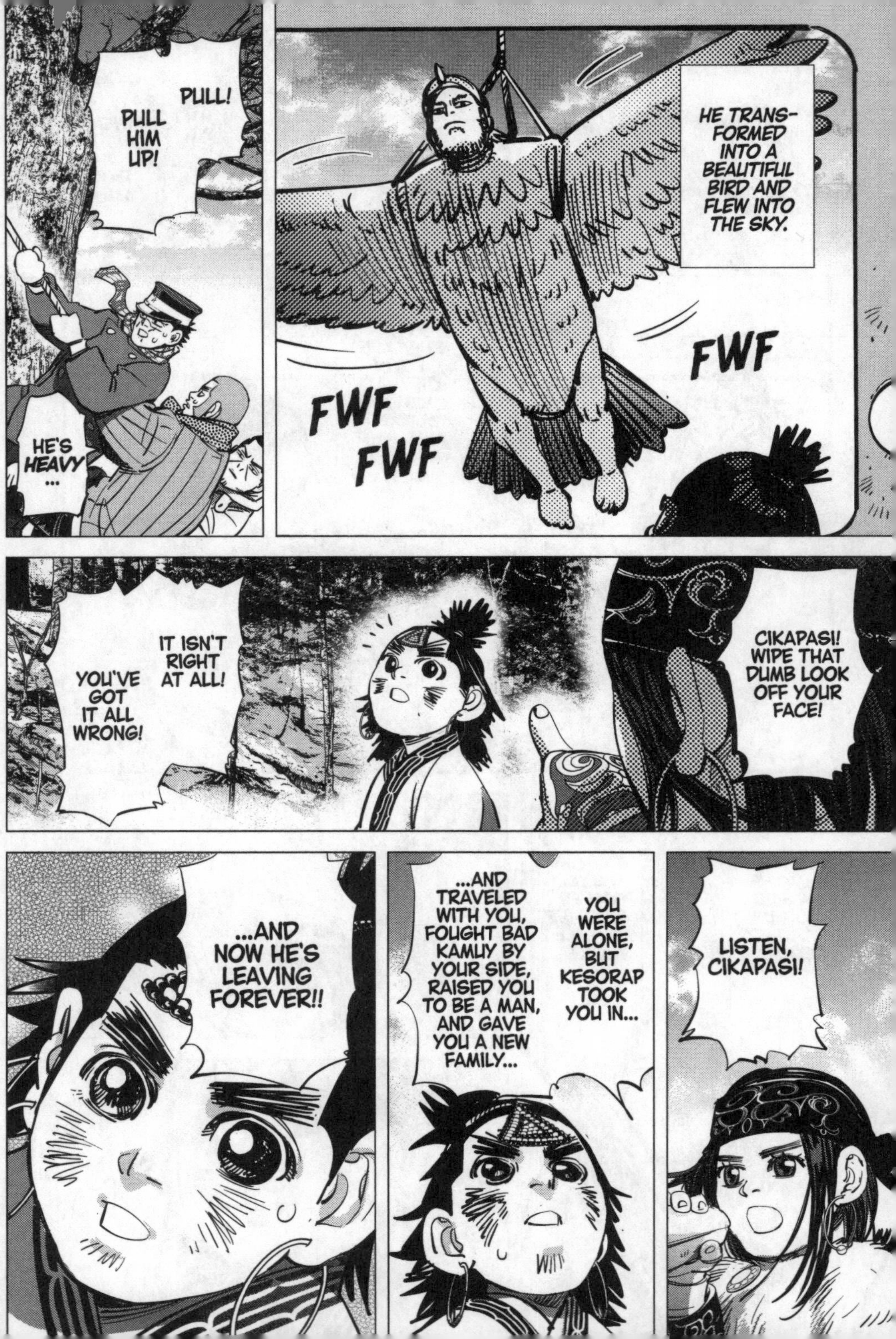
HE TRANS-FORMED INTO A BEAUTIFUL BIRD AND FLEW INTO THE SKY.
FWF
FWF
FWF
PULL!
PULL HIM UP!
HE'S HEAVY...
CIKAPASI! WIPE THAT DUMB LOOK OFF YOUR FACE!
IT ISN'T RIGHT AT ALL!
YOU'VE GOT IT ALL WRONG!
LISTEN, CIKAPASI!
YOU WERE ALONE, BUT KESORAP TOOK YOU IN...
...AND TRAVELED WITH YOU, FOUGHT BAD KAMUY BY YOUR SIDE, RAISED YOU TO BE A MAN, AND GAVE YOU A NEW FAMILY...
...AND NOW HE'S LEAVING FOREVER!!

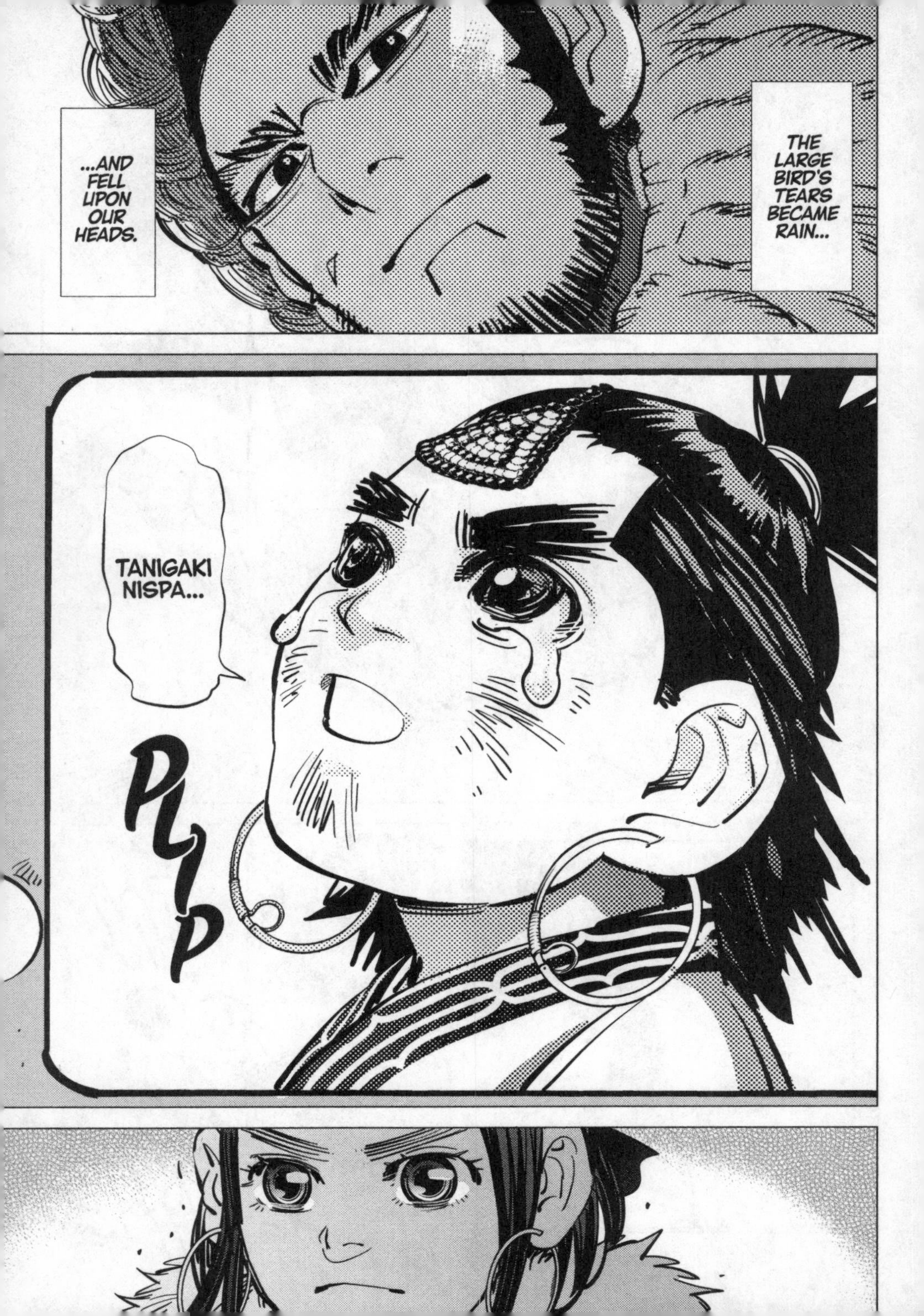
THE LARGE BIRD'S TEARS BECAME RAIN...
...AND FELL UPON OUR HEADS.
TANIGAKI NISPA...
PLIP

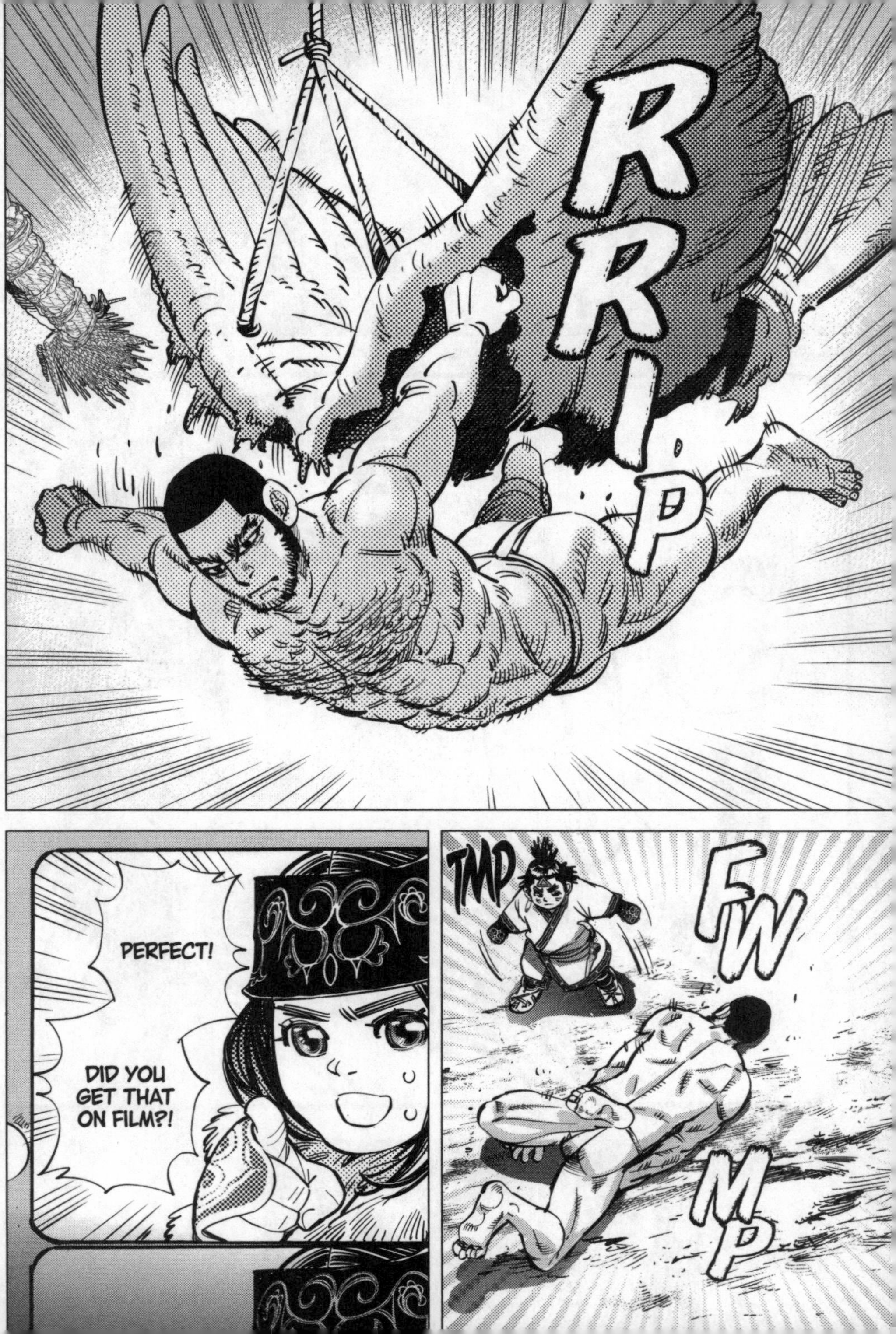
RRIP
TMP
FWMP
PERFECT!
DID YOU GET THAT ON FILM?!

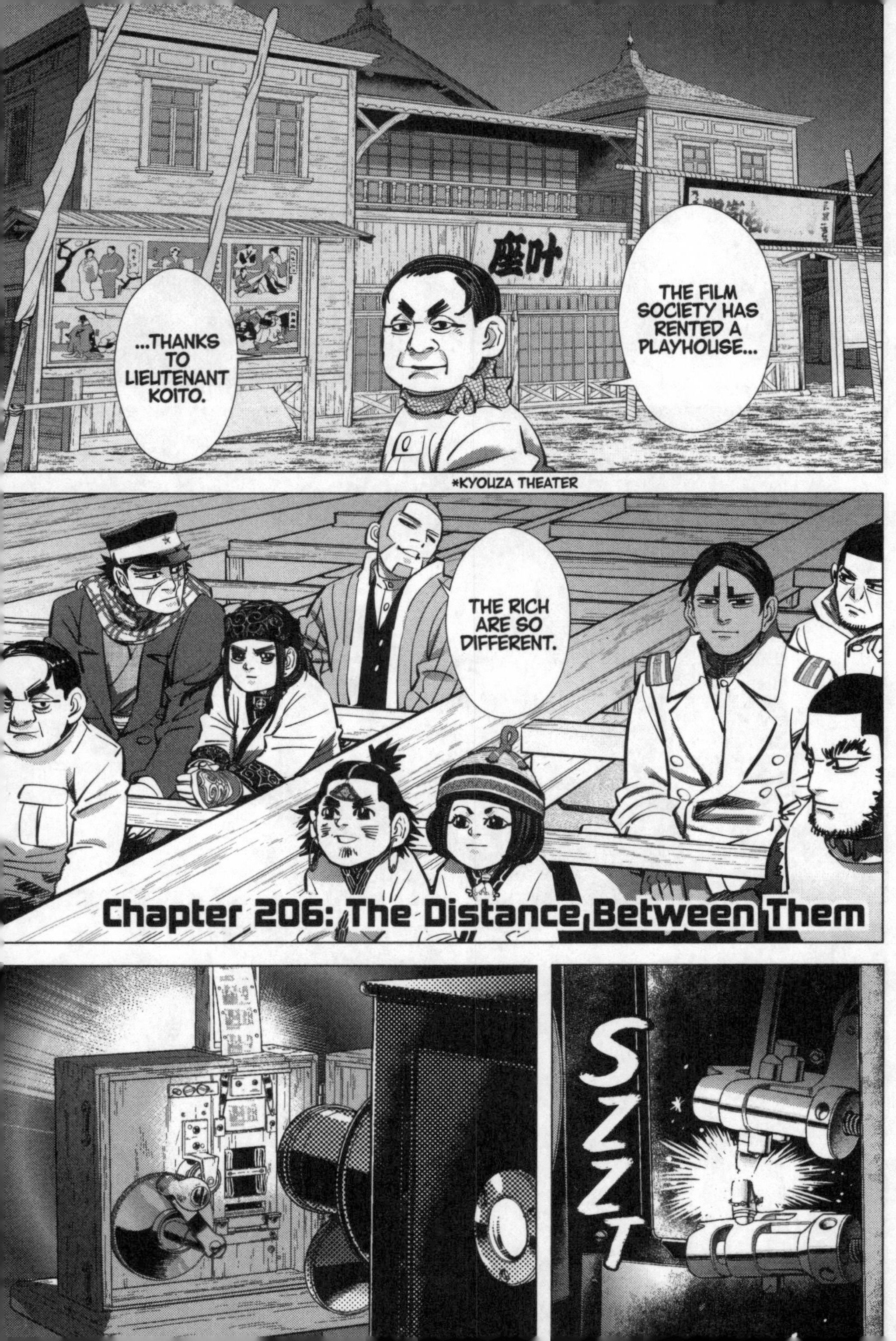
THE FILM SOCIETY HAS RENTED A PLAYHOUSE...
...THANKS TO LIEUTENANT KOITO.
叶座
*KYOUZA THEATER
THE RICH ARE SO DIFFERENT.
Chapter 206: The Distance Between Them
SZZT

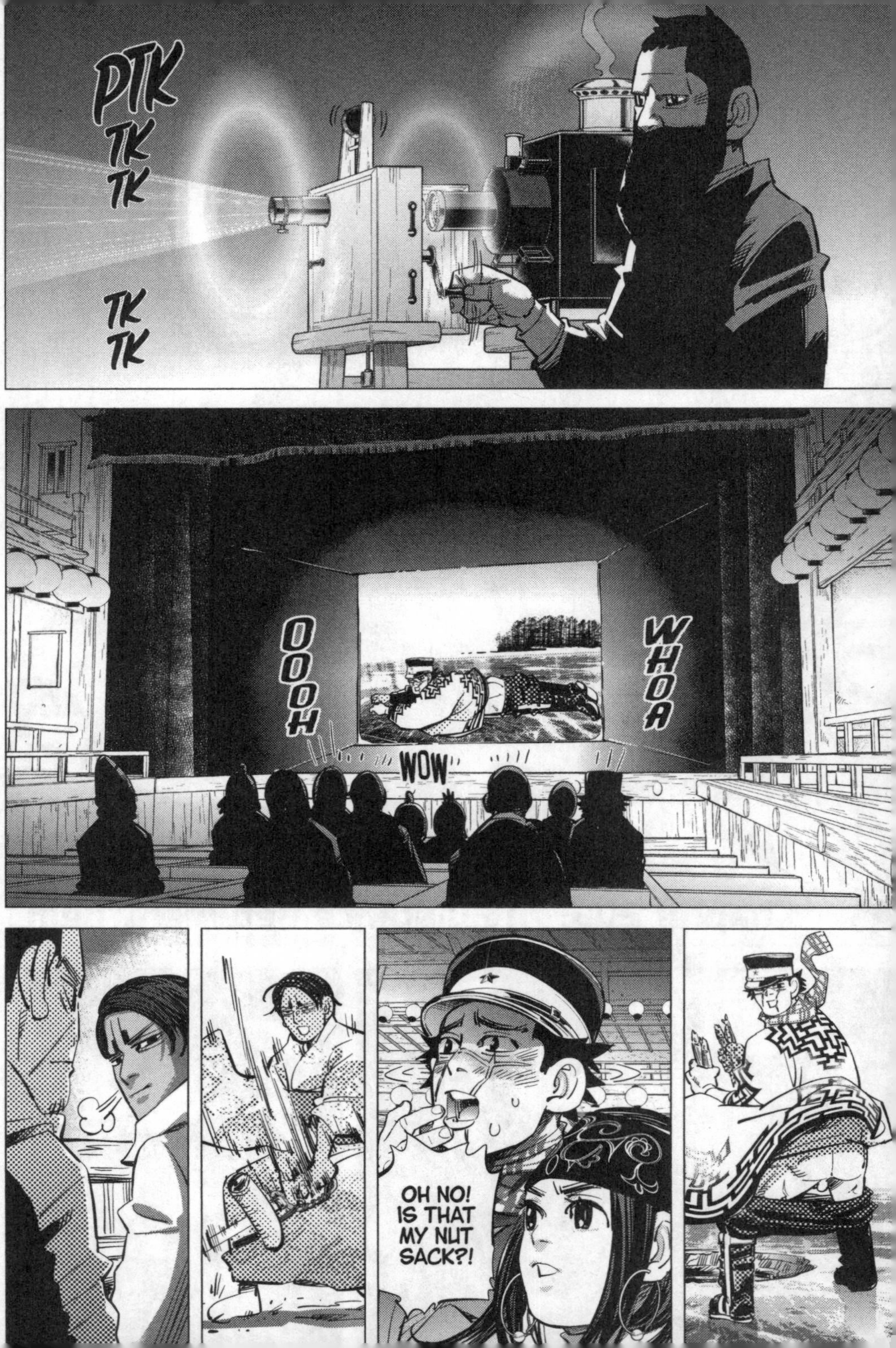
PTK
TK
TK
TK
TK
WHOA
WOW
OOOH
OH NO! IS THAT MY NUT SACK?!

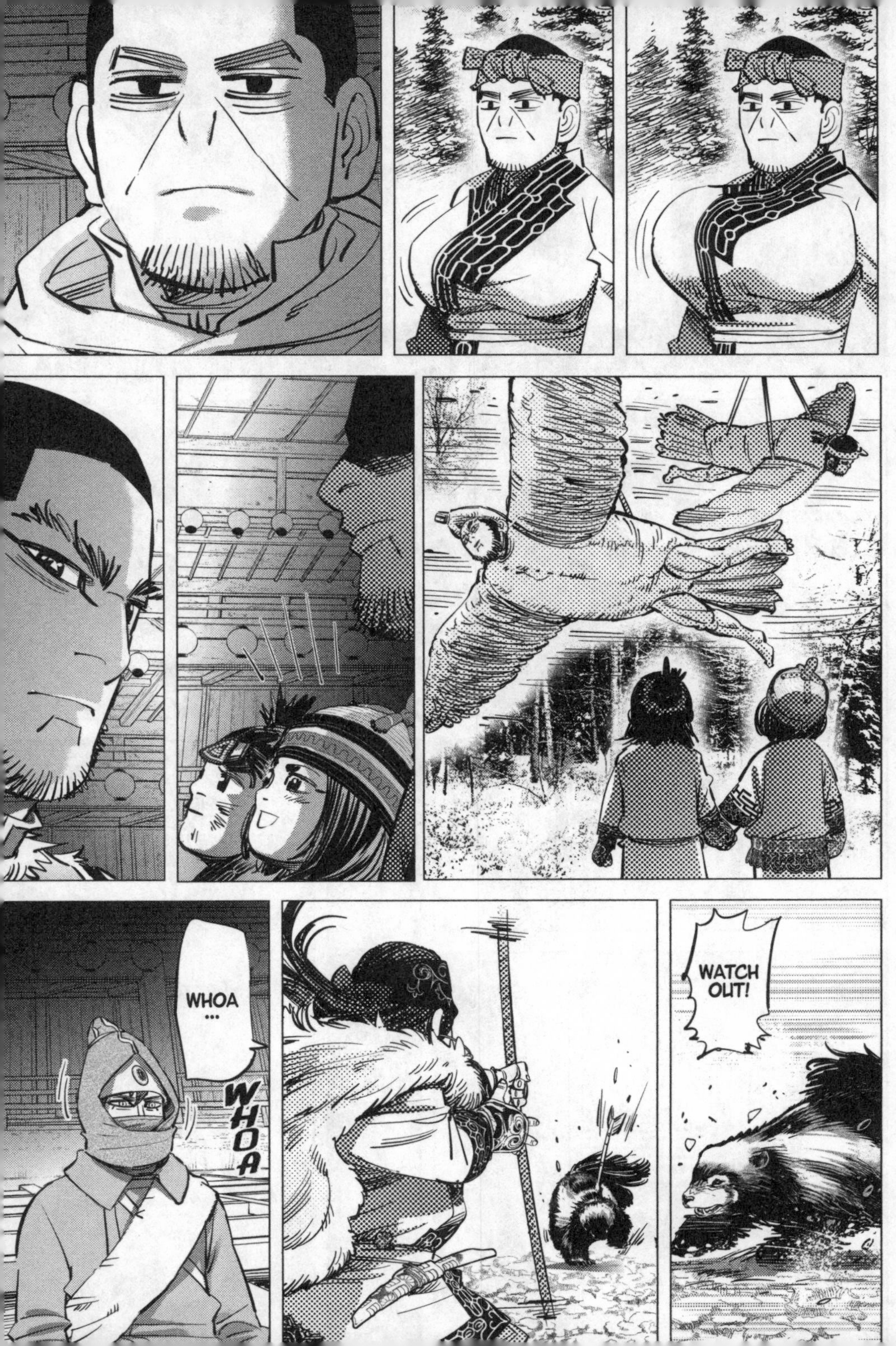
WATCH OUT!
WHOA ...
WHOA

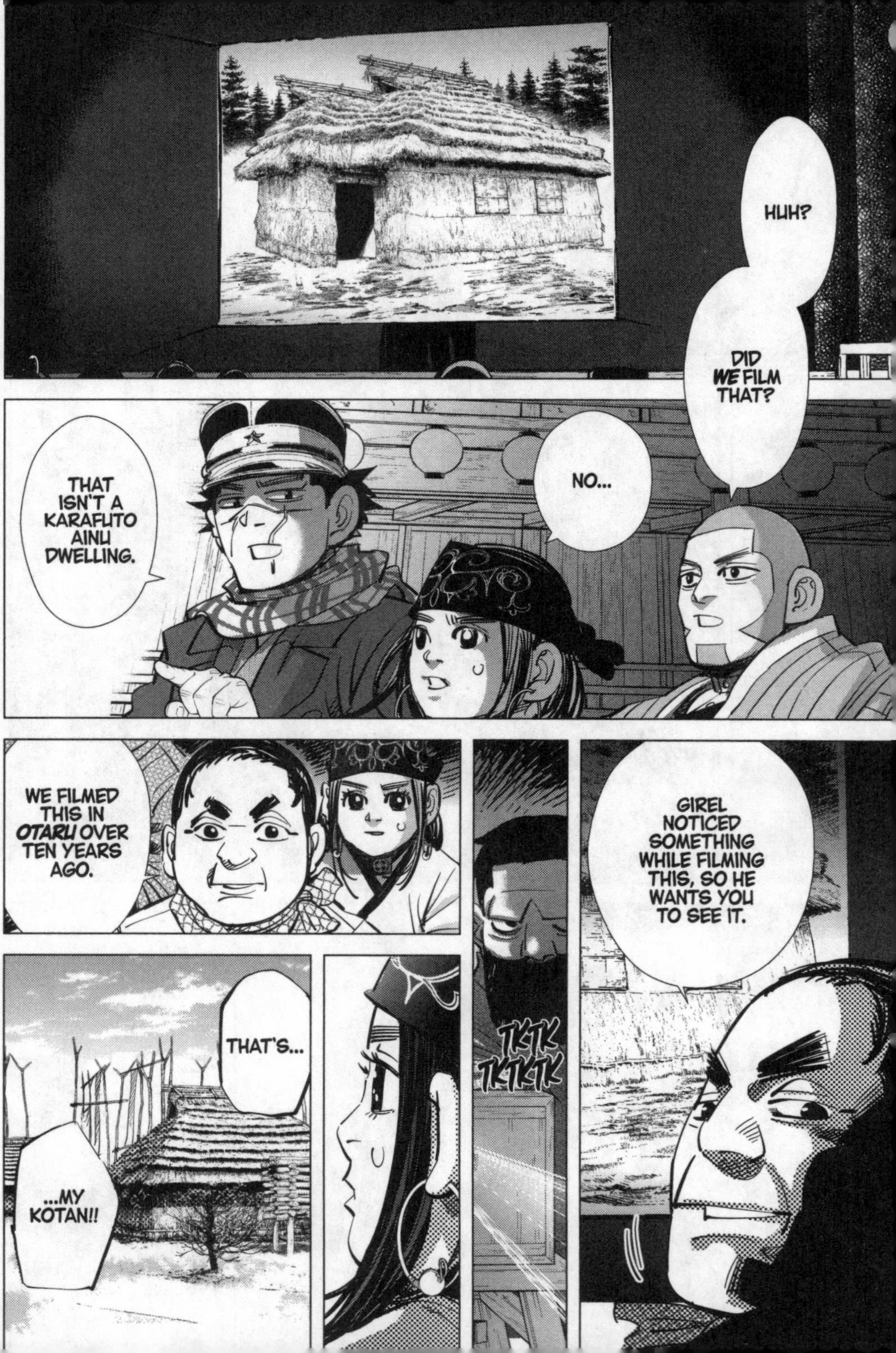
HUH?
DID WE FILM THAT?
NO...
THAT ISN'T A KARAFUTO AINU DWELLING.
GIREL NOTICED SOMETHING WHILE FILMING THIS, SO HE WANTS YOU TO SEE IT.
WE FILMED THIS IN OTARU OVER TEN YEARS AGO.
TKTK TKTKTK
THAT'S...
...MY KOTAN!!

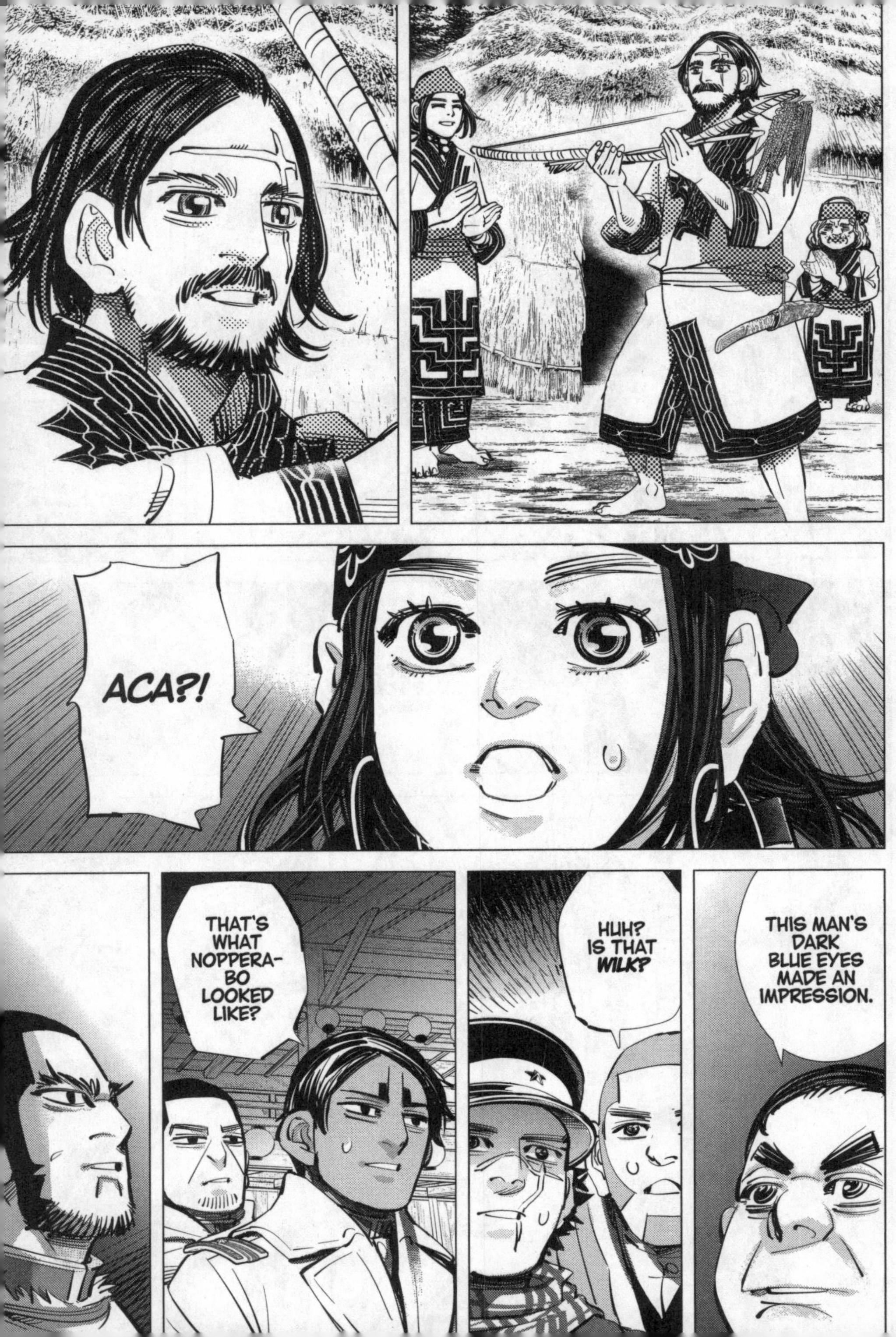
ACA?!
THIS MAN'S DARK BLUE EYES MADE AN IMPRESSION.
HUH? IS THAT *WILK*?
THAT'S WHAT NOPPERA-BO LOOKED LIKE?

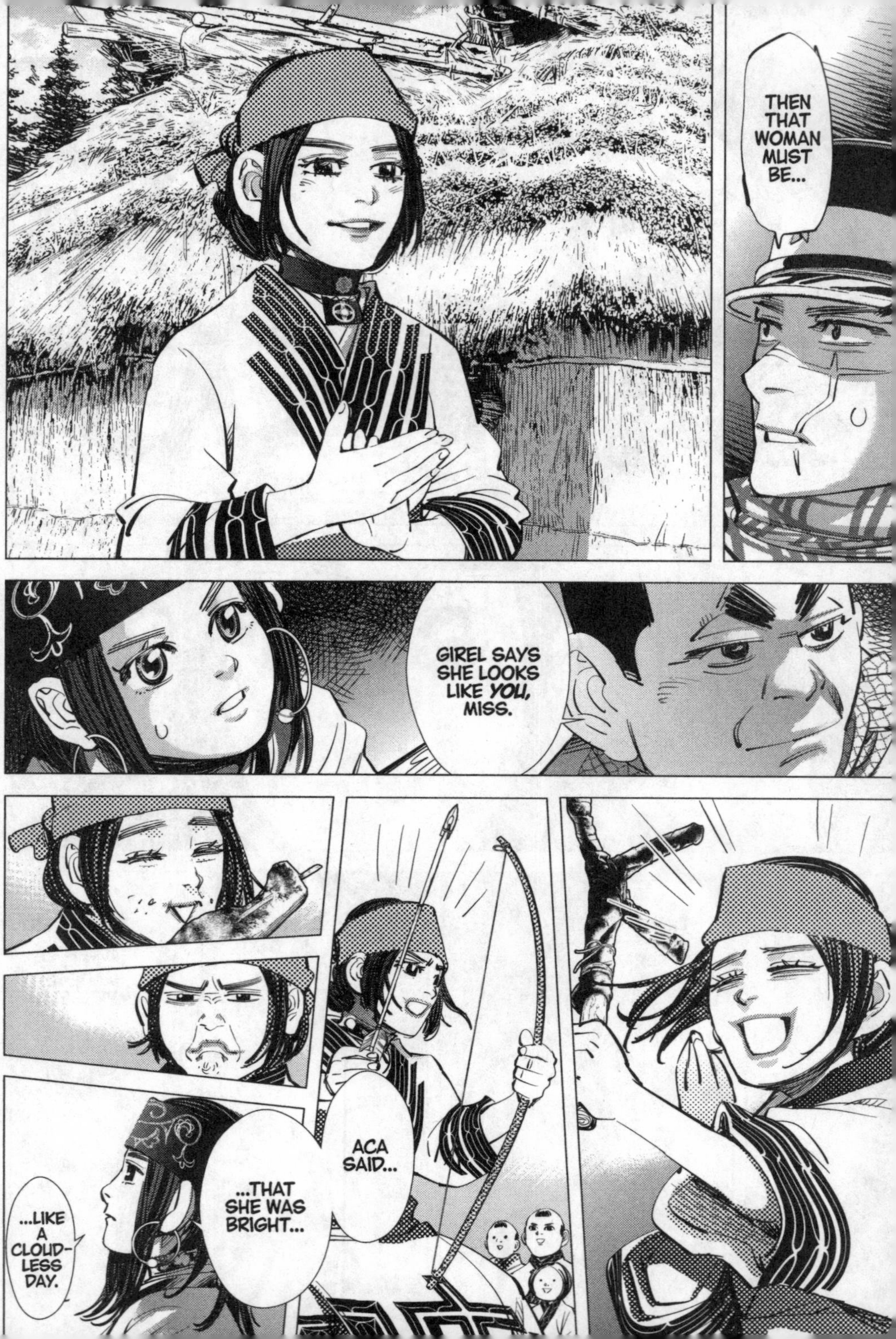
THEN THAT WOMAN MUST BE...
GIREL SAYS SHE LOOKS LIKE *YOU*, MISS.
ACA SAID...
...THAT SHE WAS BRIGHT...
...LIKE A CLOUD-LESS DAY.

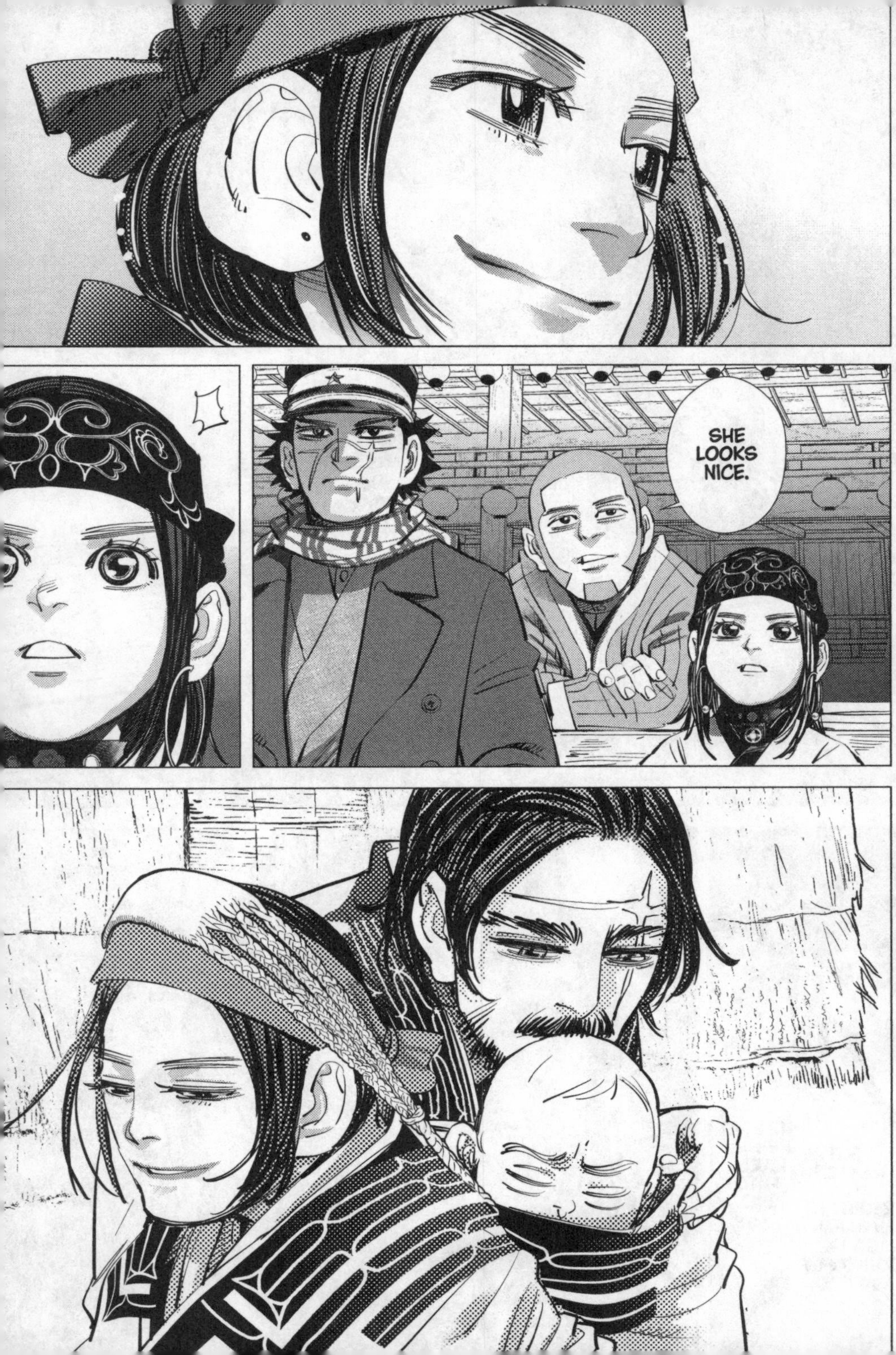
SHE LOOKS NICE.

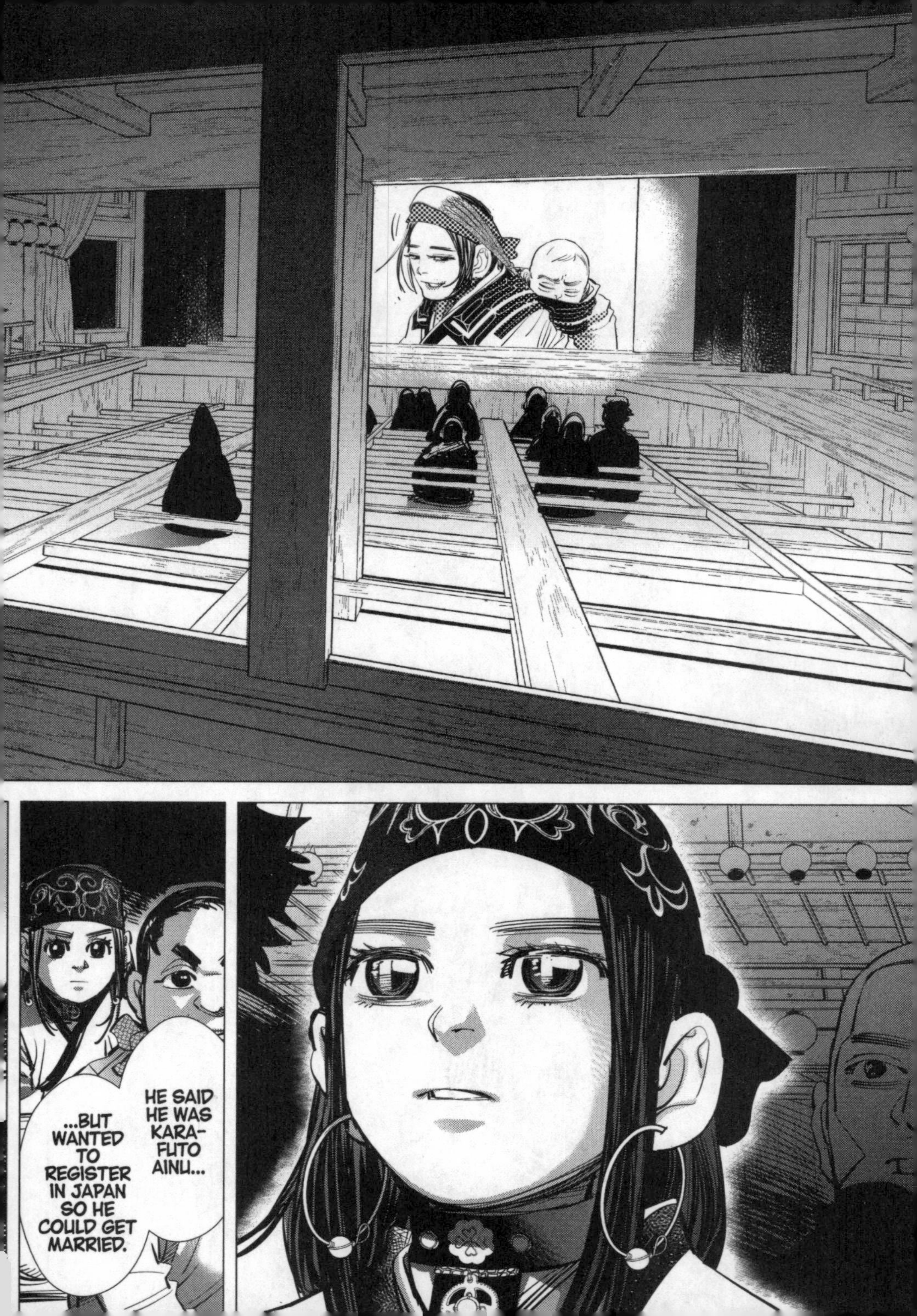
HE SAID HE WAS KARAFUTO AINU...
...BUT WANTED TO REGISTER IN JAPAN SO HE COULD GET MARRIED.

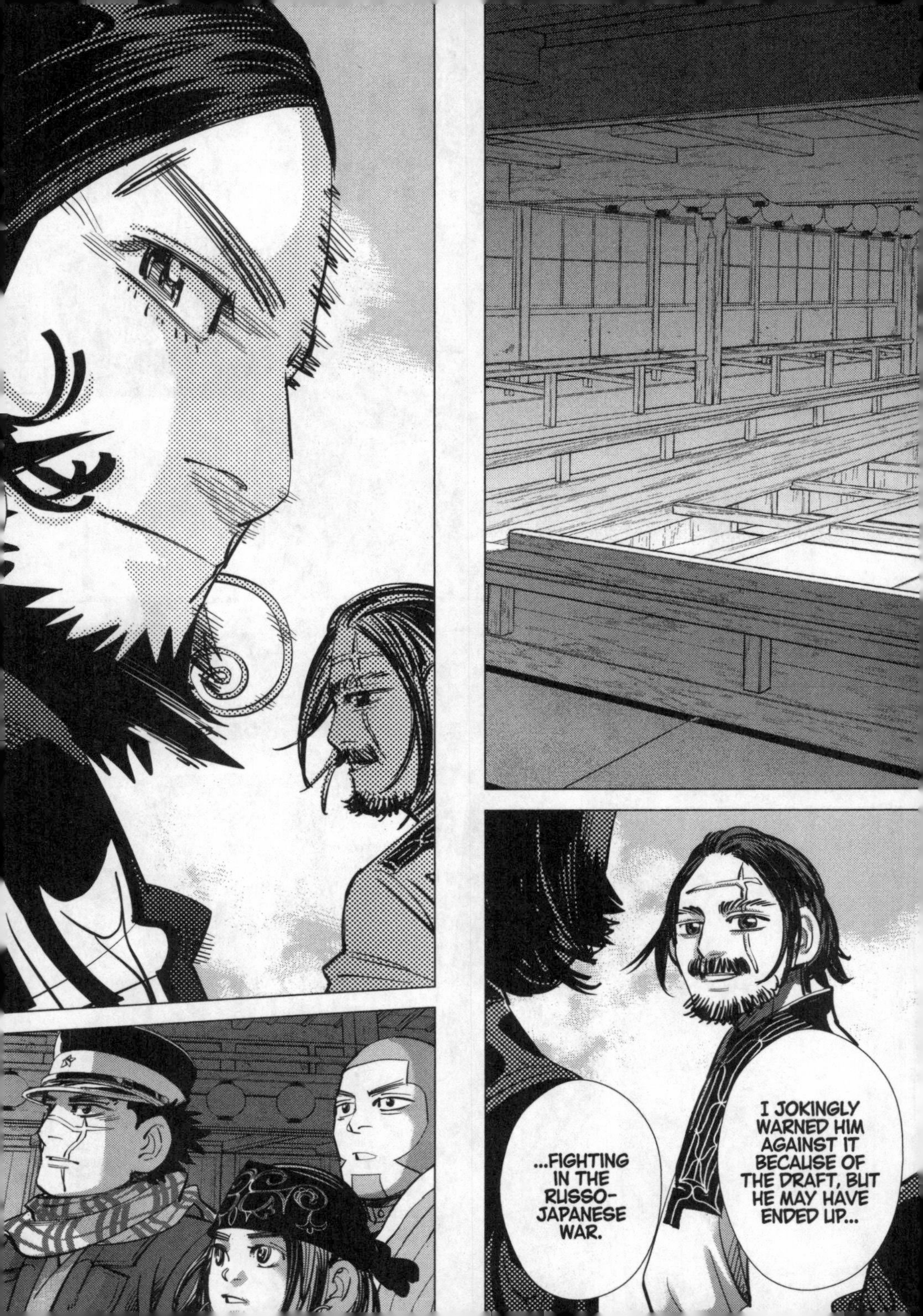
I JOKINGLY WARNED HIM AGAINST IT BECAUSE OF THE DRAFT, BUT HE MAY HAVE ENDED UP...
...FIGHTING IN THE RUSSO-JAPANESE WAR.

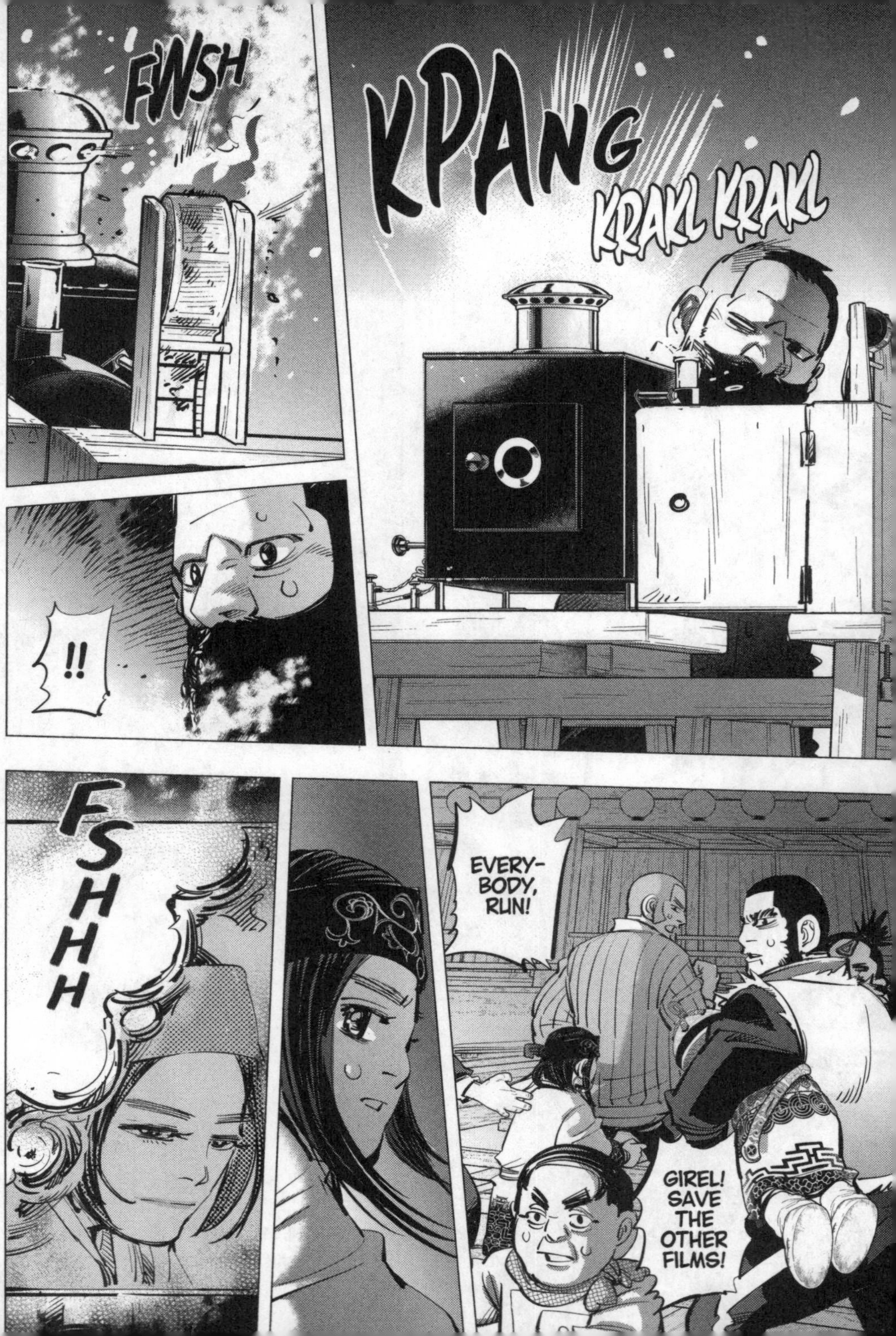
KPANG
KRAKL KRAKL
FWSH
!!
EVERY-BODY, RUN!
GIREL! SAVE THE OTHER FILMS!
FSHHH

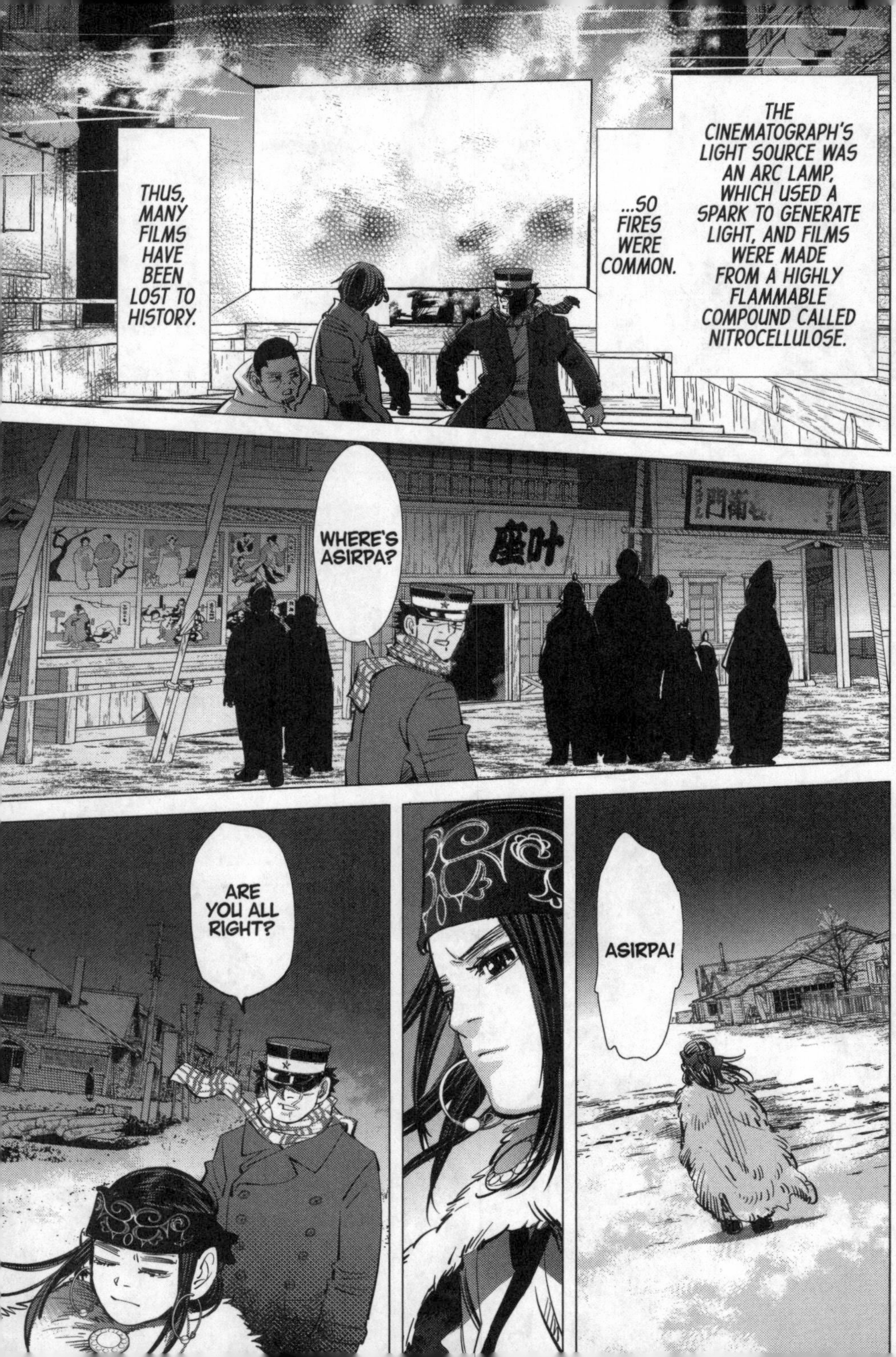
THE CINEMATOGRAPH'S LIGHT SOURCE WAS AN ARC LAMP, WHICH USED A SPARK TO GENERATE LIGHT, AND FILMS WERE MADE FROM A HIGHLY FLAMMABLE COMPOUND CALLED NITROCELLULOSE.
...SO FIRES WERE COMMON.
THUS, MANY FILMS HAVE BEEN LOST TO HISTORY.
WHERE'S ASIRPA?
ASIRPA!
ARE YOU ALL RIGHT?

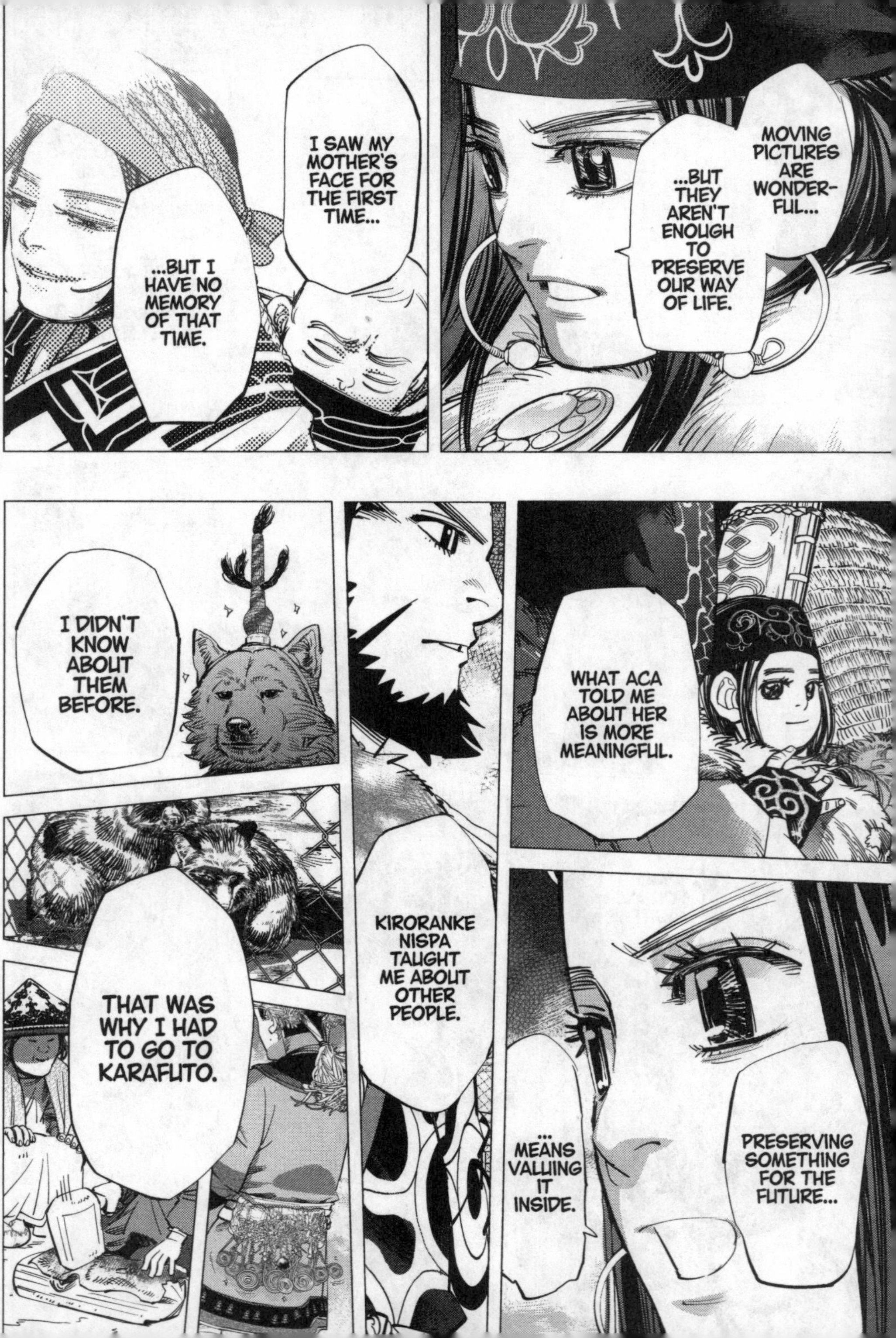
MOVING PICTURES ARE WONDER-FUL...
...BUT THEY AREN'T ENOUGH TO PRESERVE OUR WAY OF LIFE.
I SAW MY MOTHER'S FACE FOR THE FIRST TIME...
...BUT I HAVE NO MEMORY OF THAT TIME.
WHAT ACA TOLD ME ABOUT HER IS MORE MEANINGFUL.
KIRORANKE NISPA TAUGHT ME ABOUT OTHER PEOPLE.
I DIDN'T KNOW ABOUT THEM BEFORE.
THAT WAS WHY I HAD TO GO TO KARAFUTO.
PRESERVING SOMETHING FOR THE FUTURE...
...MEANS VALUING IT INSIDE.

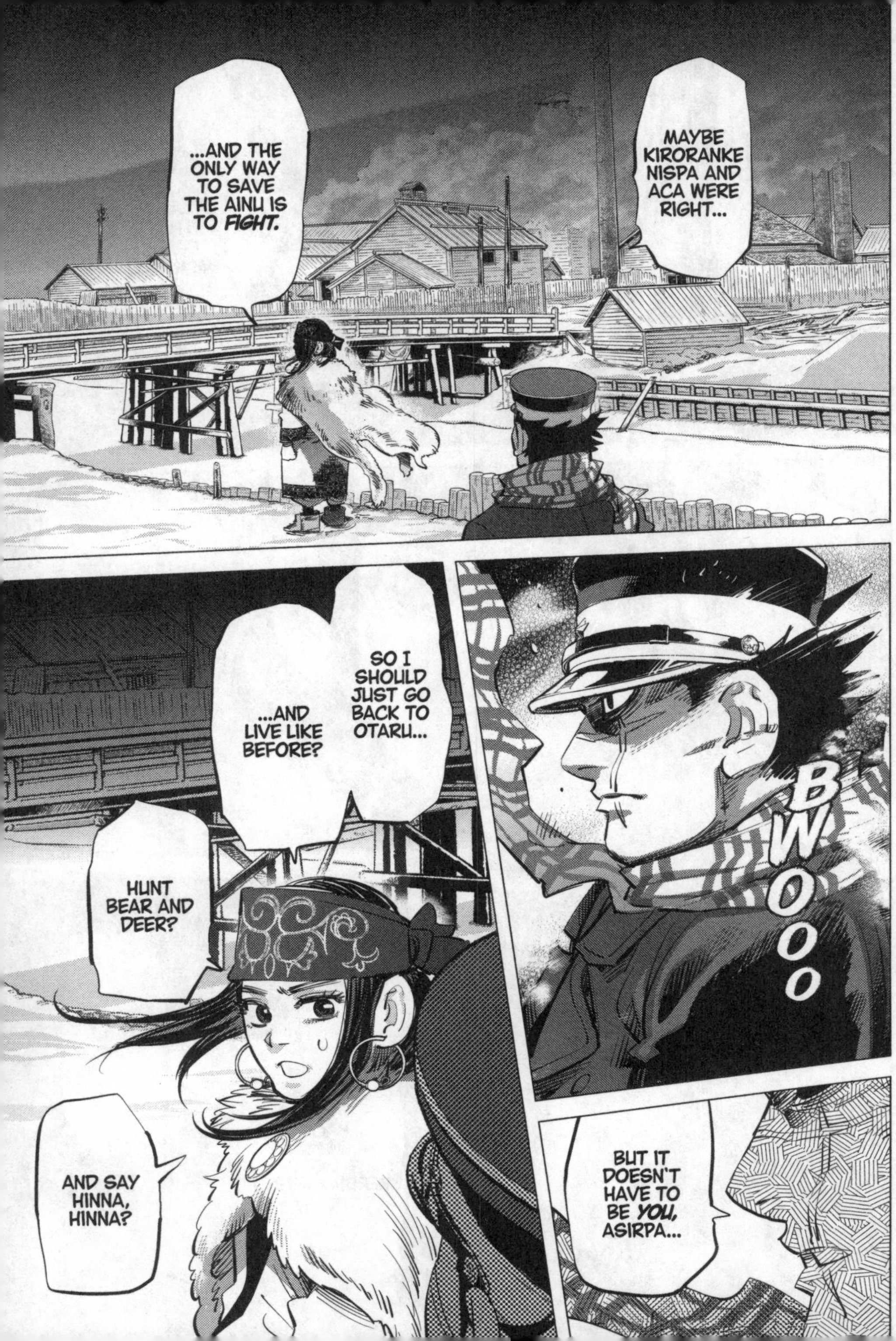

MAYBE KIRORANKE NISPA AND ACA WERE RIGHT...
...AND THE ONLY WAY TO SAVE THE AINU IS TO *FIGHT.*
BWOOOO
BUT IT DOESN'T HAVE TO BE *YOU,* ASIRPA...
SO I SHOULD JUST GO BACK TO OTARU...
...AND LIVE LIKE BEFORE?
HUNT BEAR AND DEER?
AND SAY HINNA, HINNA?

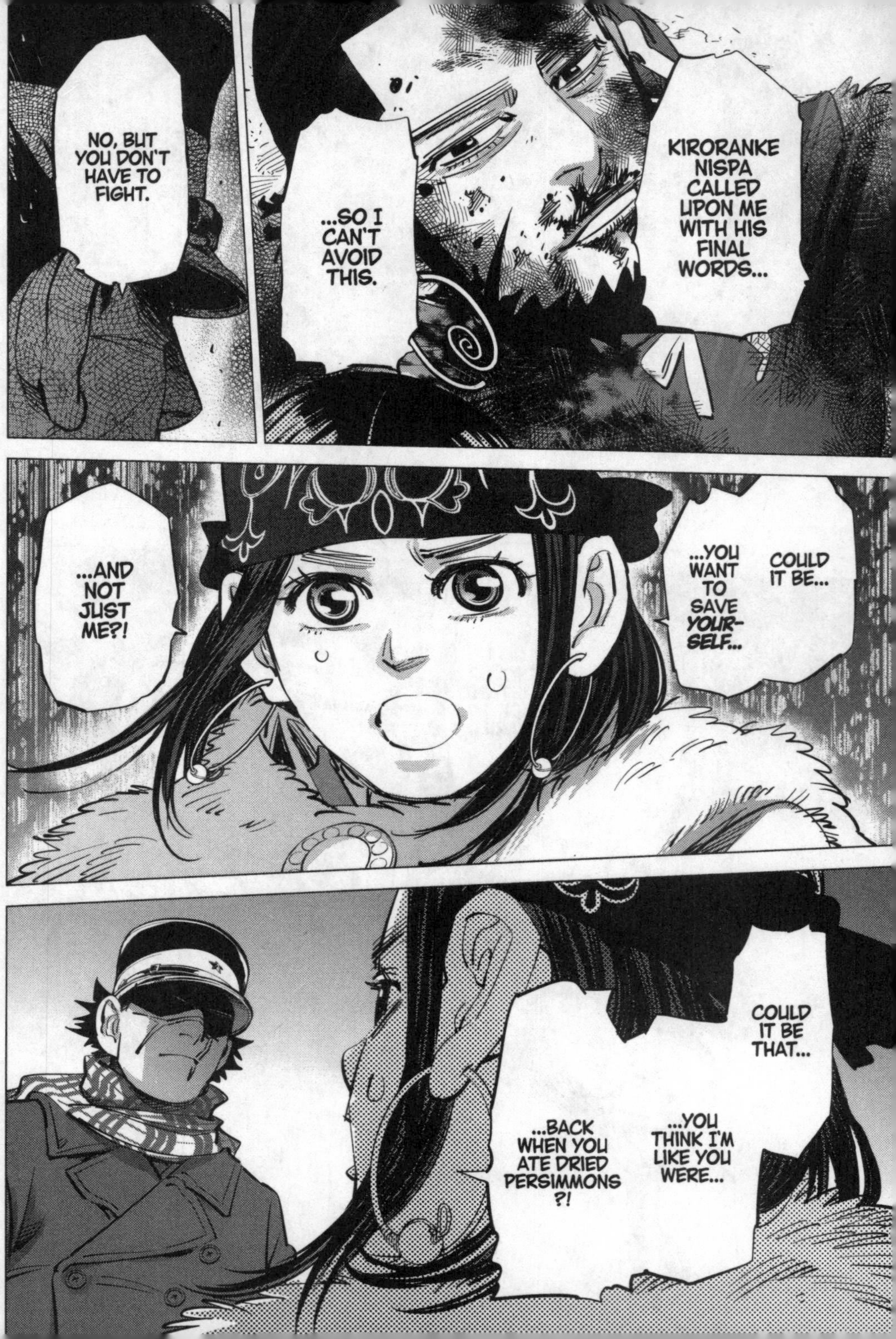
KIRORANKE NISPA CALLED UPON ME WITH HIS FINAL WORDS...
...SO I CAN'T AVOID THIS.
NO, BUT YOU DON'T HAVE TO FIGHT.
COULD IT BE...
...YOU WANT TO SAVE *YOURSELF*...
...AND NOT JUST ME?!
COULD IT BE THAT...
...YOU THINK I'M LIKE YOU WERE...
...BACK WHEN YOU ATE DRIED PERSIMMONS ?!

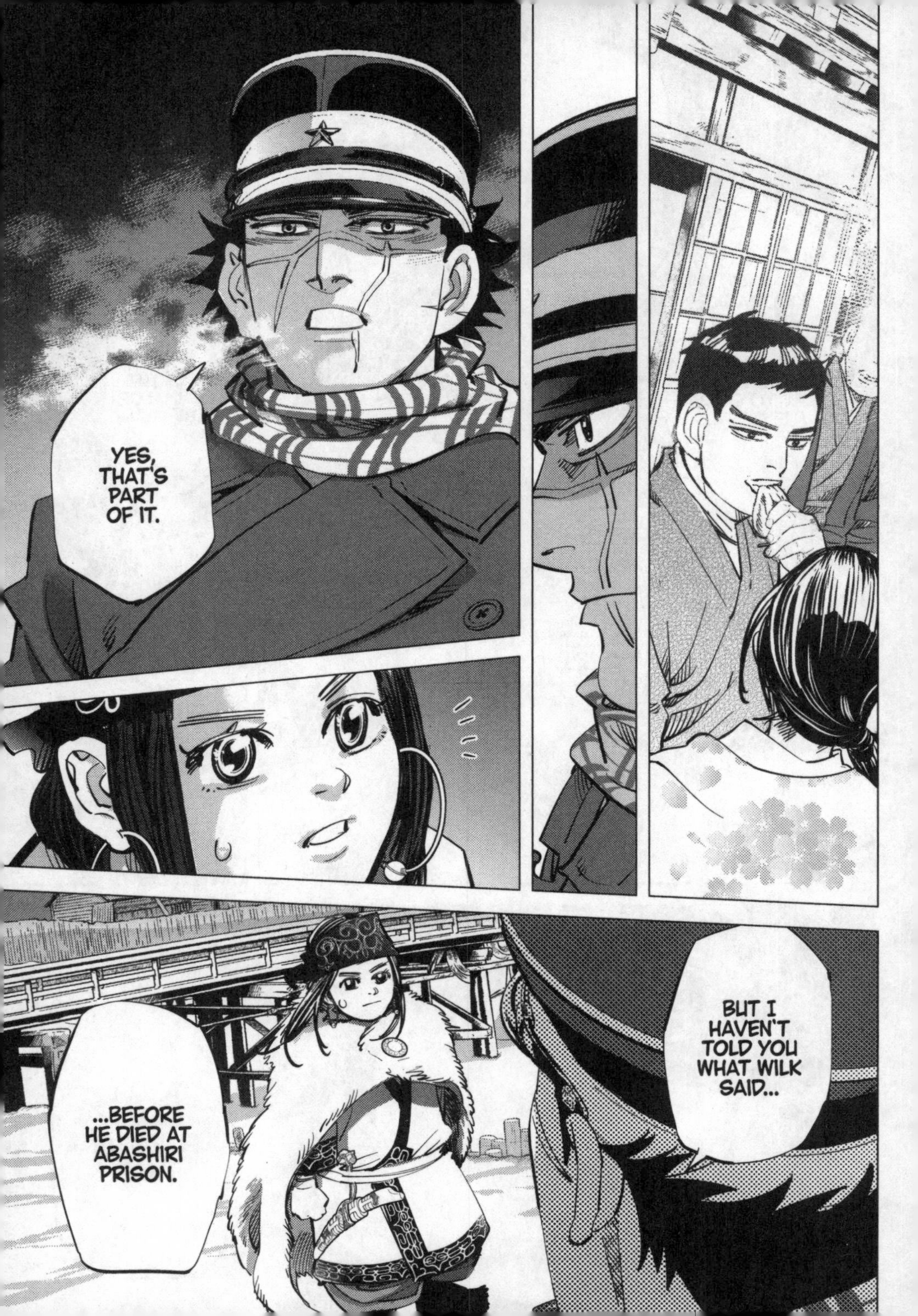
YES, THAT'S PART OF IT.
BUT I HAVEN'T TOLD YOU WHAT WILK SAID...
...BEFORE HE DIED AT ABASHIRI PRISON.

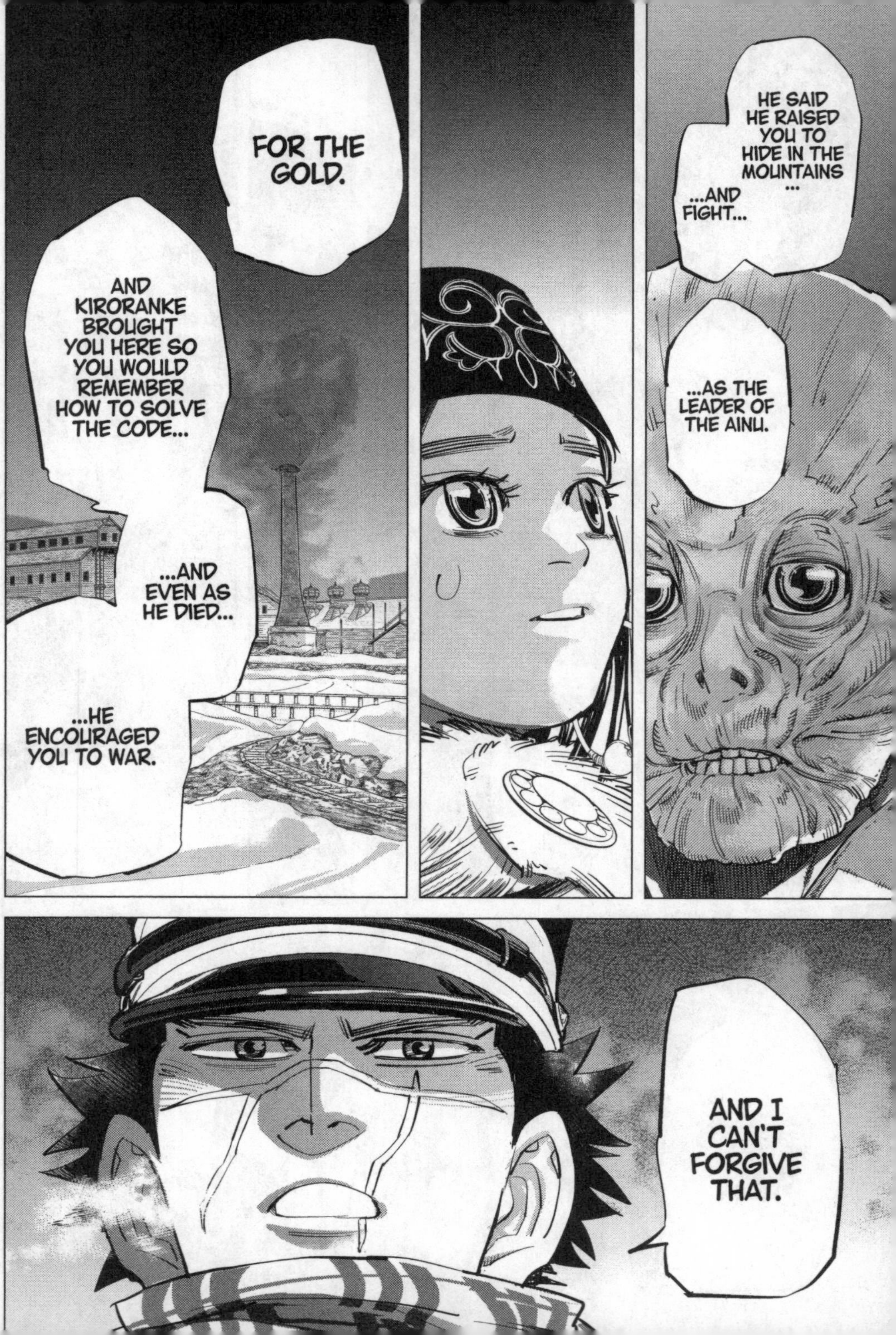
HE SAID HE RAISED YOU TO HIDE IN THE MOUNTAINS... ...AND FIGHT...
...AS THE LEADER OF THE AINU.
FOR THE GOLD.
AND KIRORANKE BROUGHT YOU HERE SO YOU WOULD REMEMBER HOW TO SOLVE THE CODE...
...AND EVEN AS HE DIED...
...HE ENCOURAGED YOU TO WAR.
AND I CAN'T FORGIVE THAT.

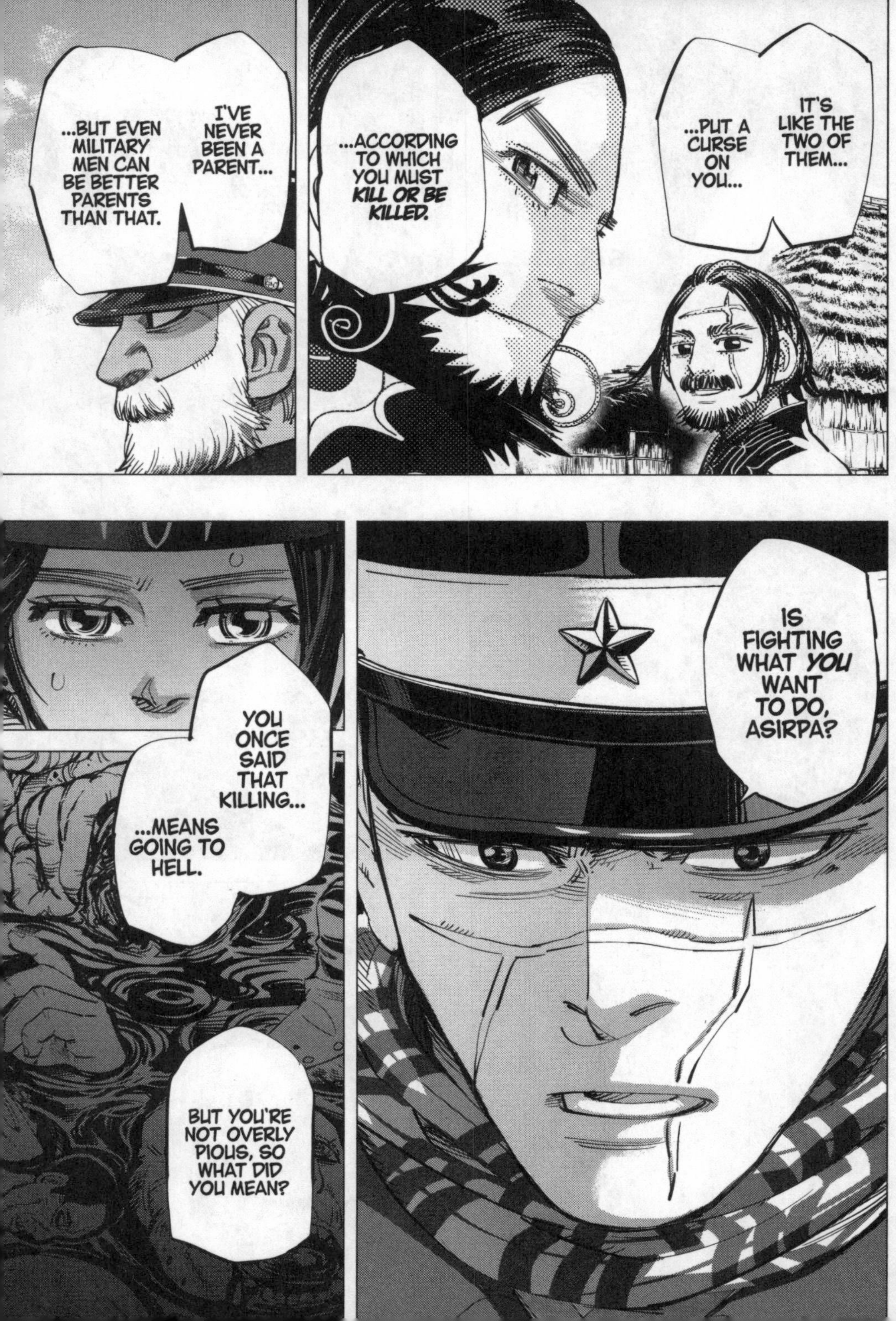
IT'S LIKE THE TWO OF THEM...
...PUT A CURSE ON YOU...
...ACCORDING TO WHICH YOU MUST *KILL OR BE KILLED.*
I'VE NEVER BEEN A PARENT...
...BUT EVEN MILITARY MEN CAN BE BETTER PARENTS THAN THAT.
IS FIGHTING WHAT *YOU* WANT TO DO, ASIRPA?
YOU ONCE SAID THAT KILLING...
...MEANS GOING TO HELL.
BUT YOU'RE NOT OVERLY PIOUS, SO WHAT DID YOU MEAN?

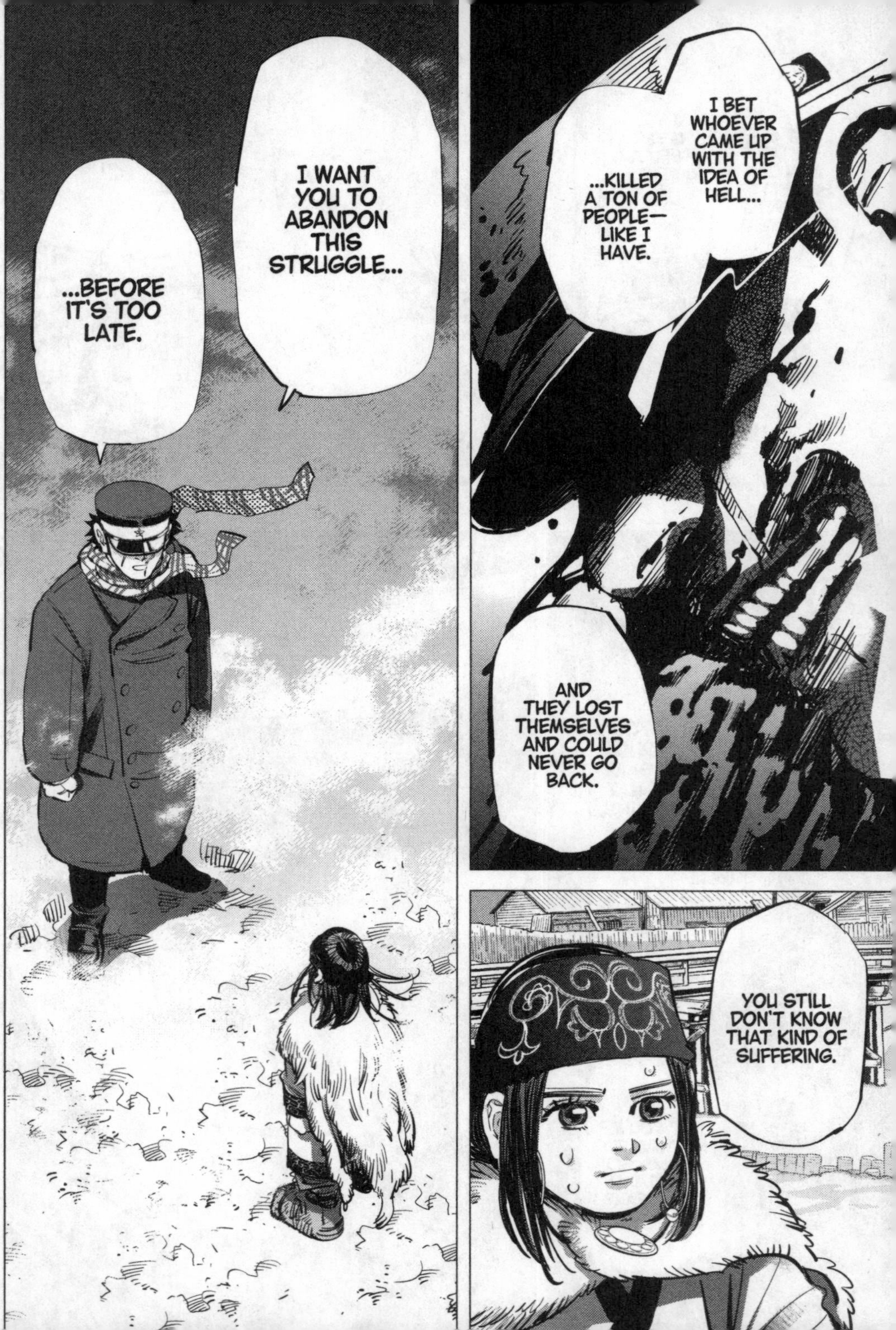
I BET WHOEVER CAME UP WITH THE IDEA OF HELL...
...KILLED A TON OF PEOPLE—LIKE I HAVE.
AND THEY LOST THEMSELVES AND COULD NEVER GO BACK.
YOU STILL DON'T KNOW THAT KIND OF SUFFERING.
I WANT YOU TO ABANDON THIS STRUGGLE...
...BEFORE IT'S TOO LATE.

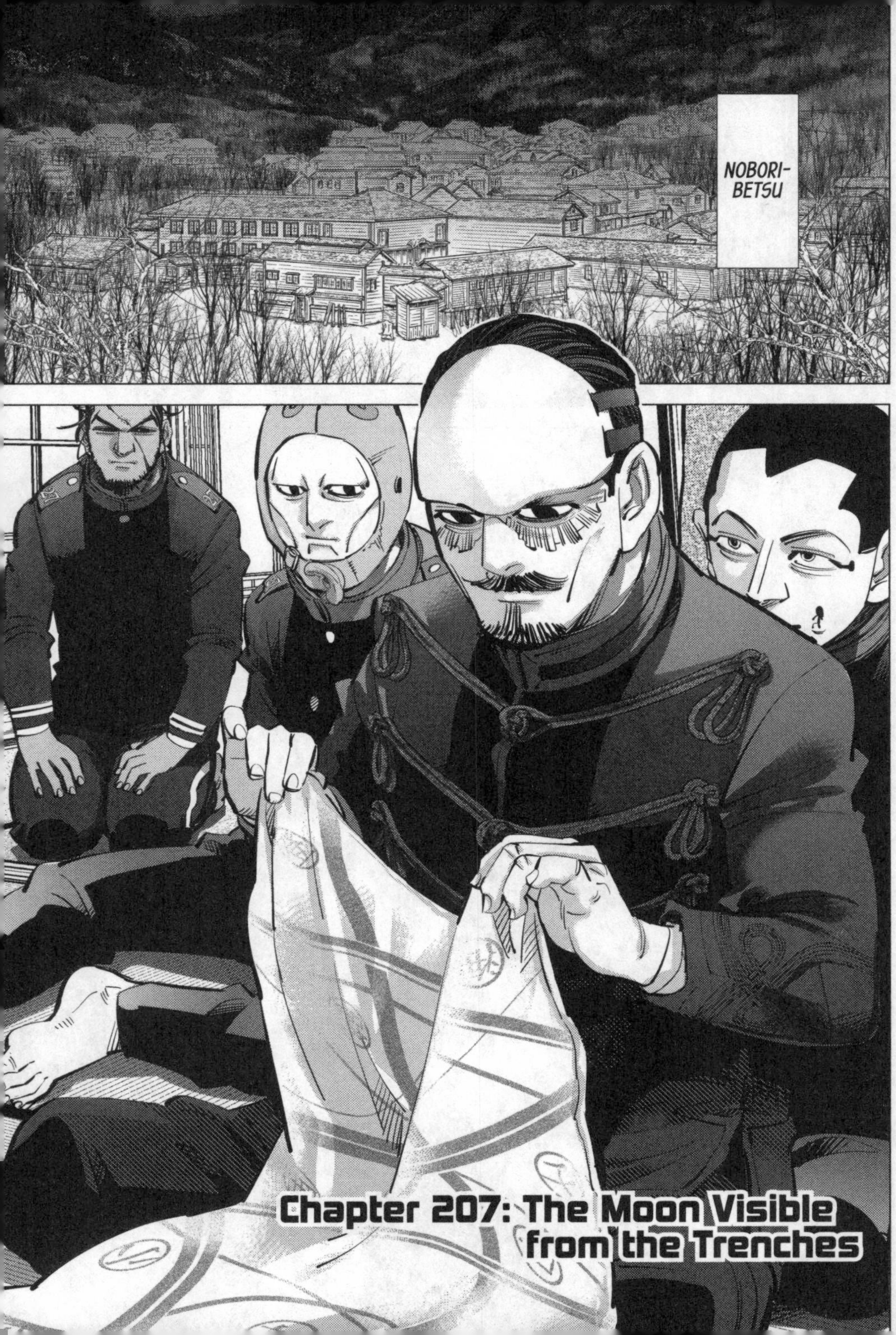
NOBORI-
BETSU
Chapter 207: The Moon Visible
from the Trenches

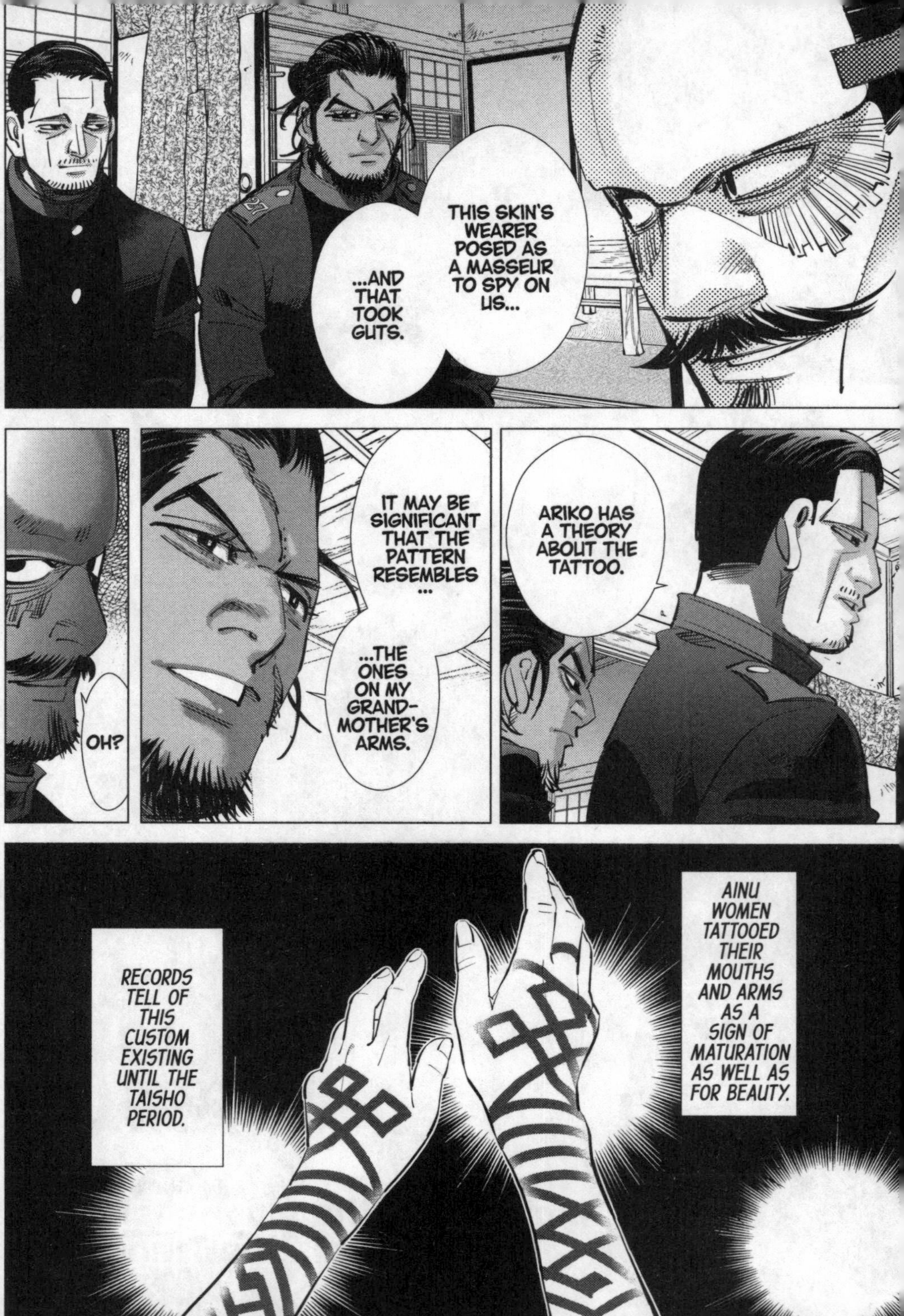
THIS SKIN'S WEARER POSED AS A MASSEUR TO SPY ON US...
...AND THAT TOOK GUTS.
ARIKO HAS A THEORY ABOUT THE TATTOO.
IT MAY BE SIGNIFICANT THAT THE PATTERN RESEMBLES...
...THE ONES ON MY GRAND-MOTHER'S ARMS.
OH?
AINU WOMEN TATTOOED THEIR MOUTHS AND ARMS AS A SIGN OF MATURATION AS WELL AS FOR BEAUTY.
RECORDS TELL OF THIS CUSTOM EXISTING UNTIL THE TAISHO PERIOD.

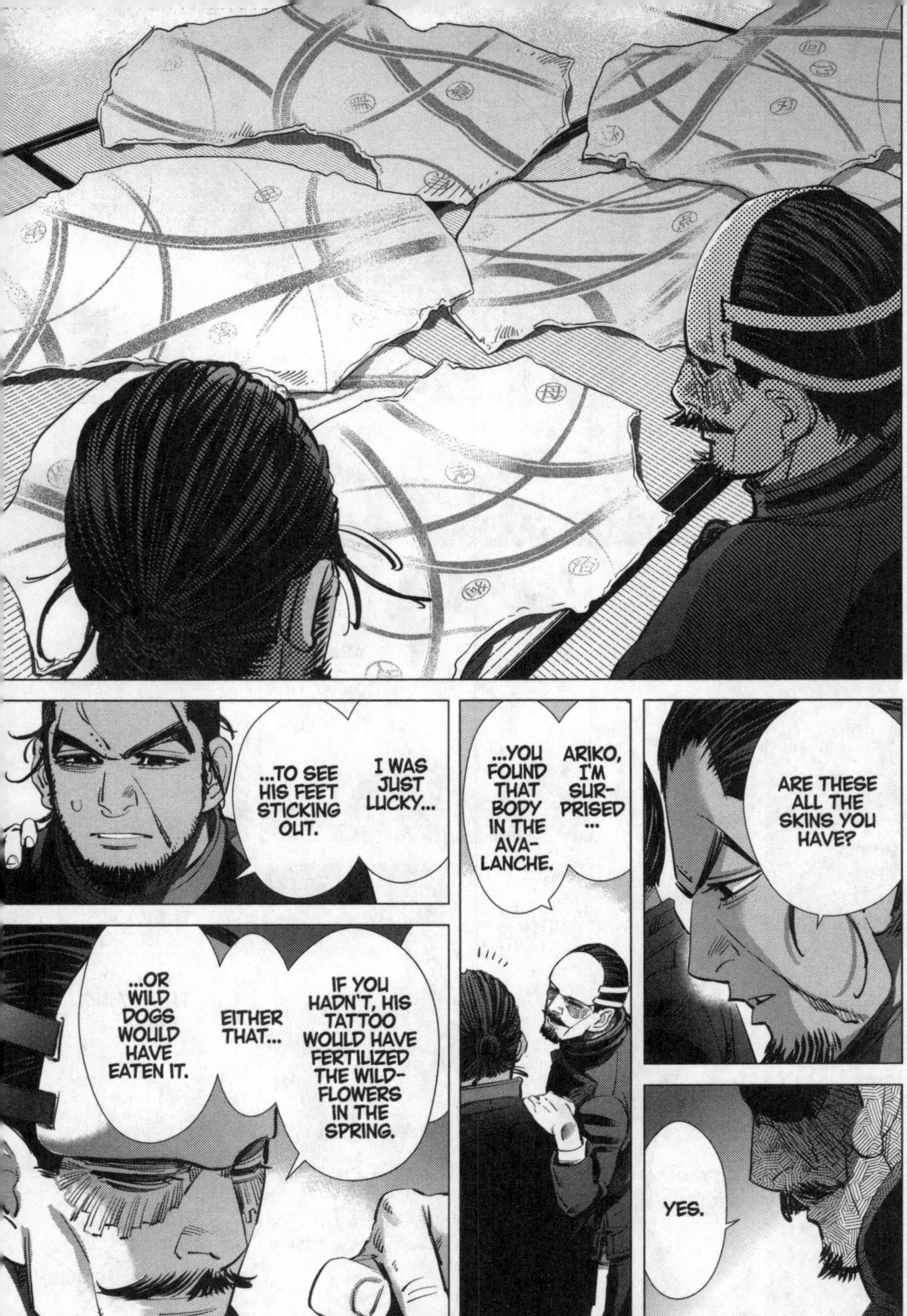
ARE THESE ALL THE SKINS YOU HAVE?
YES.
ARIKO, I'M SURPRISED...
...YOU FOUND THAT BODY IN THE AVALANCHE.
I WAS JUST LUCKY...
...TO SEE HIS FEET STICKING OUT.
IF YOU HADN'T, HIS TATTOO WOULD HAVE FERTILIZED THE WILDFLOWERS IN THE SPRING.
EITHER THAT...
...OR WILD DOGS WOULD HAVE EATEN IT.

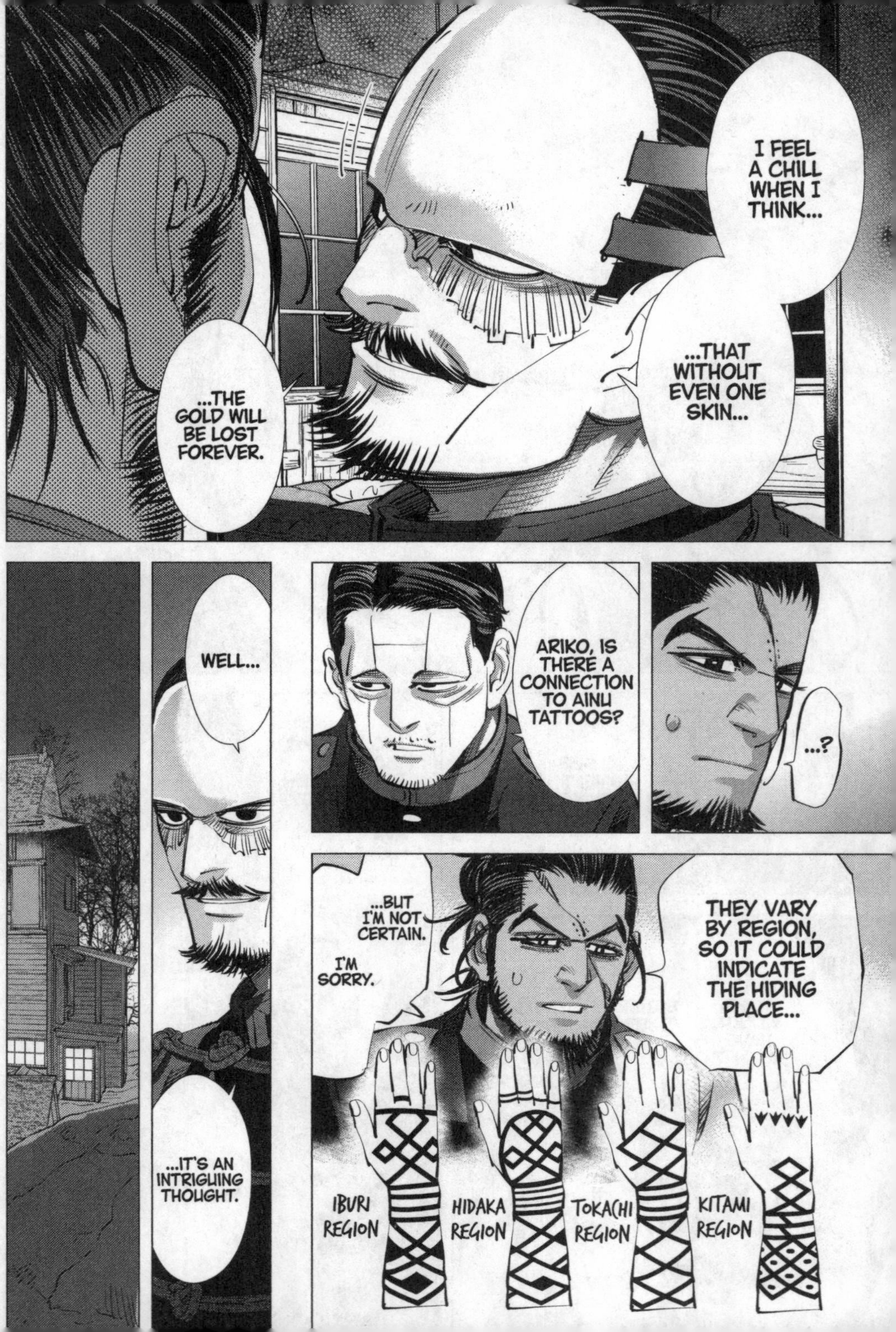
I FEEL A CHILL WHEN I THINK...
...THAT WITHOUT EVEN ONE SKIN...
...THE GOLD WILL BE LOST FOREVER.
...?
ARIKO, IS THERE A CONNECTION TO AINU TATTOOS?
THEY VARY BY REGION, SO IT COULD INDICATE THE HIDING PLACE...
...BUT I'M NOT CERTAIN.
I'M SORRY.
KITAMI REGION
TOKACHI REGION
HIDAKA REGION
IBURI REGION
WELL...
...IT'S AN INTRIGUING THOUGHT.

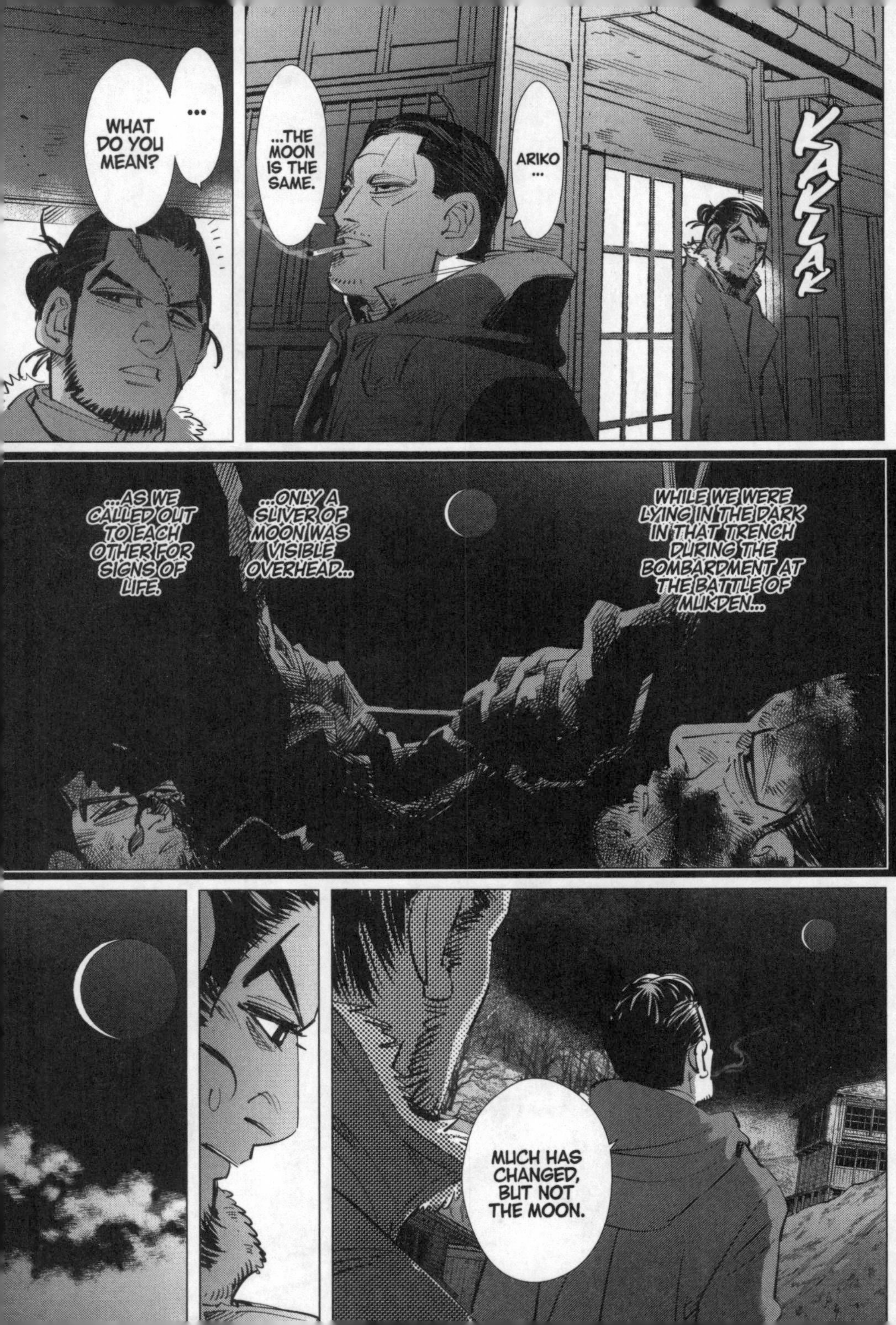
KAKLAK
ARIKO ...
...THE MOON IS THE SAME.
...
WHAT DO YOU MEAN?
WHILE WE WERE LYING IN THE DARK IN THAT TRENCH DURING THE BOMBARDMENT AT THE BATTLE OF MUKDEN...
...ONLY A SLIVER OF MOON WAS VISIBLE OVERHEAD...
...AS WE CALLED OUT TO EACH OTHER FOR SIGNS OF LIFE.
MUCH HAS CHANGED, BUT NOT THE MOON.

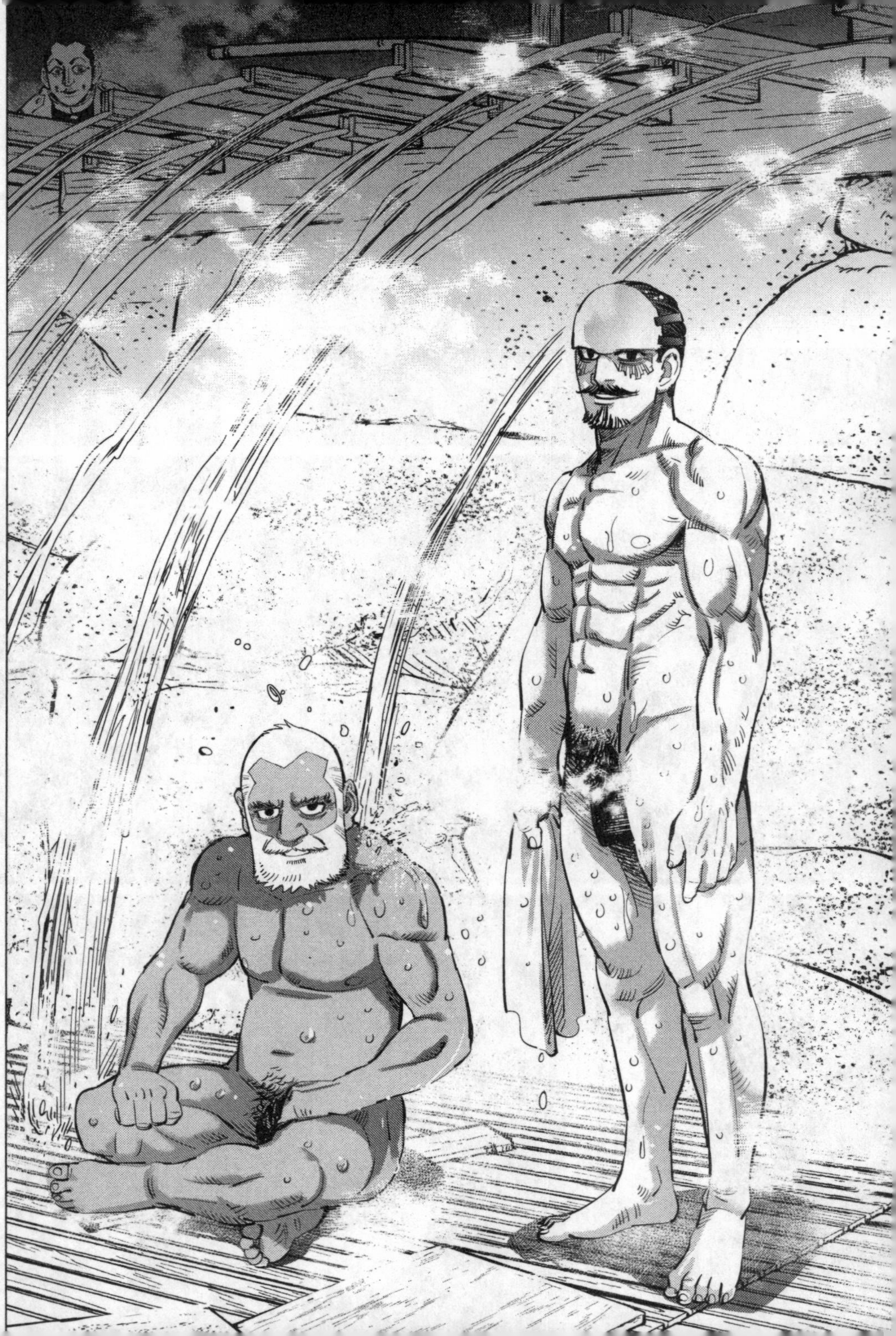

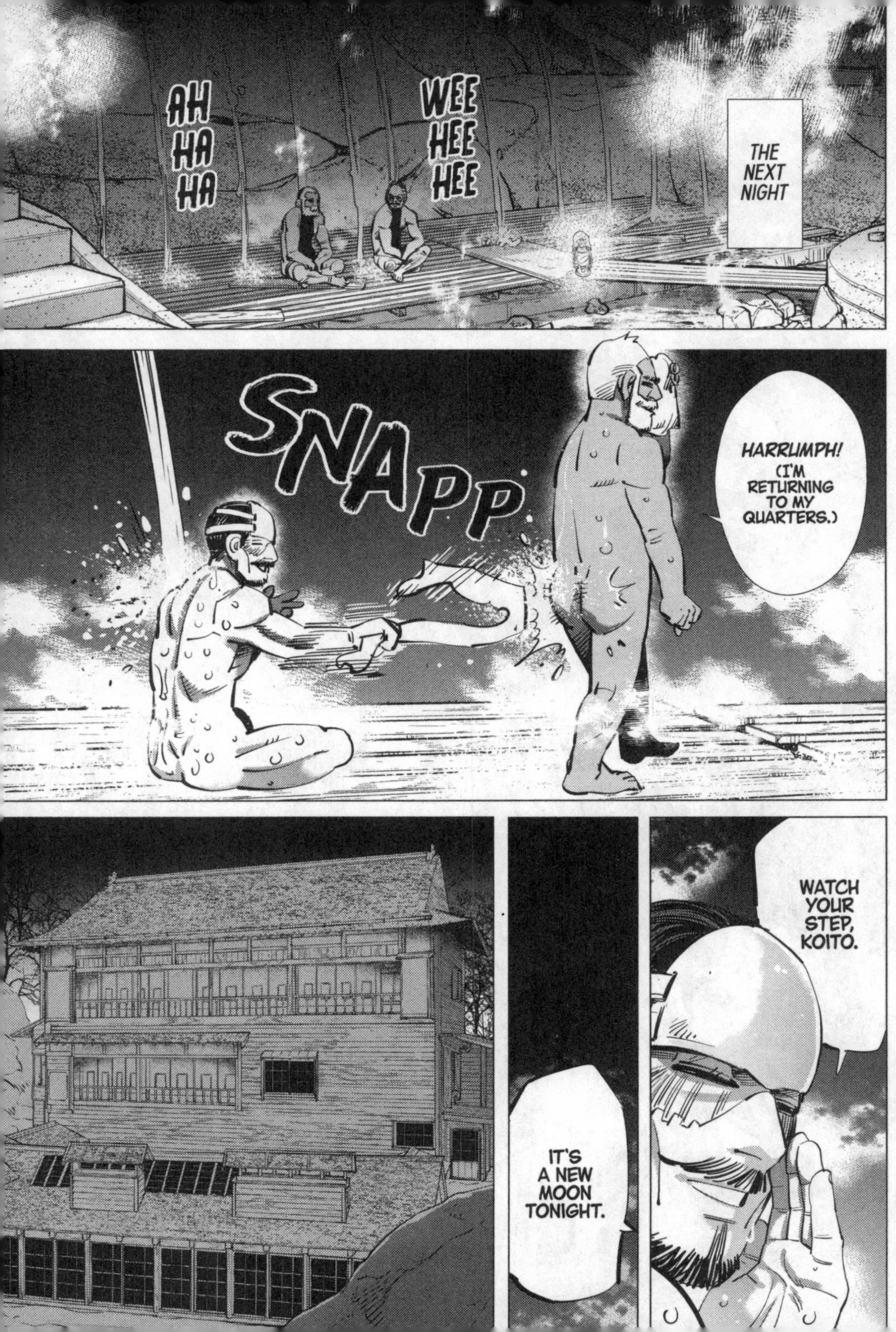
THE NEXT NIGHT
WEE HEE HEE
AH HA HA
HARRUMPH! (I'M RETURNING TO MY QUARTERS.)
SNAPP
WATCH YOUR STEP, KOITO.
IT'S A NEW MOON TONIGHT.

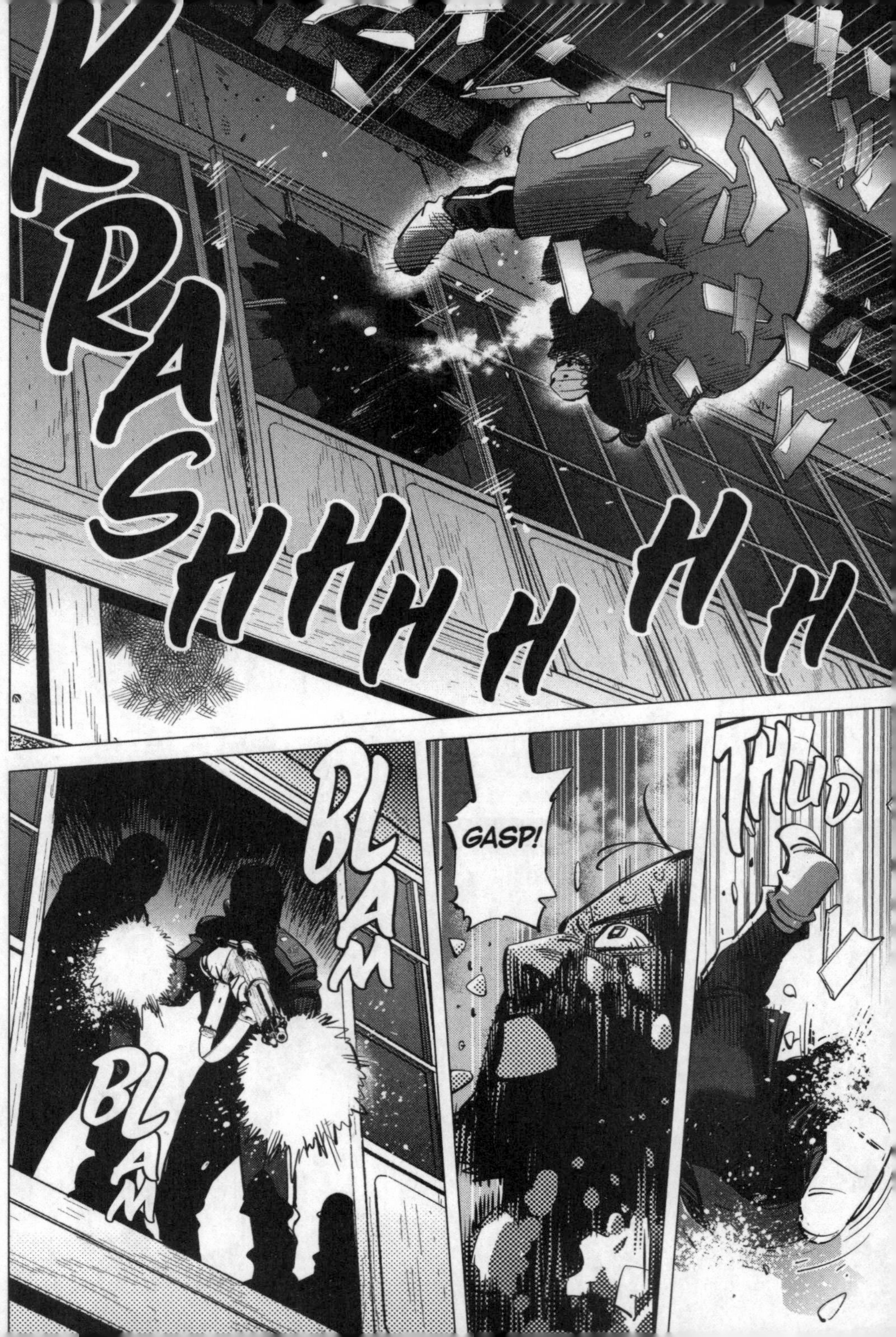
KRASHHHHHH
THUD
GASP!
BLAM
BLAM

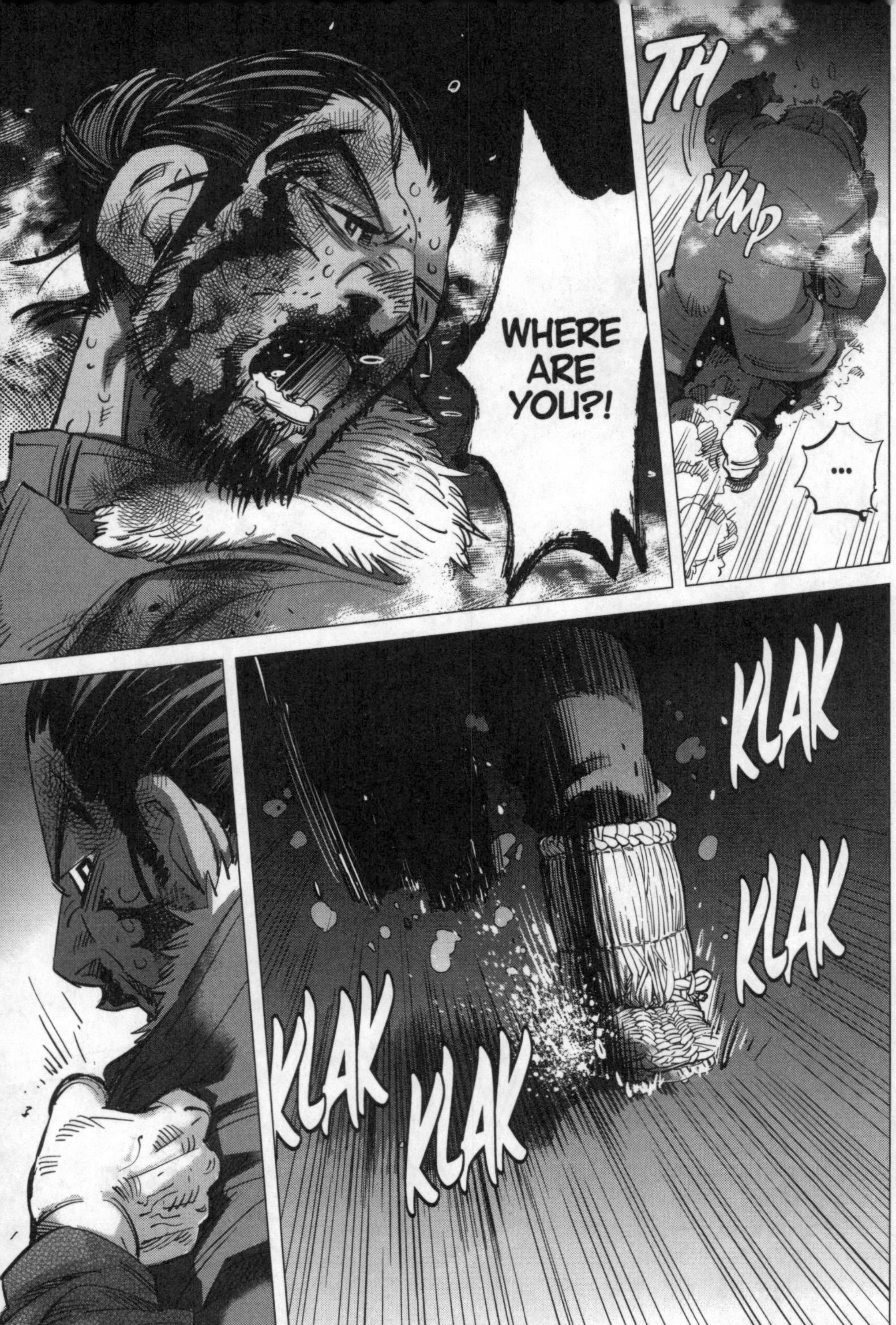
TH
WMP
...
WHERE ARE YOU?!
KLAK
KLAK
KLAK
KLAK

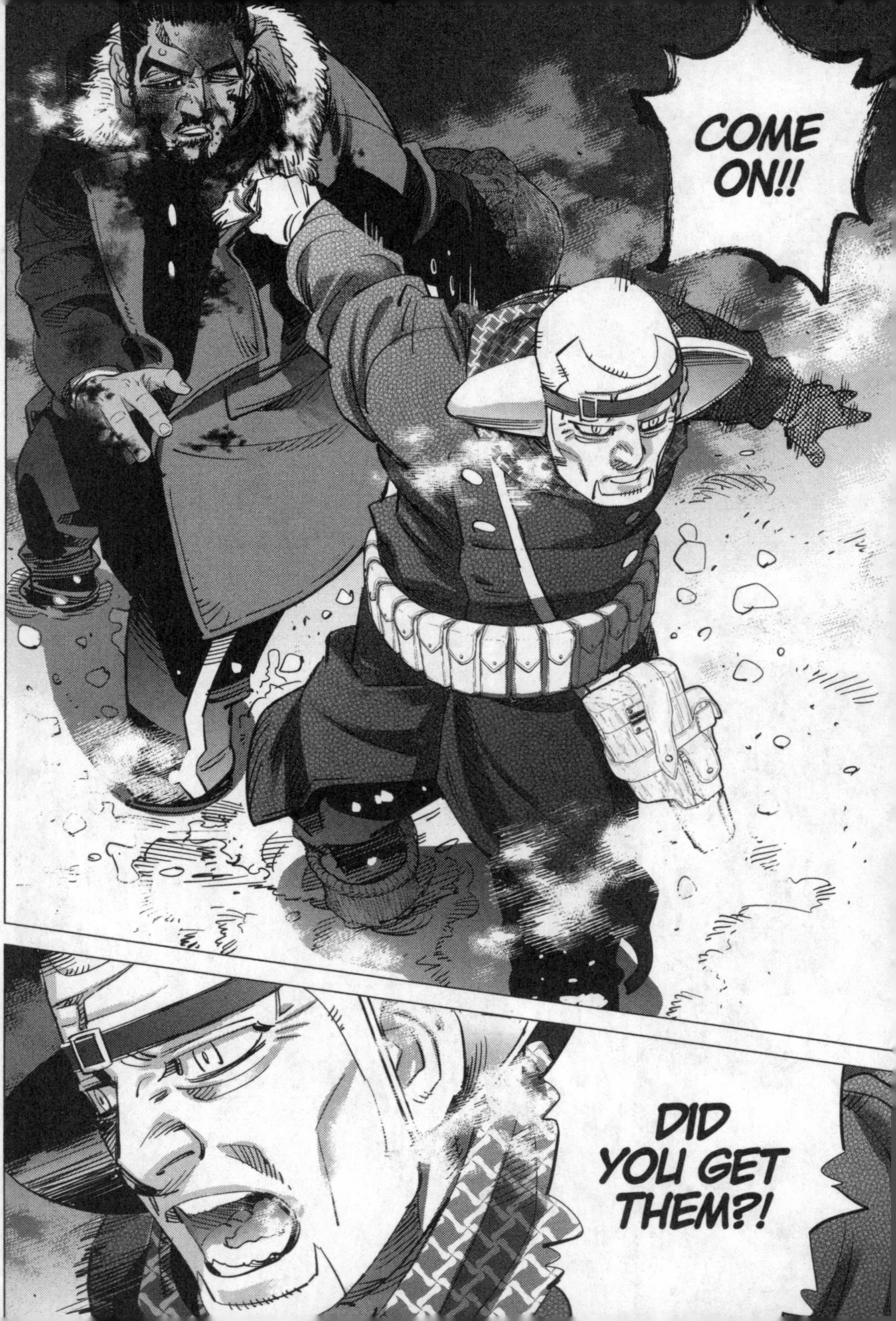
COME ON!!
DID YOU GET THEM?!

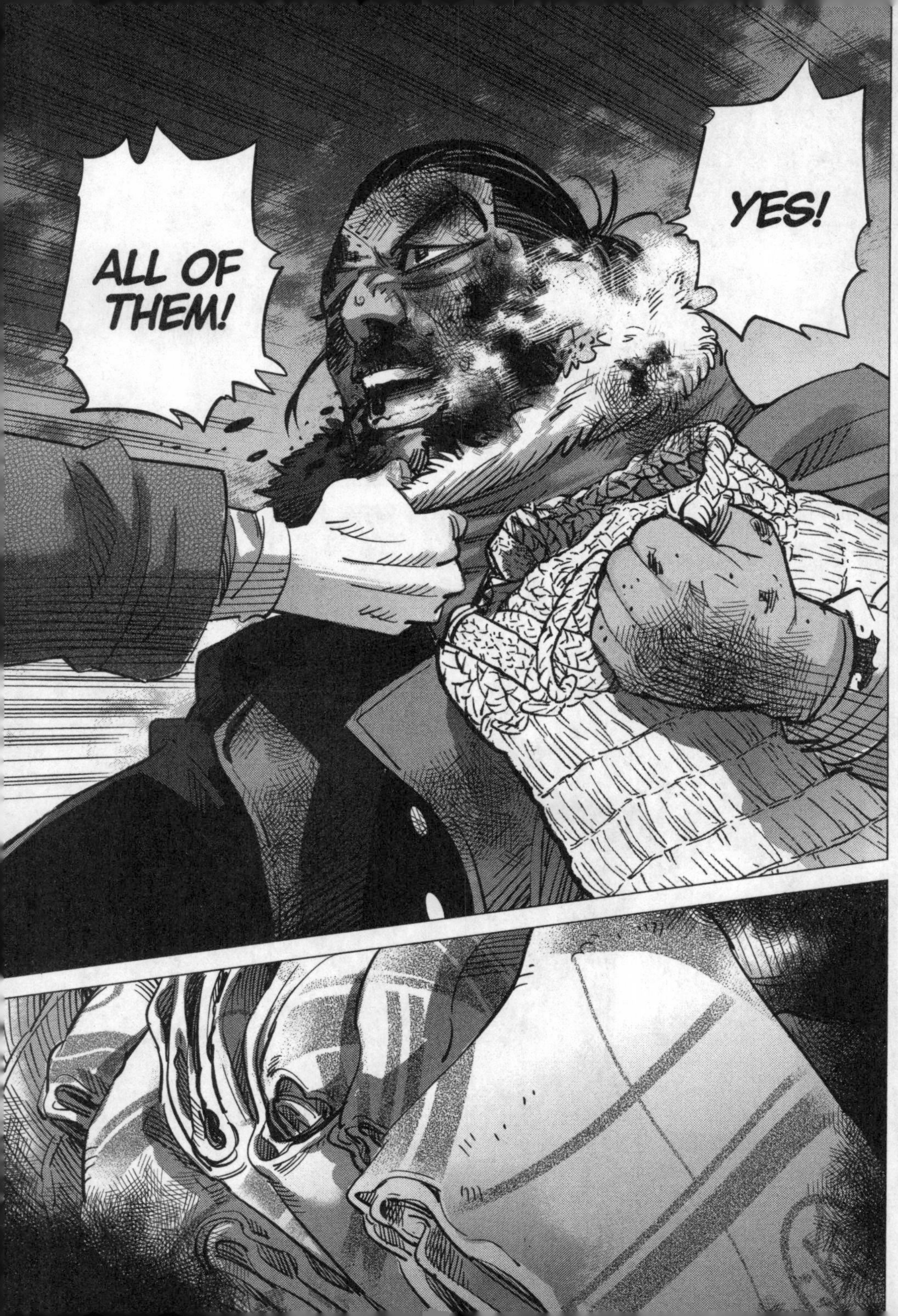
YES!
ALL OF THEM!

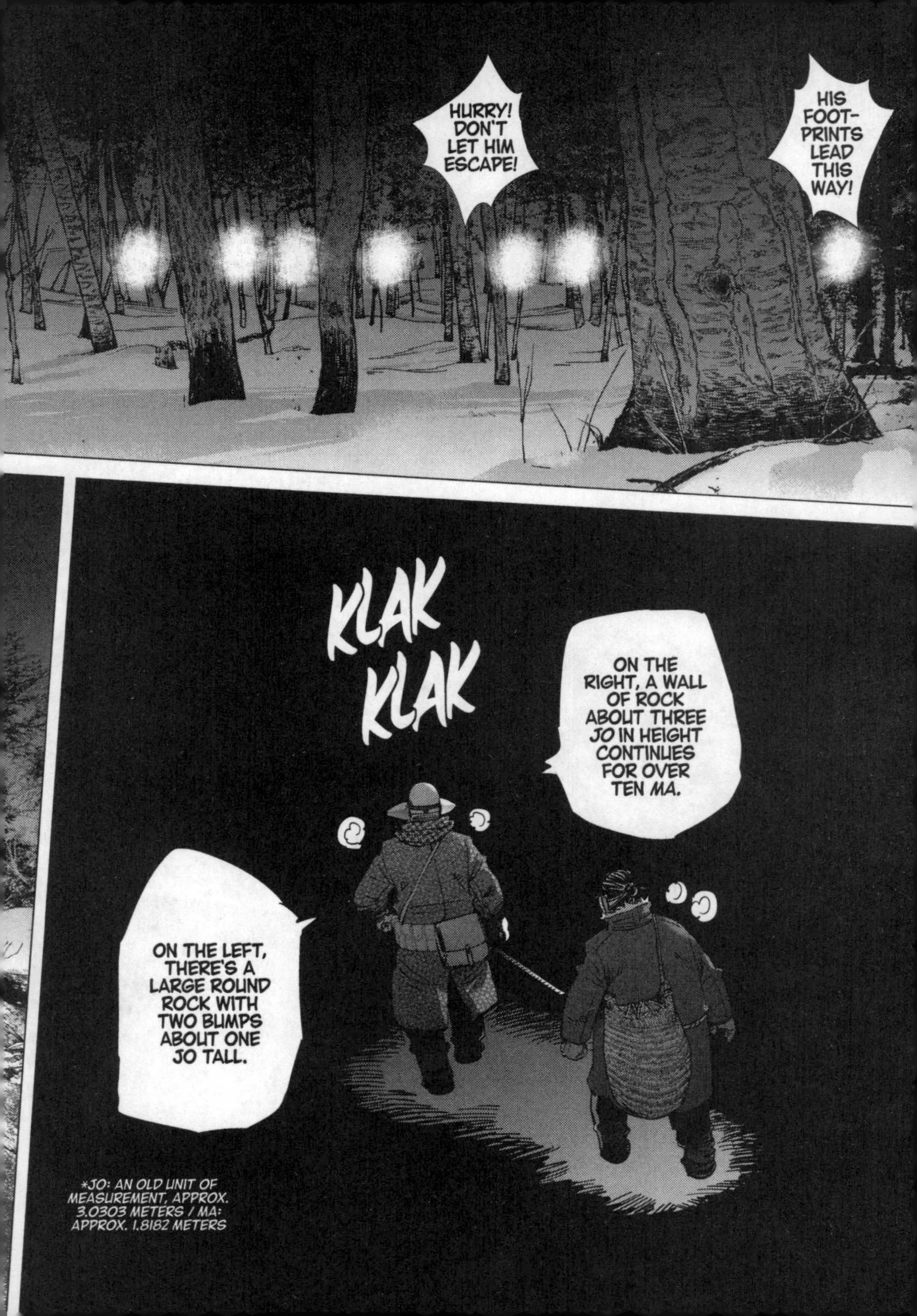
HIS FOOT-PRINTS LEAD THIS WAY!
HURRY! DON'T LET HIM ESCAPE!
KLAK KLAK
ON THE RIGHT, A WALL OF ROCK ABOUT THREE JO IN HEIGHT CONTINUES FOR OVER TEN MA.
ON THE LEFT, THERE'S A LARGE ROUND ROCK WITH TWO BUMPS ABOUT ONE JO TALL.
*JO: AN OLD UNIT OF MEASUREMENT, APPROX. 3.0303 METERS / MA: APPROX. 1.8182 METERS

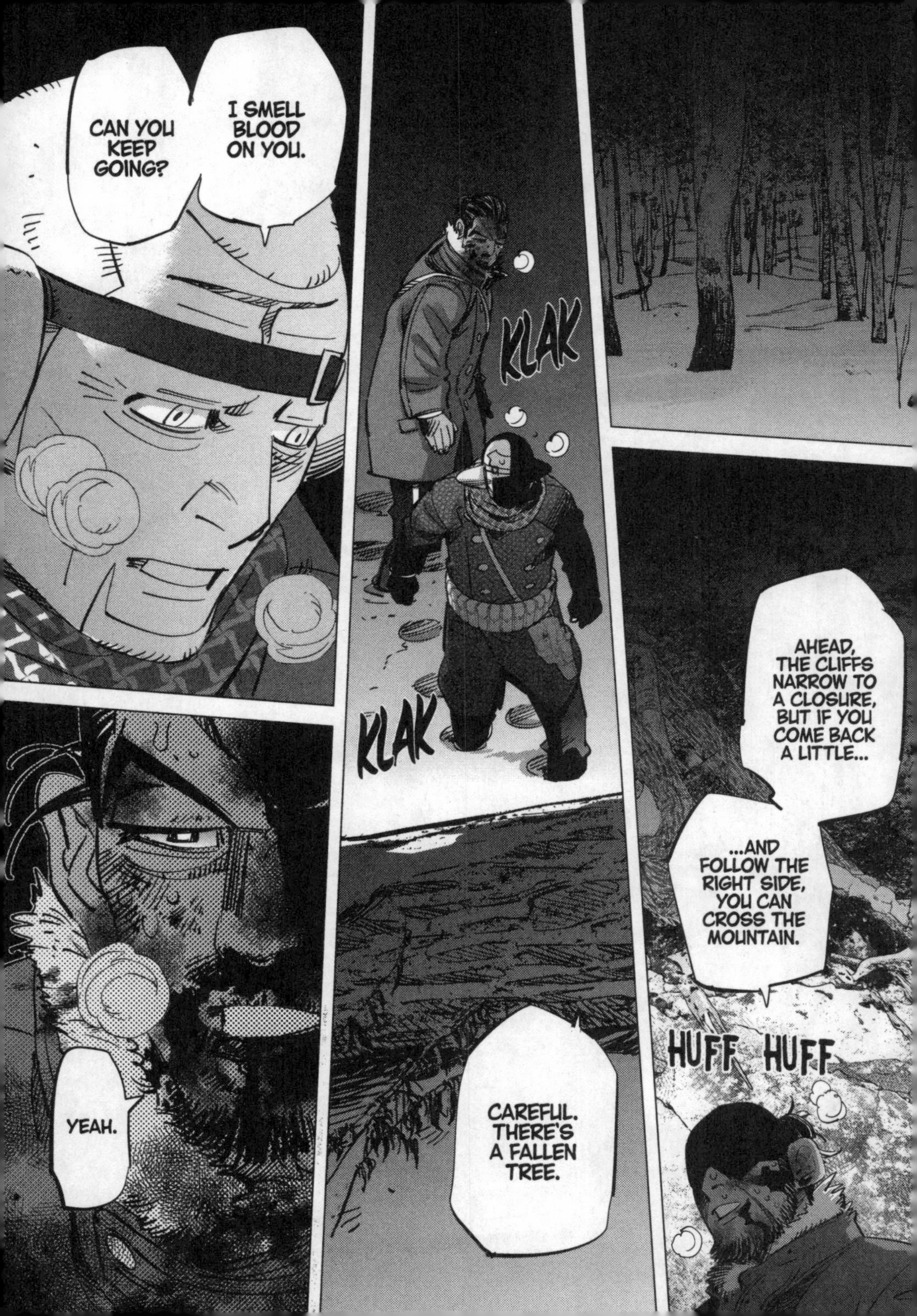
KLAK
KLAK
I SMELL BLOOD ON YOU.
CAN YOU KEEP GOING?
AHEAD, THE CLIFFS NARROW TO A CLOSURE, BUT IF YOU COME BACK A LITTLE...
...AND FOLLOW THE RIGHT SIDE, YOU CAN CROSS THE MOUNTAIN.
HUFF HUFF
CAREFUL. THERE'S A FALLEN TREE.
YEAH.

HOURS EARLIER

HAR-
RUMPH!

SNAPP

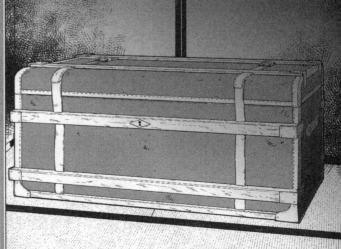

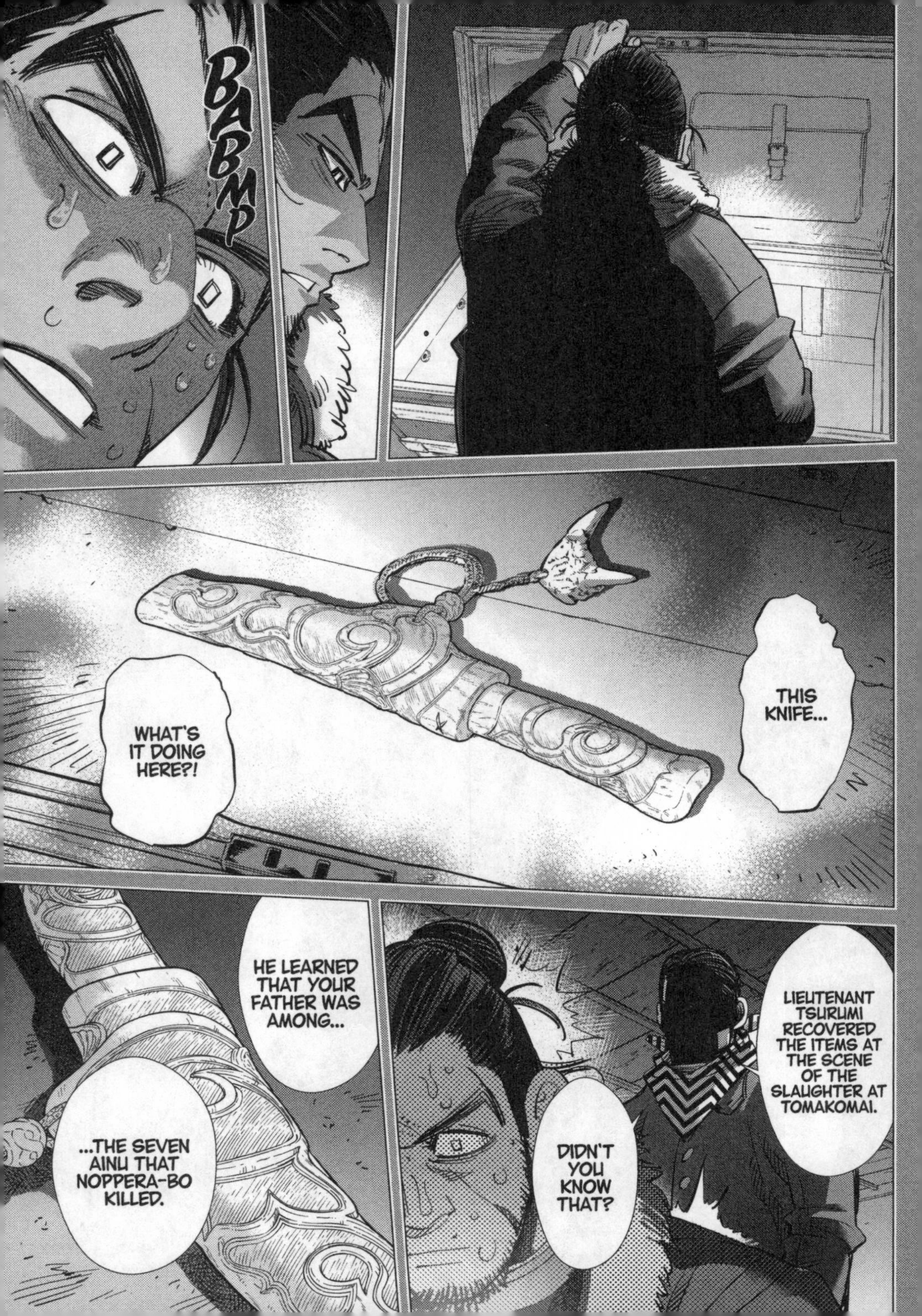
BABMP
THIS KNIFE...
WHAT'S IT DOING HERE?!
LIEUTENANT TSURUMI RECOVERED THE ITEMS AT THE SCENE OF THE SLAUGHTER AT TOMAKOMAI.
DIDN'T YOU KNOW THAT?
HE LEARNED THAT YOUR FATHER WAS AMONG...
...THE SEVEN AINU THAT NOPPERA-BO KILLED.

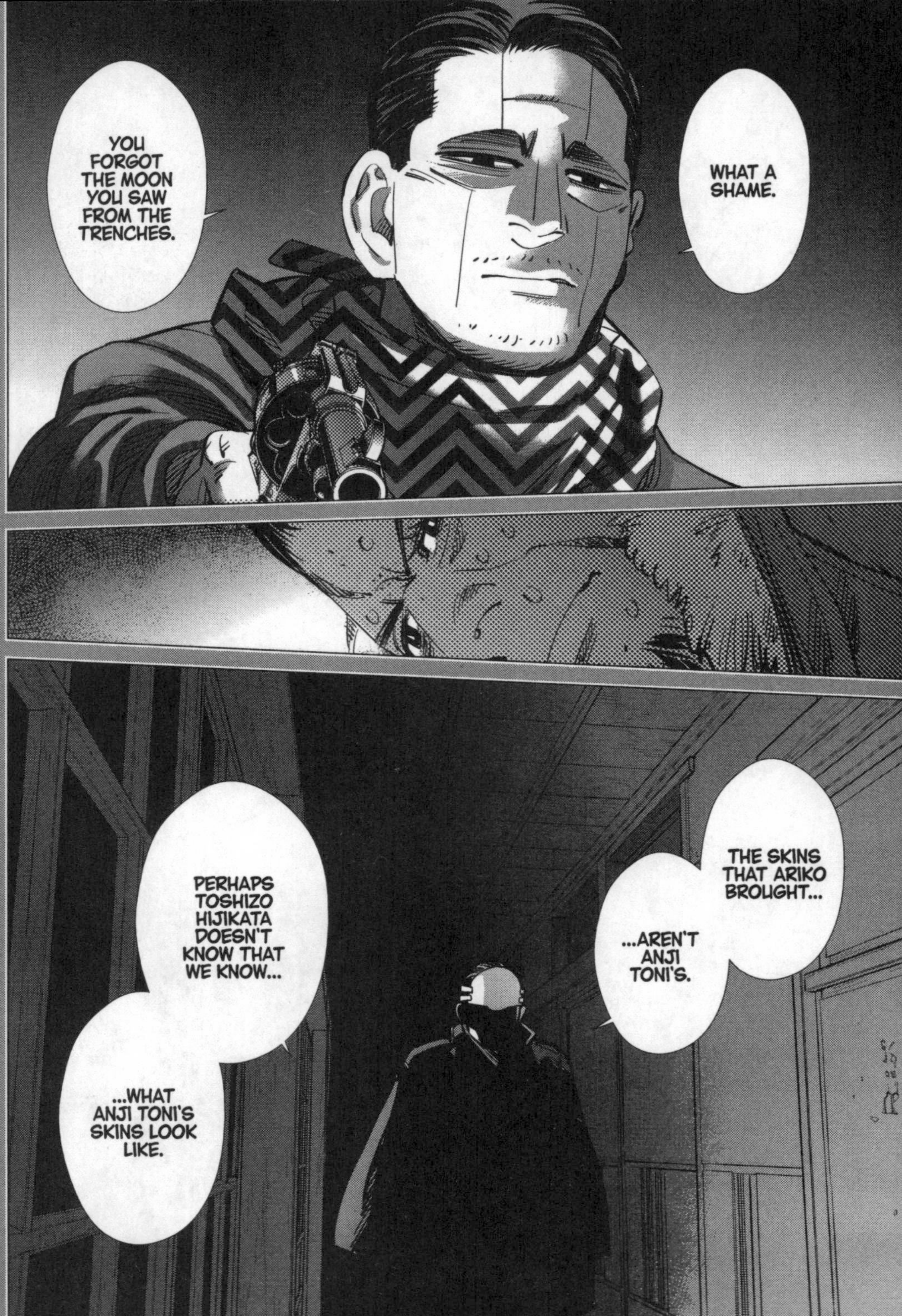
WHAT A SHAME.
YOU FORGOT THE MOON YOU SAW FROM THE TRENCHES.
THE SKINS THAT ARIKO BROUGHT...
...AREN'T ANJI TONI'S.
PERHAPS TOSHIZO HIJIKATA DOESN'T KNOW THAT WE KNOW...
...WHAT ANJI TONI'S SKINS LOOK LIKE.

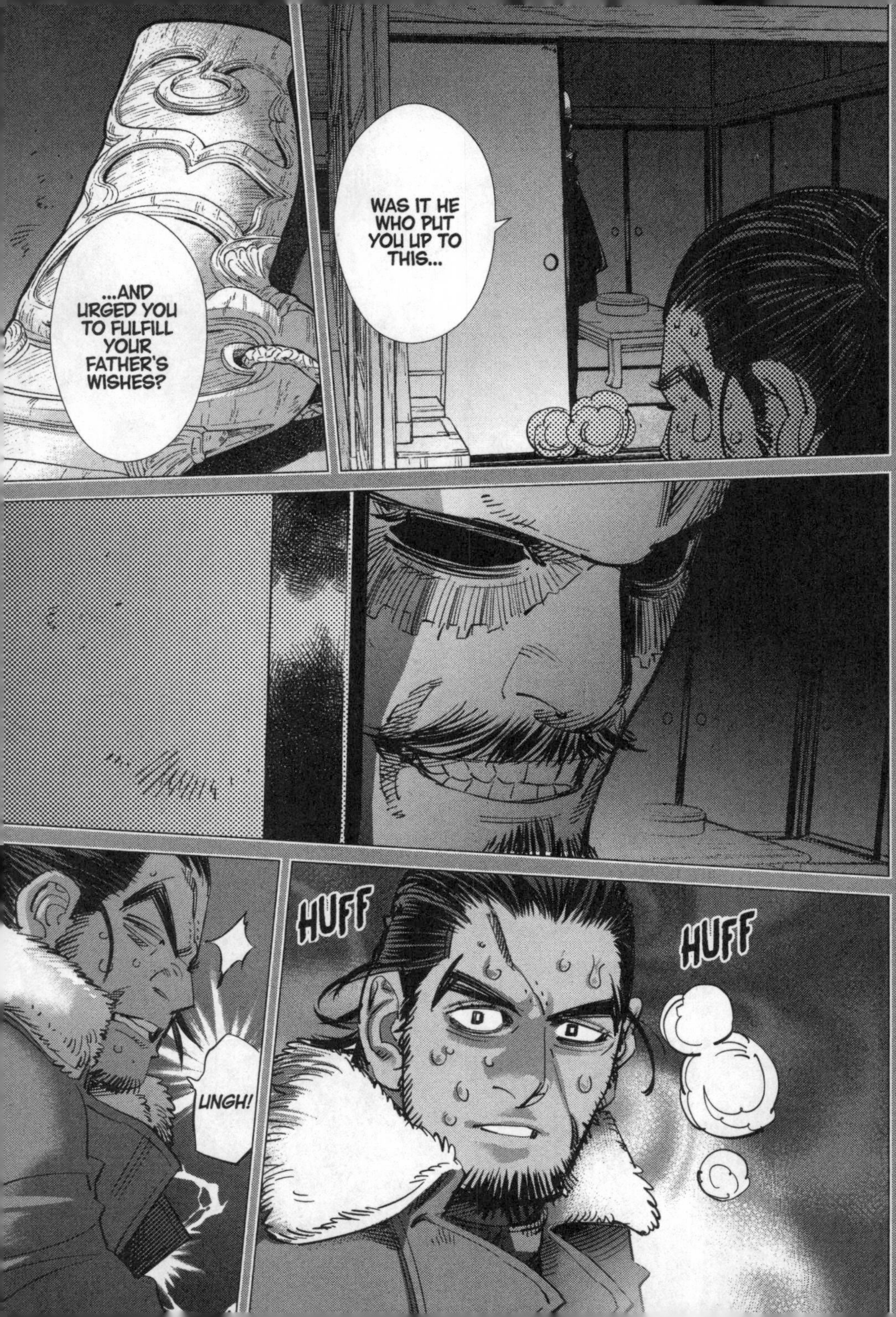
WAS IT HE WHO PUT YOU UP TO THIS...
...AND URGED YOU TO FULFILL YOUR FATHER'S WISHES?
HUFF
HUFF
UNGH!

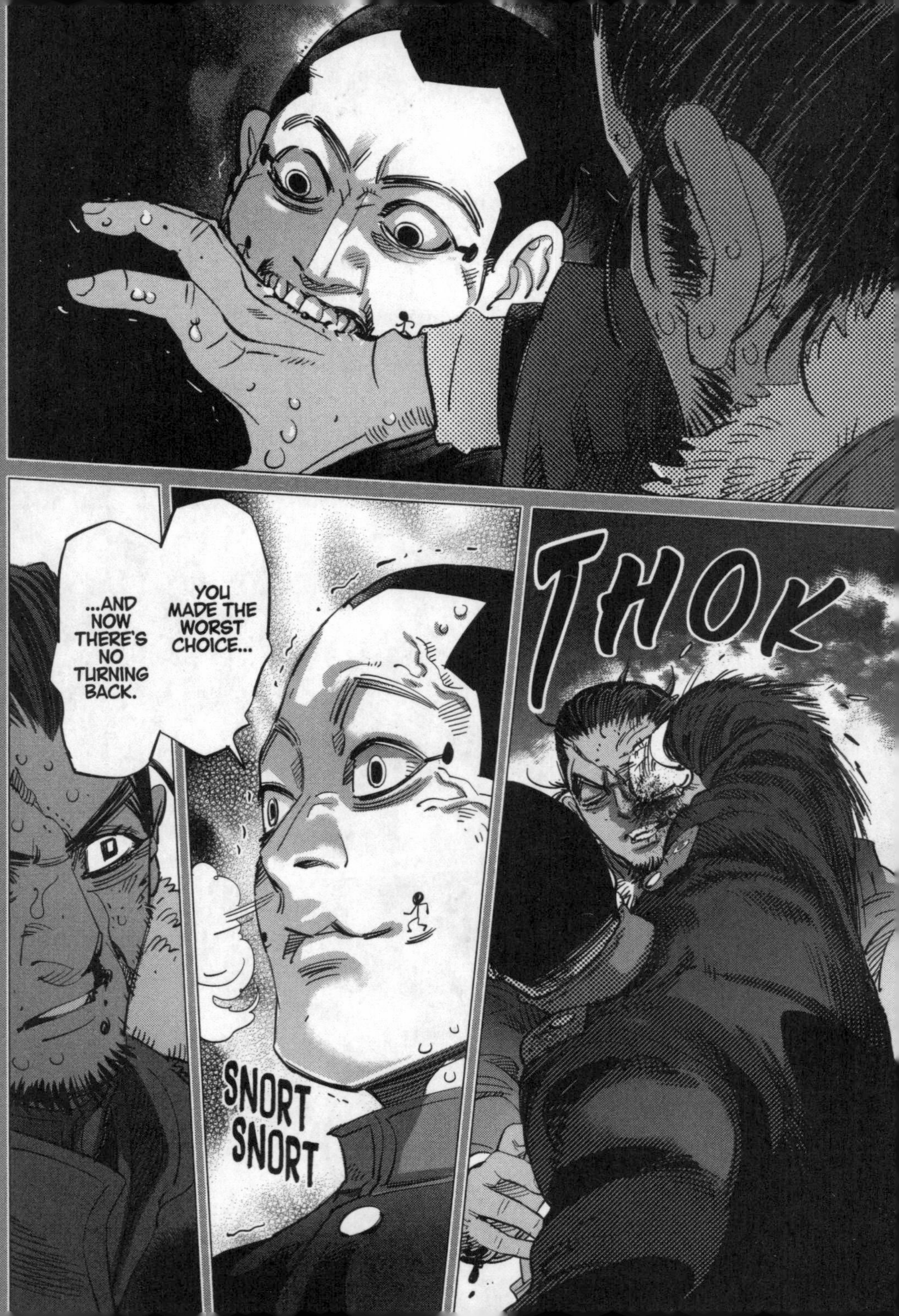
THOK
YOU MADE THE WORST CHOICE...
...AND NOW THERE'S NO TURNING BACK.
SNORT SNORT

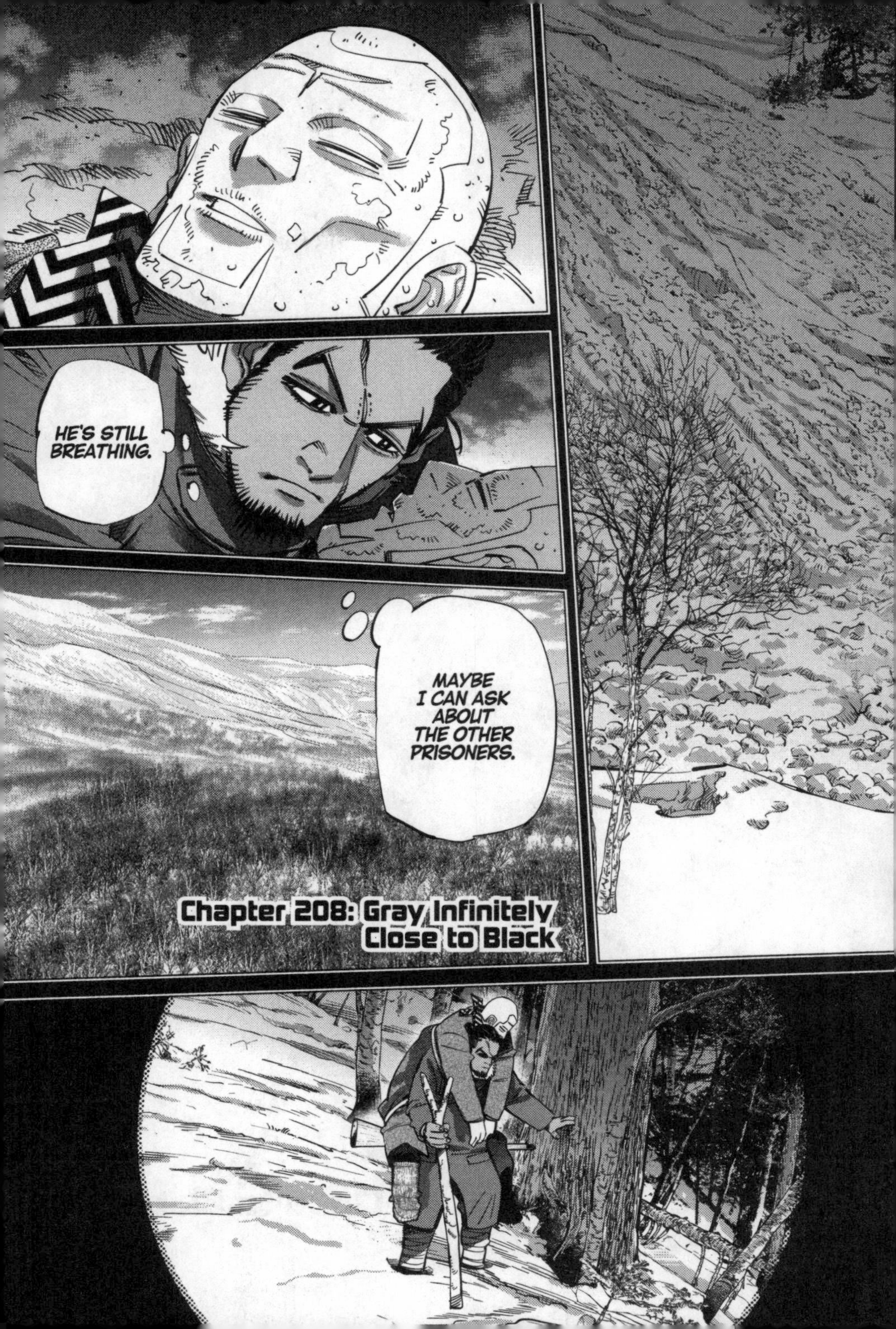
HE'S STILL BREATHING.
MAYBE I CAN ASK ABOUT THE OTHER PRISONERS.
Chapter 208: Gray Infinitely Close to Black

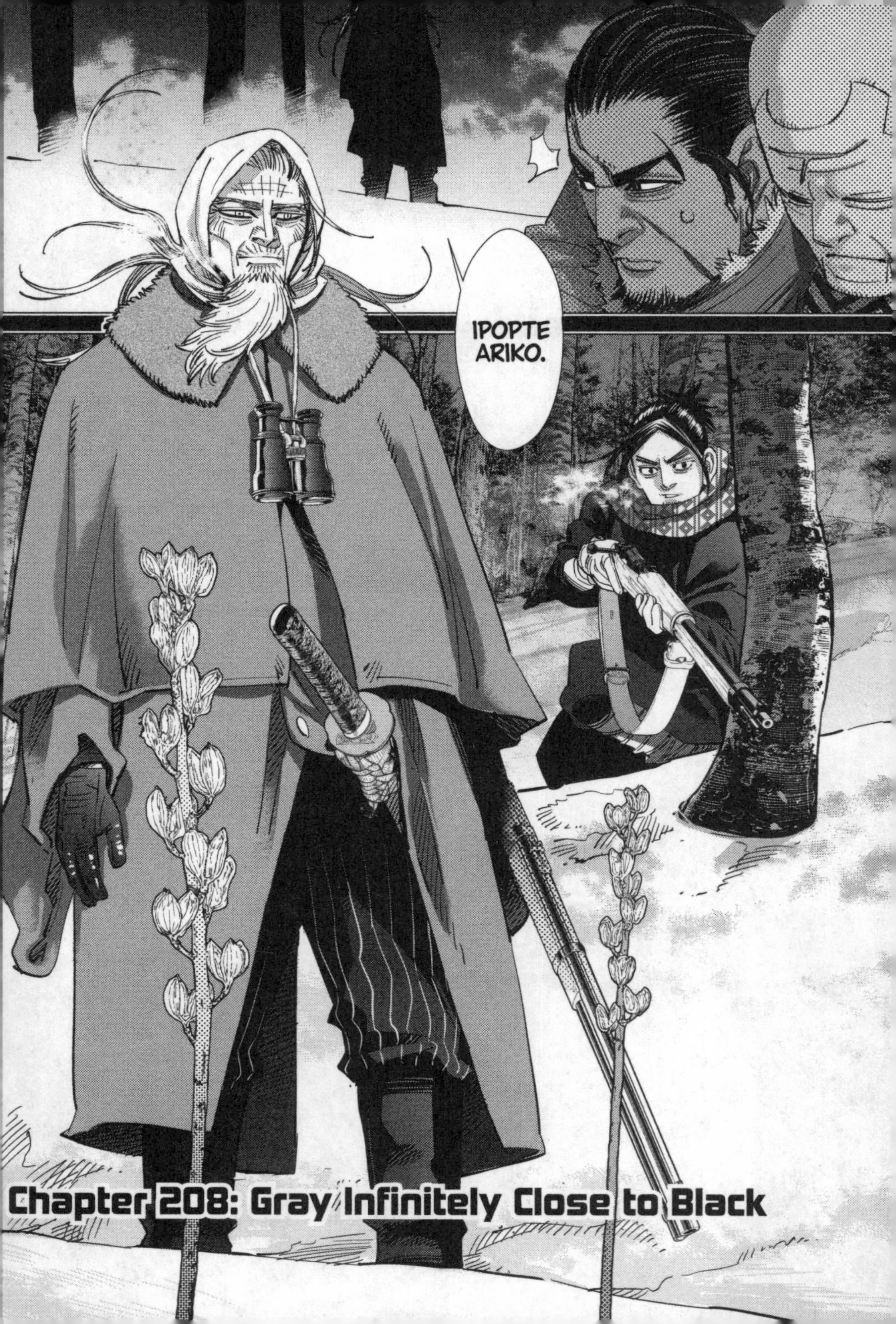
IPOPTE ARIKO.
Chapter 208: Gray Infinitely Close to Black

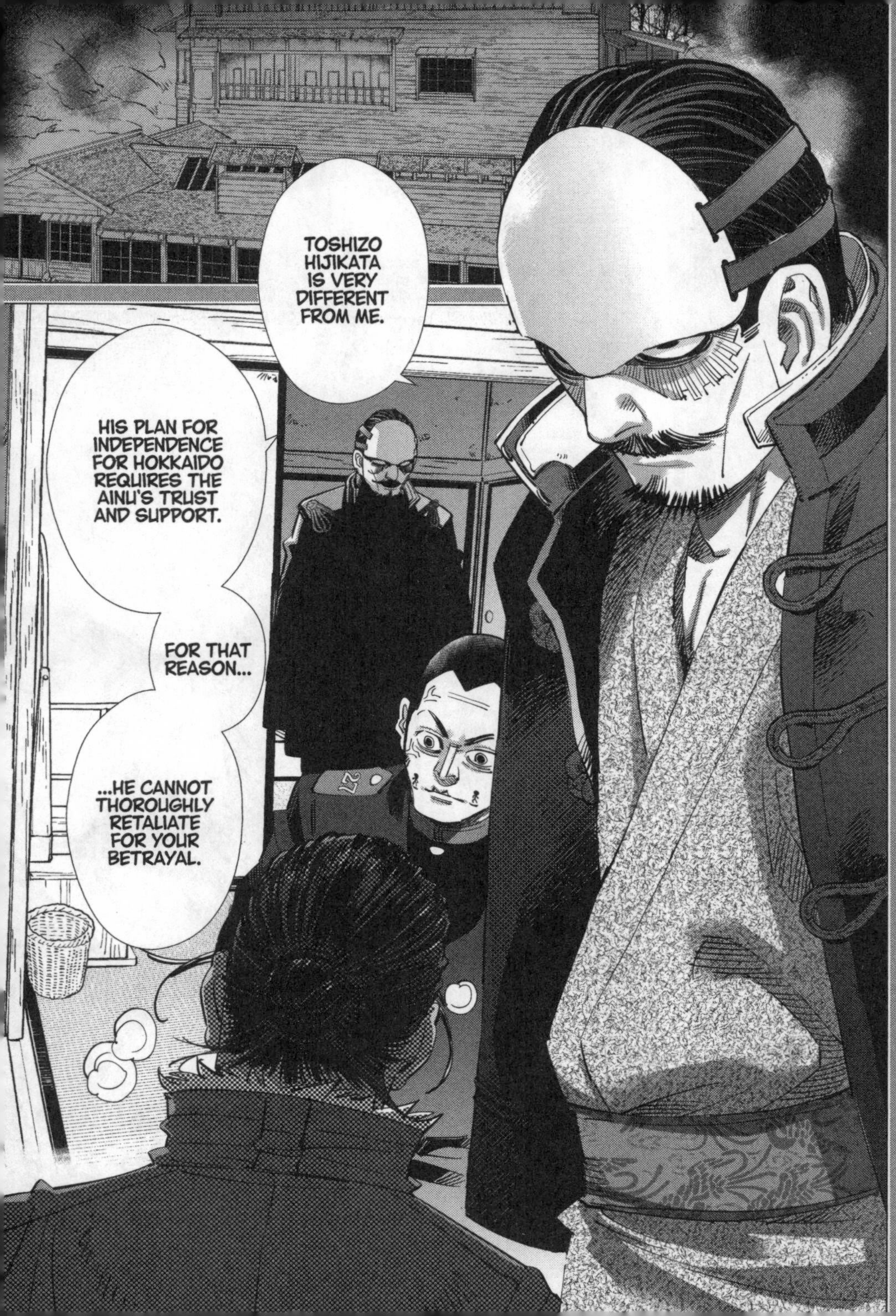
TOSHIZO HIJIKATA IS VERY DIFFERENT FROM ME.
HIS PLAN FOR INDEPENDENCE FOR HOKKAIDO REQUIRES THE AINU'S TRUST AND SUPPORT.
FOR THAT REASON...
...HE CANNOT THOROUGHLY RETALIATE FOR YOUR BETRAYAL.

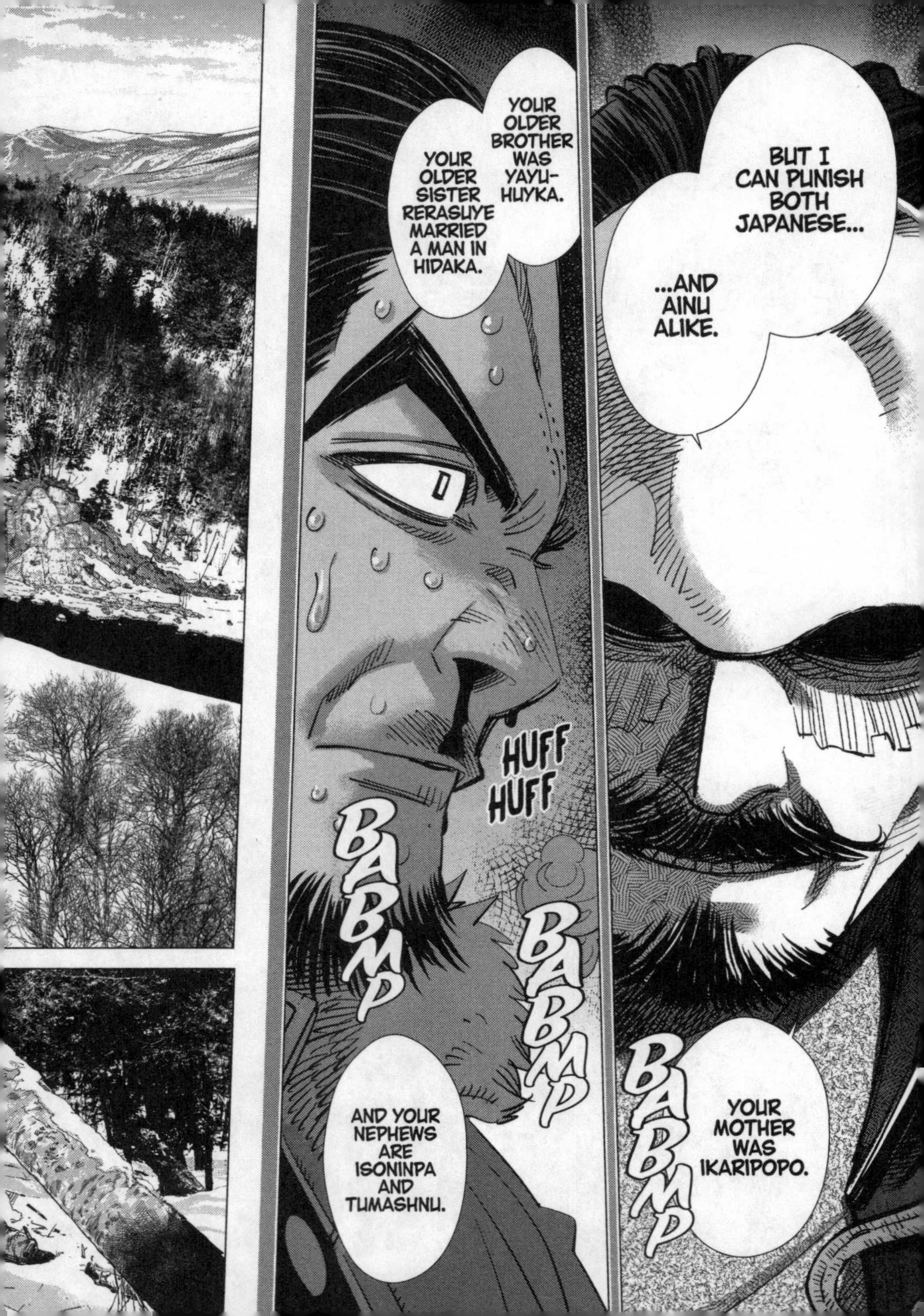
BUT I CAN PUNISH BOTH JAPANESE...
...AND AINU ALIKE.
BABMP
YOUR MOTHER WAS IKARIPOPO.
YOUR OLDER BROTHER WAS YAYU-HUYKA.
YOUR OLDER SISTER RERASUYE MARRIED A MAN IN HIDAKA.
HUFF HUFF
BABMP
BABMP
AND YOUR NEPHEWS ARE ISONINPA AND TUMASHNU.

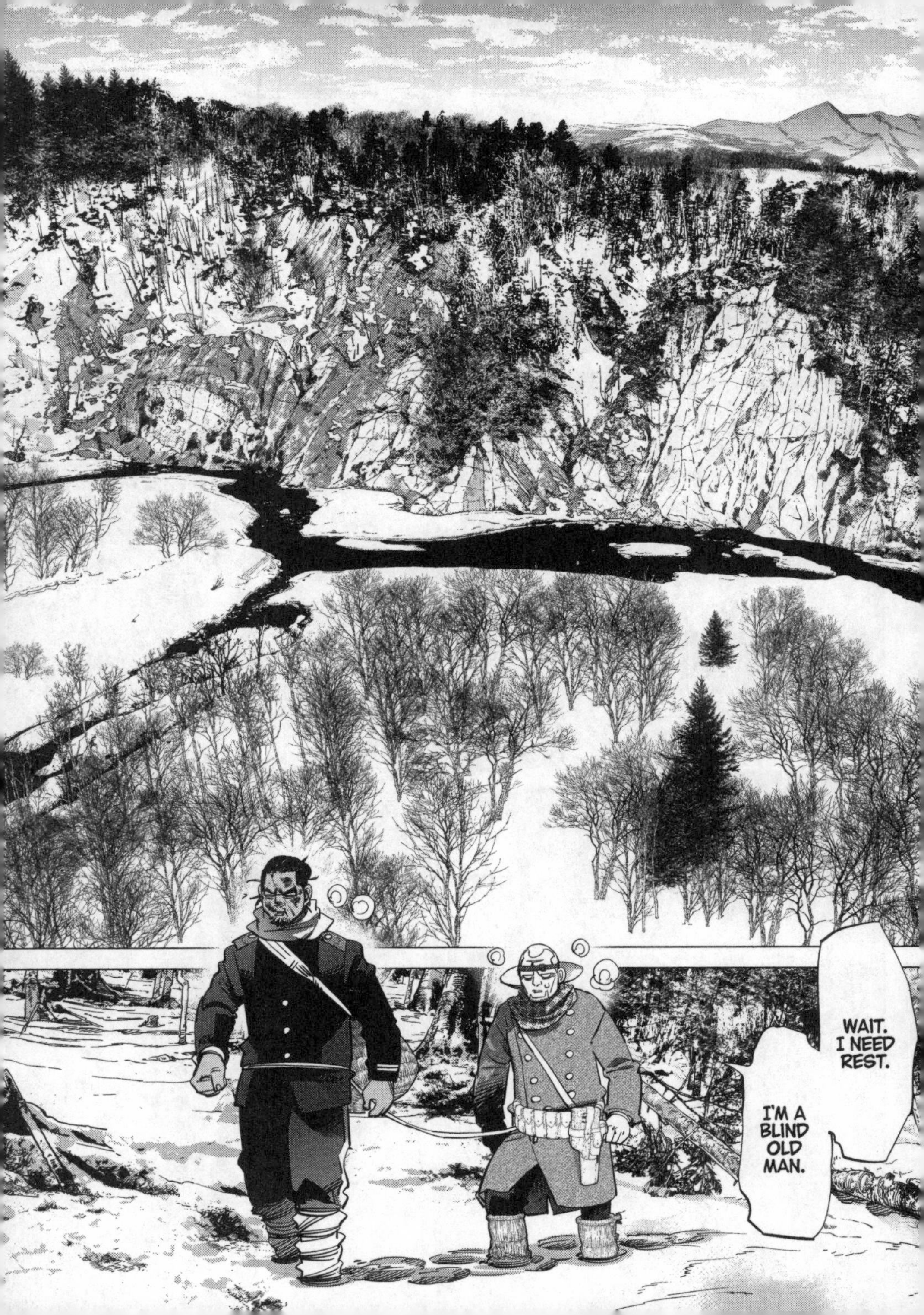
WAIT. I NEED REST.
I'M A BLIND OLD MAN.

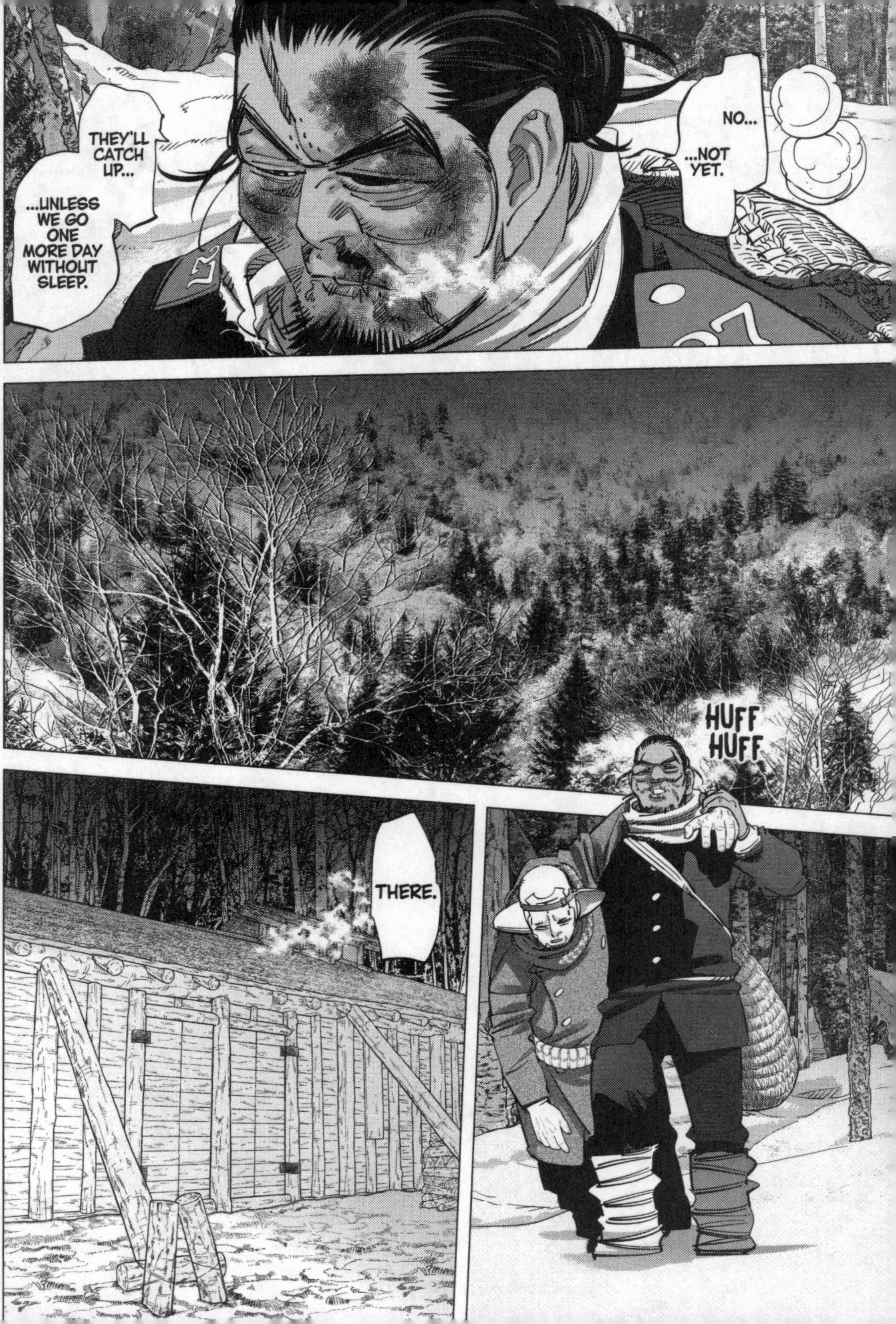
NO...
...NOT YET.
THEY'LL CATCH UP...
...UNLESS WE GO ONE MORE DAY WITHOUT SLEEP.
HUFF HUFF
THERE.

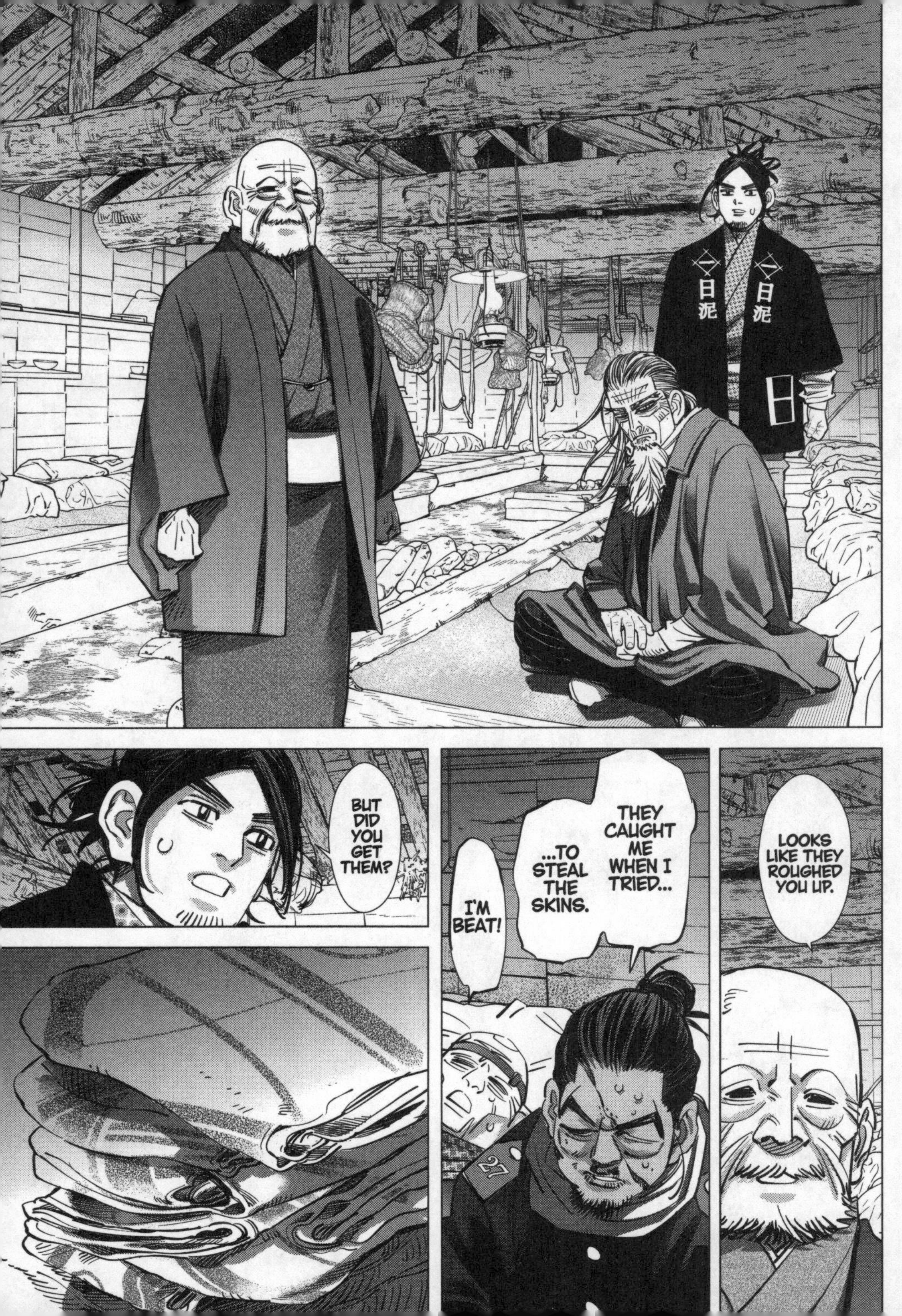
一日泥
一日泥
LOOKS LIKE THEY ROUGHED YOU UP.
THEY CAUGHT ME WHEN I TRIED...
...TO STEAL THE SKINS.
I'M BEAT!
BUT DID YOU GET THEM?

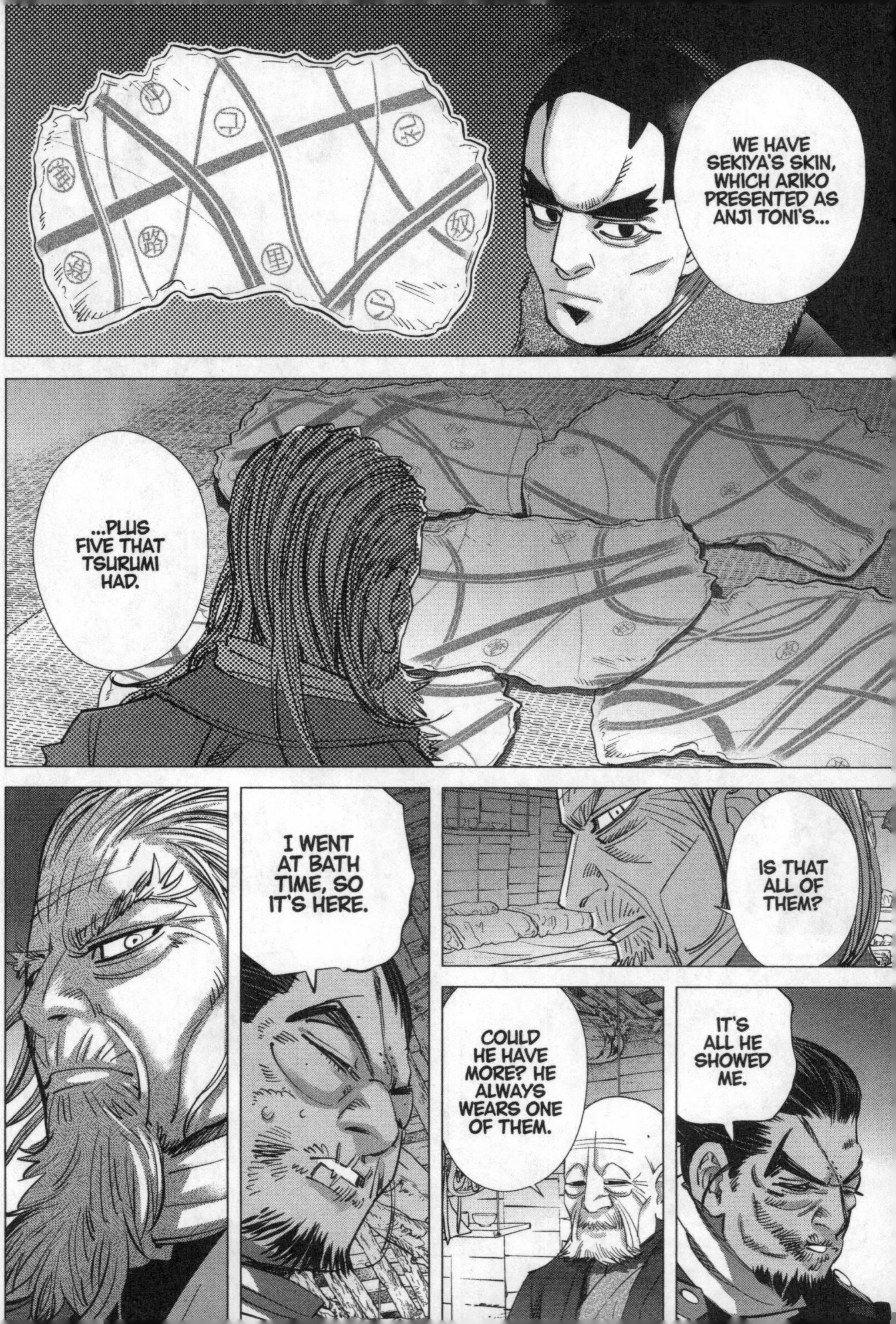
WE HAVE SEKIYA'S SKIN, WHICH ARIKO PRESENTED AS ANJI TONI'S...
...PLUS FIVE THAT TSURUMI HAD.
IS THAT ALL OF THEM?
IT'S ALL HE SHOWED ME.
COULD HE HAVE MORE? HE ALWAYS WEARS ONE OF THEM.
I WENT AT BATH TIME, SO IT'S HERE.

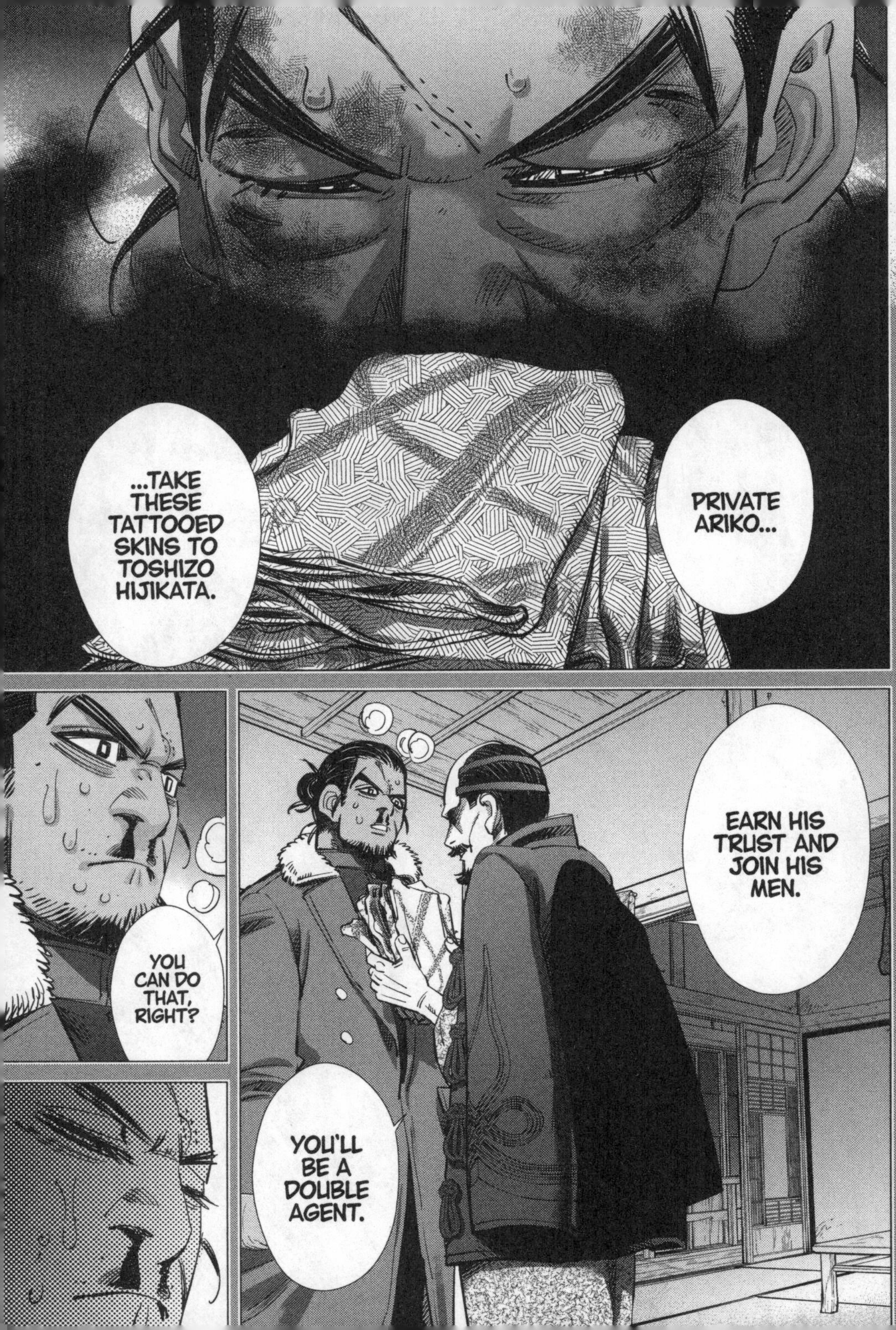
PRIVATE ARIKO...
...TAKE THESE TATTOOED SKINS TO TOSHIZO HIJIKATA.
EARN HIS TRUST AND JOIN HIS MEN.
YOU'LL BE A DOUBLE AGENT.
YOU CAN DO THAT, RIGHT?

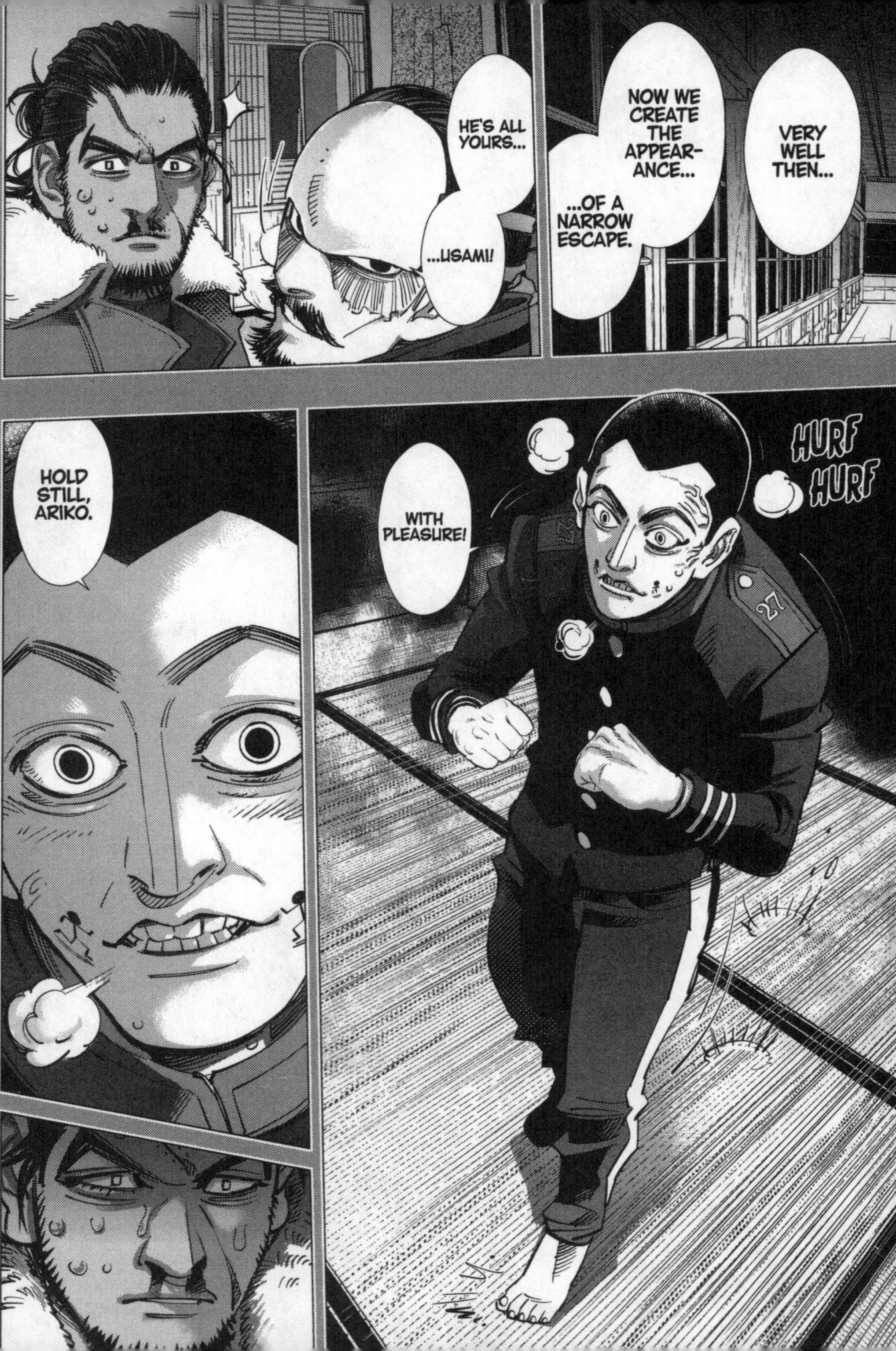
VERY WELL THEN...
NOW WE CREATE THE APPEAR-ANCE...
...OF A NARROW ESCAPE.
HE'S ALL YOURS...
...USAMI!
HURF HURF
WITH PLEASURE!
HOLD STILL, ARIKO.

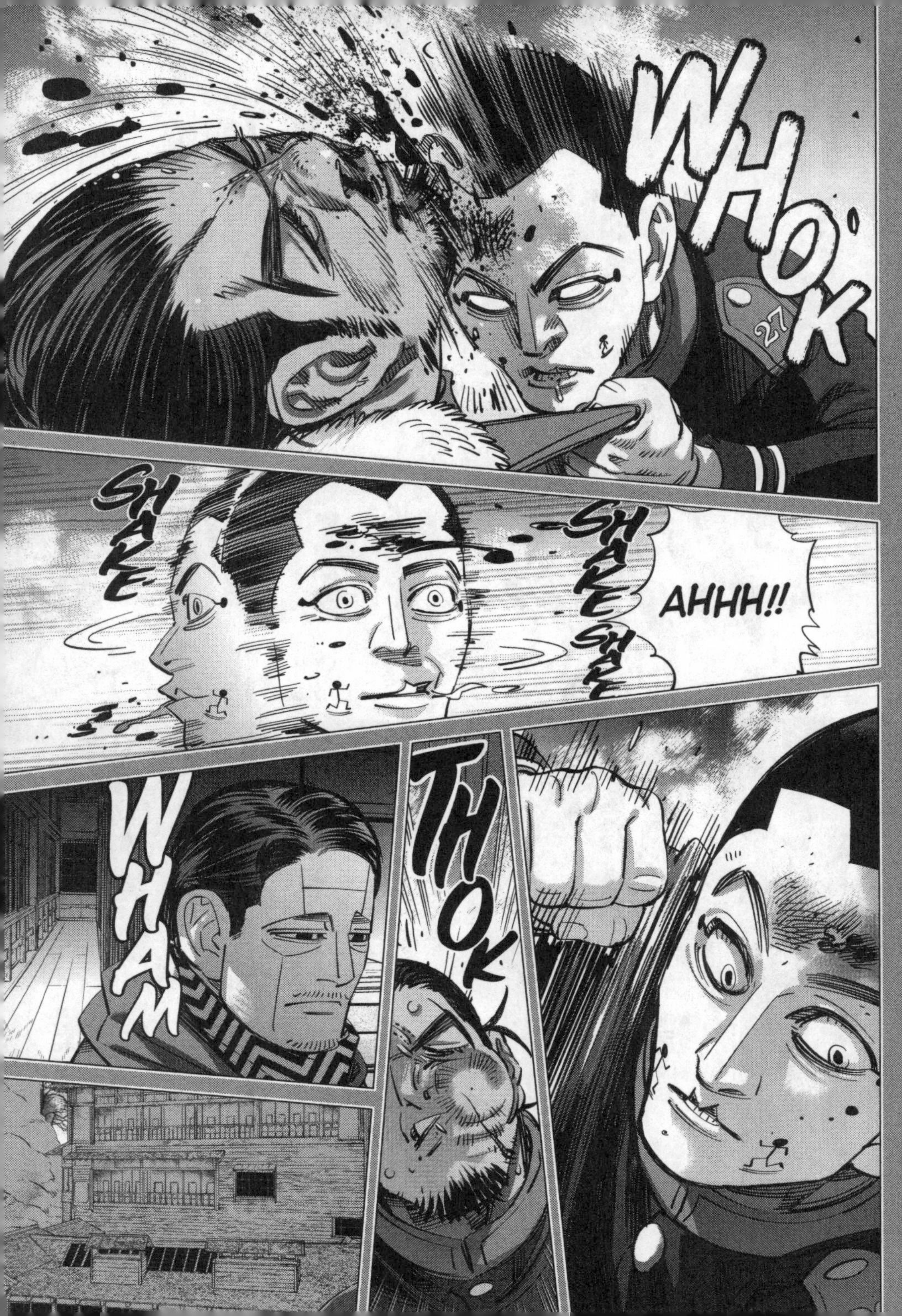
WHOK
AHHH!!
SHAKE SHAKE
SHAKE
THOK
WHAM

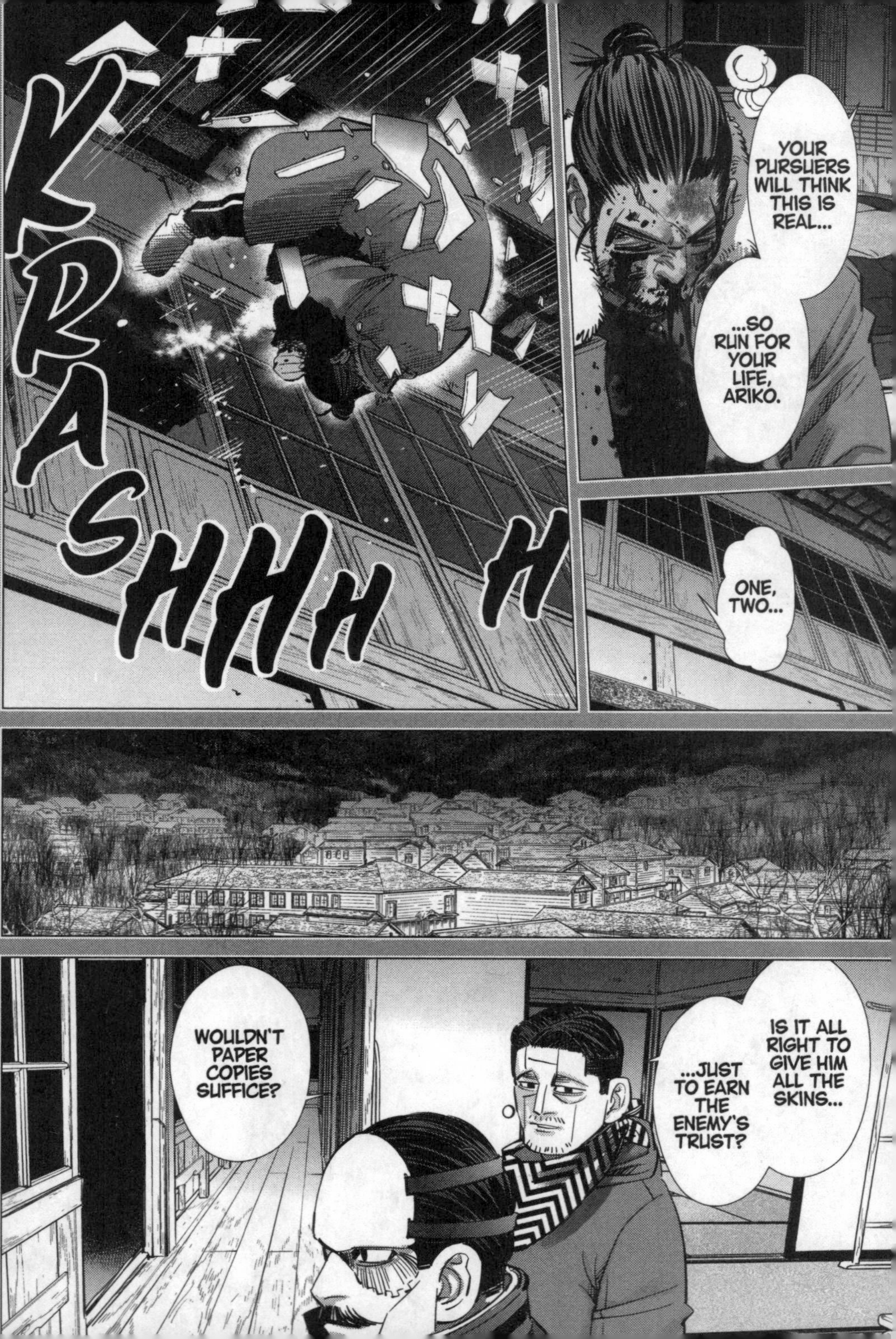
YOUR PURSUERS WILL THINK THIS IS REAL...
...SO RUN FOR YOUR LIFE, ARIKO.
ONE, TWO...
KRASHHHH
IS IT ALL RIGHT TO GIVE HIM ALL THE SKINS...
...JUST TO EARN THE ENEMY'S TRUST?
WOULDN'T PAPER COPIES SUFFICE?

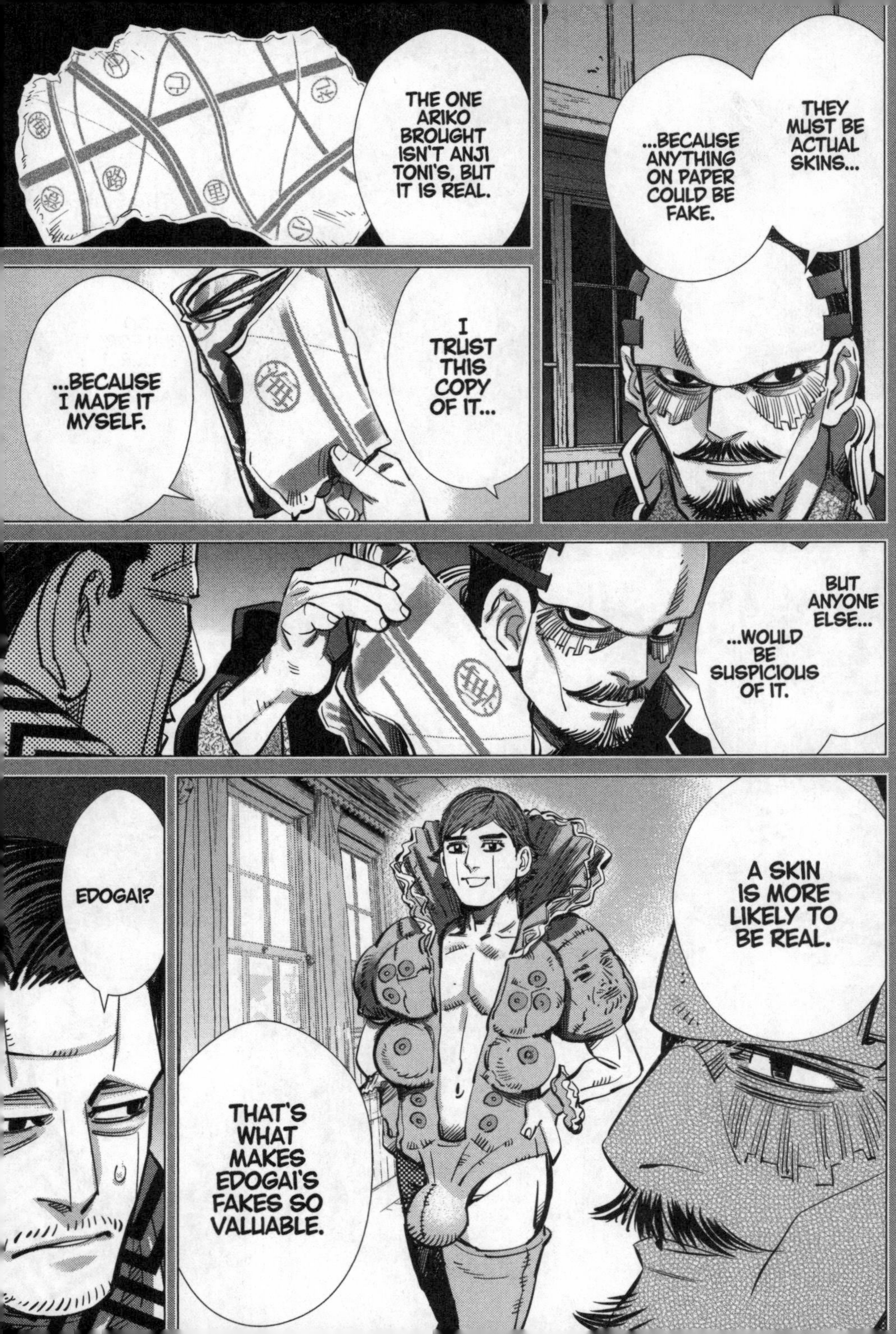
THEY MUST BE ACTUAL SKINS...
...BECAUSE ANYTHING ON PAPER COULD BE FAKE.
THE ONE ARIKO BROUGHT ISN'T ANJI TONI'S, BUT IT IS REAL.
I TRUST THIS COPY OF IT...
...BECAUSE I MADE IT MYSELF.
BUT ANYONE ELSE...
...WOULD BE SUSPICIOUS OF IT.
A SKIN IS MORE LIKELY TO BE REAL.
THAT'S WHAT MAKES EDOGAI'S FAKES SO VALUABLE.
EDOGAI?

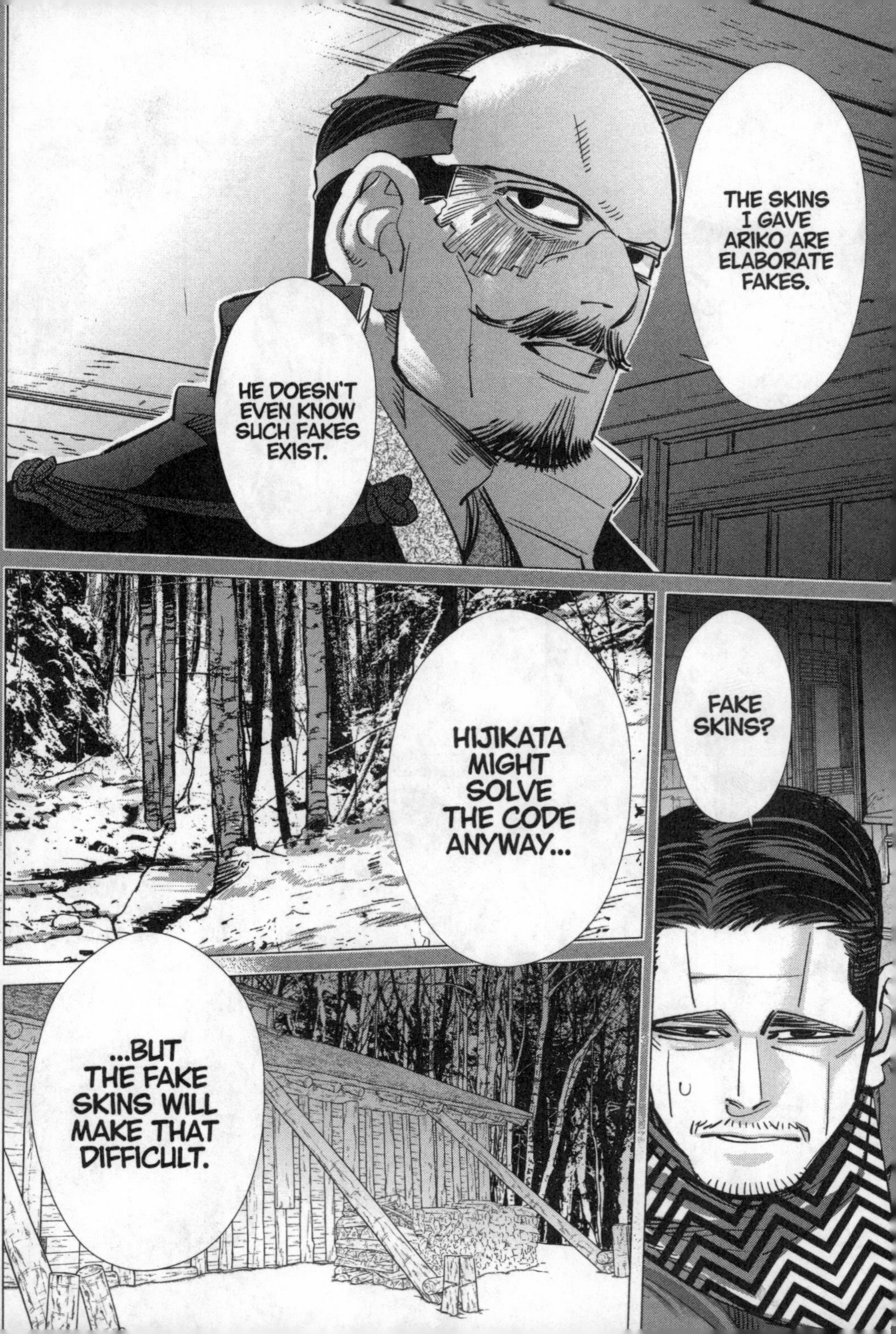
THE SKINS I GAVE ARIKO ARE ELABORATE FAKES.
HE DOESN'T EVEN KNOW SUCH FAKES EXIST.
FAKE SKINS?
HIJIKATA MIGHT SOLVE THE CODE ANYWAY...
...BUT THE FAKE SKINS WILL MAKE THAT DIFFICULT.

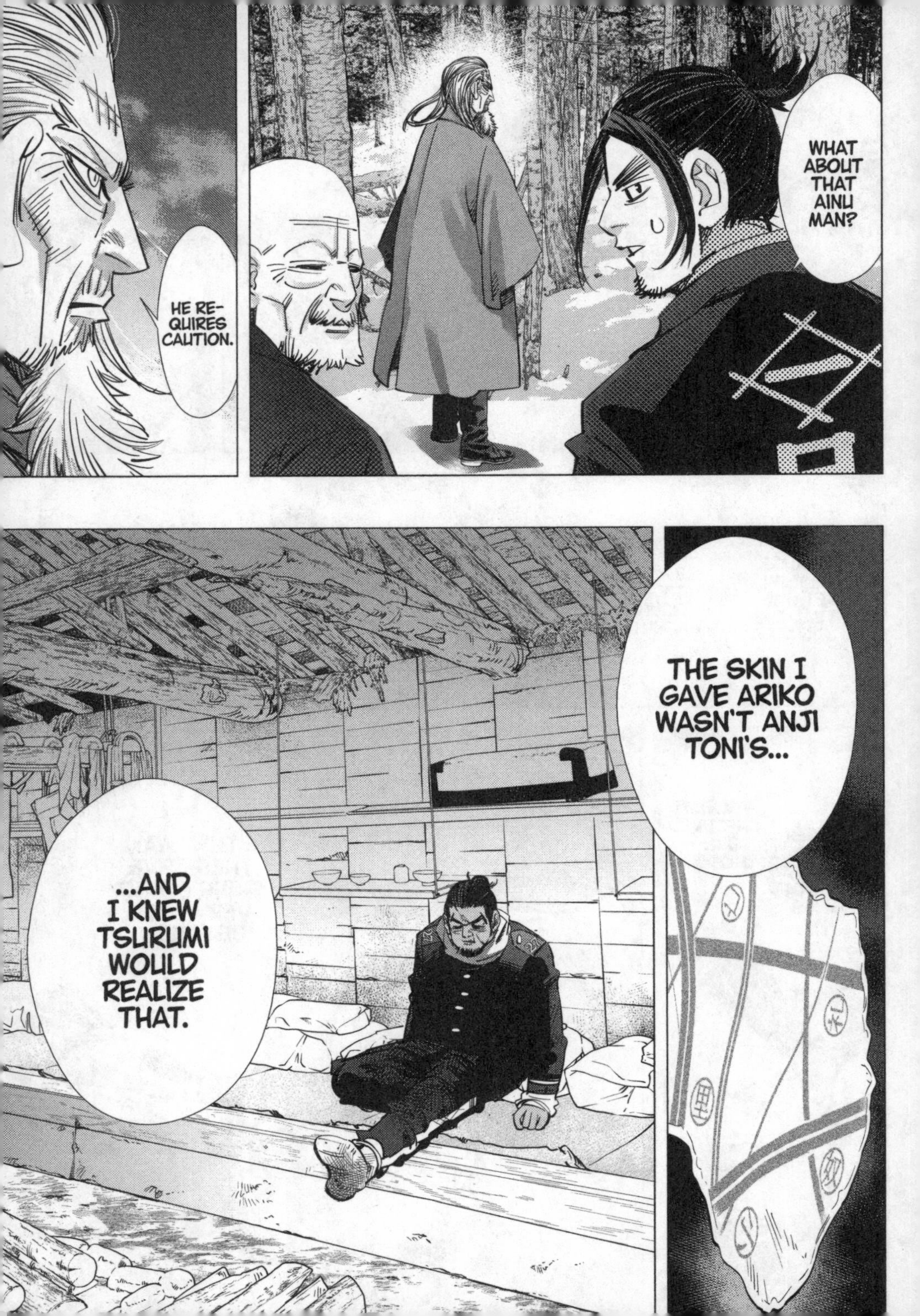
WHAT ABOUT THAT AINU MAN?
HE RE-QUIRES CAUTION.
THE SKIN I GAVE ARIKO WASN'T ANJI TONI'S...
...AND I KNEW TSURUMI WOULD REALIZE THAT.

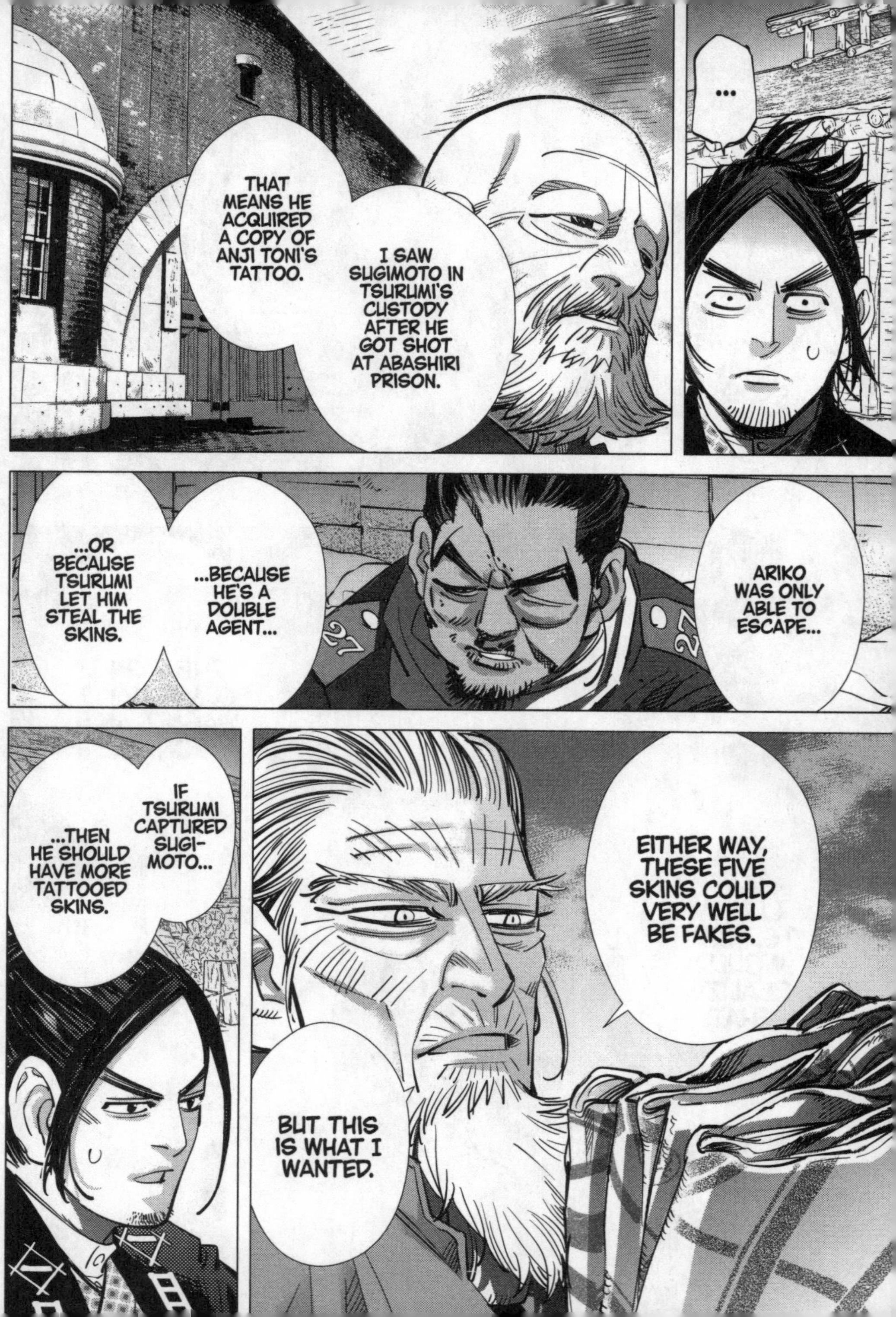
...
I SAW SUGIMOTO IN TSURUMI'S CUSTODY AFTER HE GOT SHOT AT ABASHIRI PRISON.
THAT MEANS HE ACQUIRED A COPY OF ANJI TONI'S TATTOO.
ARIKO WAS ONLY ABLE TO ESCAPE...
...BECAUSE HE'S A DOUBLE AGENT...
...OR BECAUSE TSURUMI LET HIM STEAL THE SKINS.
EITHER WAY, THESE FIVE SKINS COULD VERY WELL BE FAKES.
BUT THIS IS WHAT I WANTED.
IF TSURUMI CAPTURED SUGI-MOTO...
...THEN HE SHOULD HAVE MORE TATTOOED SKINS.

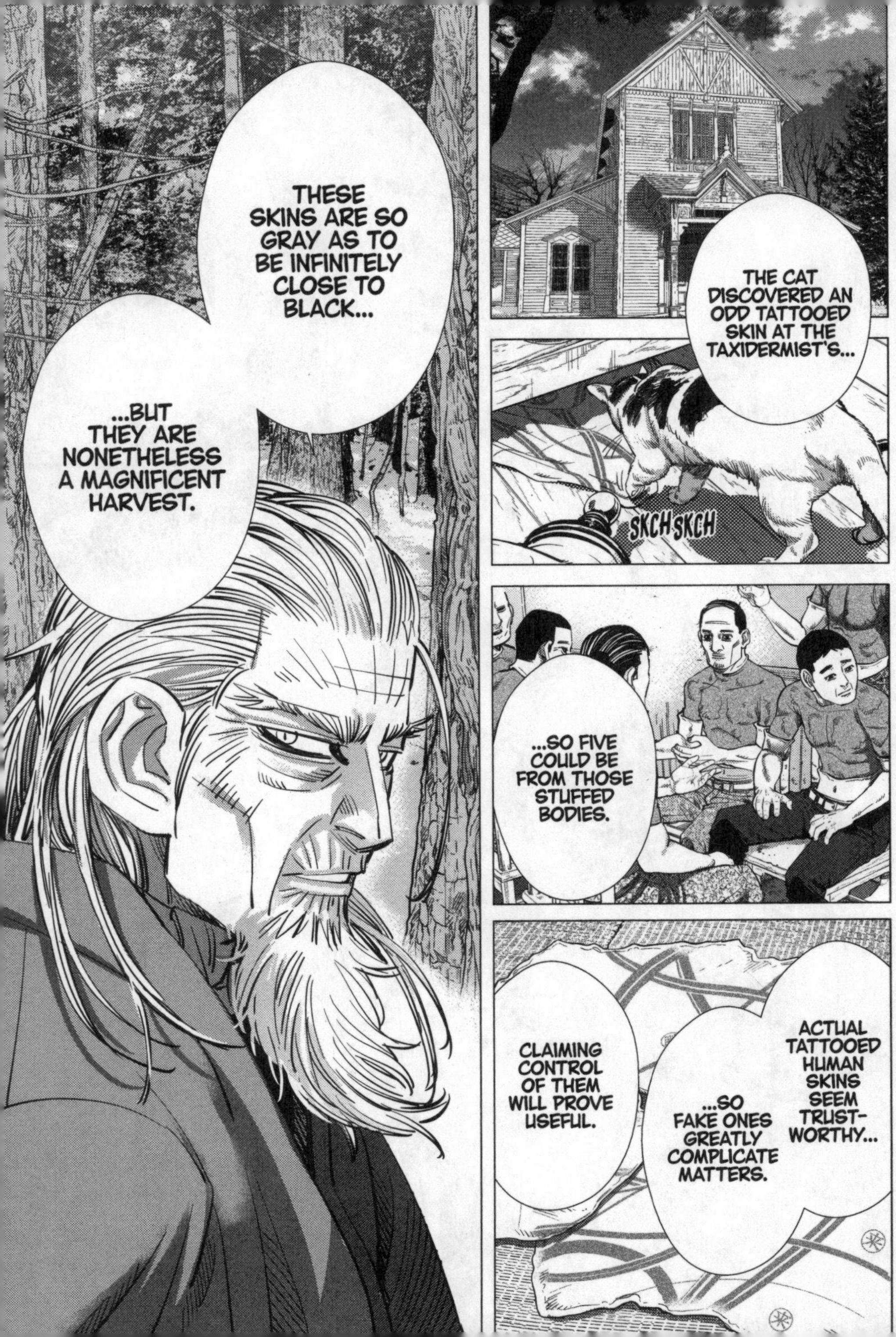
THE CAT DISCOVERED AN ODD TATTOOED SKIN AT THE TAXIDERMIST'S...
SKCH SKCH
...SO FIVE COULD BE FROM THOSE STUFFED BODIES.
ACTUAL TATTOOED HUMAN SKINS SEEM TRUST-WORTHY...
...SO FAKE ONES GREATLY COMPLICATE MATTERS.
CLAIMING CONTROL OF THEM WILL PROVE USEFUL.
THESE SKINS ARE SO GRAY AS TO BE INFINITELY CLOSE TO BLACK...
...BUT THEY ARE NONETHELESS A MAGNIFICENT HARVEST.

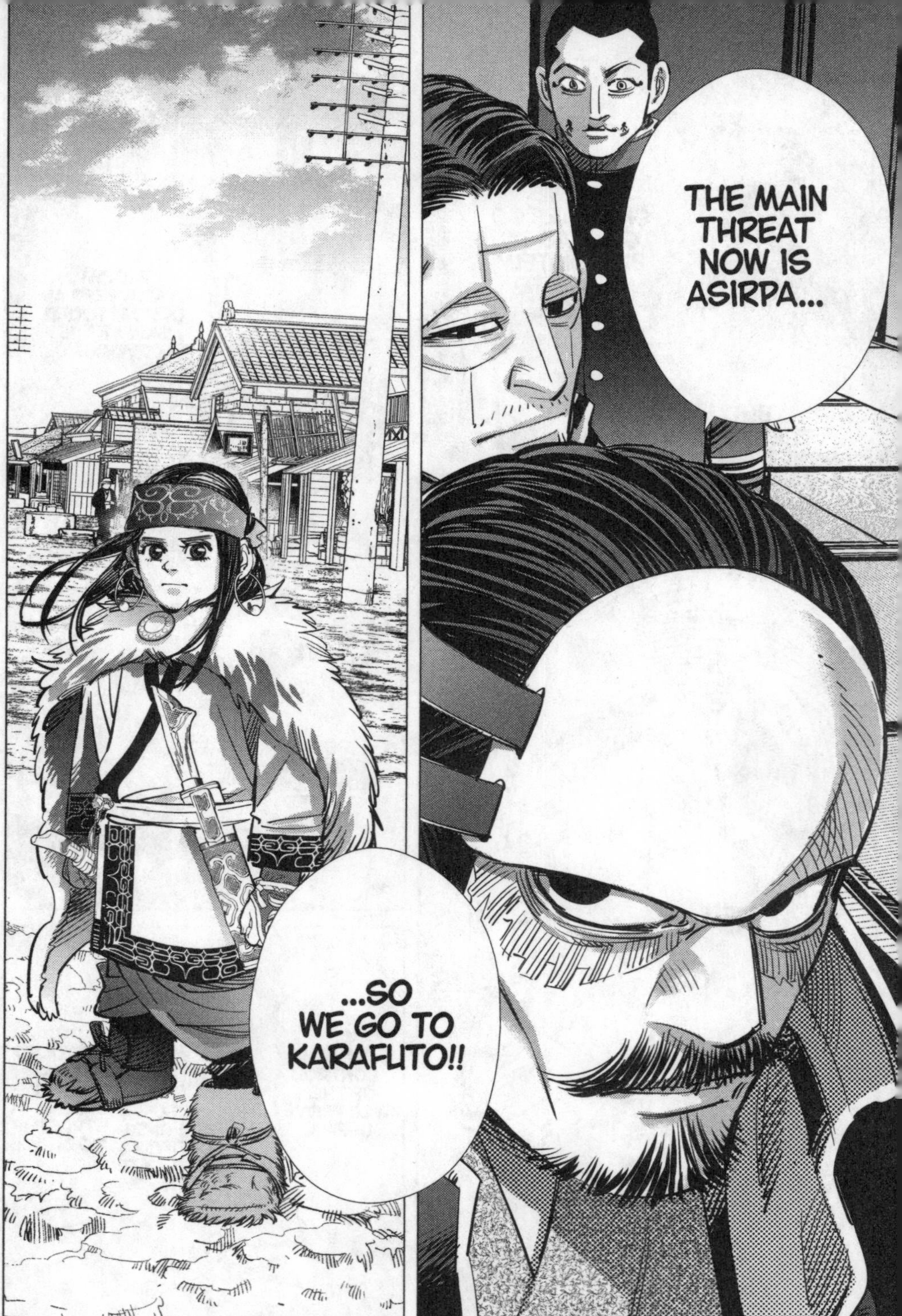
THE MAIN THREAT NOW IS ASIRPA...
...SO WE GO TO KARAFUTO!!

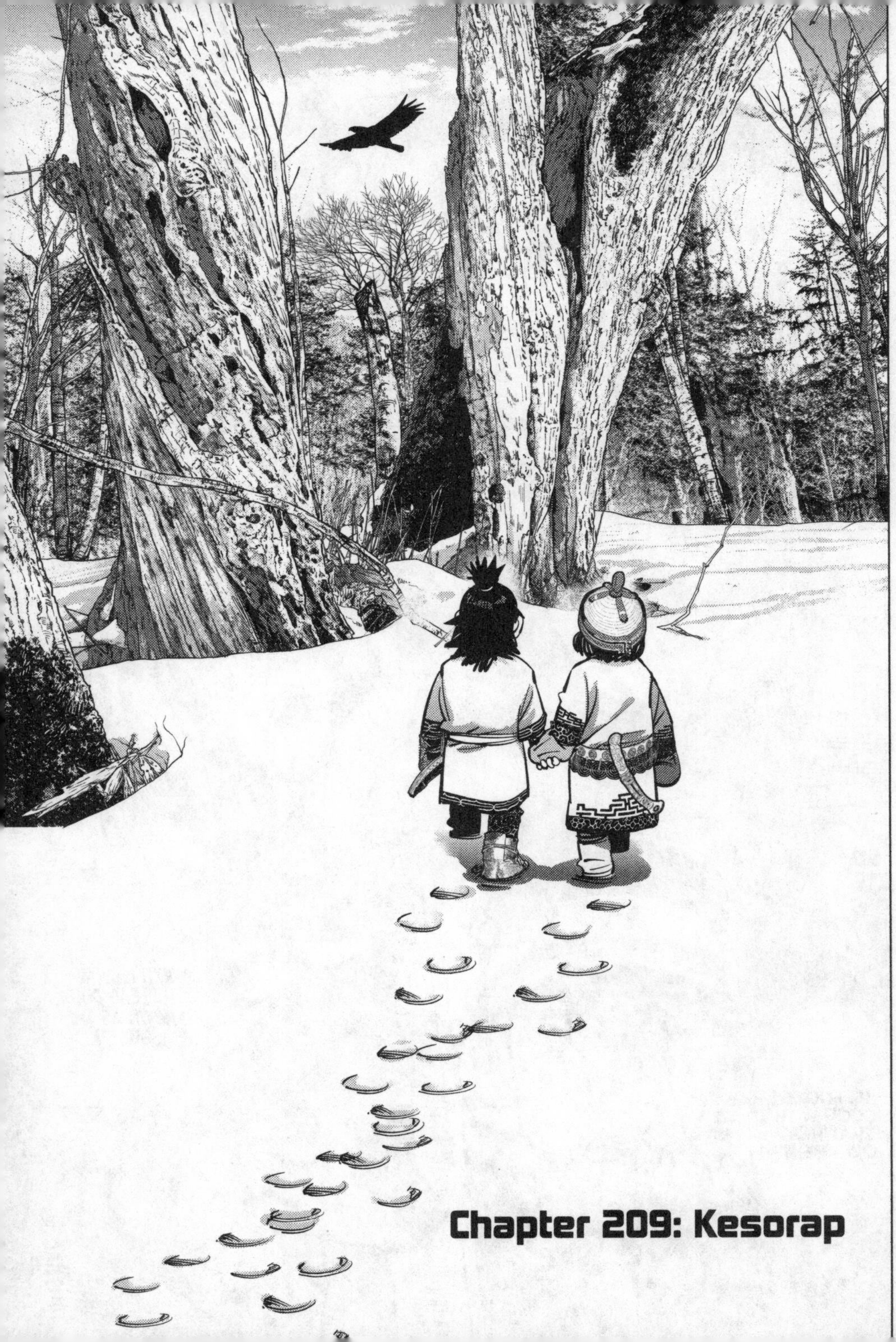

Chapter 209: Kesorap

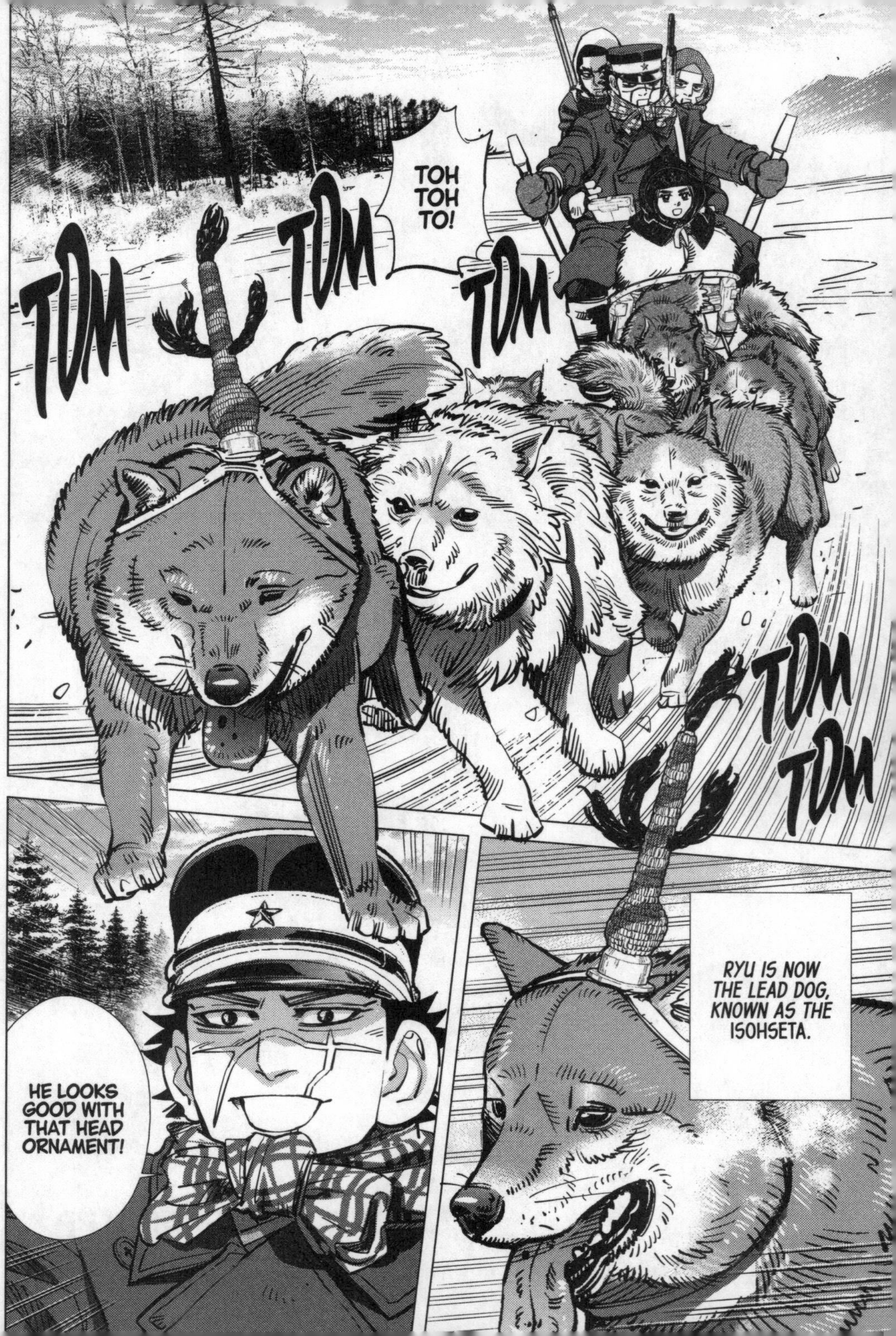
TOH TOH TO!
TOM
TOM
TOM
TOM TOM
RYU IS NOW THE LEAD DOG, KNOWN AS THE ISOHSETA.
HE LOOKS GOOD WITH THAT HEAD ORNAMENT!

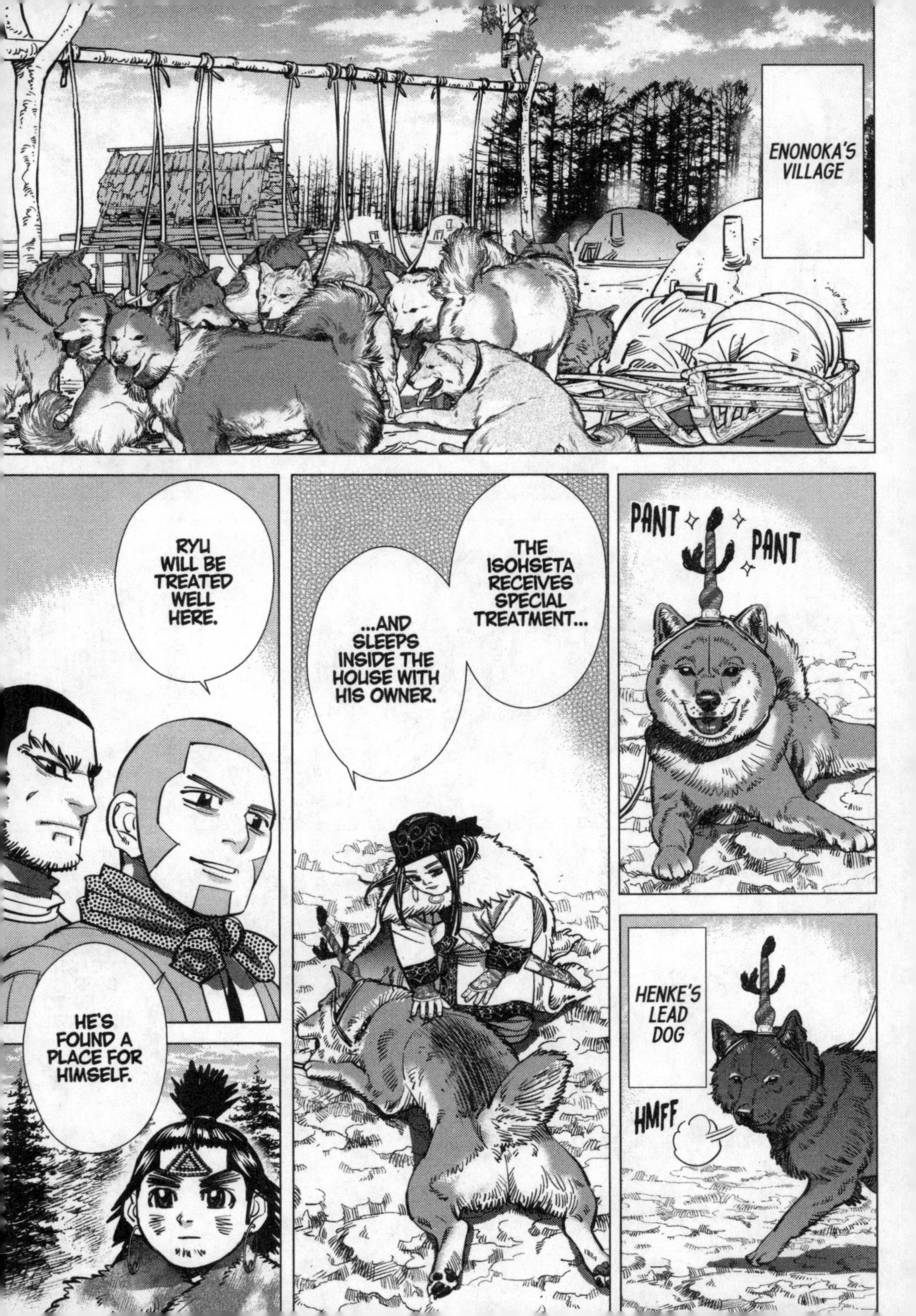
ENONOKA'S VILLAGE
PANT PANT
HENKE'S LEAD DOG
HMFF
THE ISOHSETA RECEIVES SPECIAL TREATMENT...
...AND SLEEPS INSIDE THE HOUSE WITH HIS OWNER.
RYU WILL BE TREATED WELL HERE.
HE'S FOUND A PLACE FOR HIMSELF.

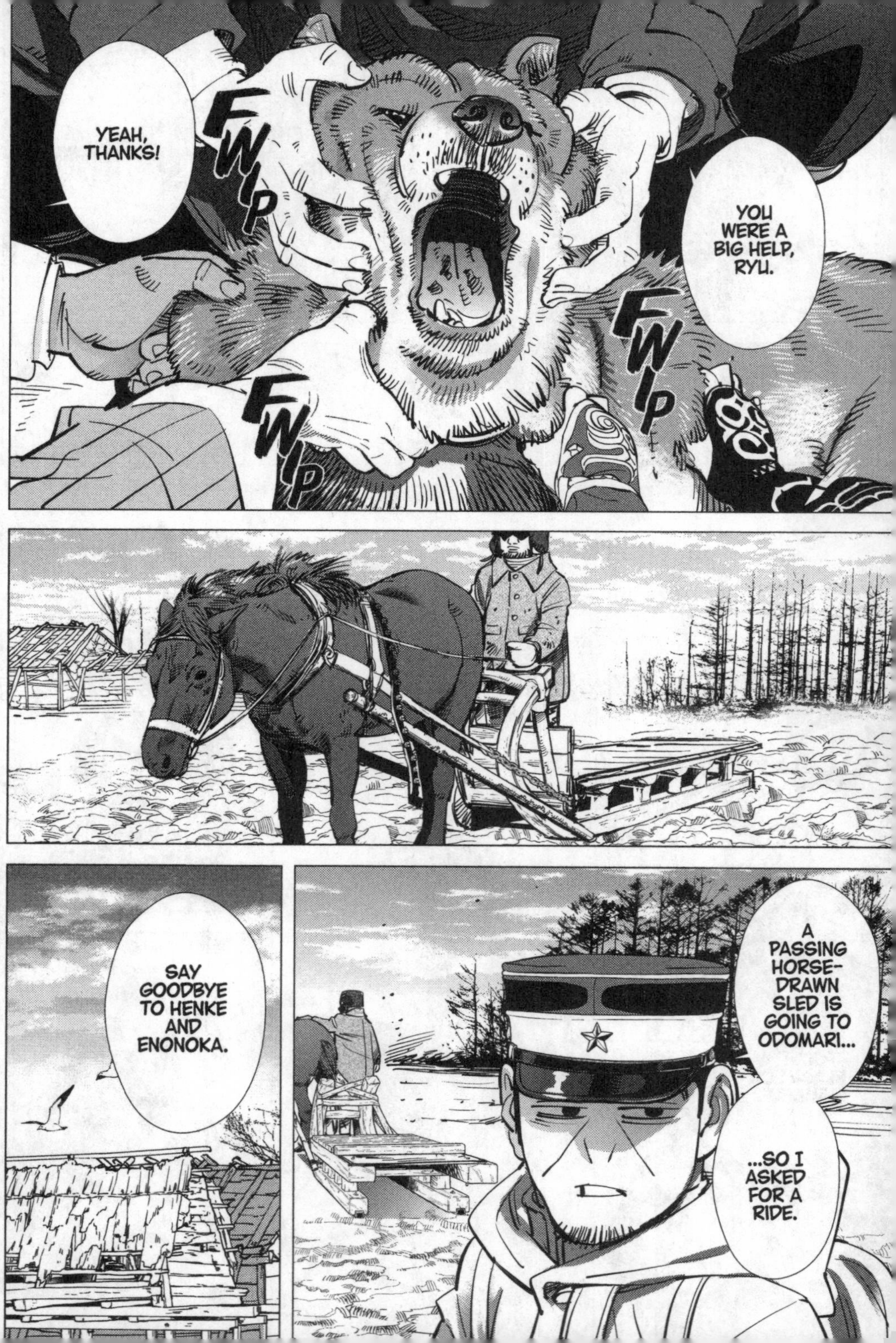
YOU WERE A BIG HELP, RYU.
YEAH, THANKS!
FWIP
FWIP
FWIP
A PASSING HORSE-DRAWN SLED IS GOING TO ODOMARI...
...SO I ASKED FOR A RIDE.
SAY GOODBYE TO HENKE AND ENONOKA.

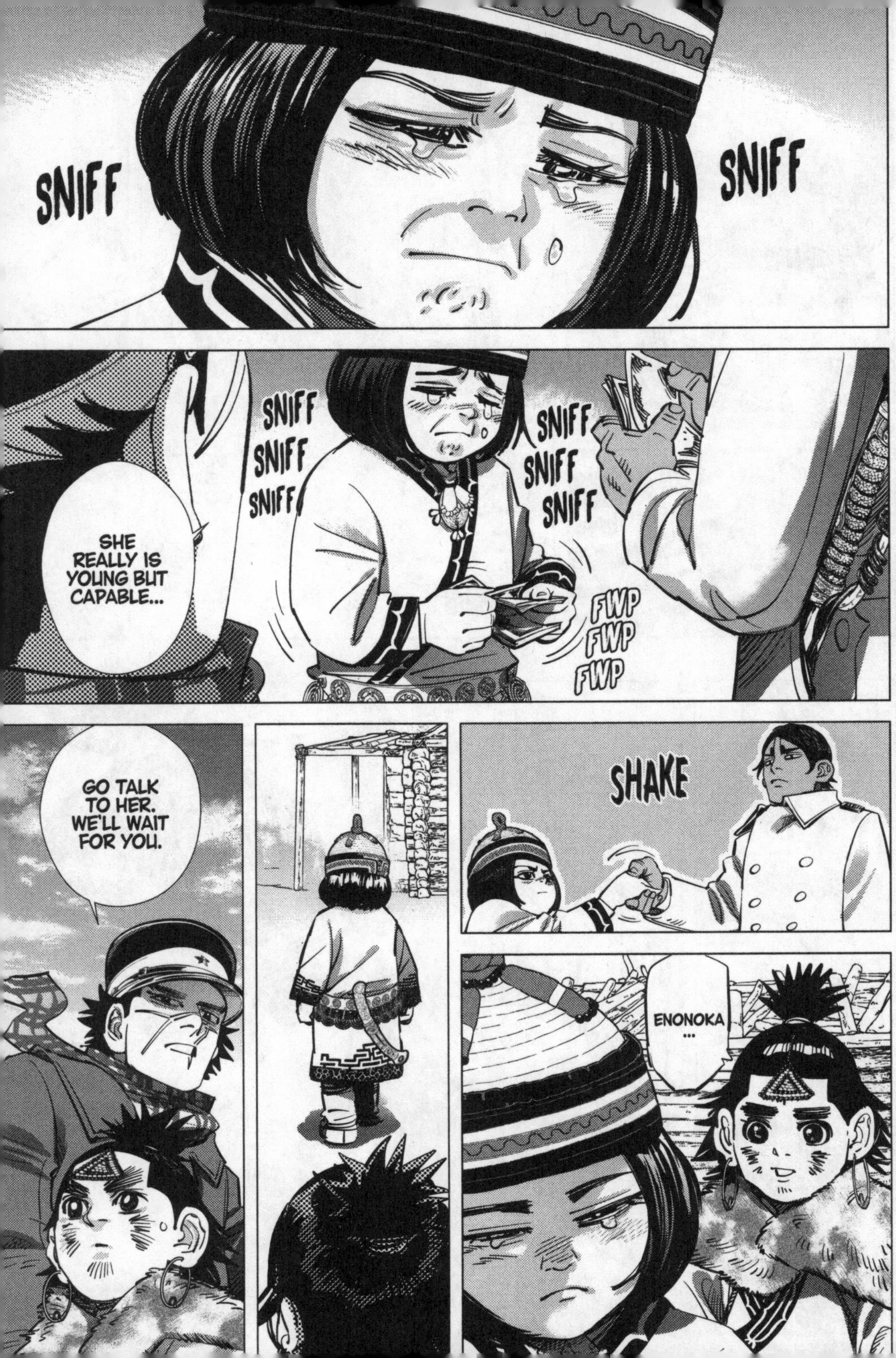
SNIFF
SNIFF
SNIFF
SNIFF
SNIFF
SNIFF
SNIFF
SNIFF
FWP
FWP
FWP
SHE REALLY IS YOUNG BUT CAPABLE...
SHAKE
ENONOKA ...
GO TALK TO HER. WE'LL WAIT FOR YOU.

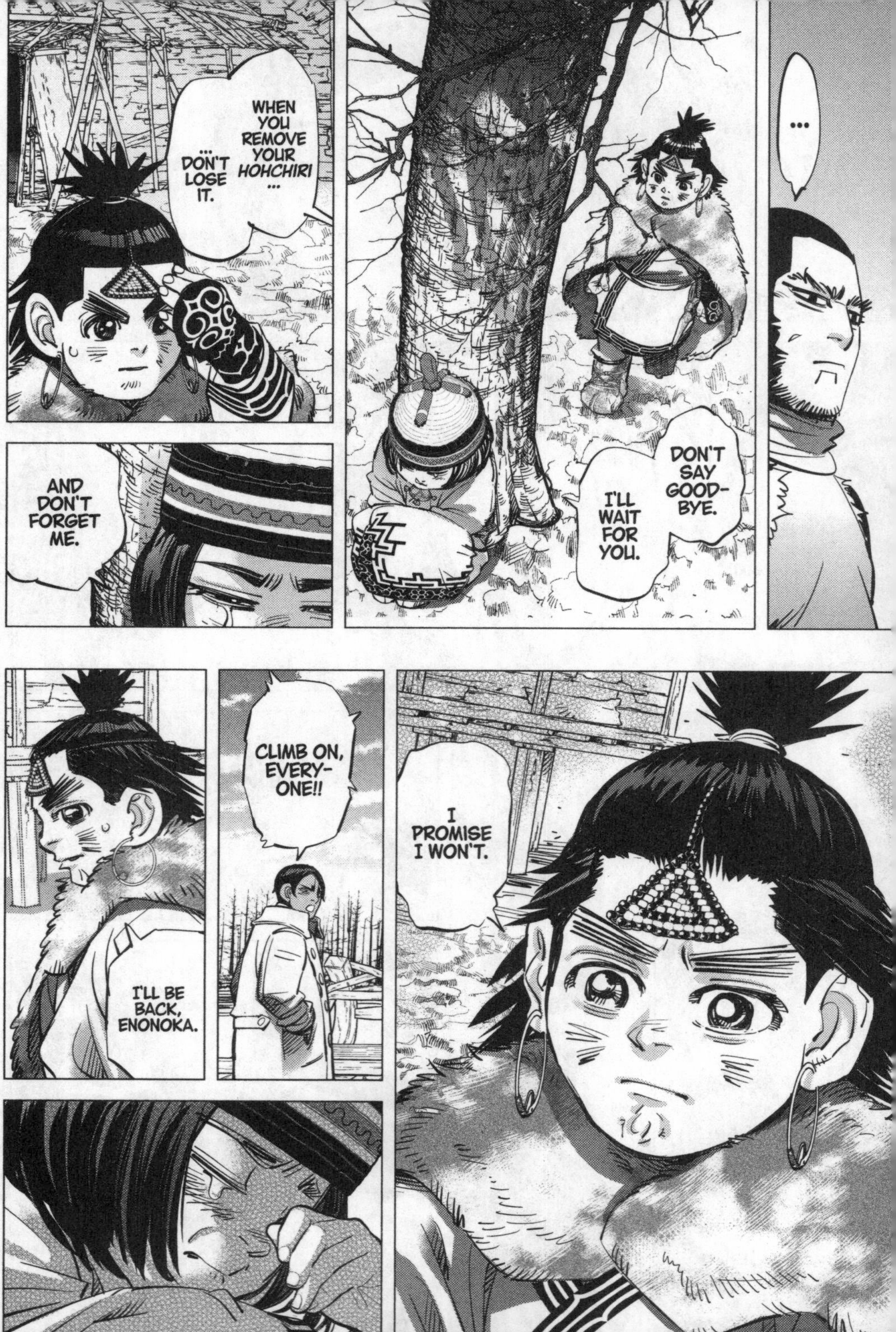
...
DON'T SAY GOOD-BYE.
I'LL WAIT FOR YOU.
WHEN YOU REMOVE YOUR HOHCHIRI...
...DON'T LOSE IT.
AND DON'T FORGET ME.
I PROMISE I WON'T.
CLIMB ON, EVERYONE!!
I'LL BE BACK, ENONOKA.

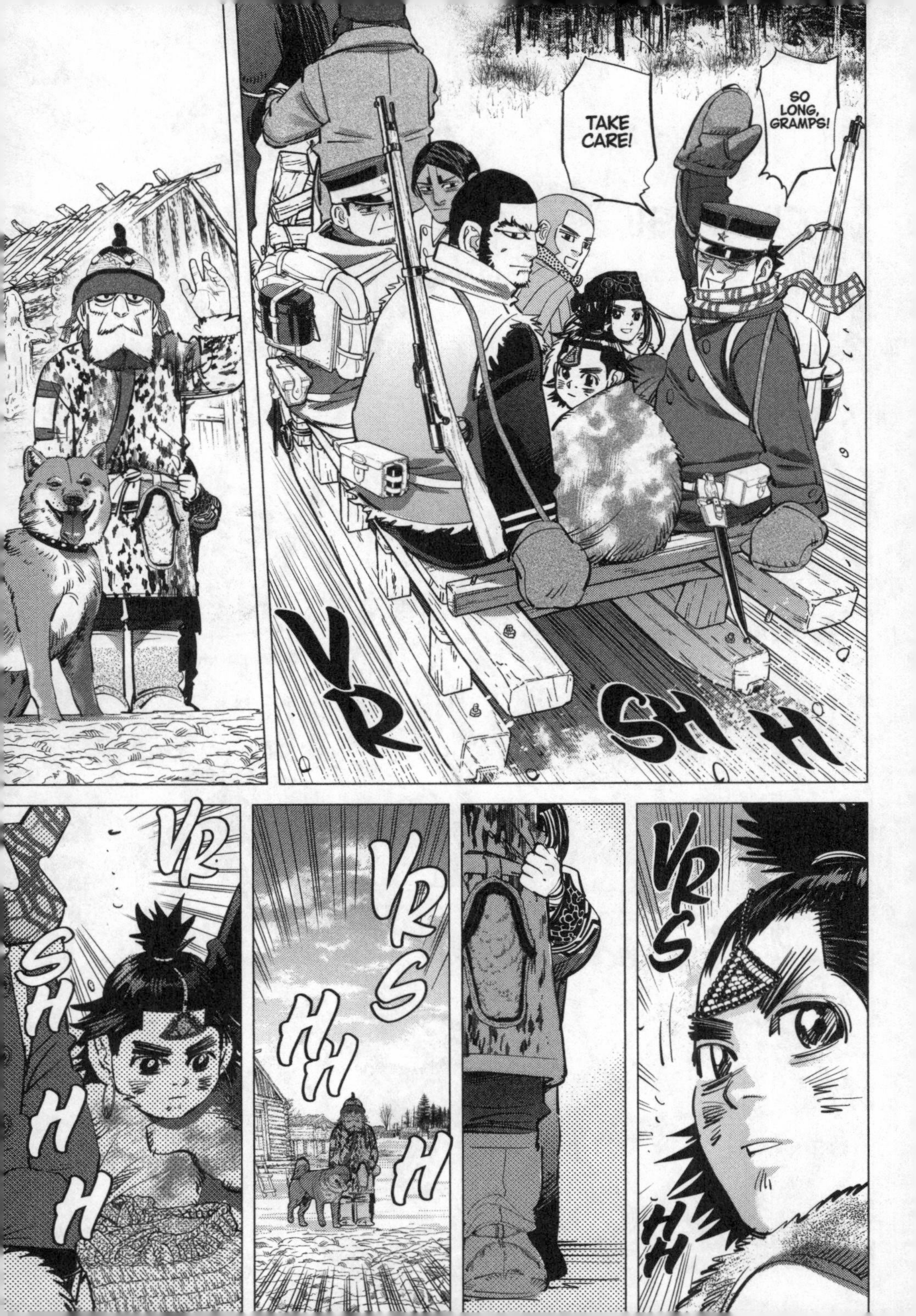
SO LONG, GRAMPS!
TAKE CARE!
VR
SHH
VRS
HH
VRS
HH
H
VR
SHHH

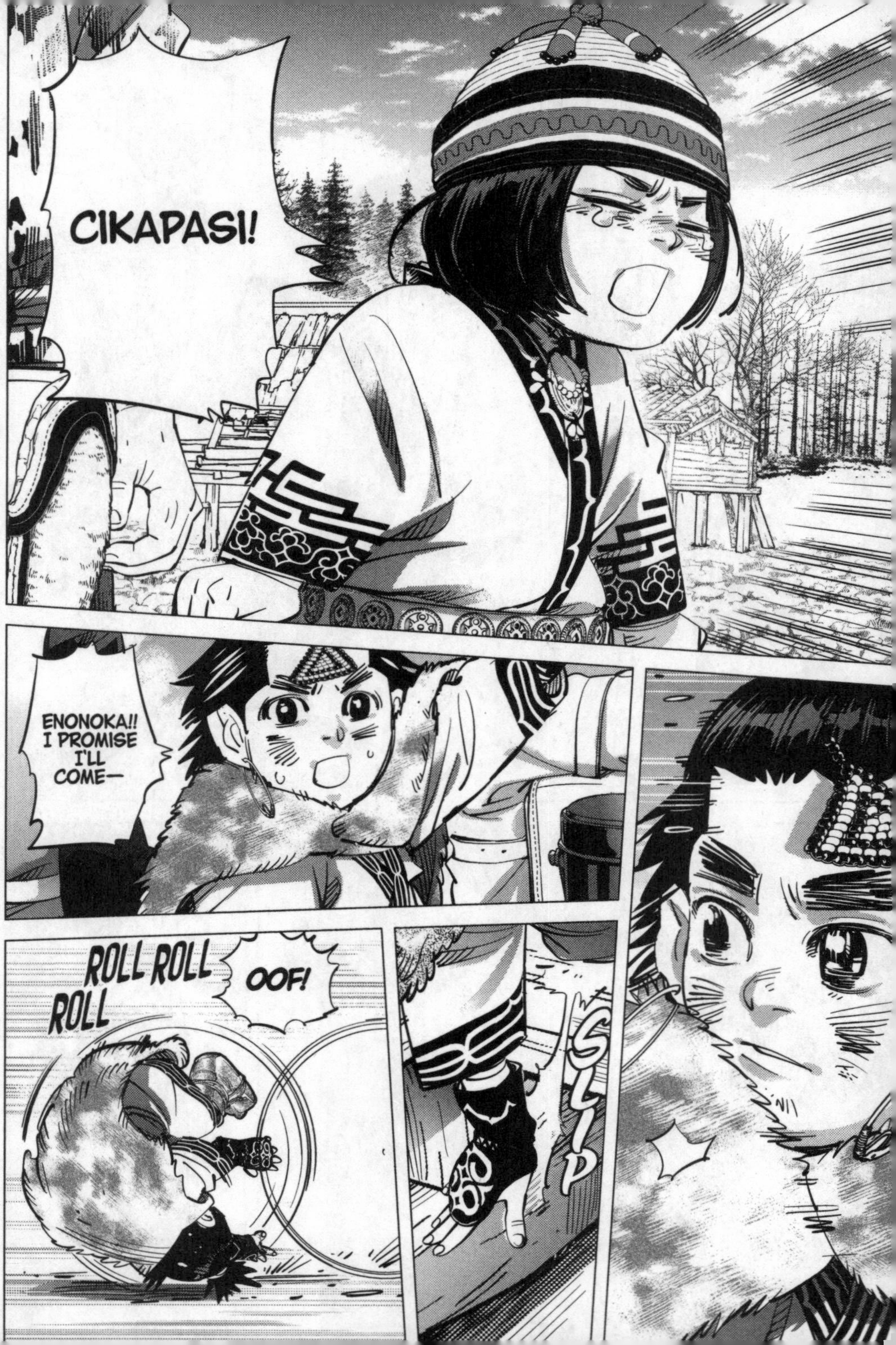
CIKAPASI!
ENONOKA!! I PROMISE I'LL COME—
SLIP
ROLL ROLL ROLL
OOF!

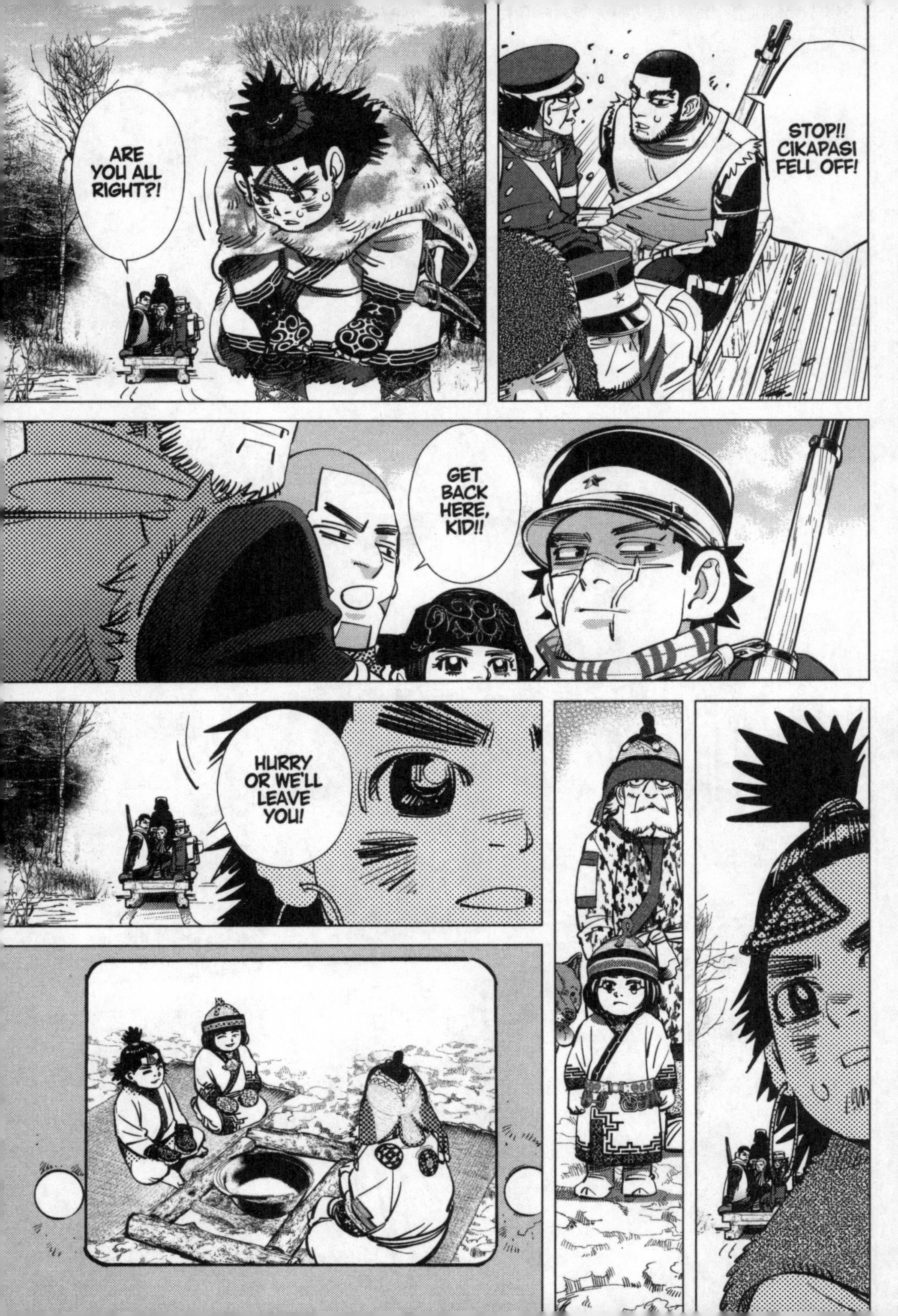
STOP!! CIKAPASI FELL OFF!
ARE YOU ALL RIGHT?!
GET BACK HERE, KID!!
HURRY OR WE'LL LEAVE YOU!

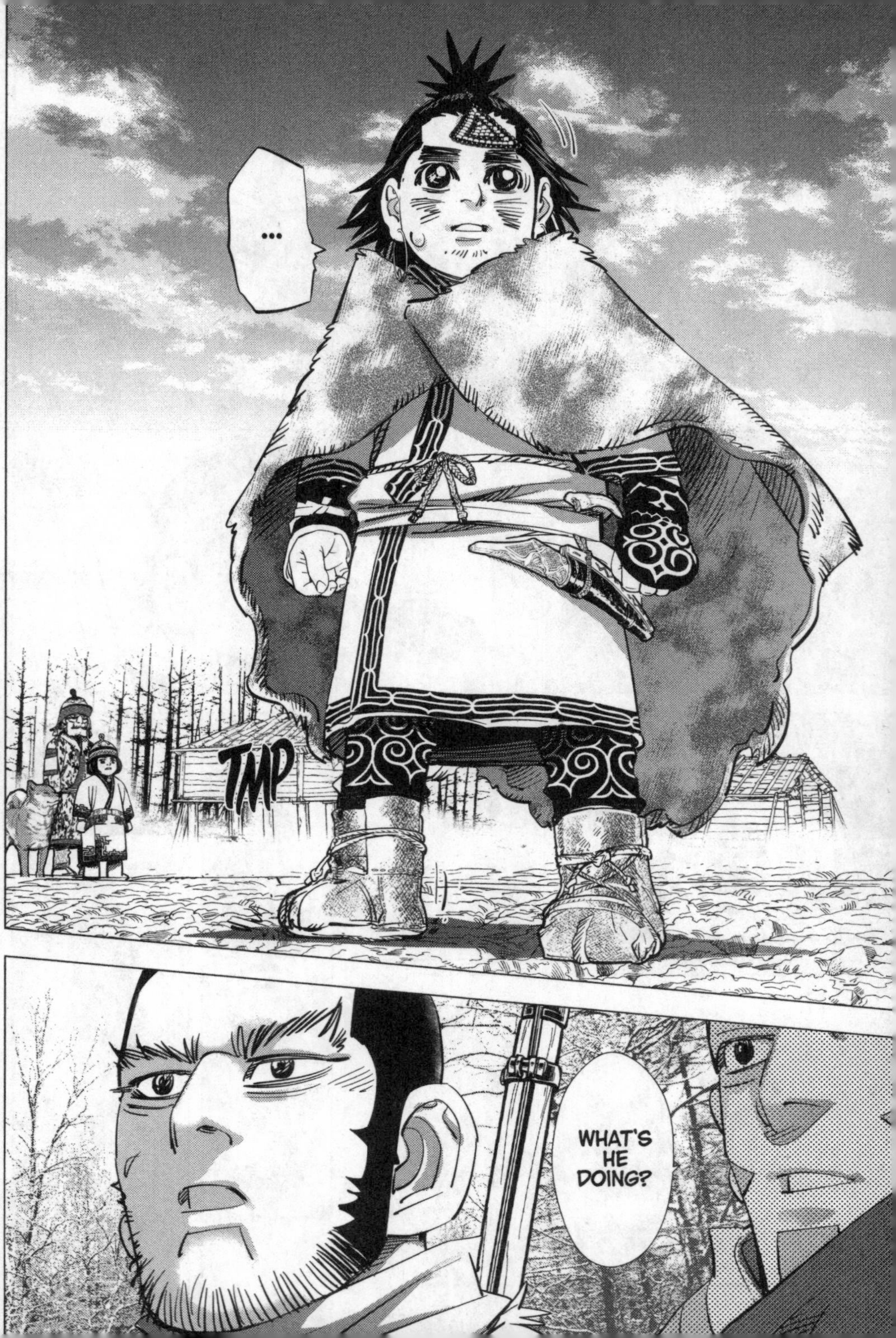
...
TMP
WHAT'S HE DOING?

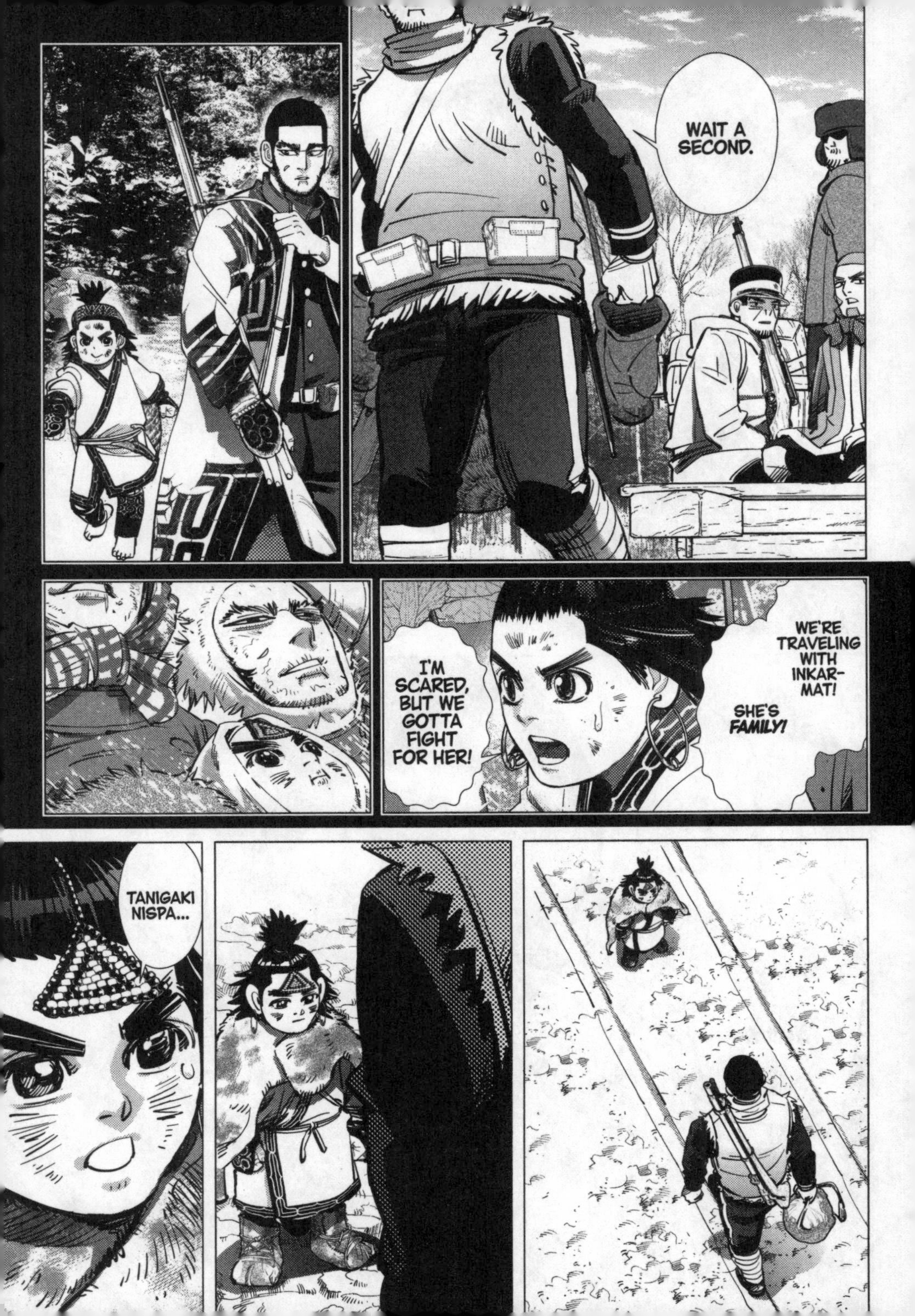
WAIT A SECOND.
WE'RE TRAVELING WITH INKARMAT!
SHE'S FAMILY!
I'M SCARED, BUT WE GOTTA FIGHT FOR HER!
TANIGAKI NISPA...

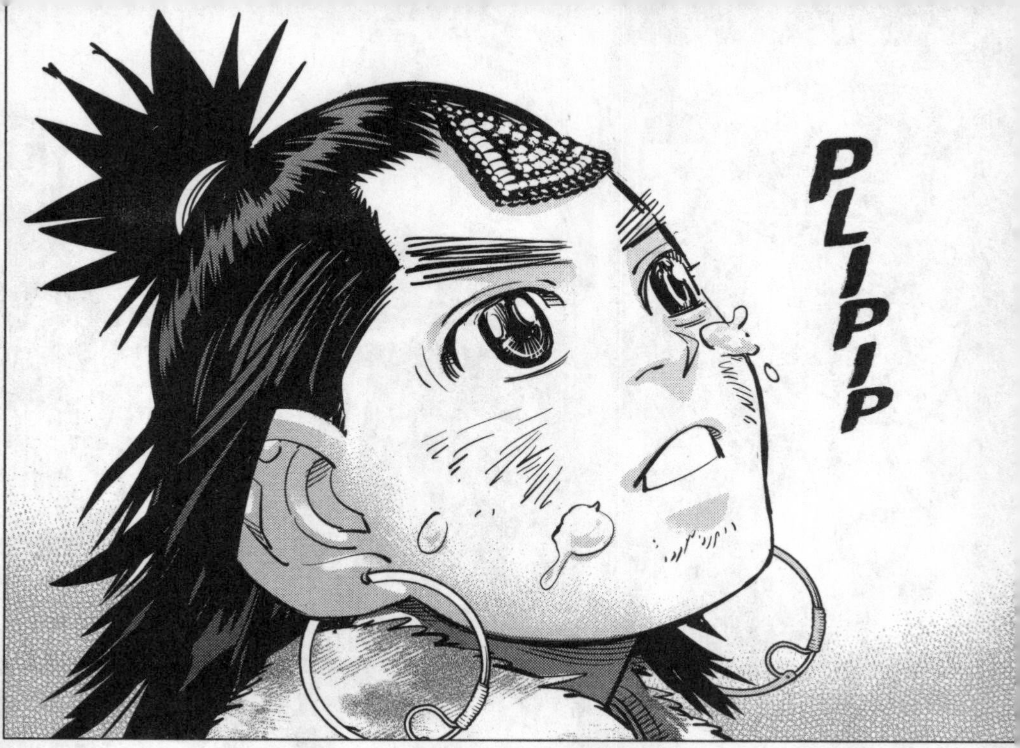
PLIPIP

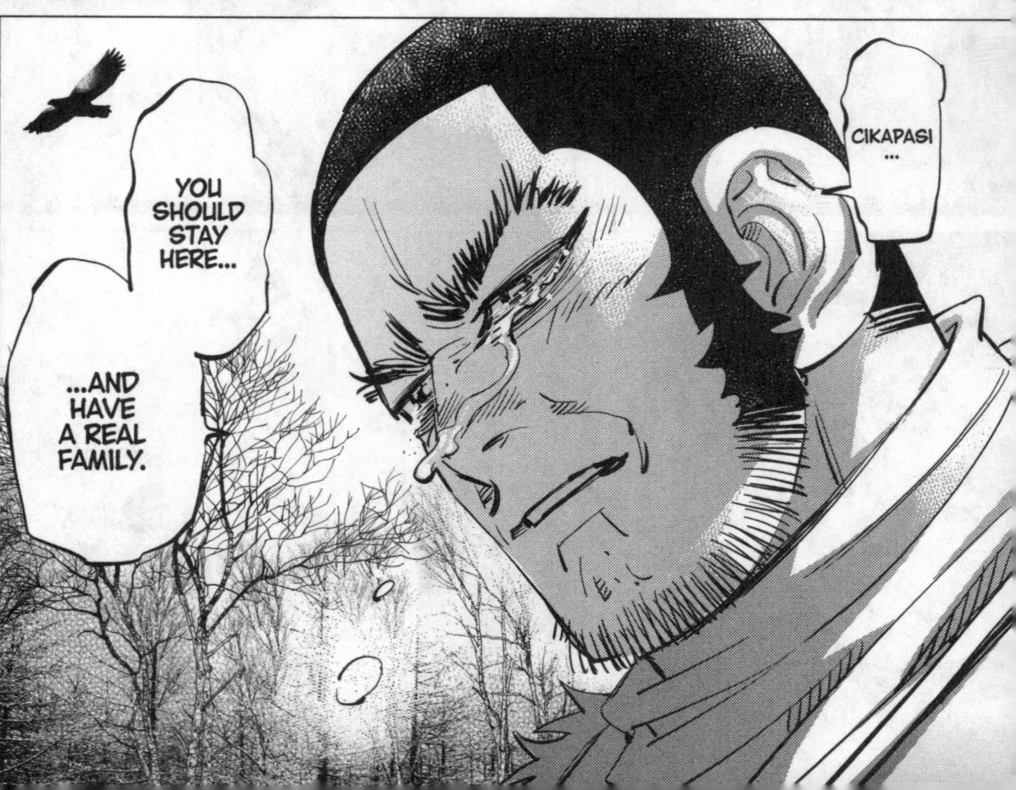
CIKAPASI ...
YOU SHOULD STAY HERE...
...AND HAVE A REAL FAMILY.

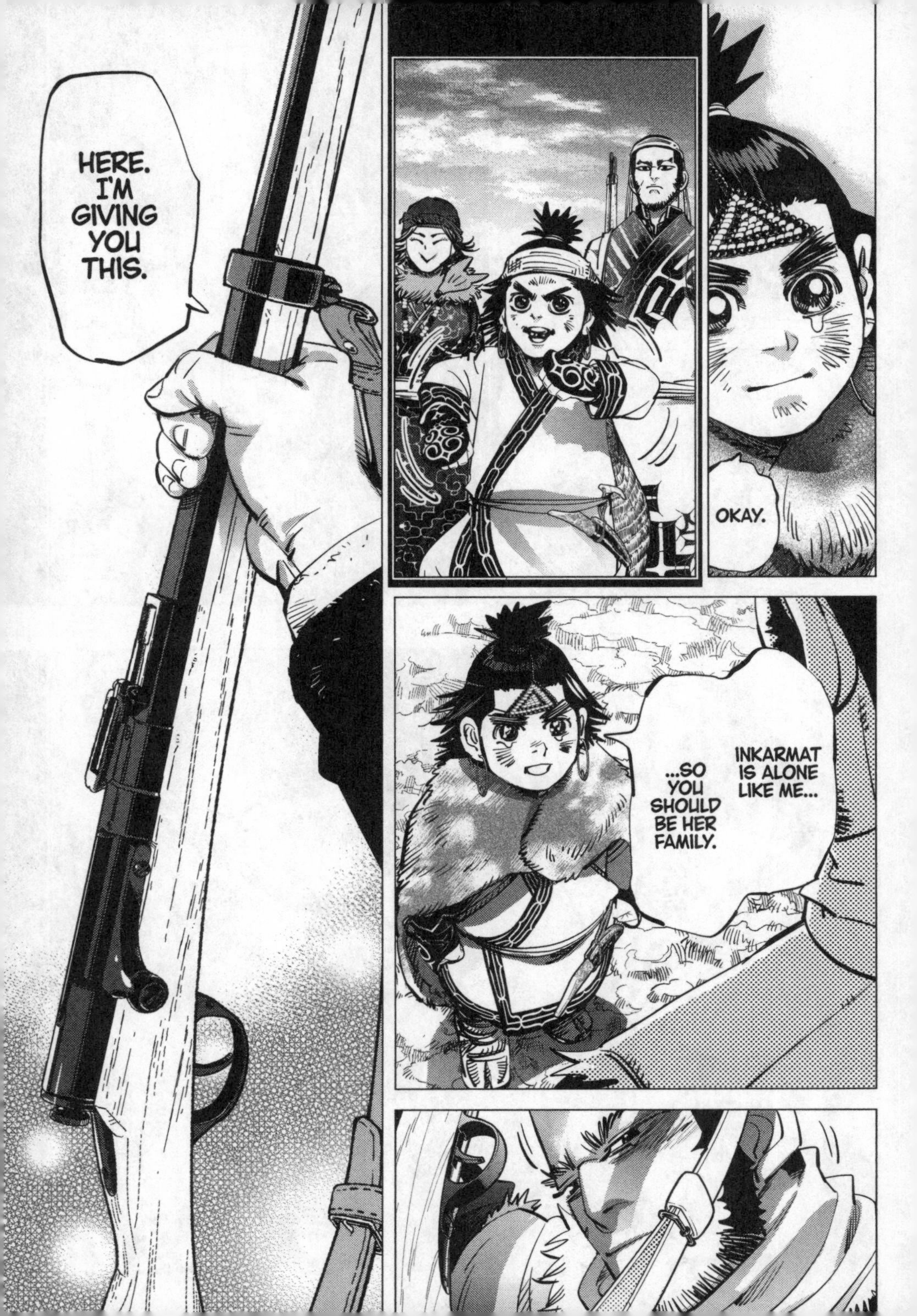
OKAY.
INKARMAT IS ALONE LIKE ME...
...SO YOU SHOULD BE HER FAMILY.
HERE. I'M GIVING YOU THIS.

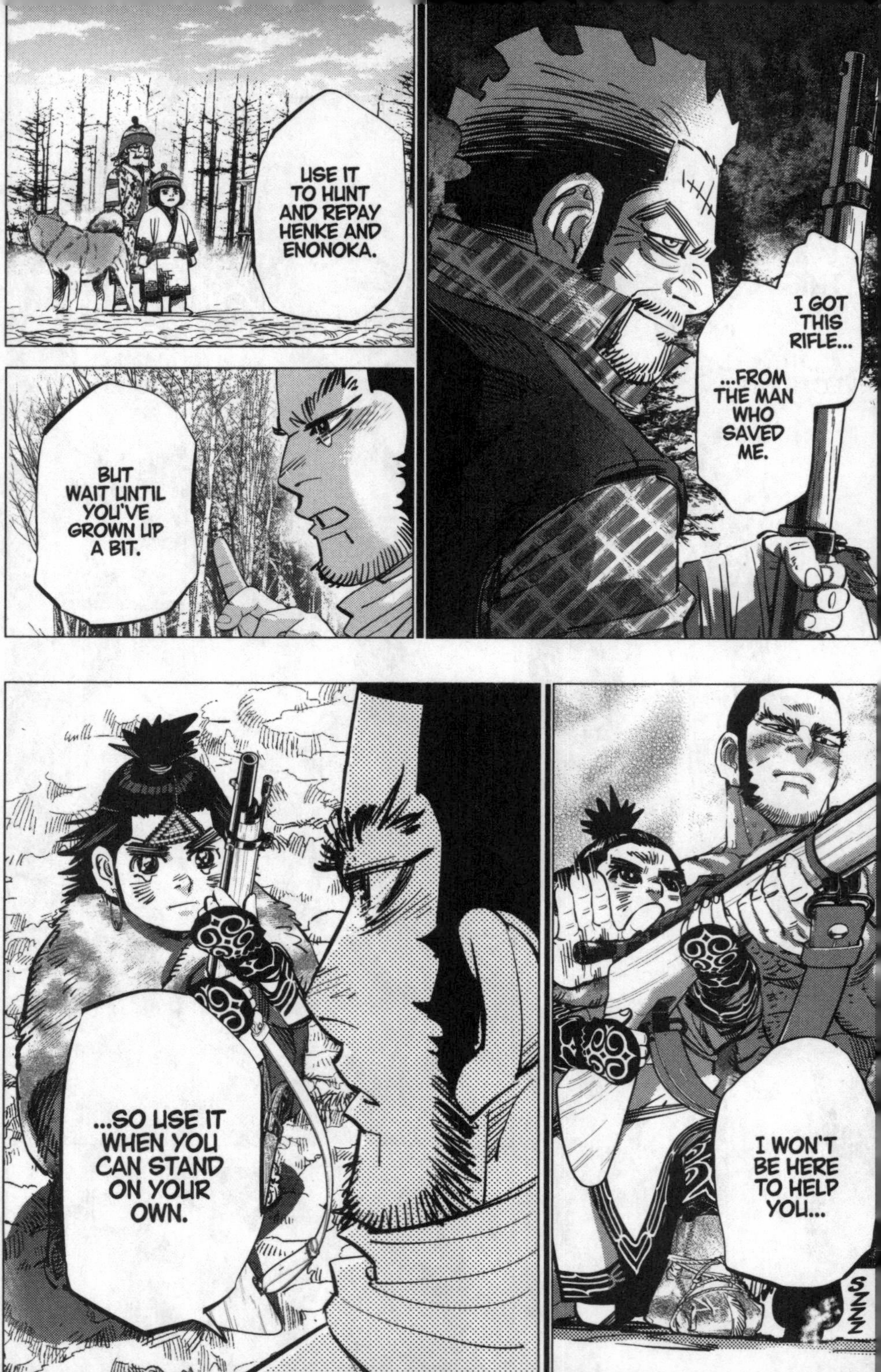
I GOT THIS RIFLE...
...FROM THE MAN WHO SAVED ME.
USE IT TO HUNT AND REPAY HENKE AND ENONOKA.
BUT WAIT UNTIL YOU'VE GROWN UP A BIT.
I WON'T BE HERE TO HELP YOU...
SZZZ
...SO USE IT WHEN YOU CAN STAND ON YOUR OWN.

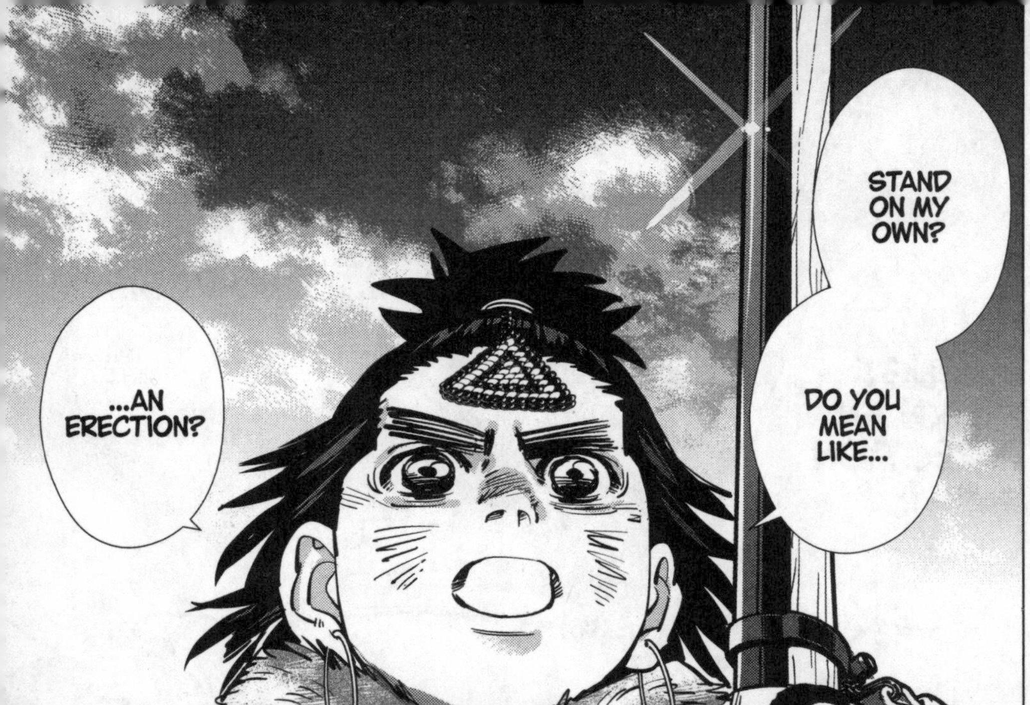
STAND ON MY OWN?
DO YOU MEAN LIKE...
...AN ERECTION?
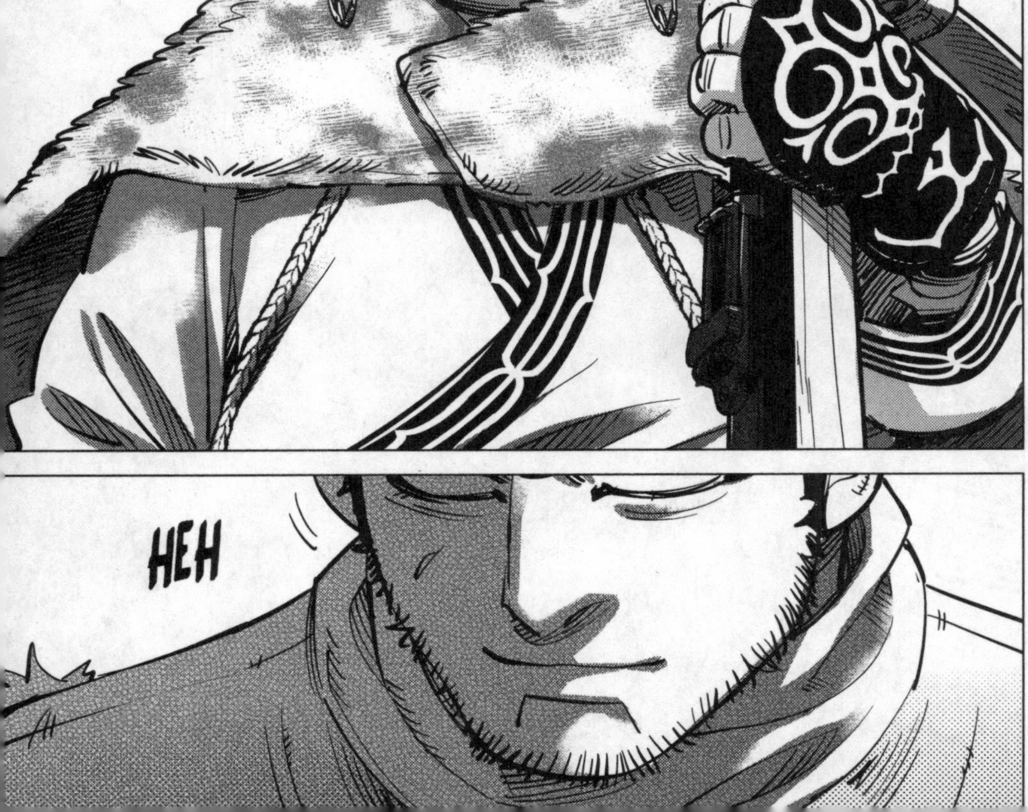
HEH

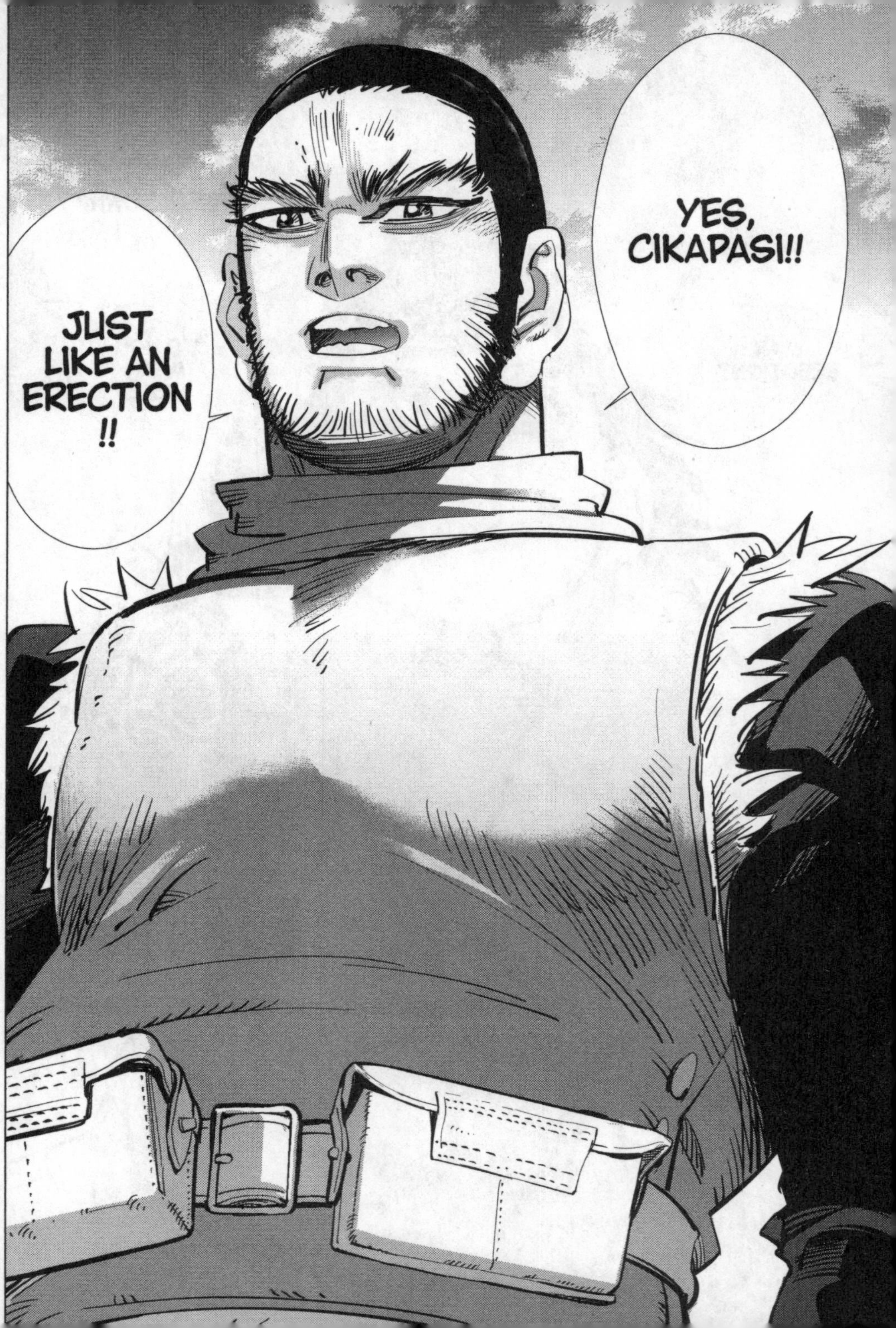
YES, CIKAPASI!!
JUST LIKE AN ERECTION !!

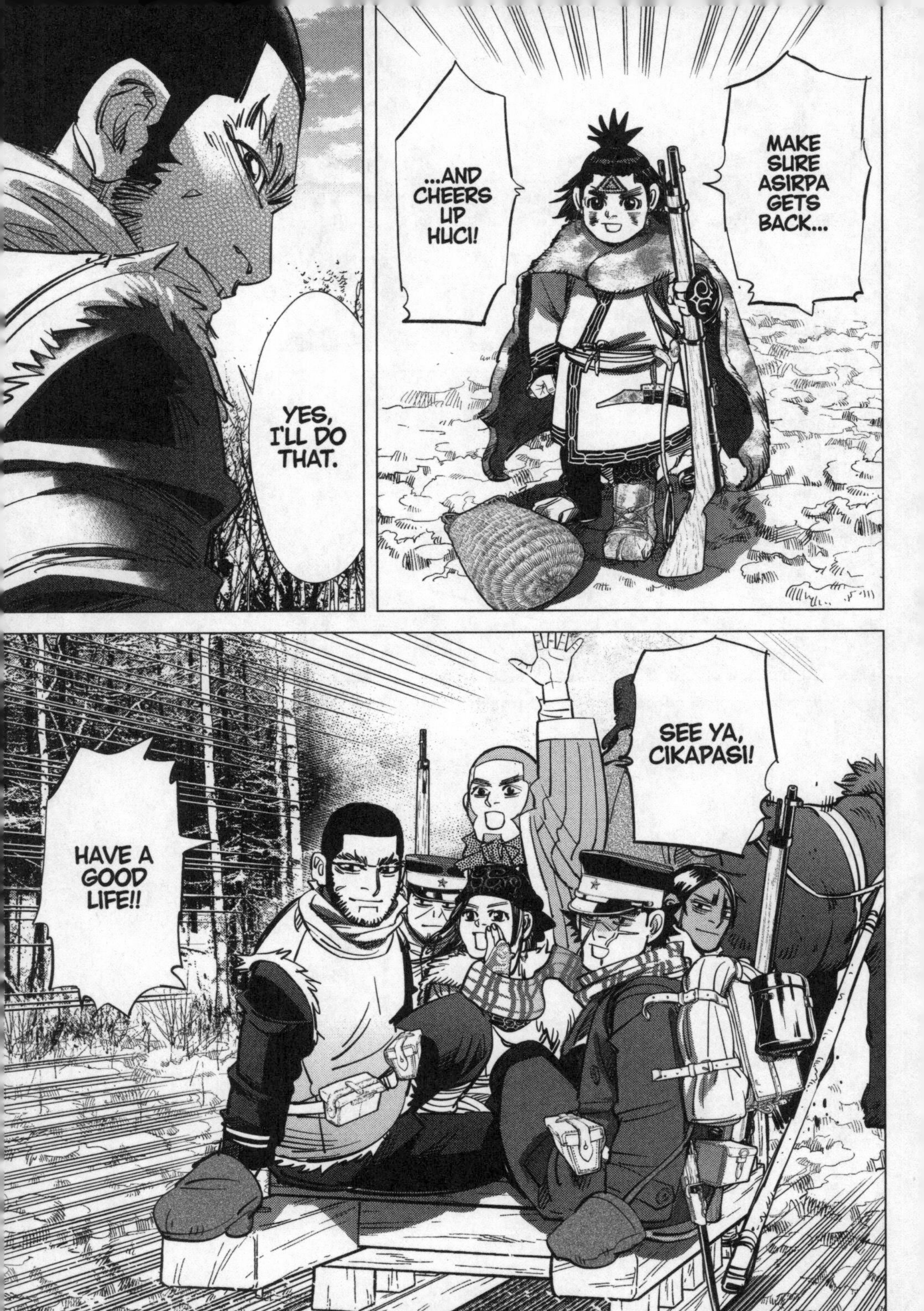
MAKE SURE ASIRPA GETS BACK...
...AND CHEERS UP HUCI!
YES, I'LL DO THAT.
SEE YA, CIKAPASI!
HAVE A GOOD LIFE!!

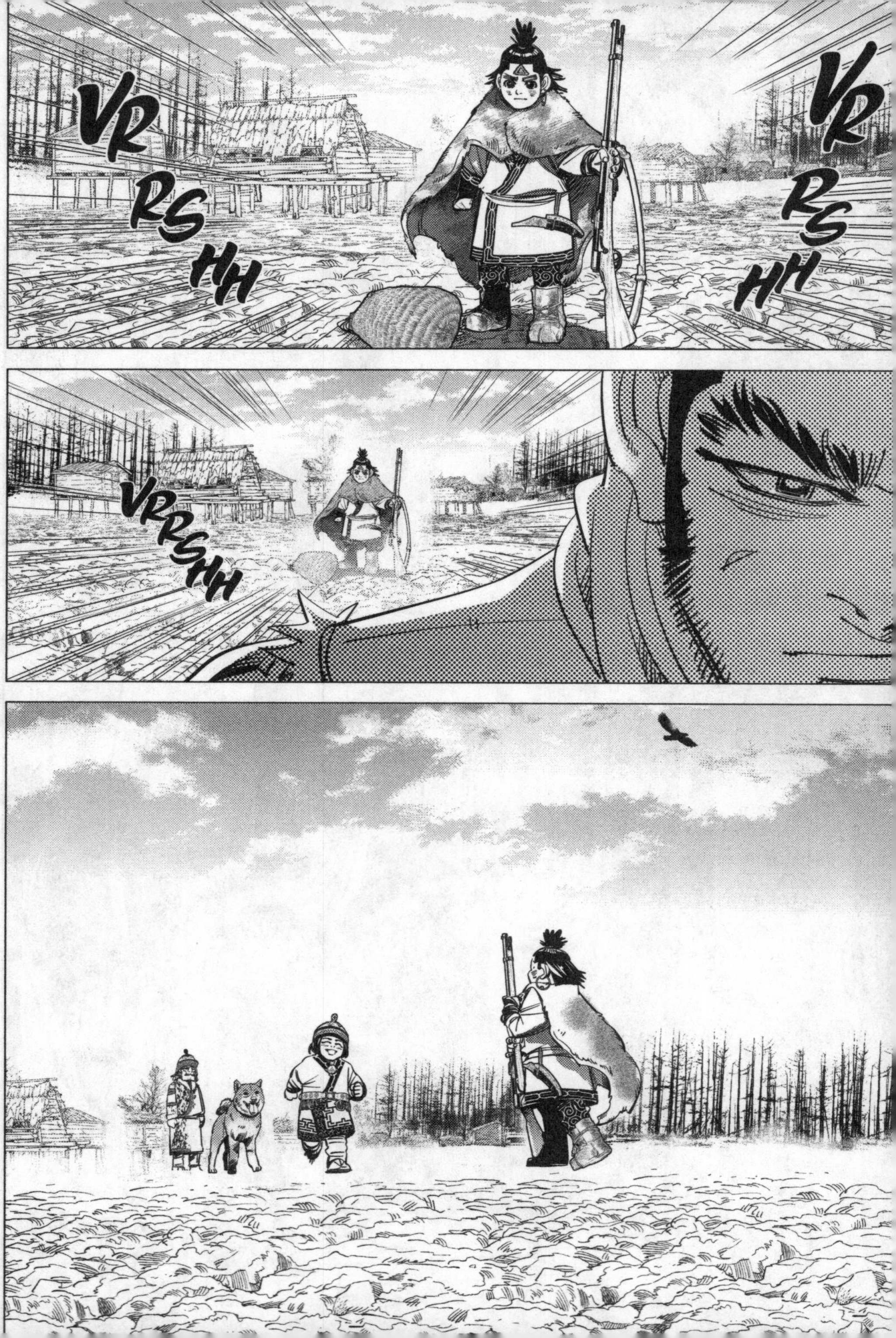
VRRSHH
VRRSHH
VRRRSHH

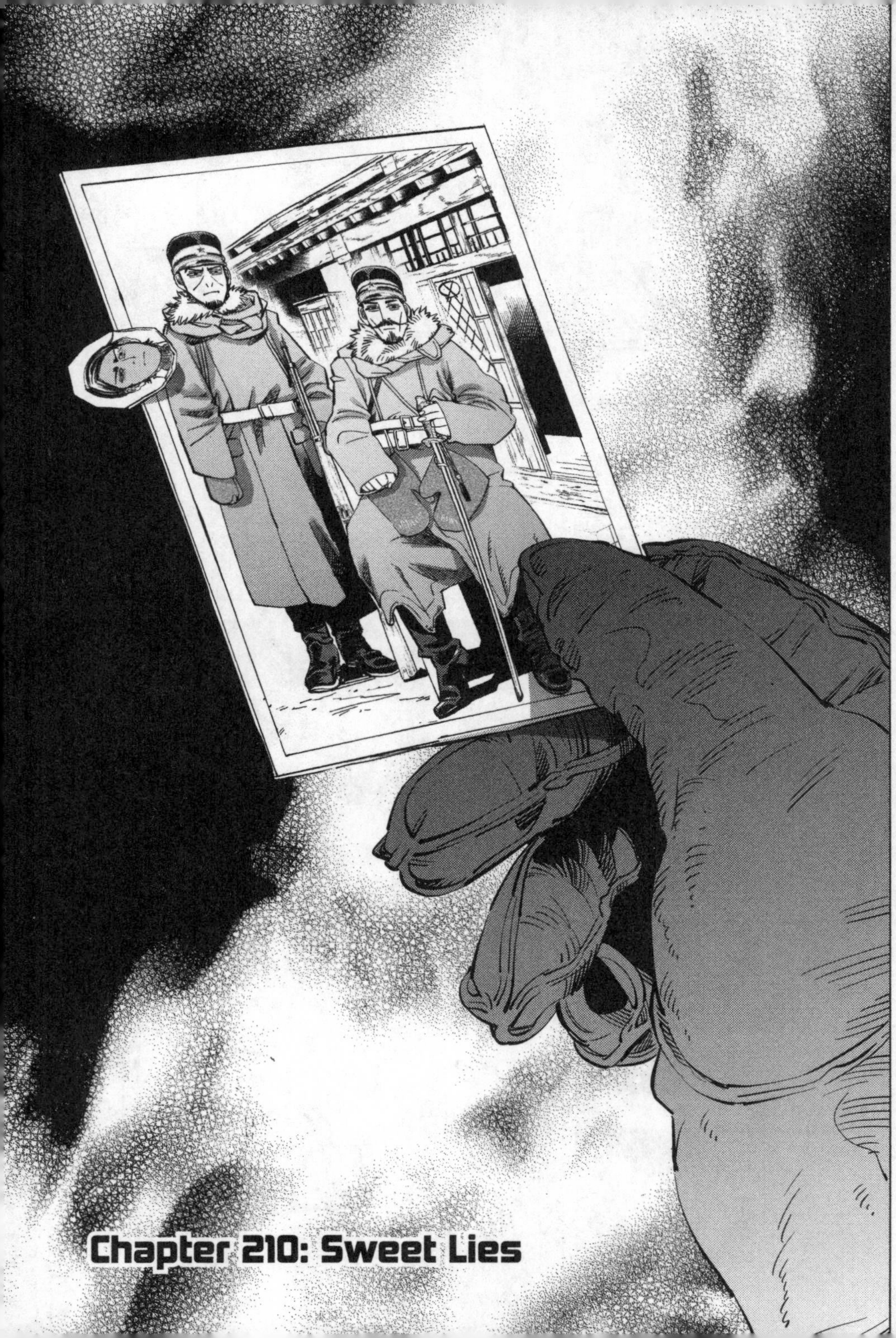
Chapter 210: Sweet Lies

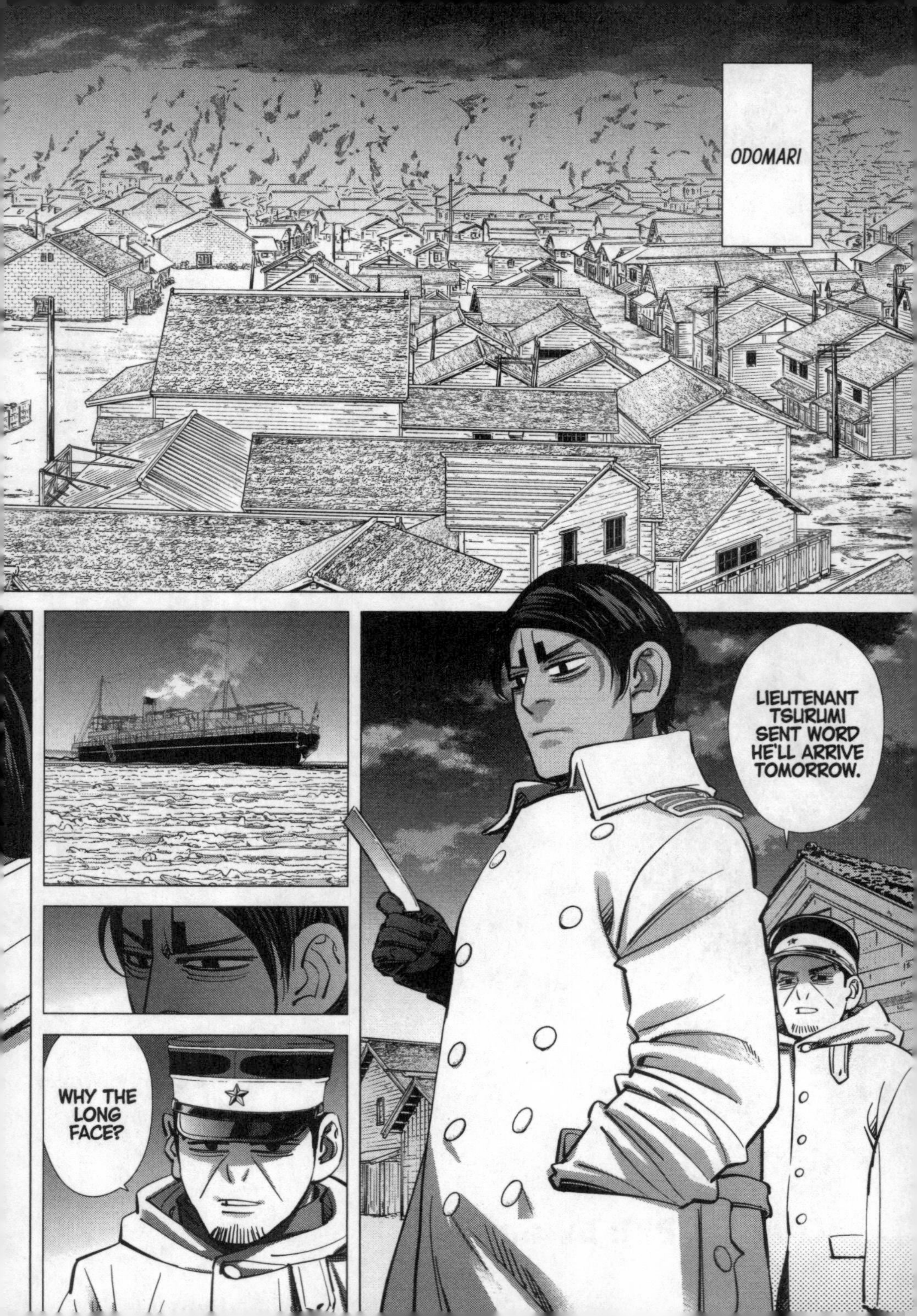
ODOMARI
LIEUTENANT TSURUMI SENT WORD HE'LL ARRIVE TOMORROW.
WHY THE LONG FACE?

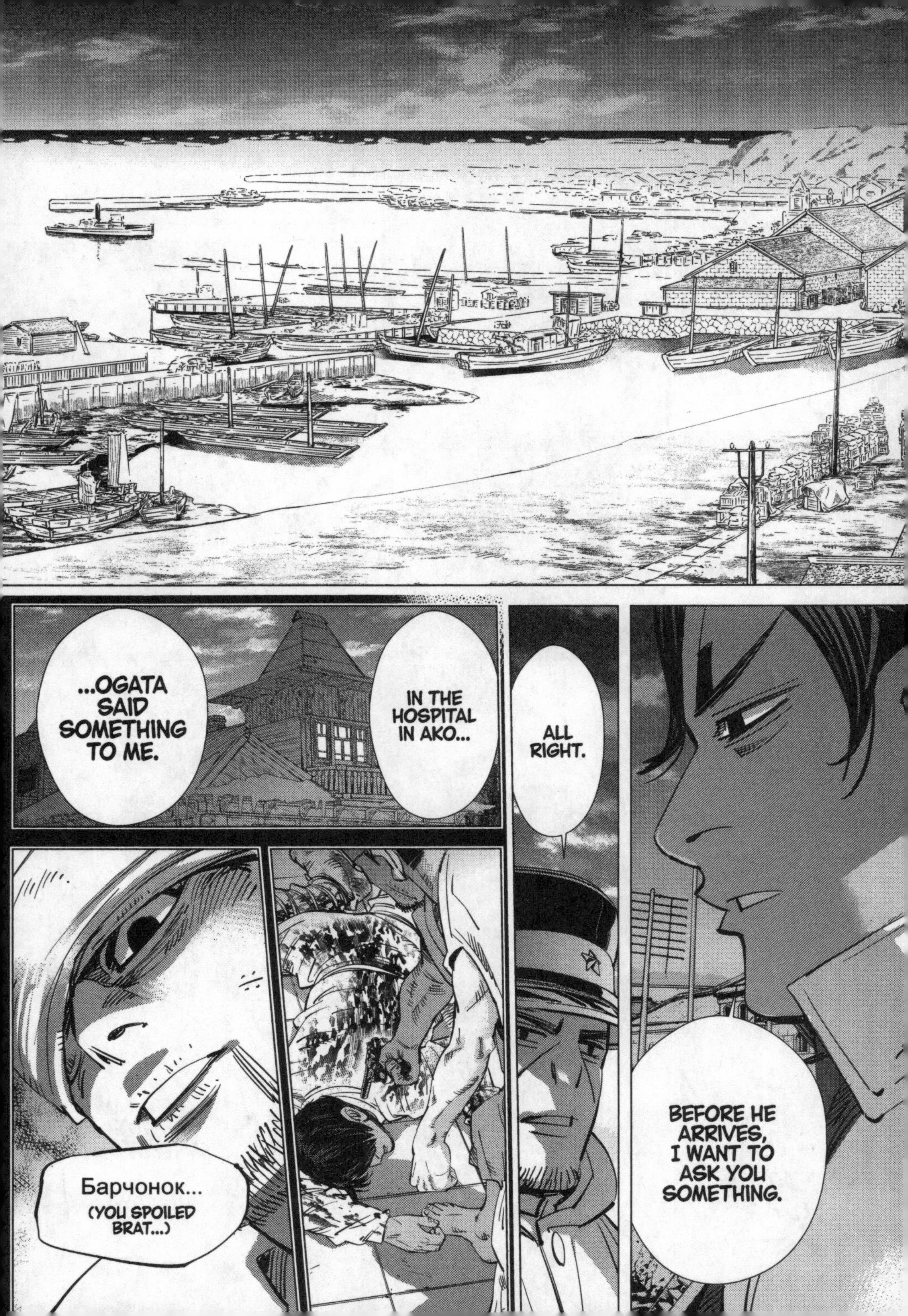
BEFORE HE ARRIVES, I WANT TO ASK YOU SOMETHING.
ALL RIGHT.
IN THE HOSPITAL IN AKO...
...OGATA SAID SOMETHING TO ME.
Барчонок...
(YOU SPOILED BRAT...)

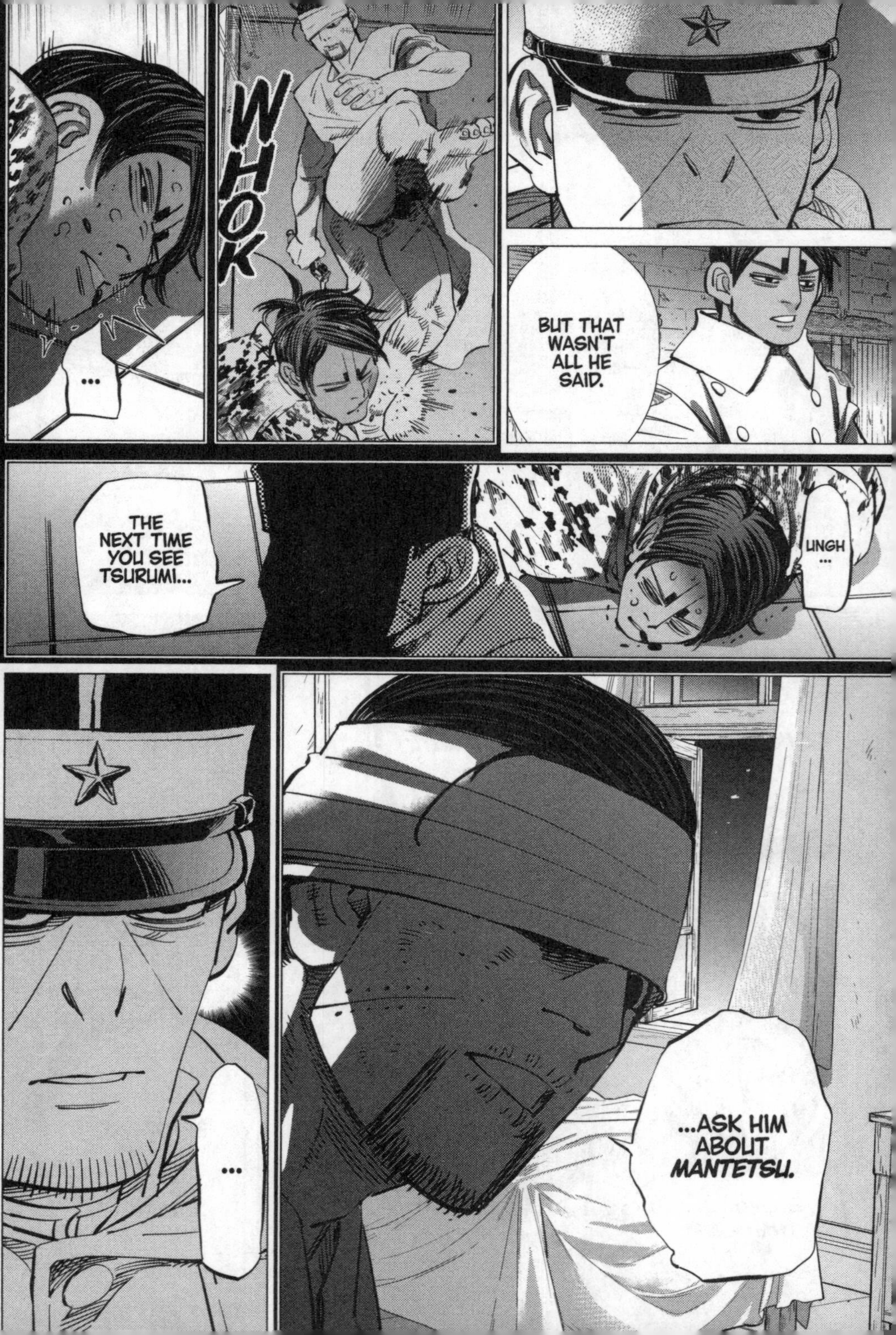
BUT THAT WASN'T ALL HE SAID.
WHOK
...
UNGH ...
THE NEXT TIME YOU SEE TSURUMI...
...ASK HIM ABOUT MANTETSU.
...

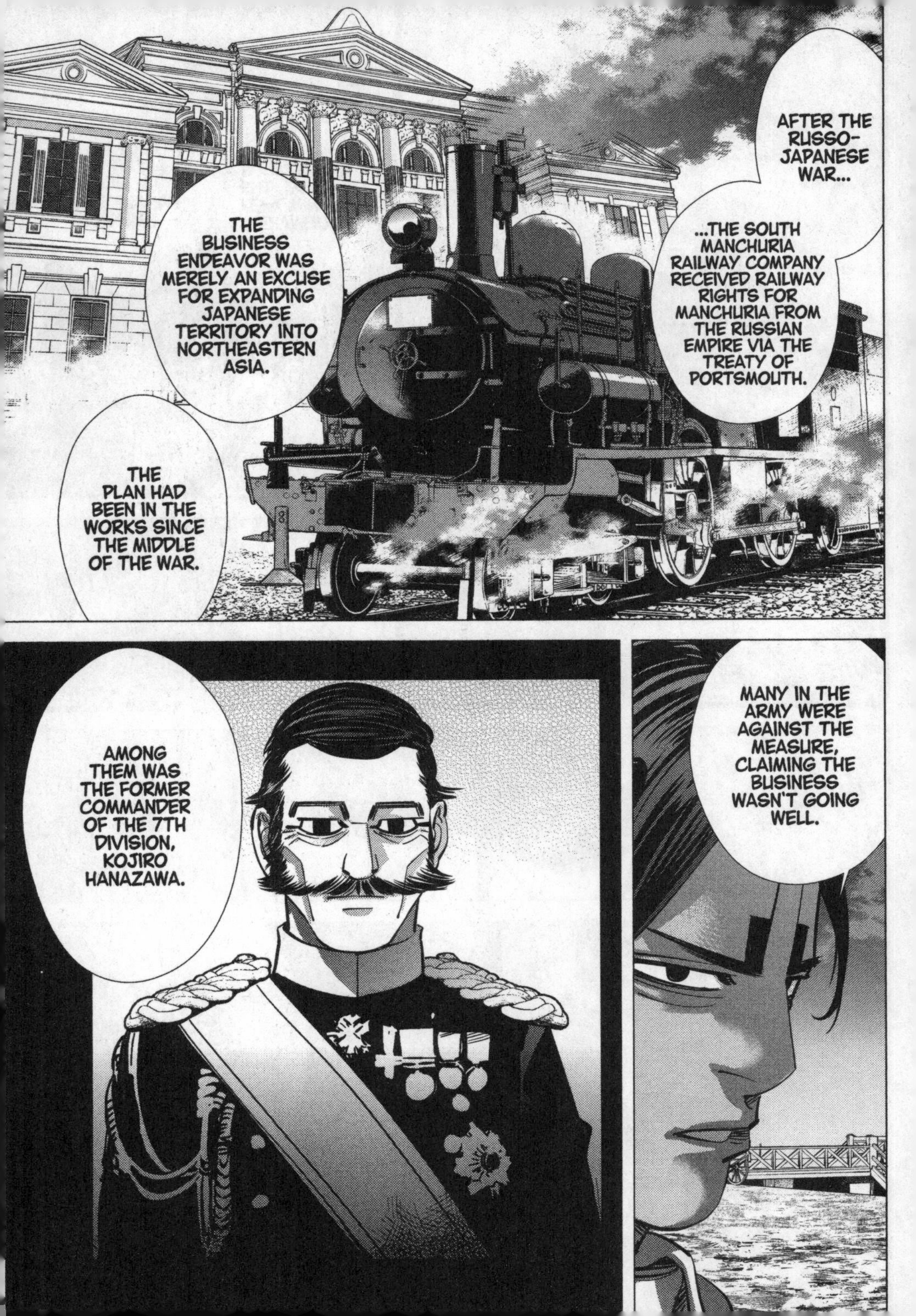
AFTER THE RUSSO-JAPANESE WAR...
...THE SOUTH MANCHURIA RAILWAY COMPANY RECEIVED RAILWAY RIGHTS FOR MANCHURIA FROM THE RUSSIAN EMPIRE VIA THE TREATY OF PORTSMOUTH.
THE BUSINESS ENDEAVOR WAS MERELY AN EXCUSE FOR EXPANDING JAPANESE TERRITORY INTO NORTHEASTERN ASIA.
THE PLAN HAD BEEN IN THE WORKS SINCE THE MIDDLE OF THE WAR.
MANY IN THE ARMY WERE AGAINST THE MEASURE, CLAIMING THE BUSINESS WASN'T GOING WELL.
AMONG THEM WAS THE FORMER COMMANDER OF THE 7TH DIVISION, KOJIRO HANAZAWA.

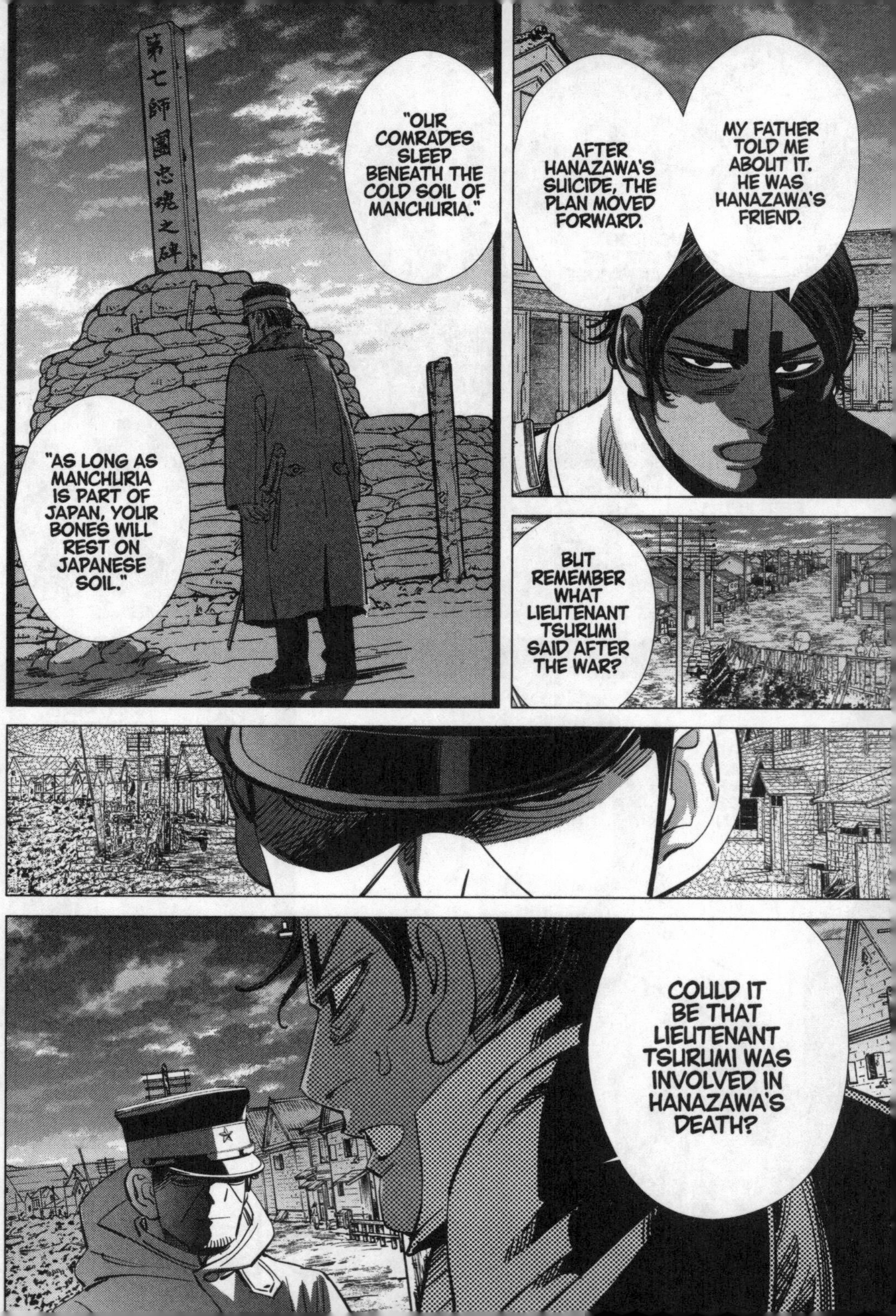
MY FATHER TOLD ME ABOUT IT. HE WAS HANAZAWA'S FRIEND.
AFTER HANAZAWA'S SUICIDE, THE PLAN MOVED FORWARD.
BUT REMEMBER WHAT LIEUTENANT TSURUMI SAID AFTER THE WAR?
第七師團忠魂之碑
"OUR COMRADES SLEEP BENEATH THE COLD SOIL OF MANCHURIA."
"AS LONG AS MANCHURIA IS PART OF JAPAN, YOUR BONES WILL REST ON JAPANESE SOIL."
COULD IT BE THAT LIEUTENANT TSURUMI WAS INVOLVED IN HANAZAWA'S DEATH?

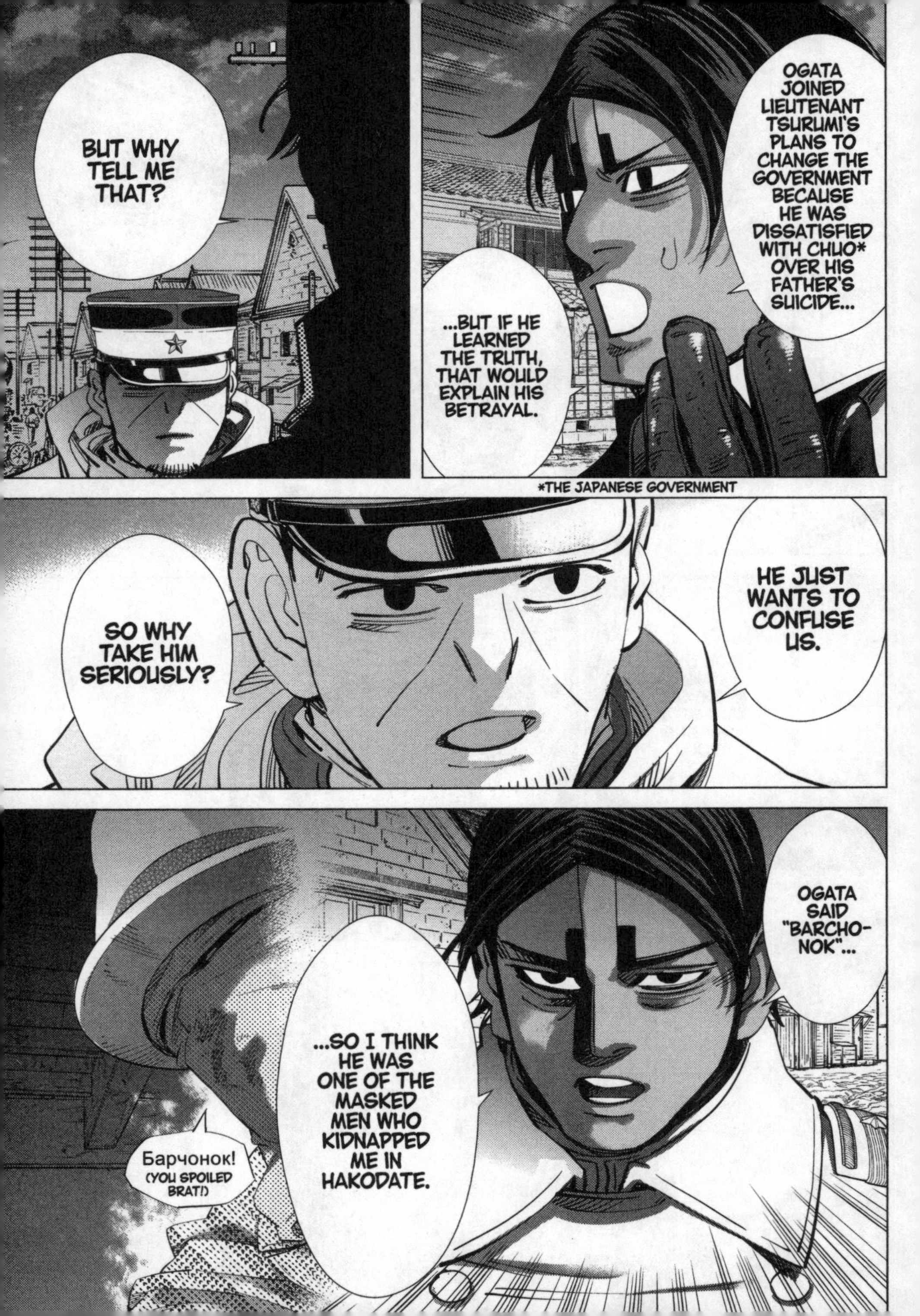
OGATA JOINED LIEUTENANT TSURUMI'S PLANS TO CHANGE THE GOVERNMENT BECAUSE HE WAS DISSATISFIED WITH CHUO* OVER HIS FATHER'S SUICIDE...
...BUT IF HE LEARNED THE TRUTH, THAT WOULD EXPLAIN HIS BETRAYAL.
BUT WHY TELL ME THAT?
*THE JAPANESE GOVERNMENT
HE JUST WANTS TO CONFUSE US.
SO WHY TAKE HIM SERIOUSLY?
OGATA SAID "BARCHO-NOK"...
...SO I THINK HE WAS ONE OF THE MASKED MEN WHO KIDNAPPED ME IN HAKODATE.
Барчонок! (YOU SPOILED BRAT!)

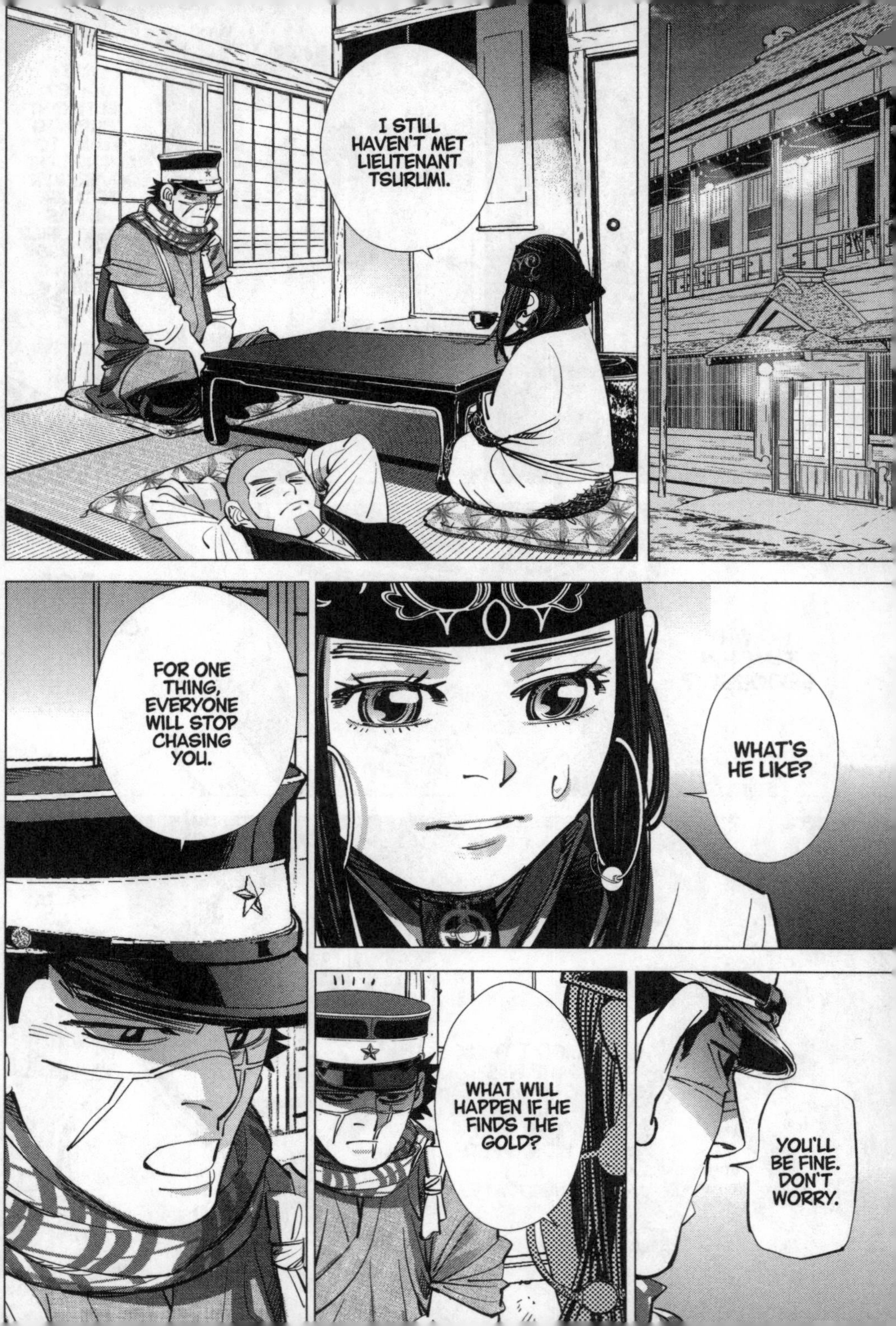
I STILL HAVEN'T MET LIEUTENANT TSURUMI.
WHAT'S HE LIKE?
YOU'LL BE FINE. DON'T WORRY.
WHAT WILL HAPPEN IF HE FINDS THE GOLD?
FOR ONE THING, EVERYONE WILL STOP CHASING YOU.

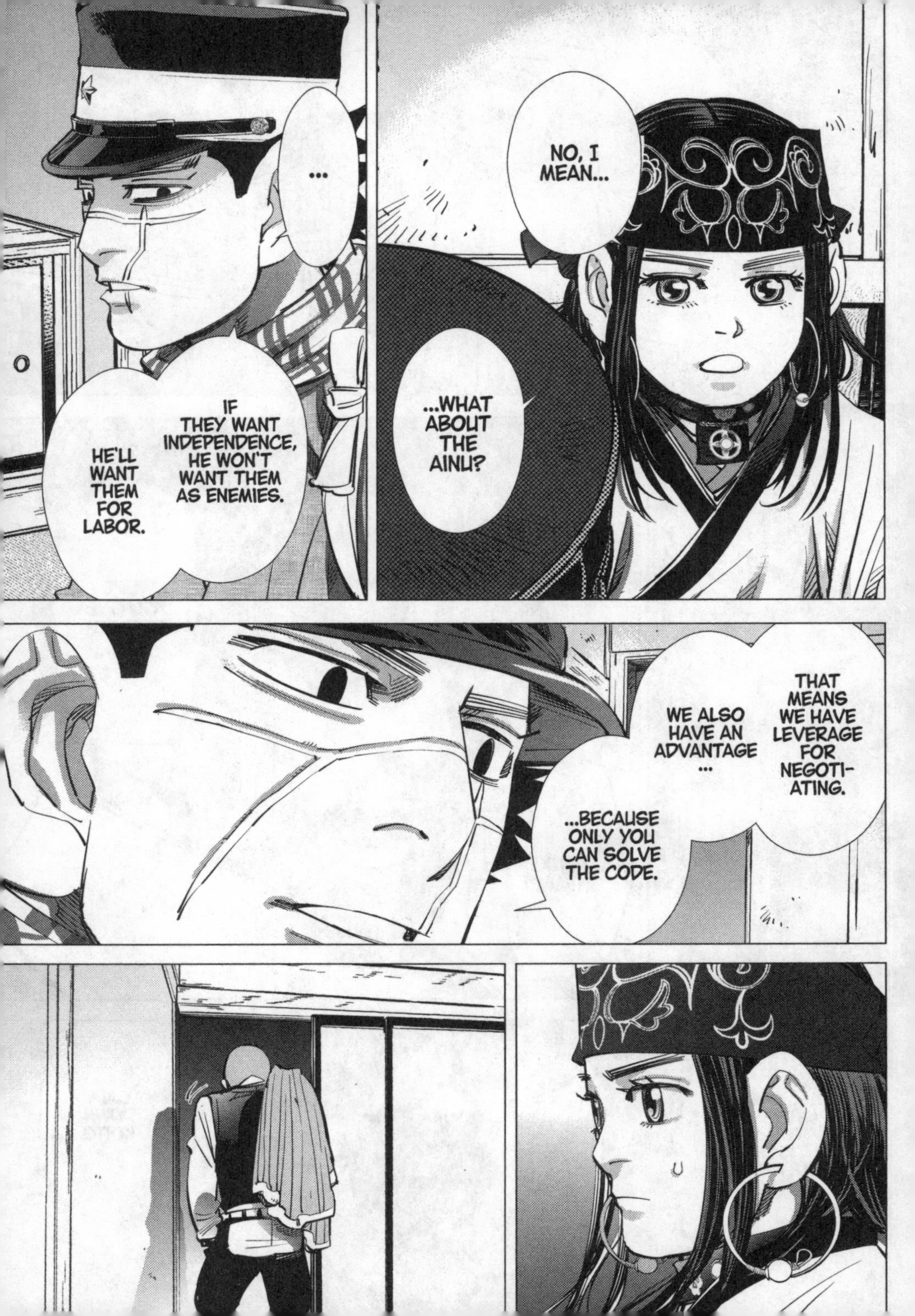
NO, I MEAN...
...WHAT ABOUT THE AINU?
...
IF THEY WANT INDEPENDENCE, HE WON'T WANT THEM AS ENEMIES.
HE'LL WANT THEM FOR LABOR.
THAT MEANS WE HAVE LEVERAGE FOR NEGOTI-ATING.
WE ALSO HAVE AN ADVANTAGE...
...BECAUSE ONLY YOU CAN SOLVE THE CODE.

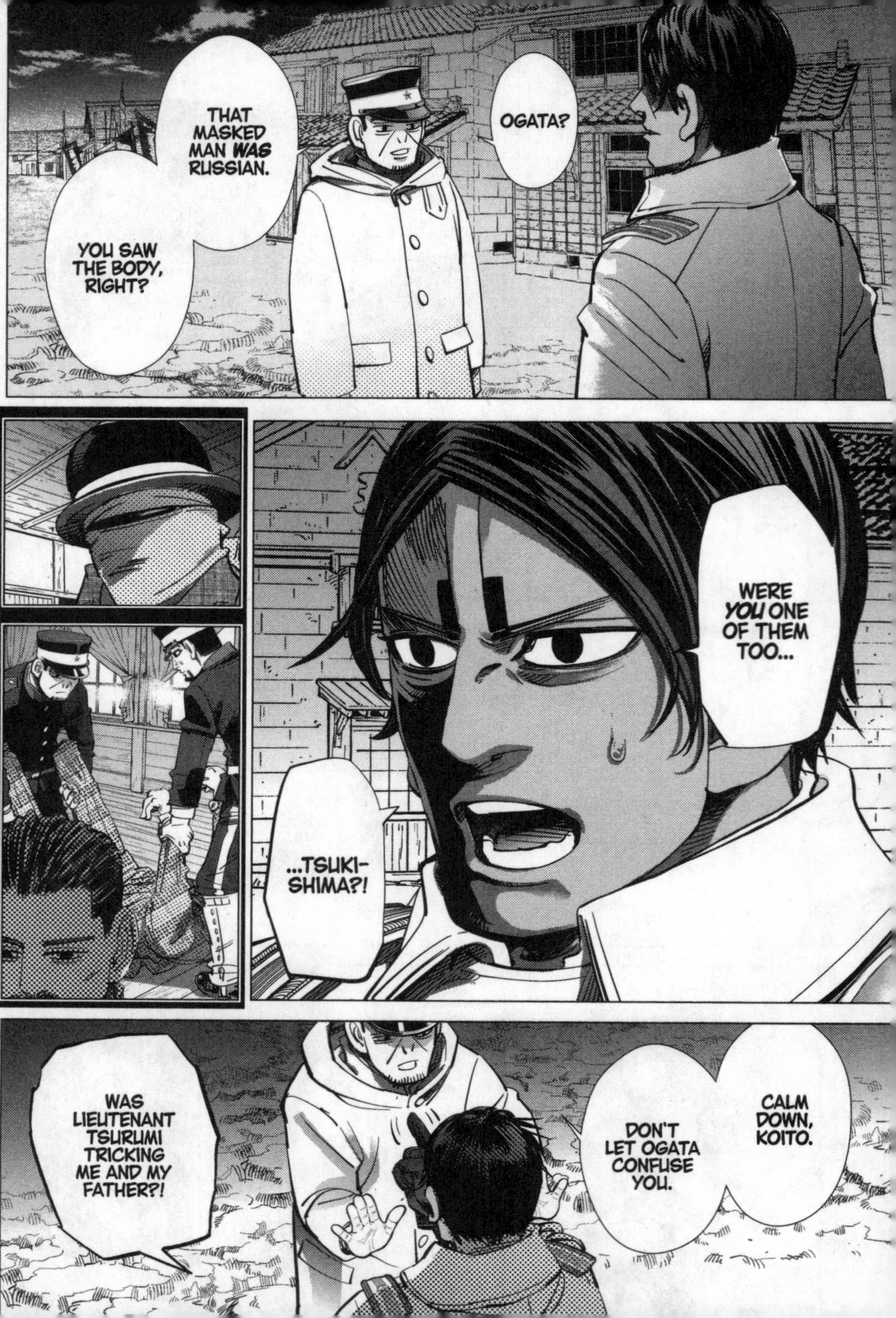
OGATA?
THAT MASKED MAN WAS RUSSIAN.
YOU SAW THE BODY, RIGHT?
WERE YOU ONE OF THEM TOO...
...TSUKI-SHIMA?!
CALM DOWN, KOITO.
DON'T LET OGATA CONFUSE YOU.
WAS LIEUTENANT TSURUMI TRICKING ME AND MY FATHER?!

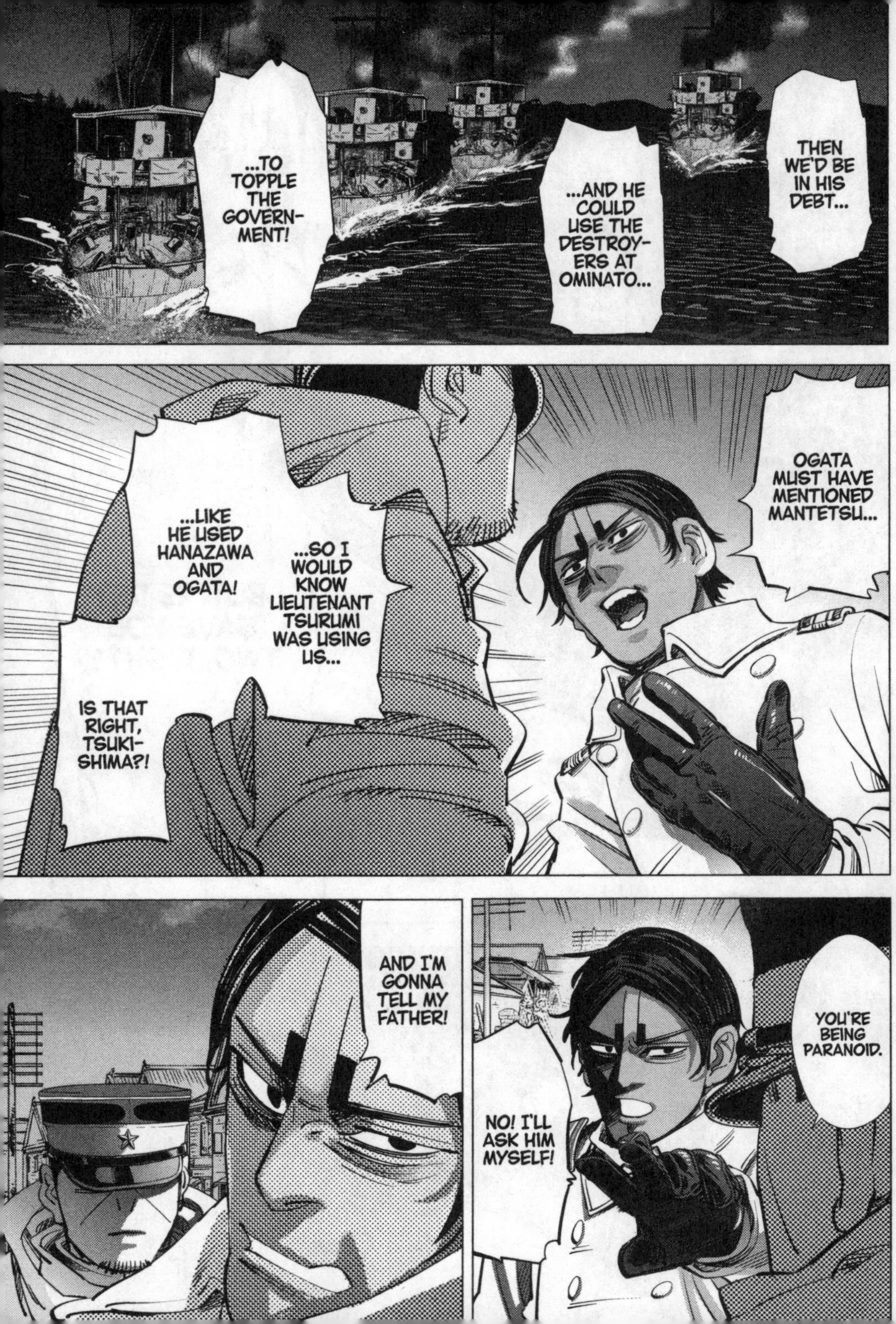
THEN WE'D BE IN HIS DEBT...
...AND HE COULD USE THE DESTROYERS AT OMINATO...
...TO TOPPLE THE GOVERNMENT!
OGATA MUST HAVE MENTIONED MANTETSU...
...SO I WOULD KNOW LIEUTENANT TSURUMI WAS USING US...
...LIKE HE USED HANAZAWA AND OGATA!
IS THAT RIGHT, TSUKISHIMA?!
YOU'RE BEING PARANOID.
NO! I'LL ASK HIM MYSELF!
AND I'M GONNA TELL MY FATHER!

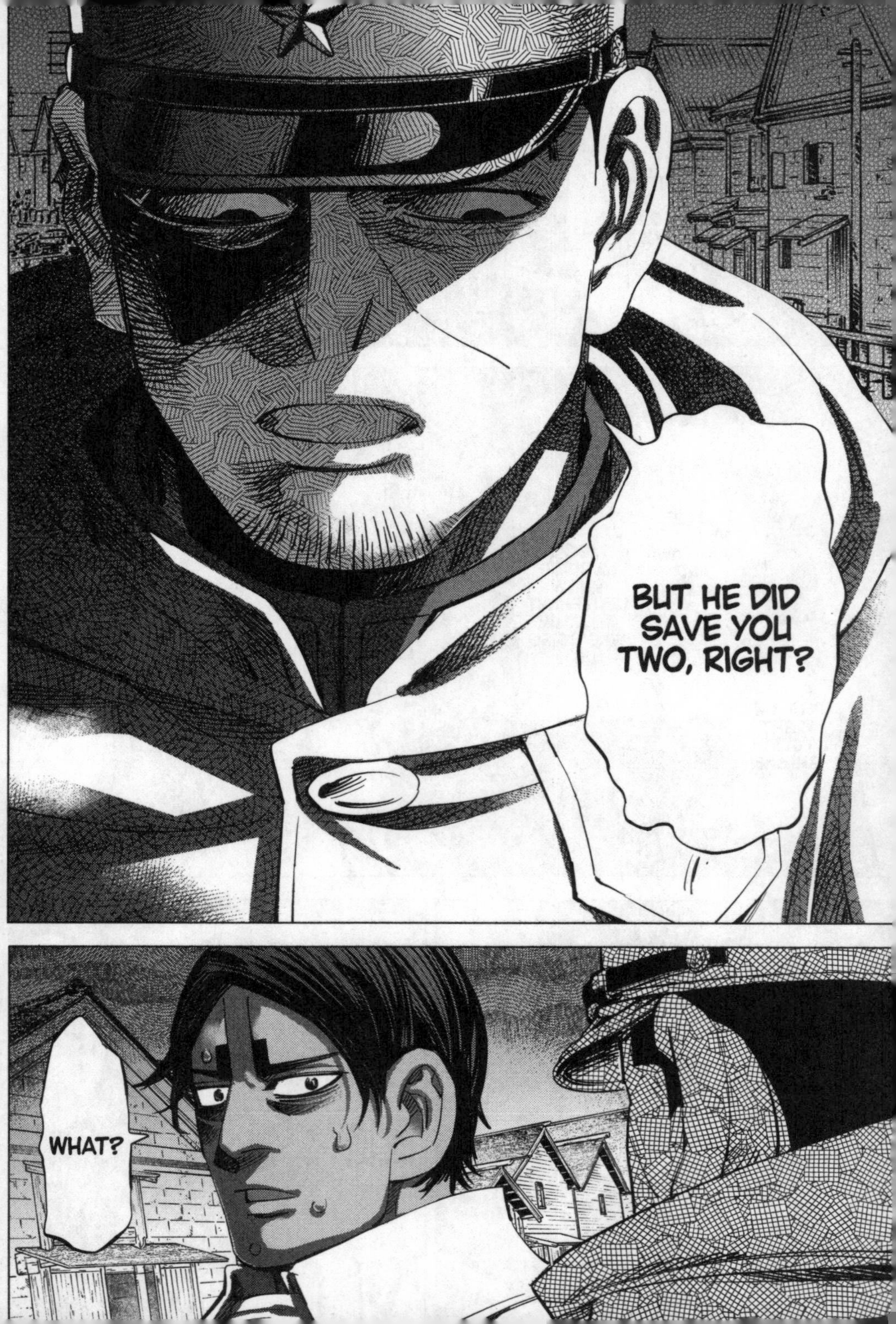
BUT HE DID SAVE YOU TWO, RIGHT?
WHAT?

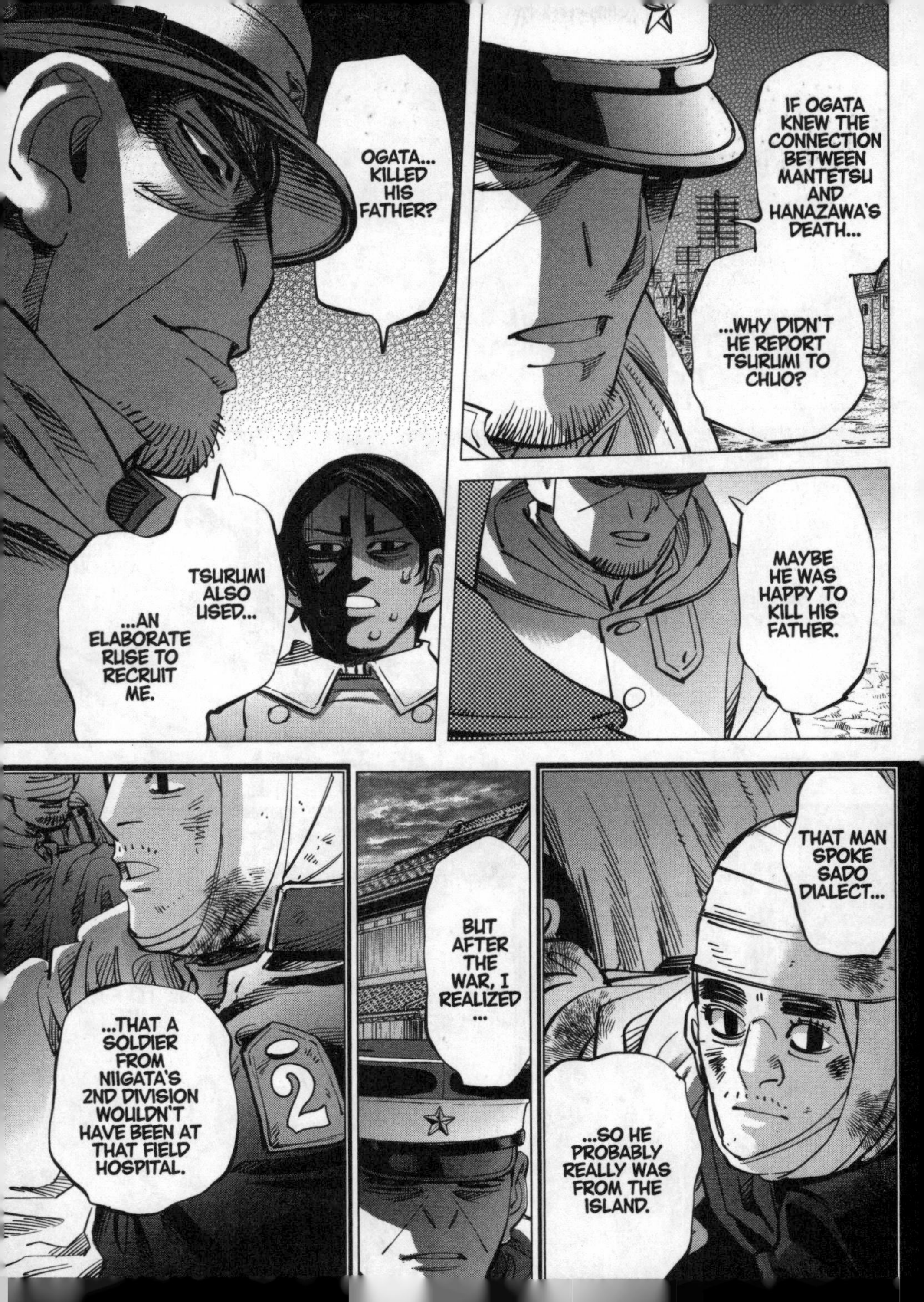

IF OGATA KNEW THE CONNECTION BETWEEN MANTETSU AND HANAZAWA'S DEATH...
...WHY DIDN'T HE REPORT TSURUMI TO CHUO?
MAYBE HE WAS HAPPY TO KILL HIS FATHER.
OGATA... KILLED HIS FATHER?
TSURUMI ALSO USED...
...AN ELABORATE RUSE TO RECRUIT ME.
THAT MAN SPOKE SADO DIALECT...
...SO HE PROBABLY REALLY WAS FROM THE ISLAND.
BUT AFTER THE WAR, I REALIZED ...
...THAT A SOLDIER FROM NIIGATA'S 2ND DIVISION WOULDN'T HAVE BEEN AT THAT FIELD HOSPITAL.

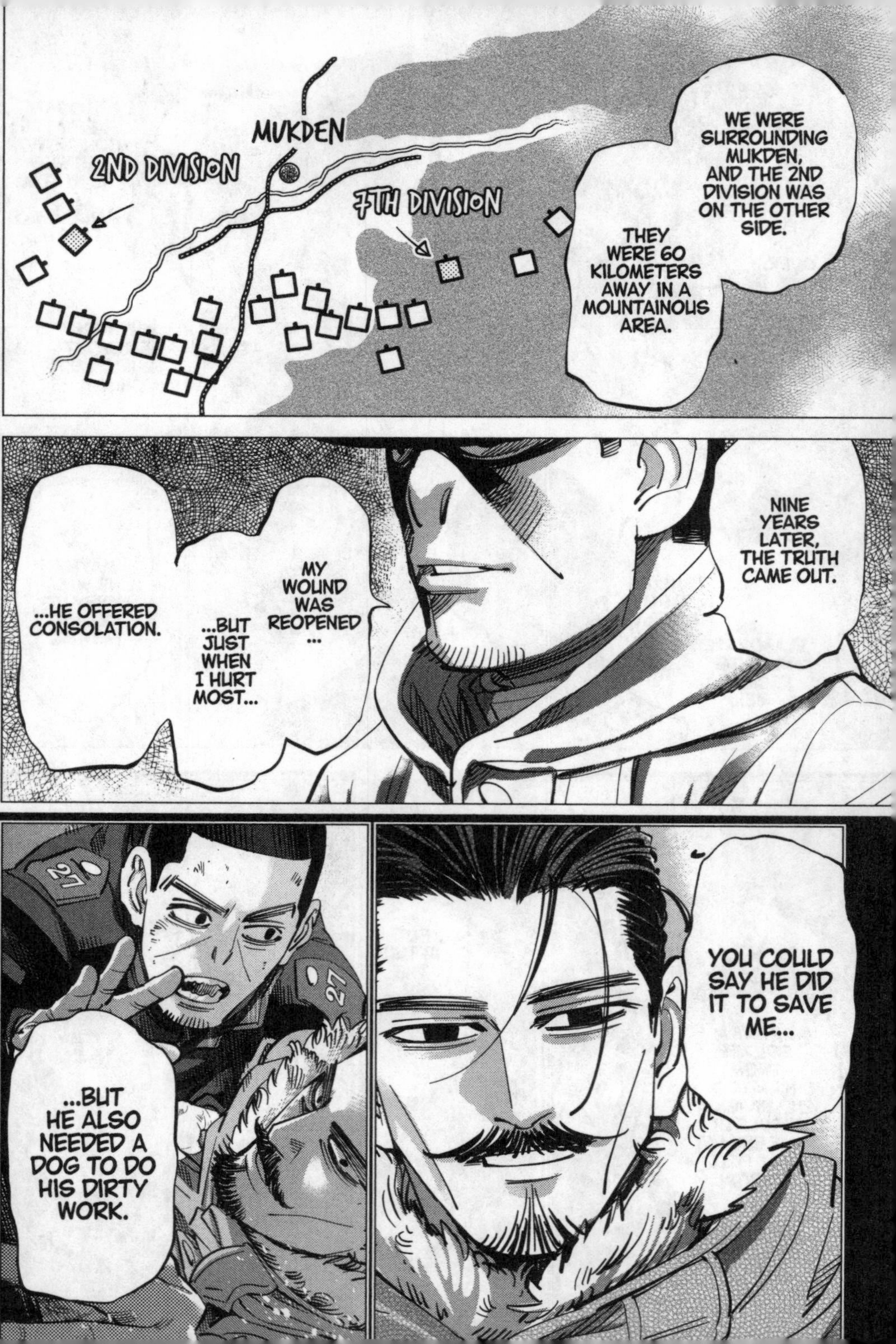
WE WERE SURROUNDING MUKDEN, AND THE 2ND DIVISION WAS ON THE OTHER SIDE.
THEY WERE 60 KILOMETERS AWAY IN A MOUNTAINOUS AREA.
MUKDEN
2ND DIVISION
7TH DIVISION
NINE YEARS LATER, THE TRUTH CAME OUT.
MY WOUND WAS REOPENED...
...BUT JUST WHEN I HURT MOST...
...HE OFFERED CONSOLATION.
YOU COULD SAY HE DID IT TO SAVE ME...
...BUT HE ALSO NEEDED A DOG TO DO HIS DIRTY WORK.

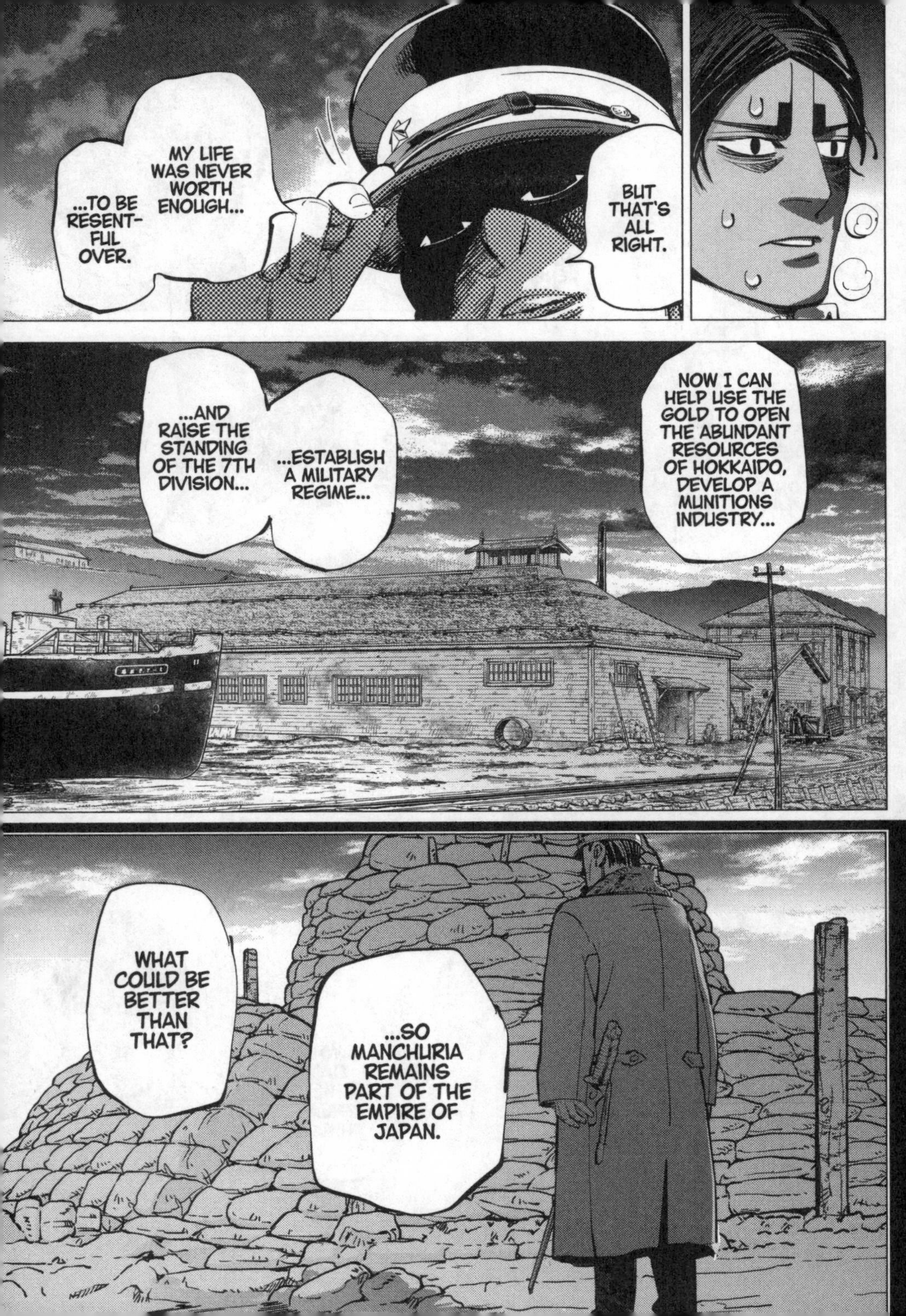
BUT THAT'S ALL RIGHT.
MY LIFE WAS NEVER WORTH ENOUGH...
...TO BE RESENTFUL OVER.
NOW I CAN HELP USE THE GOLD TO OPEN THE ABUNDANT RESOURCES OF HOKKAIDO, DEVELOP A MUNITIONS INDUSTRY...
...ESTABLISH A MILITARY REGIME...
...AND RAISE THE STANDING OF THE 7TH DIVISION...
...SO MANCHURIA REMAINS PART OF THE EMPIRE OF JAPAN.
WHAT COULD BE BETTER THAN THAT?

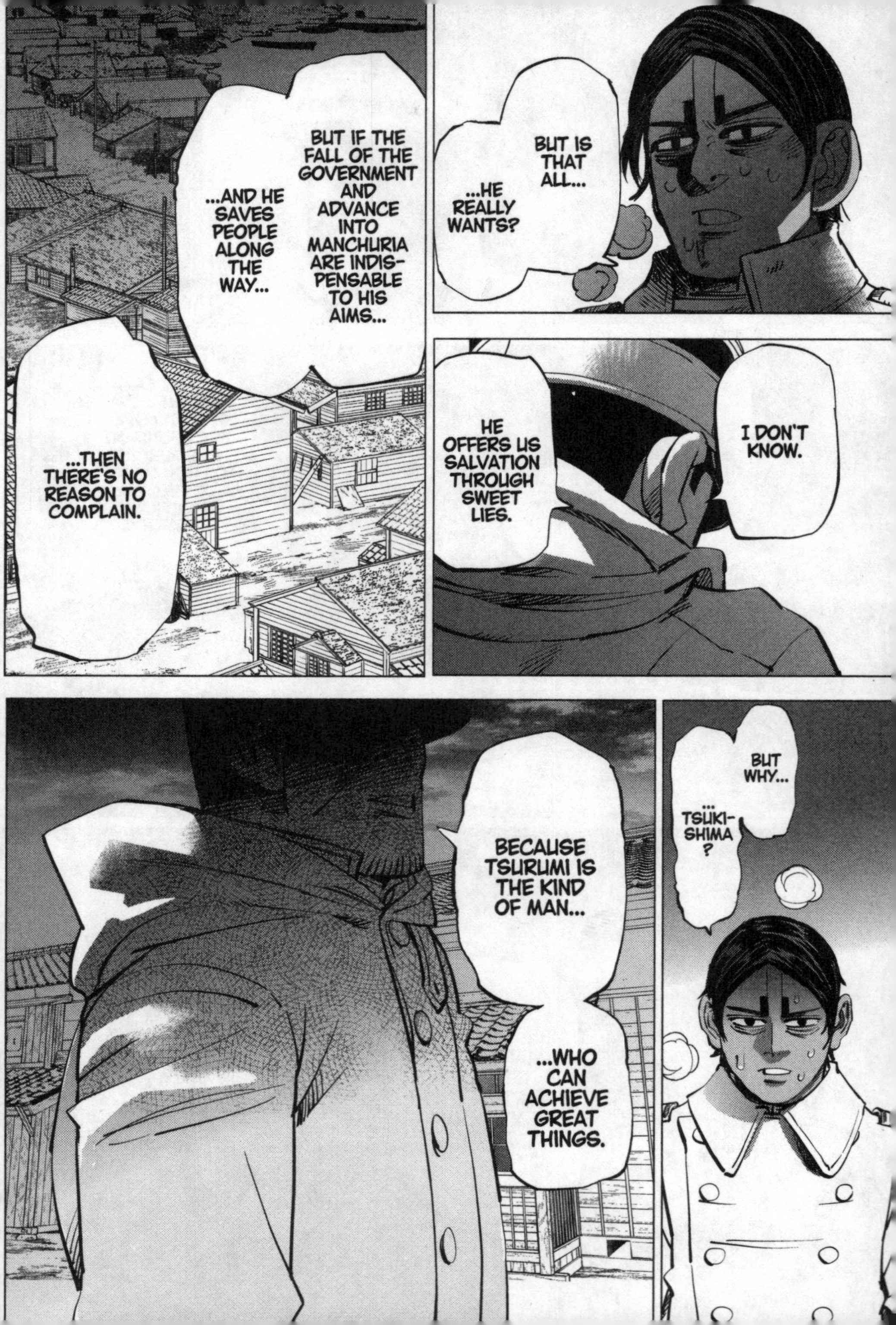
BUT IS THAT ALL...
...HE REALLY WANTS?
I DON'T KNOW.
HE OFFERS US SALVATION THROUGH SWEET LIES.
BUT IF THE FALL OF THE GOVERNMENT AND ADVANCE INTO MANCHURIA ARE INDIS-PENSABLE TO HIS AIMS...
...AND HE SAVES PEOPLE ALONG THE WAY...
...THEN THERE'S NO REASON TO COMPLAIN.
BUT WHY...
...TSUKISHIMA?
BECAUSE TSURUMI IS THE KIND OF MAN...
...WHO CAN ACHIEVE GREAT THINGS.

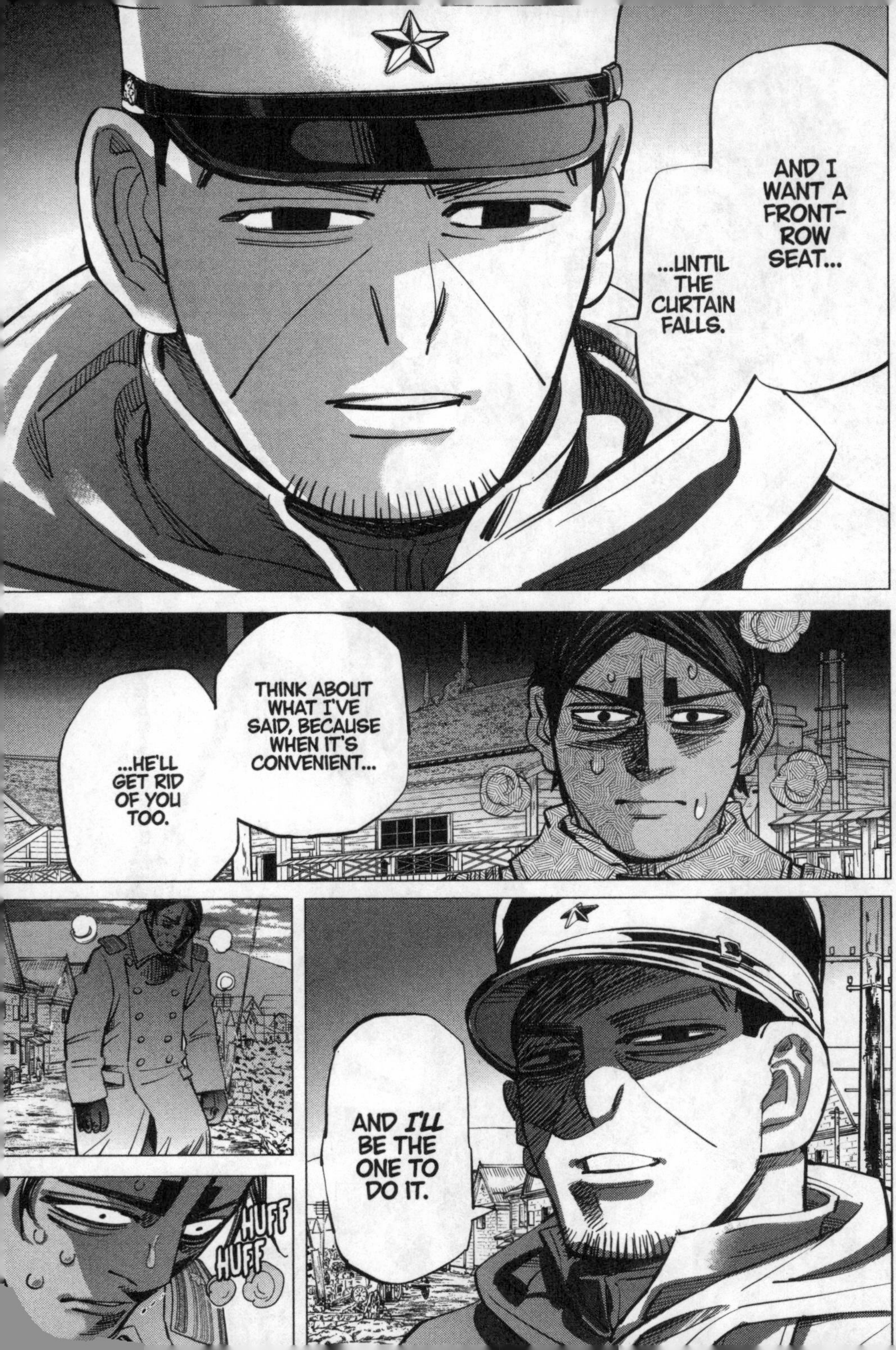
AND I WANT A FRONT-ROW SEAT...
...UNTIL THE CURTAIN FALLS.
THINK ABOUT WHAT I'VE SAID, BECAUSE WHEN IT'S CONVENIENT...
...HE'LL GET RID OF YOU TOO.
AND I'LL BE THE ONE TO DO IT.
HUFF
HUFF

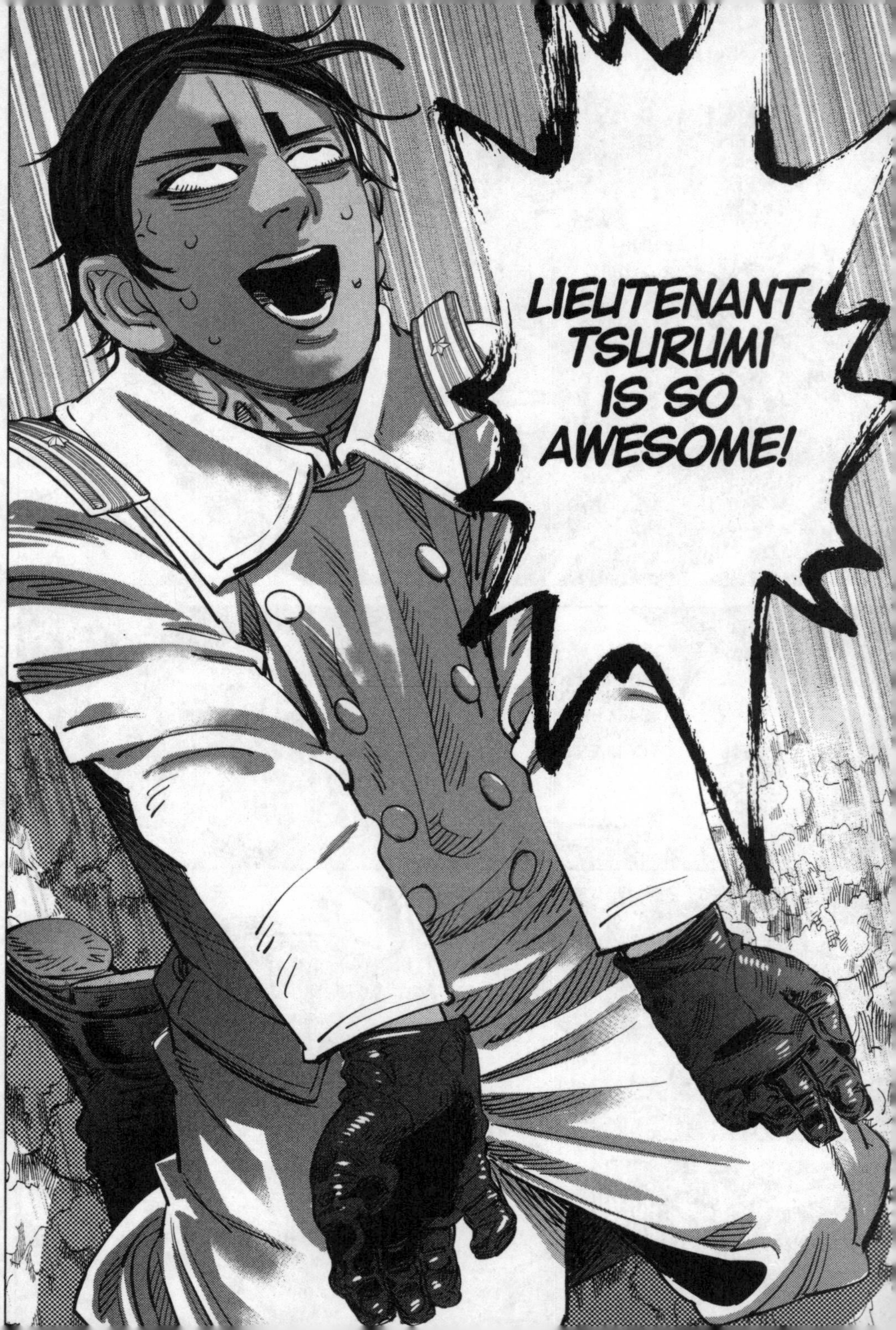
LIEUTENANT TSURUMI IS SO AWESOME!

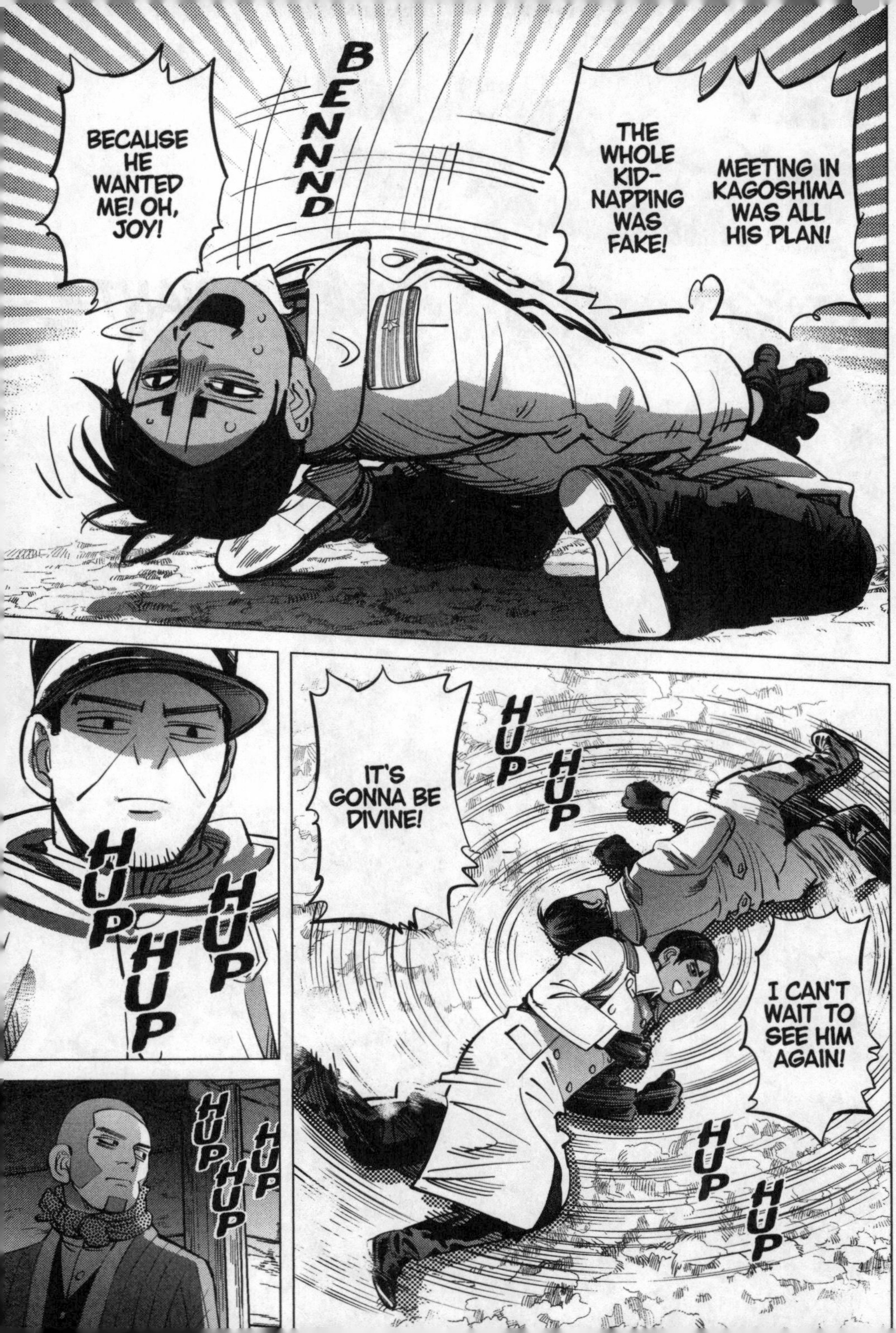
MEETING IN KAGOSHIMA WAS ALL HIS PLAN!
THE WHOLE KID-NAPPING WAS FAKE!
BENNND
BECAUSE HE WANTED ME! OH, JOY!
HUP HUP
HUP HUP
IT'S GONNA BE DIVINE!
I CAN'T WAIT TO SEE HIM AGAIN!
HUP HUP
HUP HUP
HUP HUP
HUP HUP
HUP HUP
HUP HUP

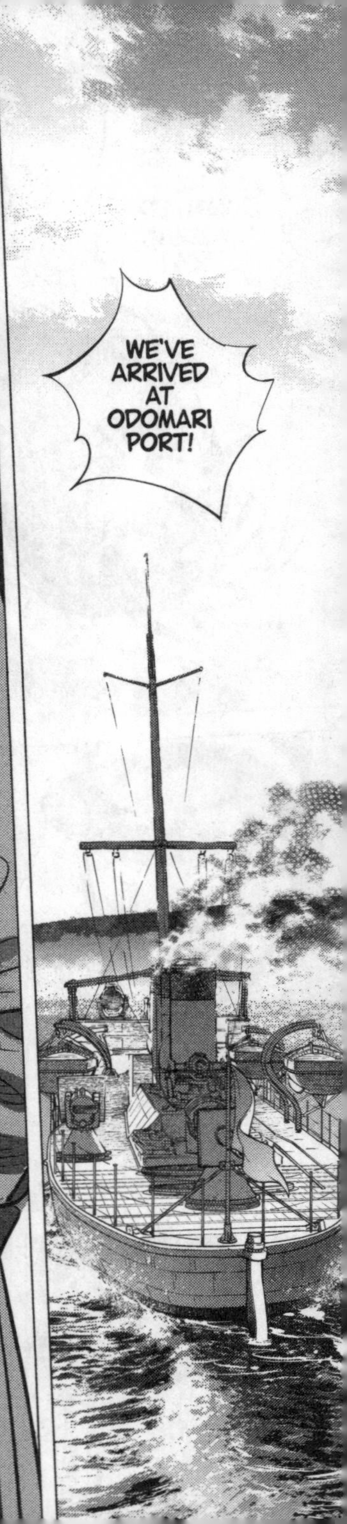
WE'VE ARRIVED AT ODOMARI PORT!
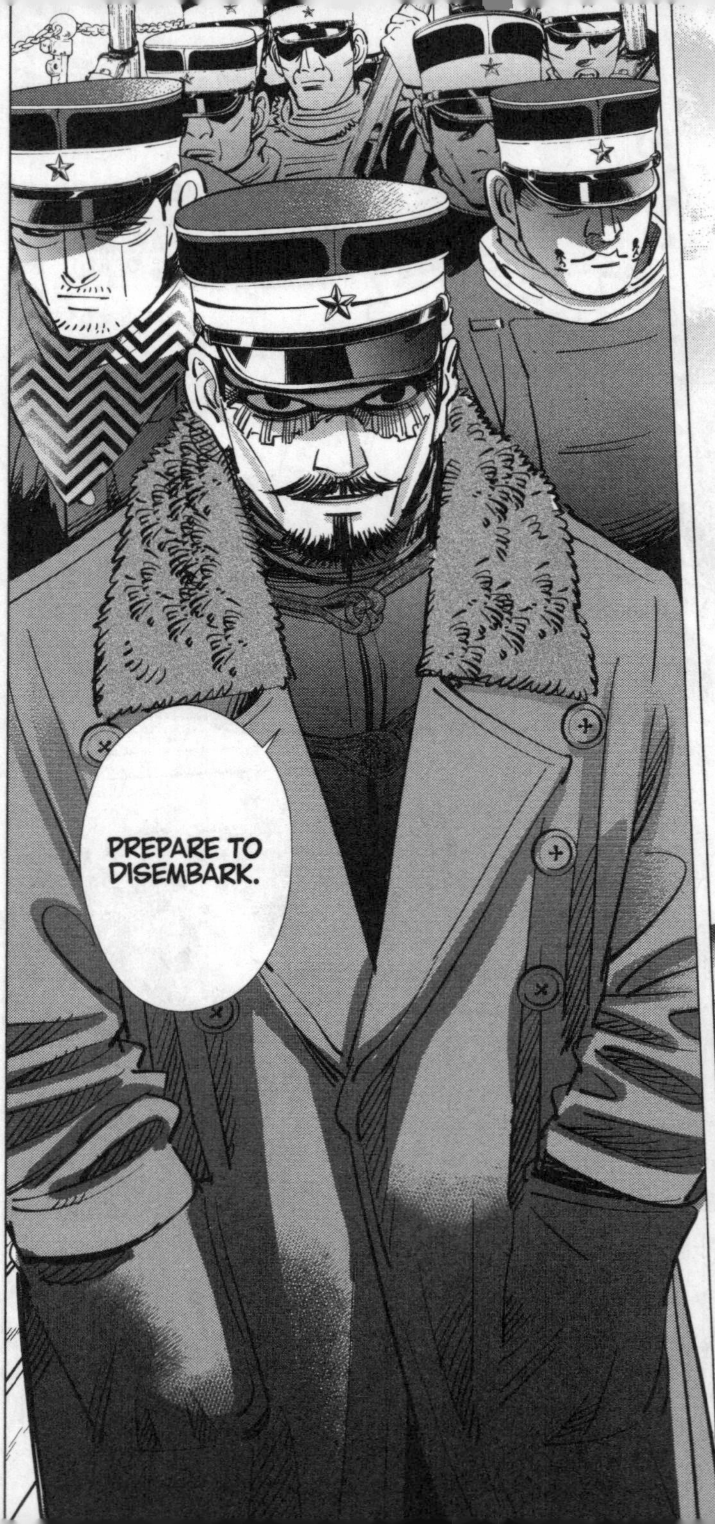
PREPARE TO DISEMBARK.

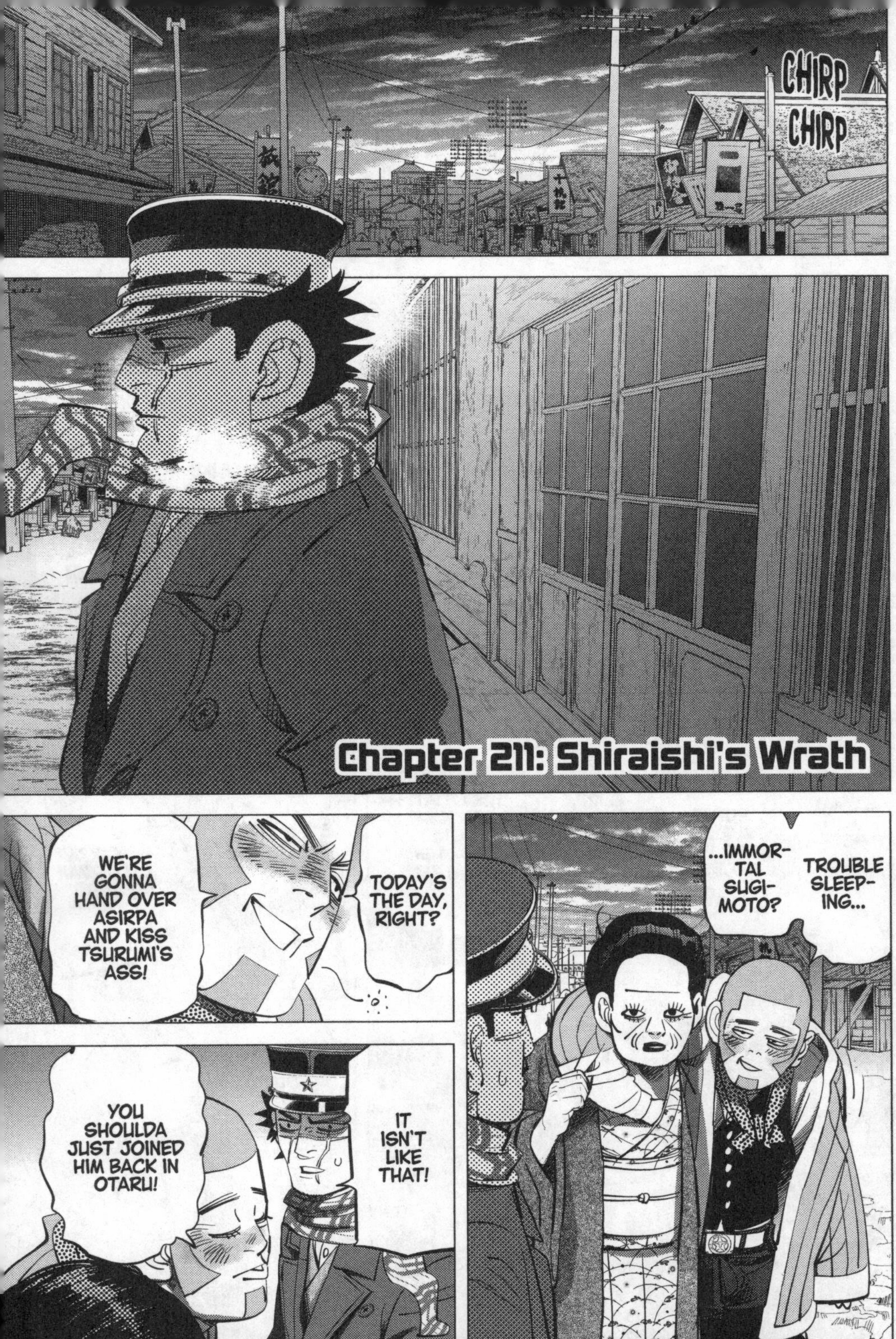
CHIRP
CHIRP
Chapter 211: Shiraishi's Wrath
TROUBLE SLEEPING...
...IMMORTAL SUGIMOTO?
TODAY'S THE DAY, RIGHT?
WE'RE GONNA HAND OVER ASIRPA AND KISS TSURUMI'S ASS!
IT ISN'T LIKE THAT!
YOU SHOULDA JUST JOINED HIM BACK IN OTARU!

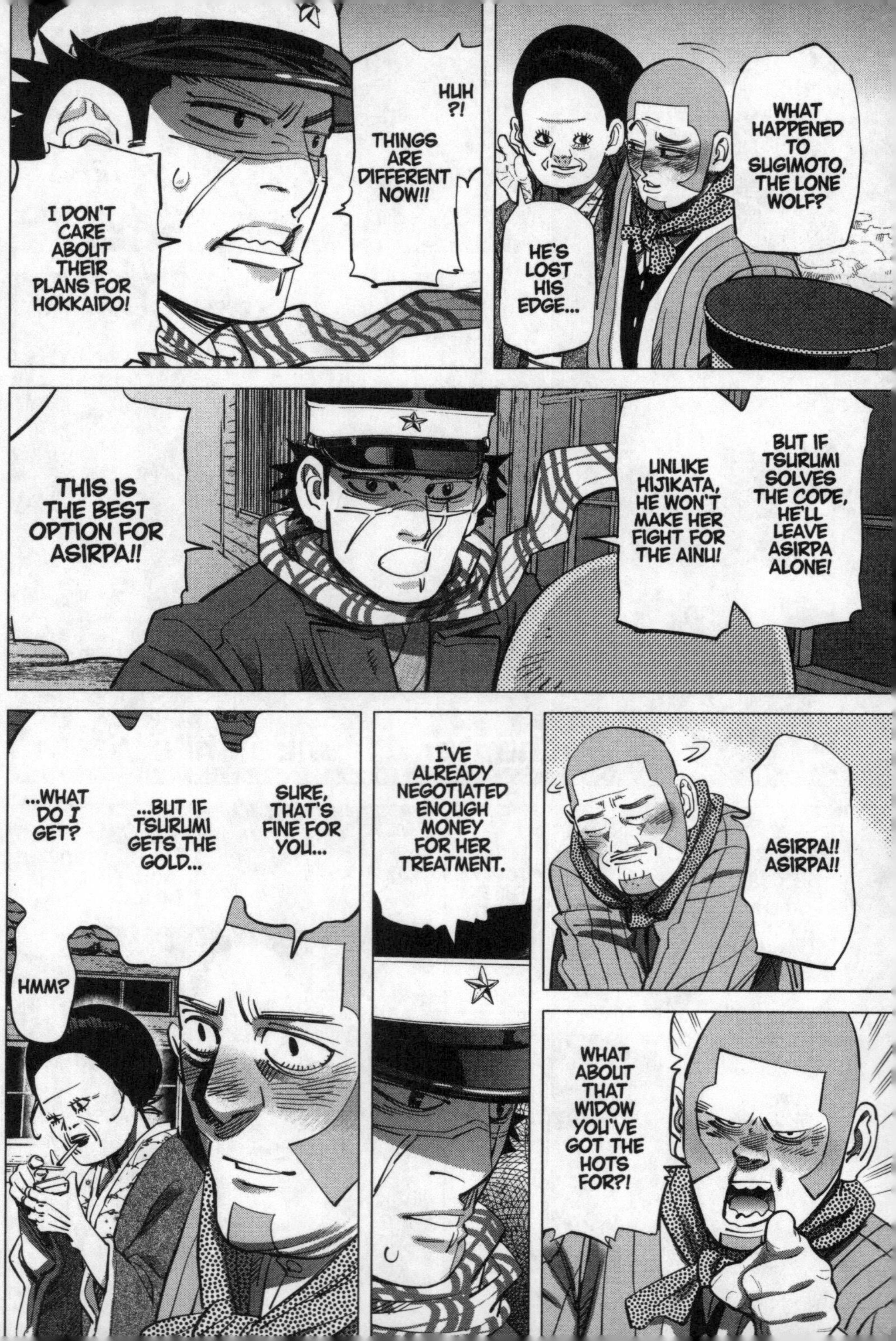
WHAT HAPPENED TO SUGIMOTO, THE LONE WOLF?
HE'S LOST HIS EDGE...
HUH ?!
THINGS ARE DIFFERENT NOW!!
I DON'T CARE ABOUT THEIR PLANS FOR HOKKAIDO!
BUT IF TSURUMI SOLVES THE CODE, HE'LL LEAVE ASIRPA ALONE!
UNLIKE HIJIKATA, HE WON'T MAKE HER FIGHT FOR THE AINU!
THIS IS THE BEST OPTION FOR ASIRPA!!
ASIRPA!! ASIRPA!!
WHAT ABOUT THAT WIDOW YOU'VE GOT THE HOTS FOR?!
I'VE ALREADY NEGOTIATED ENOUGH MONEY FOR HER TREATMENT.
SURE, THAT'S FINE FOR YOU...
...BUT IF TSURUMI GETS THE GOLD...
...WHAT DO I GET?
HMM?

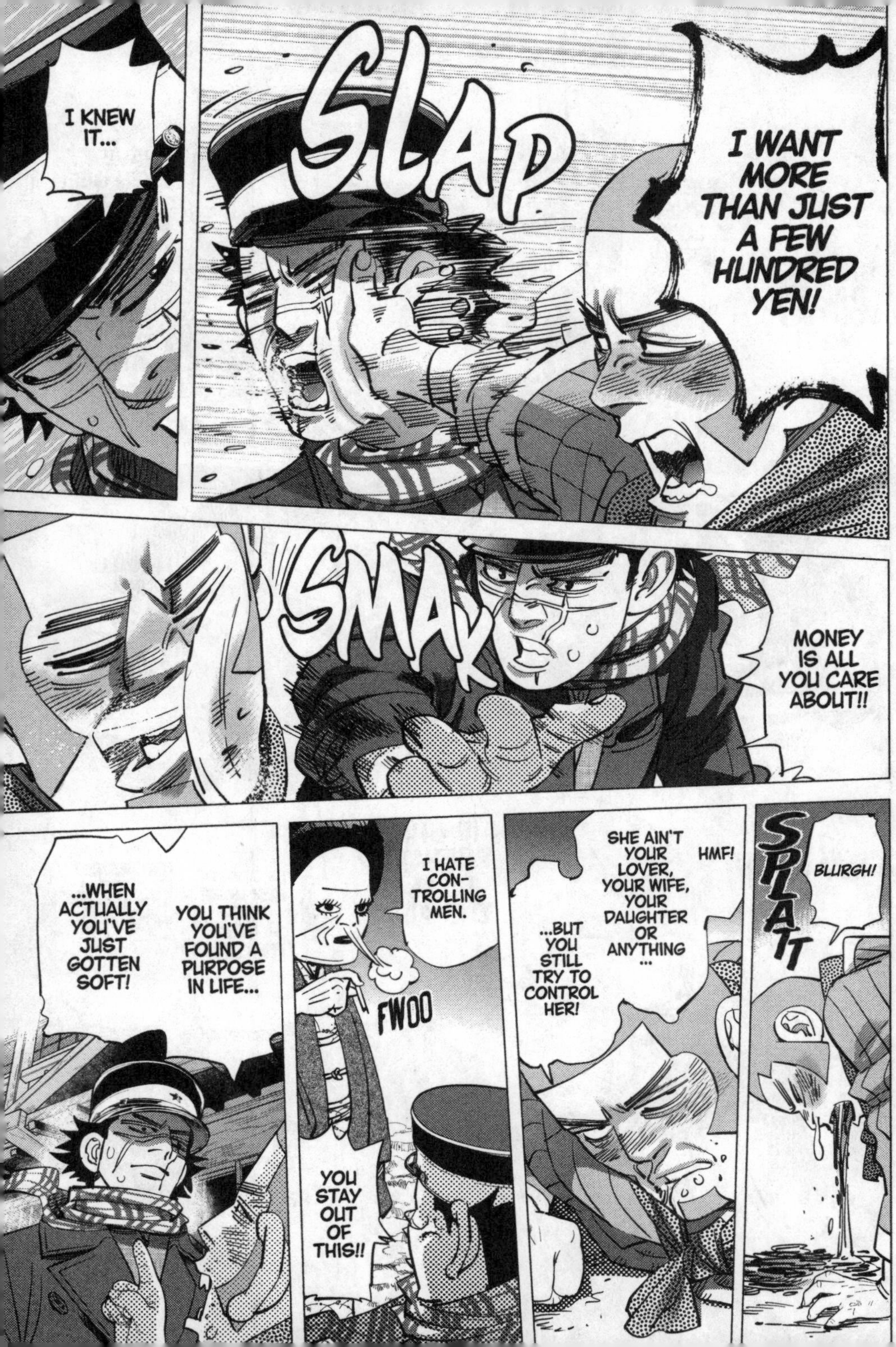
I WANT MORE THAN JUST A FEW HUNDRED YEN!
SLAP
I KNEW IT...
SMAK
MONEY IS ALL YOU CARE ABOUT!!
SPLATT
BLURGH!
HMF!
SHE AIN'T YOUR LOVER, YOUR WIFE, YOUR DAUGHTER OR ANYTHING...
...BUT YOU STILL TRY TO CONTROL HER!
I HATE CON-TROLLING MEN.
FWOO
YOU STAY OUT OF THIS!!
YOU THINK YOU'VE FOUND A PURPOSE IN LIFE...
...WHEN ACTUALLY YOU'VE JUST GOTTEN SOFT!

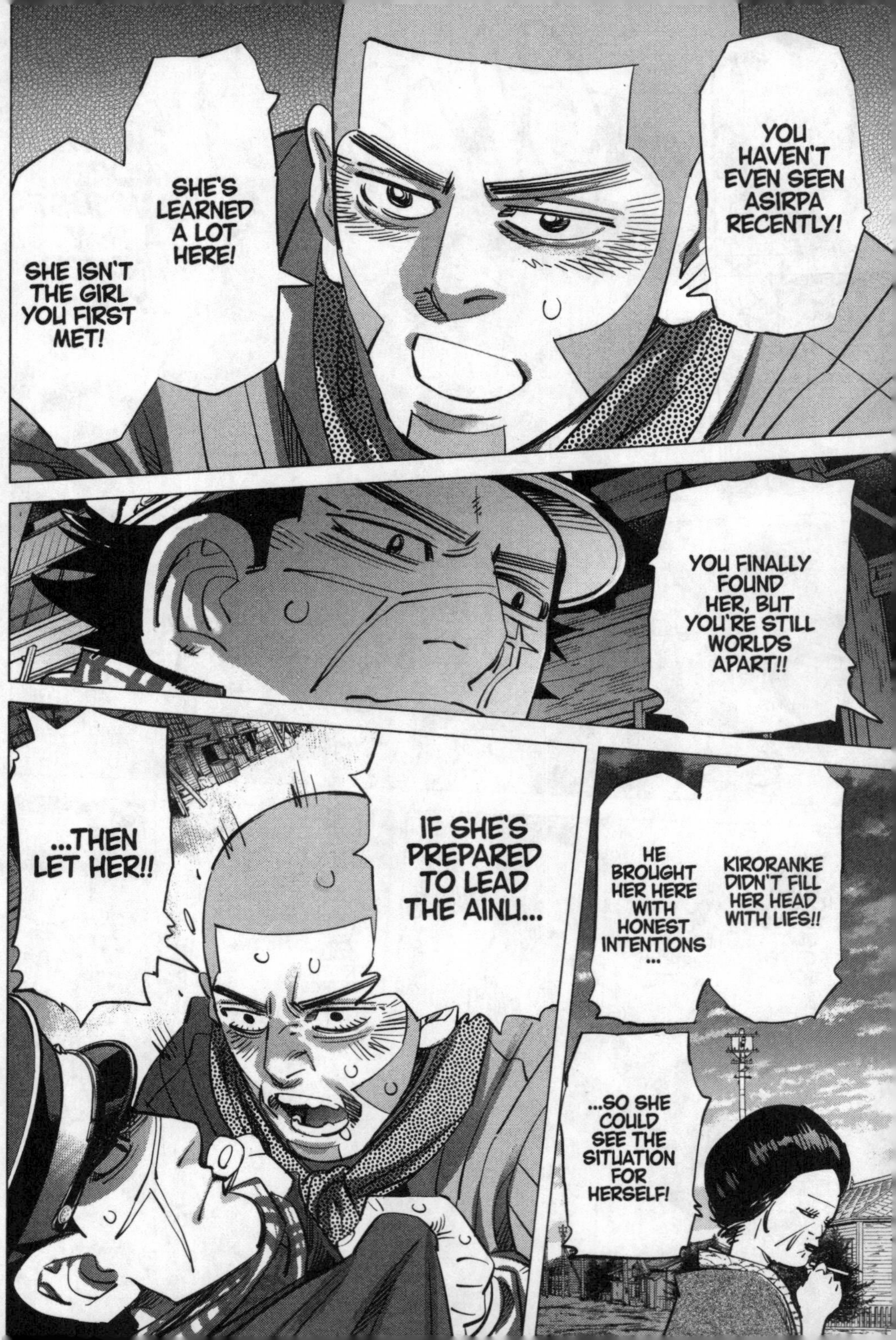
YOU HAVEN'T EVEN SEEN ASIRPA RECENTLY!
SHE'S LEARNED A LOT HERE!
SHE ISN'T THE GIRL YOU FIRST MET!
YOU FINALLY FOUND HER, BUT YOU'RE STILL WORLDS APART!!
KIRORANKE DIDN'T FILL HER HEAD WITH LIES!!
HE BROUGHT HER HERE WITH HONEST INTENTIONS...
...SO SHE COULD SEE THE SITUATION FOR HERSELF!
IF SHE'S PREPARED TO LEAD THE AINU...
...THEN LET HER!!

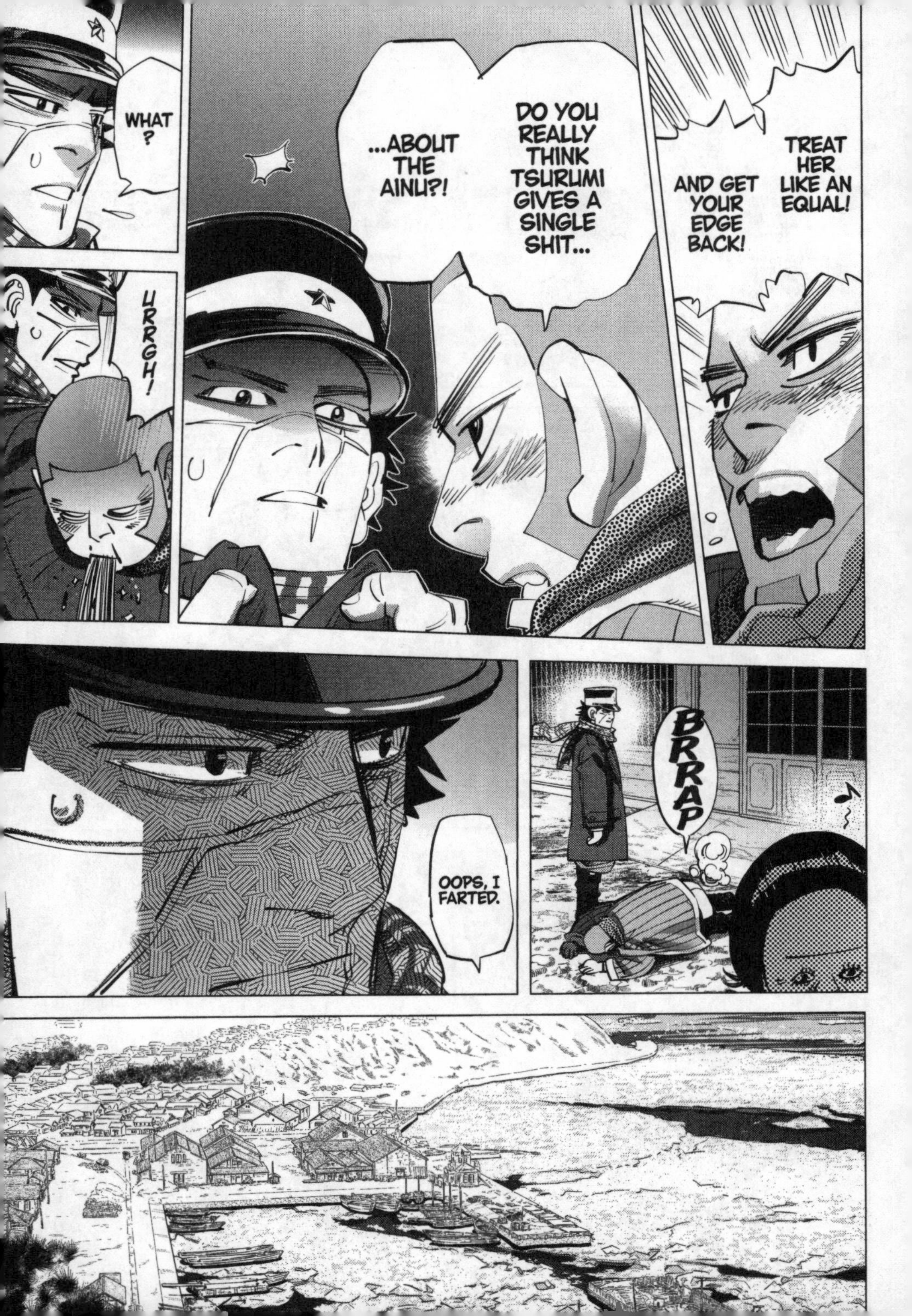
TREAT HER LIKE AN EQUAL!
AND GET YOUR EDGE BACK!
DO YOU REALLY THINK TSURUMI GIVES A SINGLE SHIT...
...ABOUT THE AINU?!
WHAT?
URRGH!
BRRAP
OOPS, I FARTED.

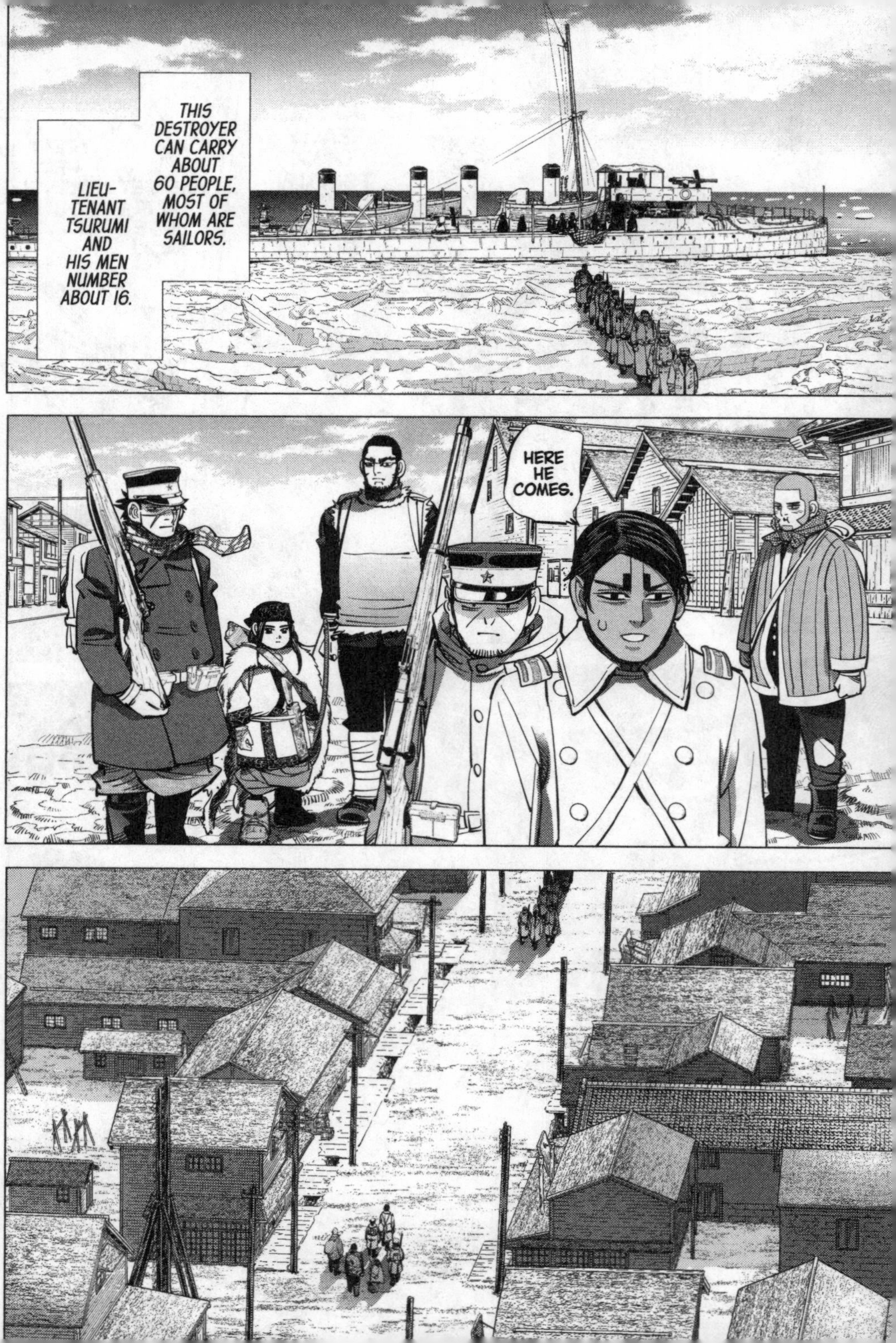
THIS DESTROYER CAN CARRY ABOUT 60 PEOPLE, MOST OF WHOM ARE SAILORS.
LIEU-TENANT TSURUMI AND HIS MEN NUMBER ABOUT 16.
HERE HE COMES.

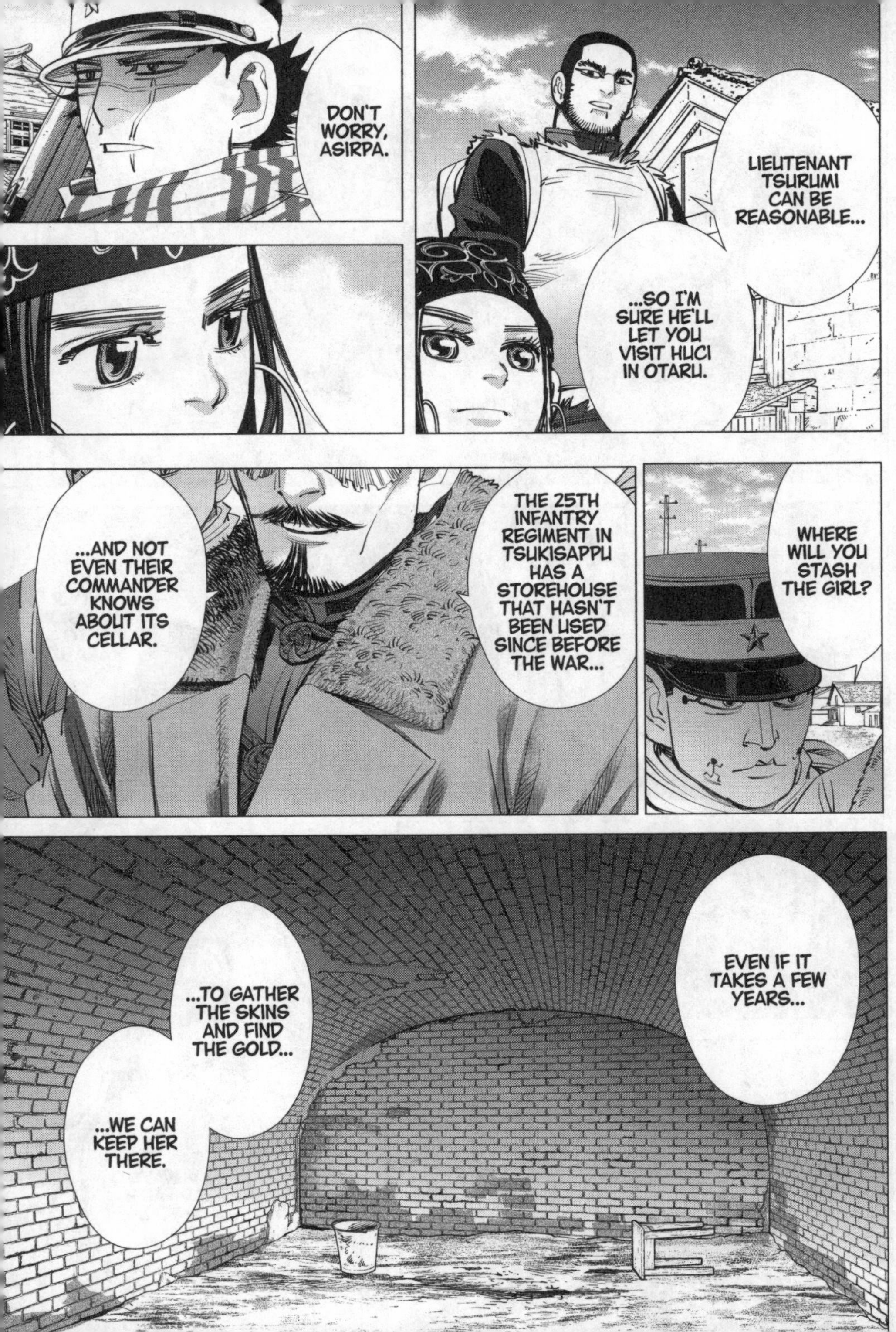
LIEUTENANT TSURUMI CAN BE REASONABLE...
...SO I'M SURE HE'LL LET YOU VISIT HUCI IN OTARU.
DON'T WORRY, ASIRPA.
WHERE WILL YOU STASH THE GIRL?
THE 25TH INFANTRY REGIMENT IN TSUKISAPPU HAS A STOREHOUSE THAT HASN'T BEEN USED SINCE BEFORE THE WAR...
...AND NOT EVEN THEIR COMMANDER KNOWS ABOUT ITS CELLAR.
EVEN IF IT TAKES A FEW YEARS...
...TO GATHER THE SKINS AND FIND THE GOLD...
...WE CAN KEEP HER THERE.

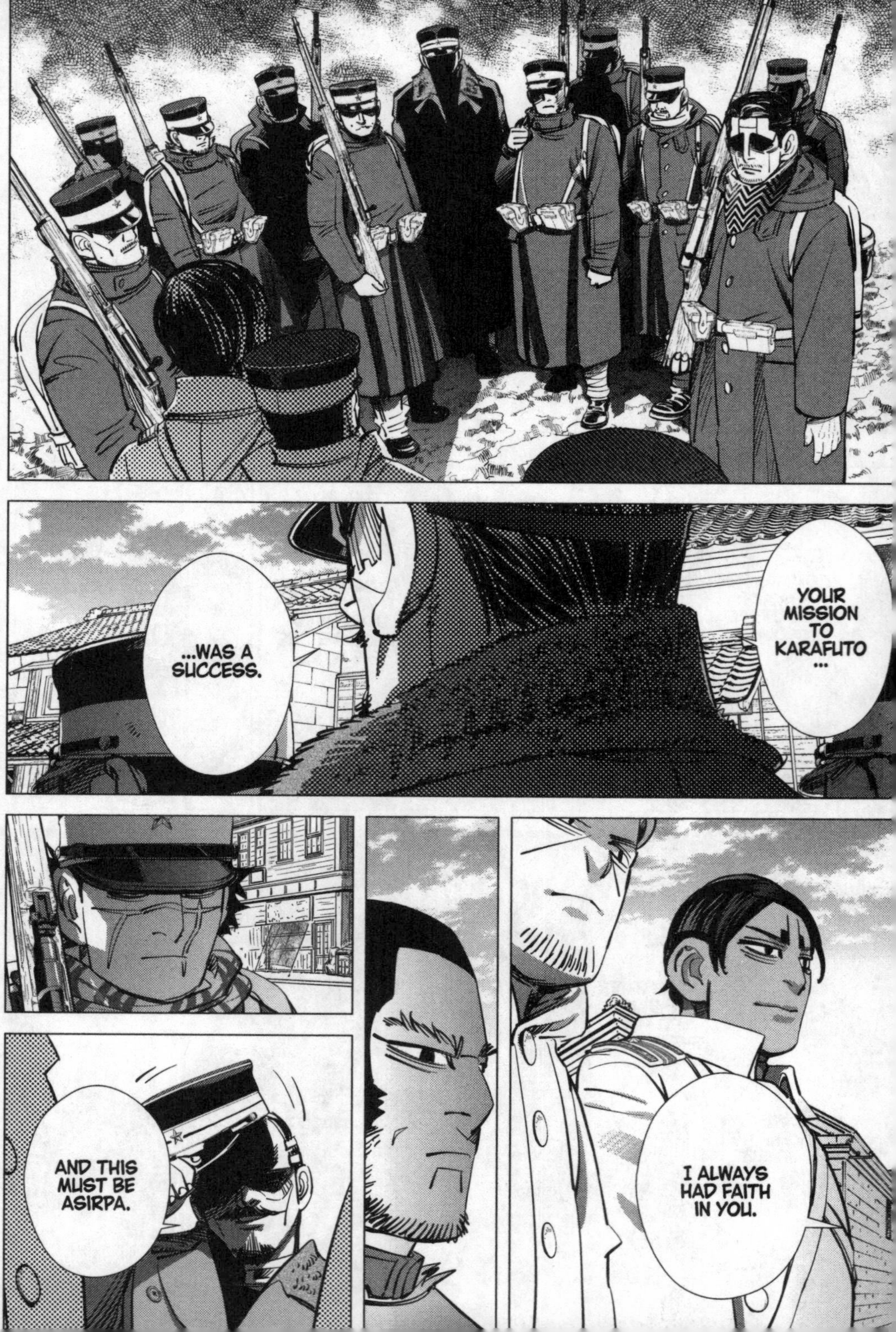
YOUR MISSION TO KARAFUTO ...
...WAS A SUCCESS.
I ALWAYS HAD FAITH IN YOU.
AND THIS MUST BE ASIRPA.

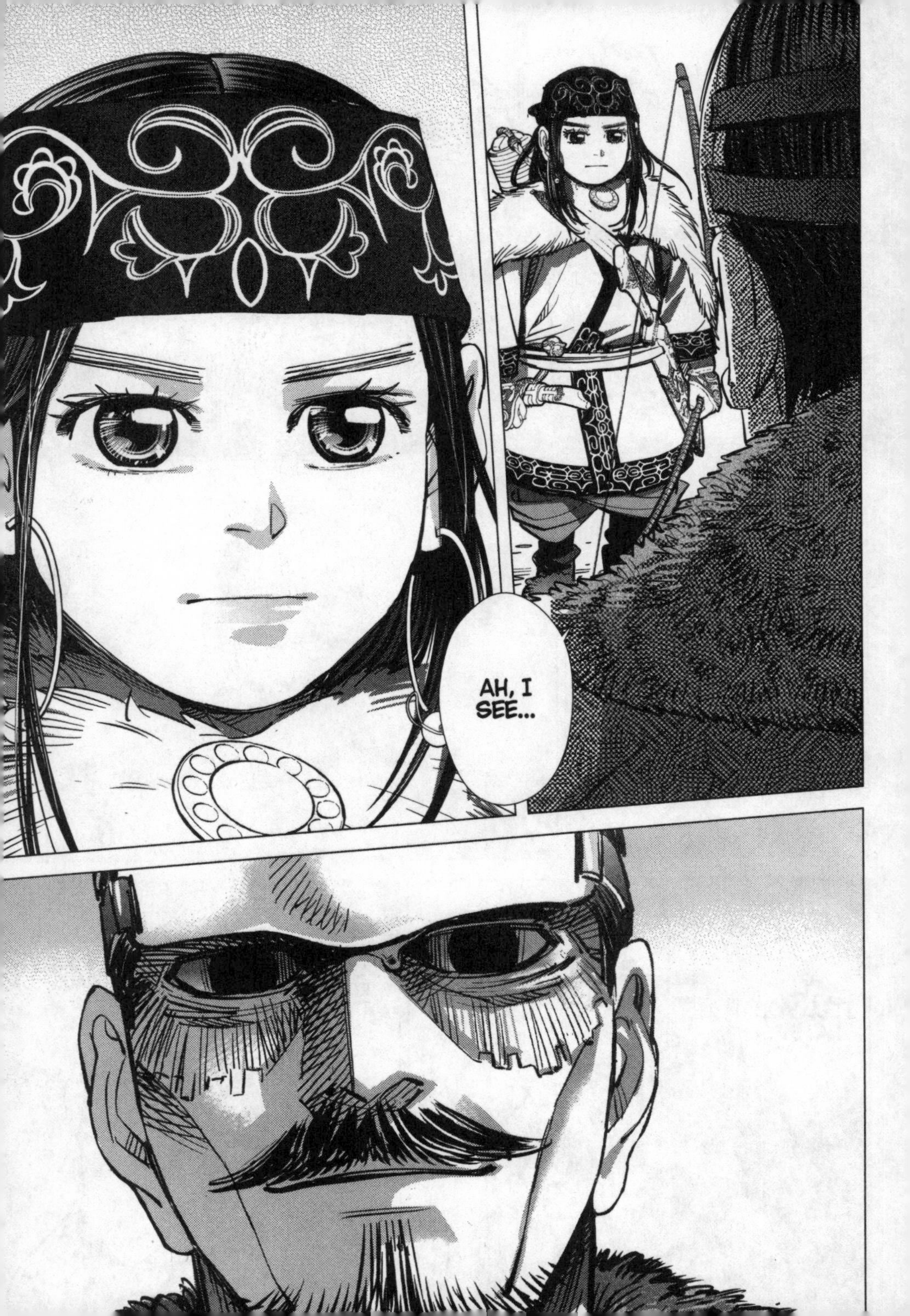
AH, I SEE...

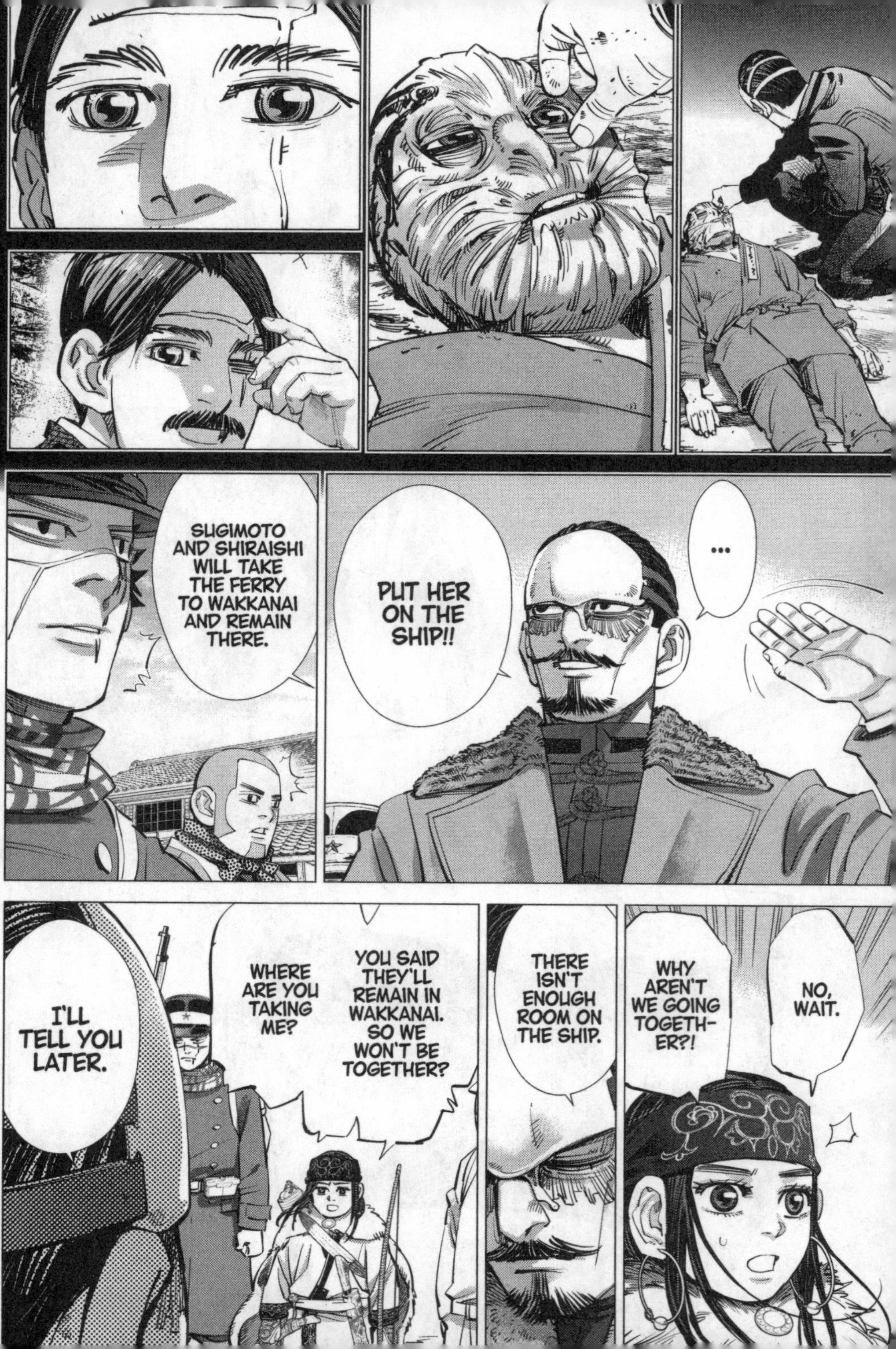
...
PUT HER ON THE SHIP!!
SUGIMOTO AND SHIRAISHI WILL TAKE THE FERRY TO WAKKANAI AND REMAIN THERE.
NO, WAIT.
WHY AREN'T WE GOING TOGETH-ER?!
THERE ISN'T ENOUGH ROOM ON THE SHIP.
YOU SAID THEY'LL REMAIN IN WAKKANAI. SO WE WON'T BE TOGETHER?
WHERE ARE YOU TAKING ME?
I'LL TELL YOU LATER.

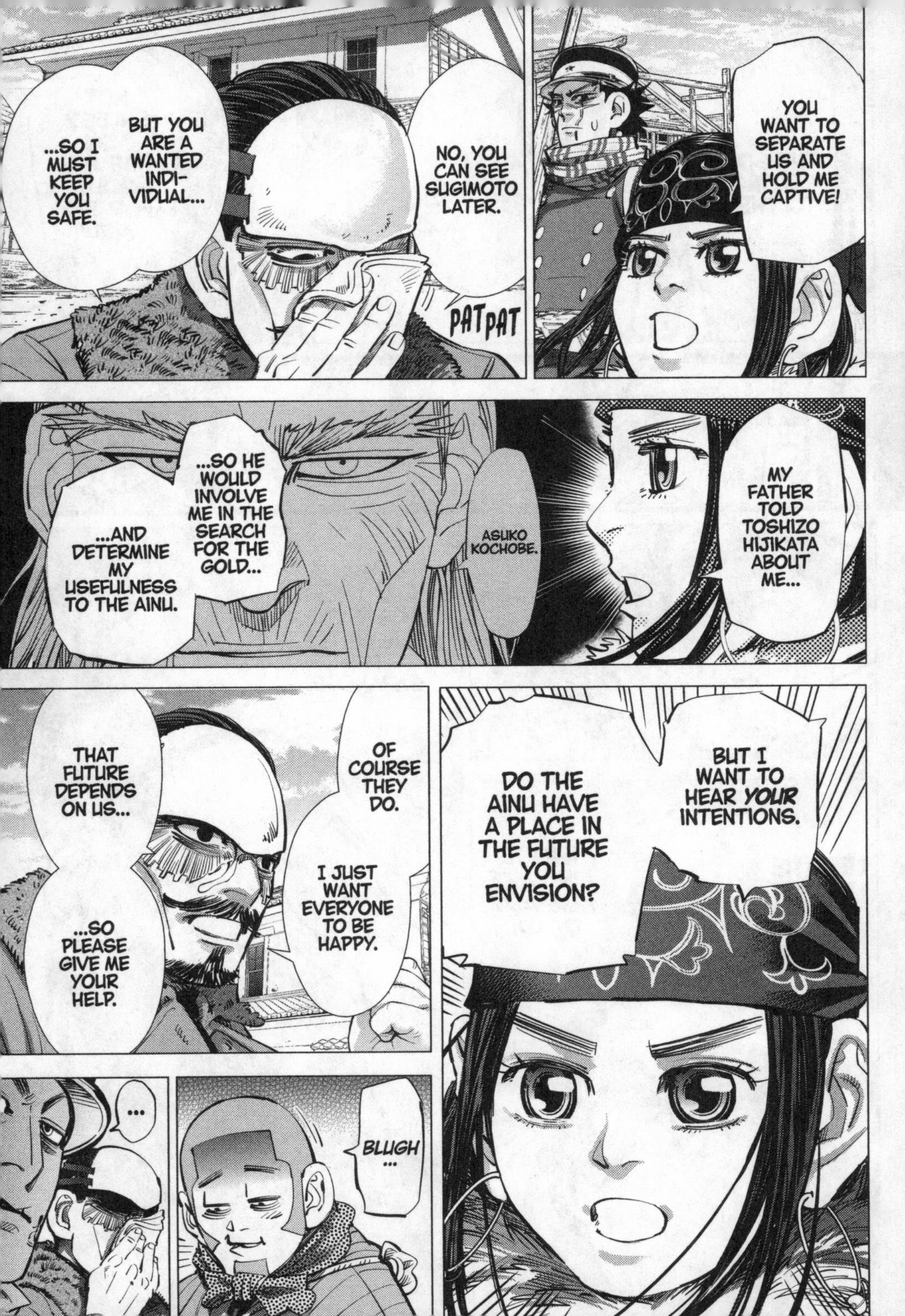
YOU WANT TO SEPARATE US AND HOLD ME CAPTIVE!
NO, YOU CAN SEE SUGIMOTO LATER.
BUT YOU ARE A WANTED INDIVIDUAL...
...SO I MUST KEEP YOU SAFE.
PAT PAT
MY FATHER TOLD TOSHIZO HIJIKATA ABOUT ME...
ASUKO KOCHOBE.
...SO HE WOULD INVOLVE ME IN THE SEARCH FOR THE GOLD...
...AND DETERMINE MY USEFULNESS TO THE AINU.
BUT I WANT TO HEAR *YOUR* INTENTIONS.
DO THE AINU HAVE A PLACE IN THE FUTURE YOU ENVISION?
OF COURSE THEY DO.
I JUST WANT EVERYONE TO BE HAPPY.
THAT FUTURE DEPENDS ON US...
...SO PLEASE GIVE ME YOUR HELP.
BLUGH...
...

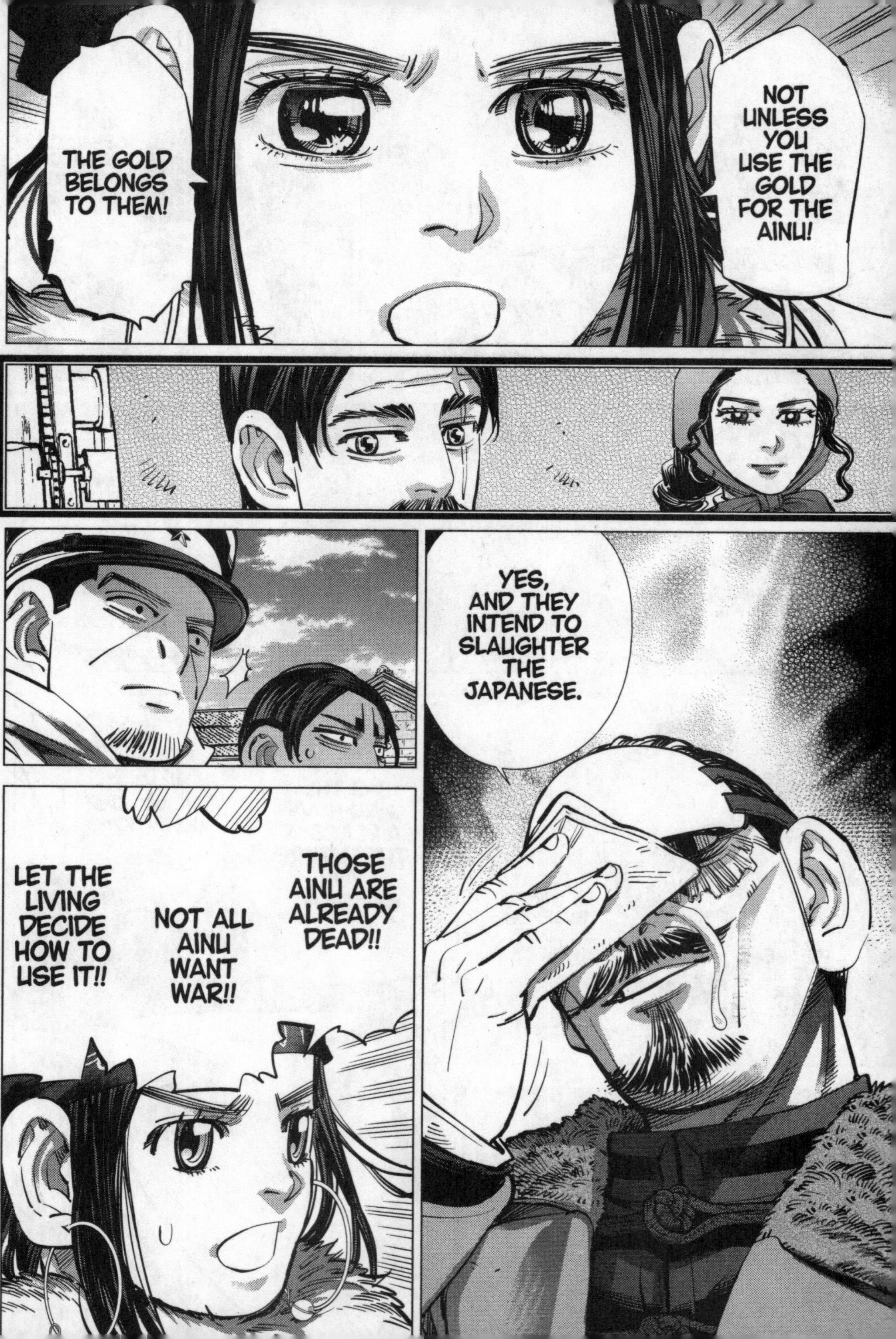
NOT UNLESS YOU USE THE GOLD FOR THE AINU!
THE GOLD BELONGS TO THEM!
YES, AND THEY INTEND TO SLAUGHTER THE JAPANESE.
THOSE AINU ARE ALREADY DEAD!!
NOT ALL AINU WANT WAR!!
LET THE LIVING DECIDE HOW TO USE IT!!

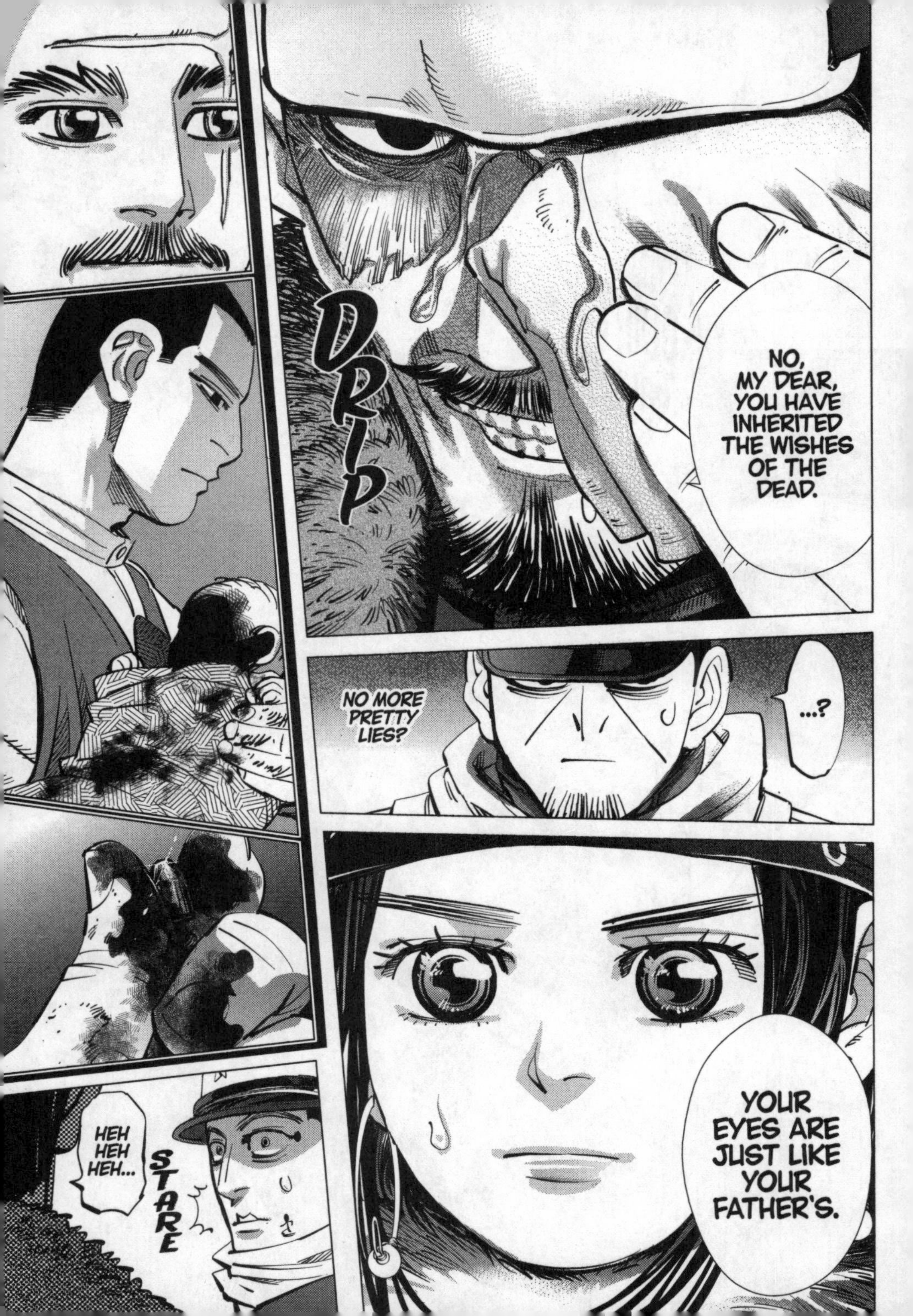
NO, MY DEAR, YOU HAVE INHERITED THE WISHES OF THE DEAD.
DRIP
...?
NO MORE PRETTY LIES?
YOUR EYES ARE JUST LIKE YOUR FATHER'S.
HEH HEH HEH...
STARE

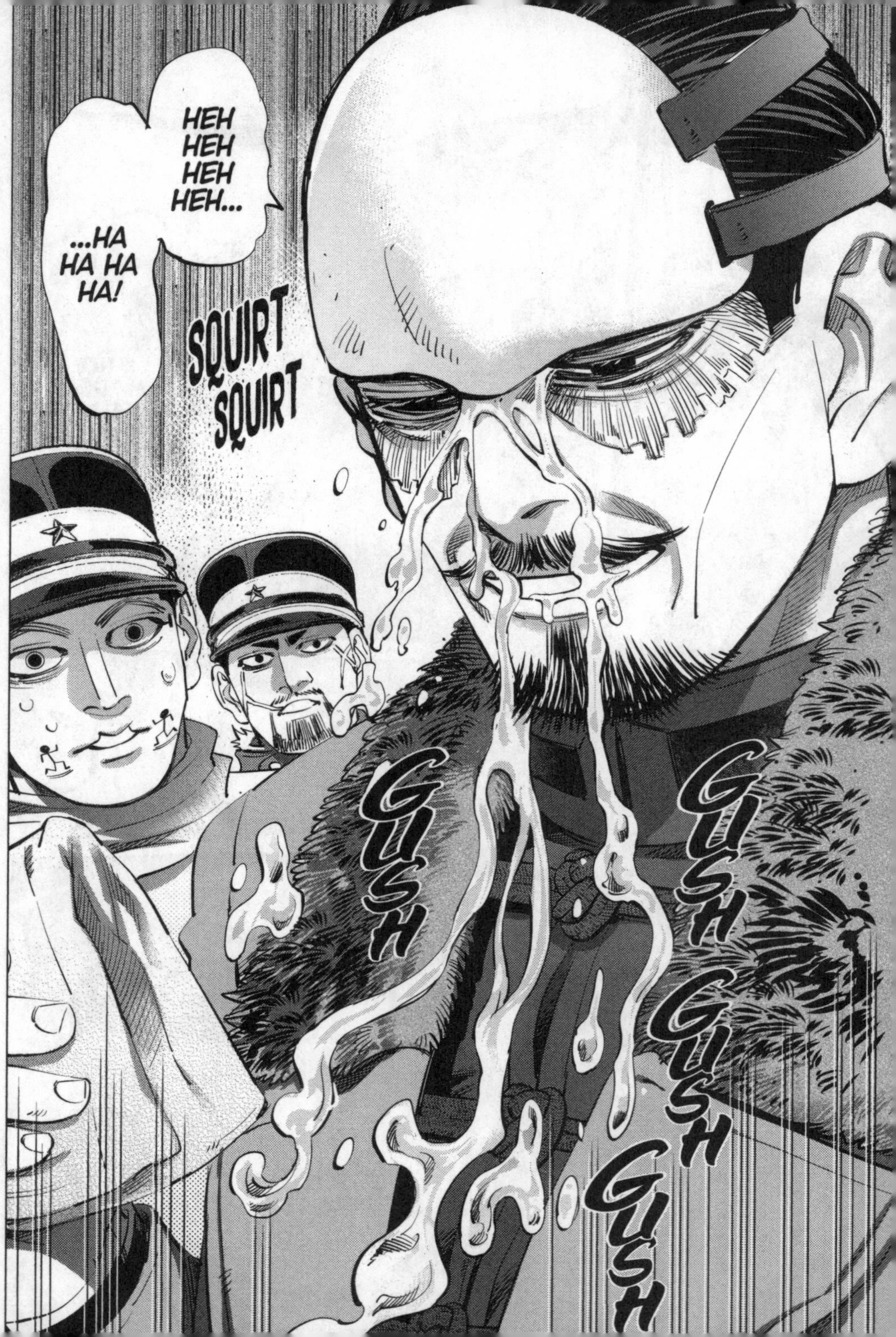

HEH HEH HEH HEH...
...HA HA HA HA!
SQUIRT SQUIRT
GUSH GUSH GUSH
GUSH GUSH

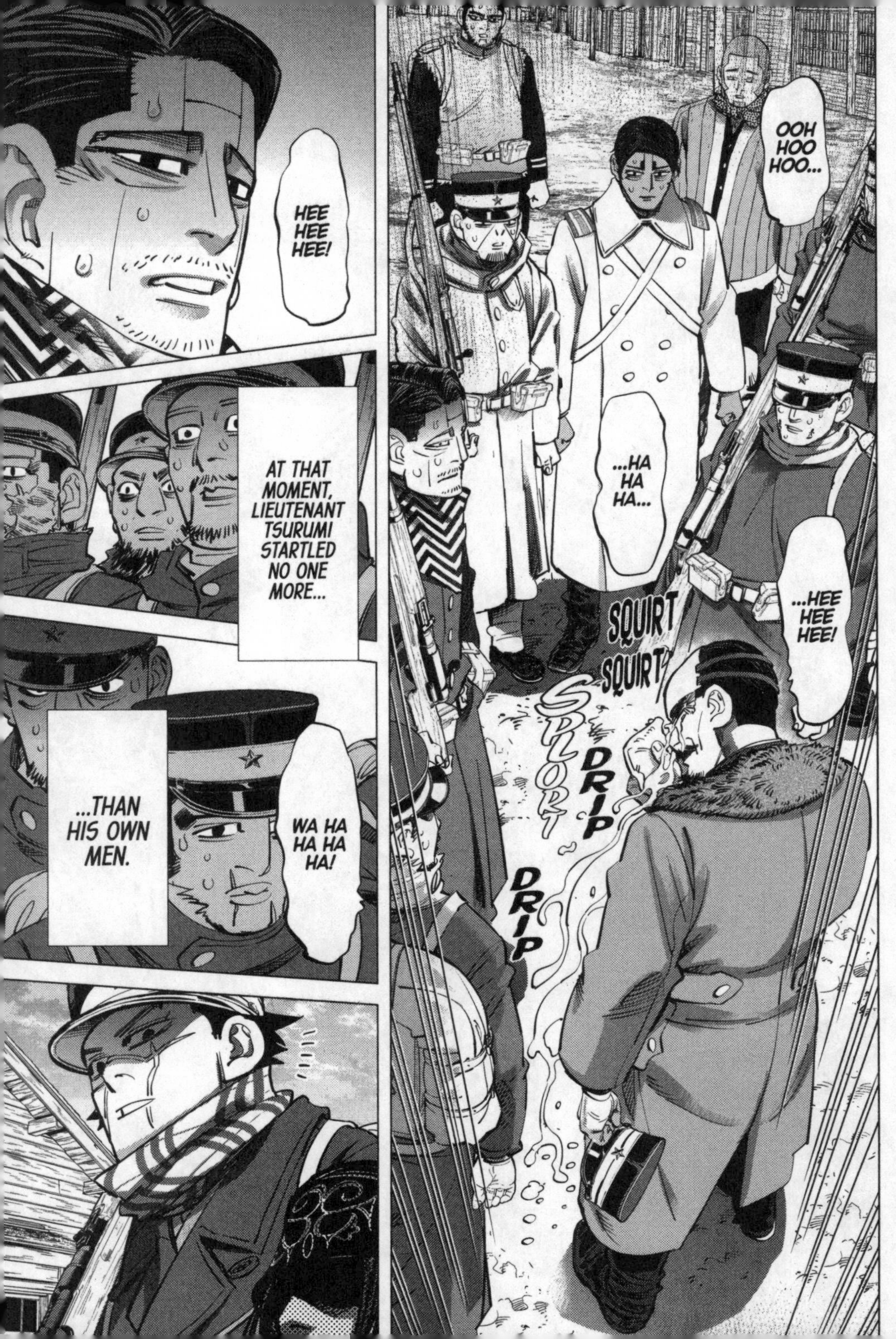
OOH HOO HOO...
...HA HA HA...
...HEE HEE HEE!
SQUIRT
SQUIRT
SPLORT
DRIP DRIP
DRIP DRIP
HEE HEE HEE!
AT THAT MOMENT, LIEUTENANT TSURUMI STARTLED NO ONE MORE...
WA HA HA HA HA!
...THAN HIS OWN MEN.

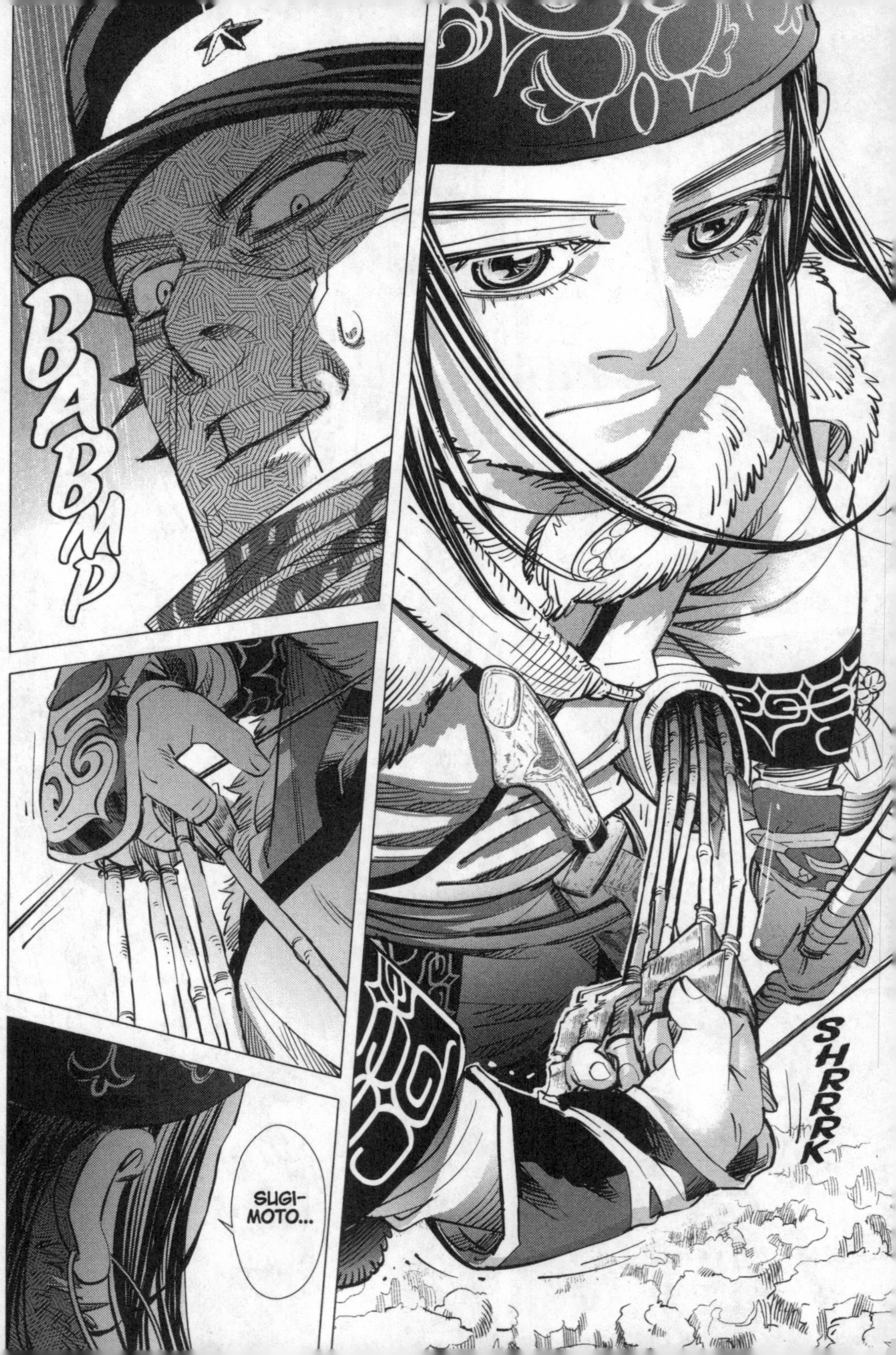
SHRRRK
BABMP
SUGI-MOTO...

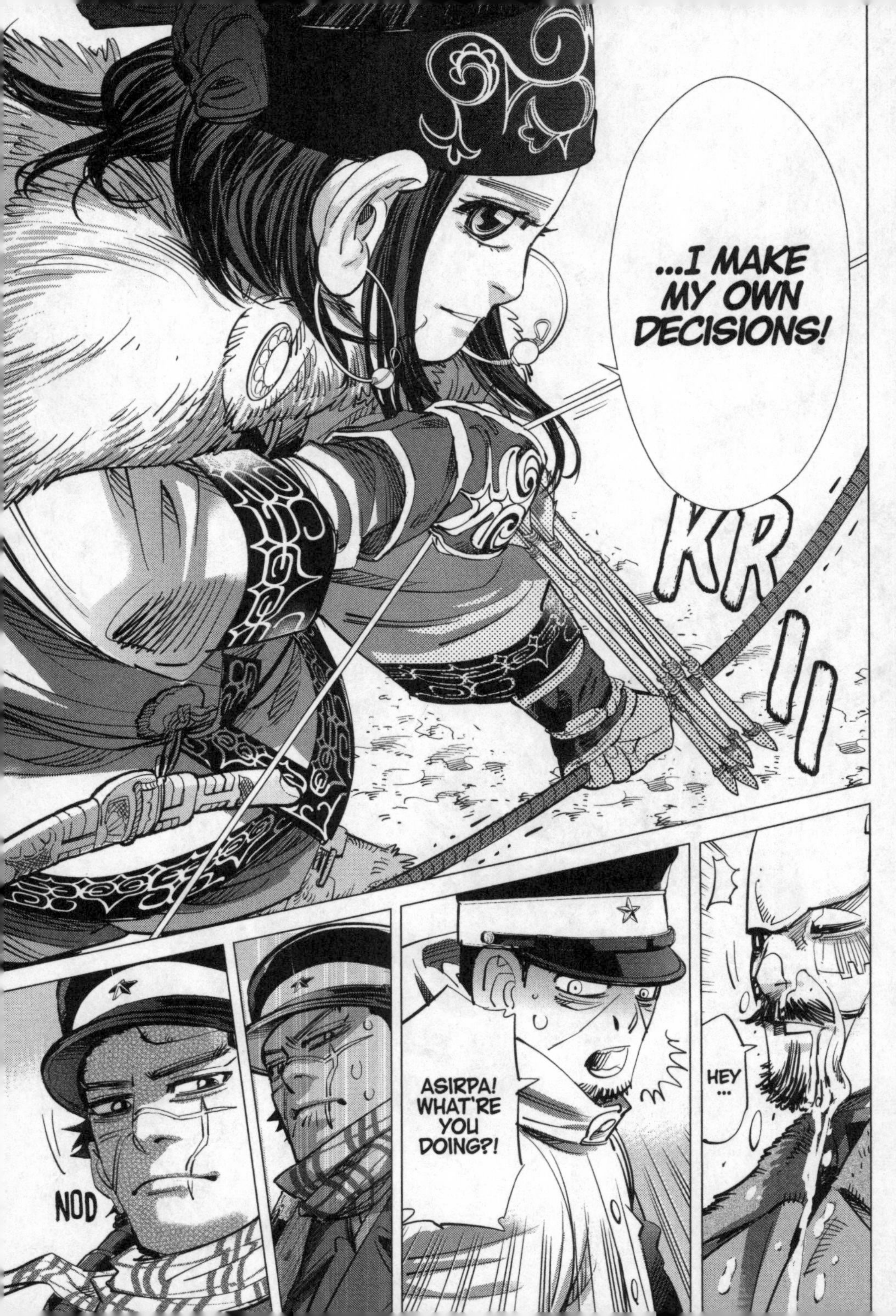
...I MAKE MY OWN DECISIONS!
KRII
HEY ...
ASIRPA! WHAT'RE YOU DOING?!
NOD

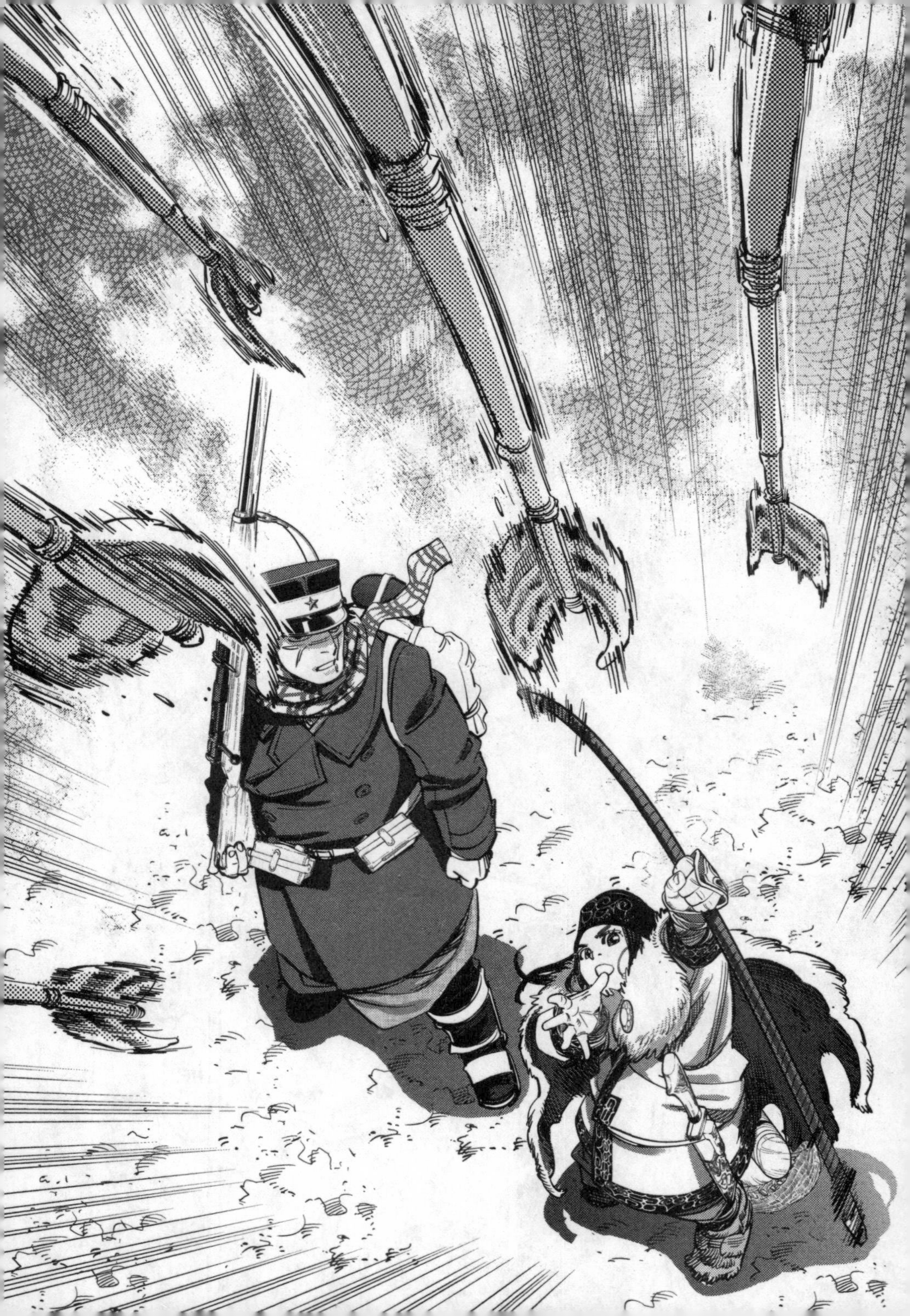

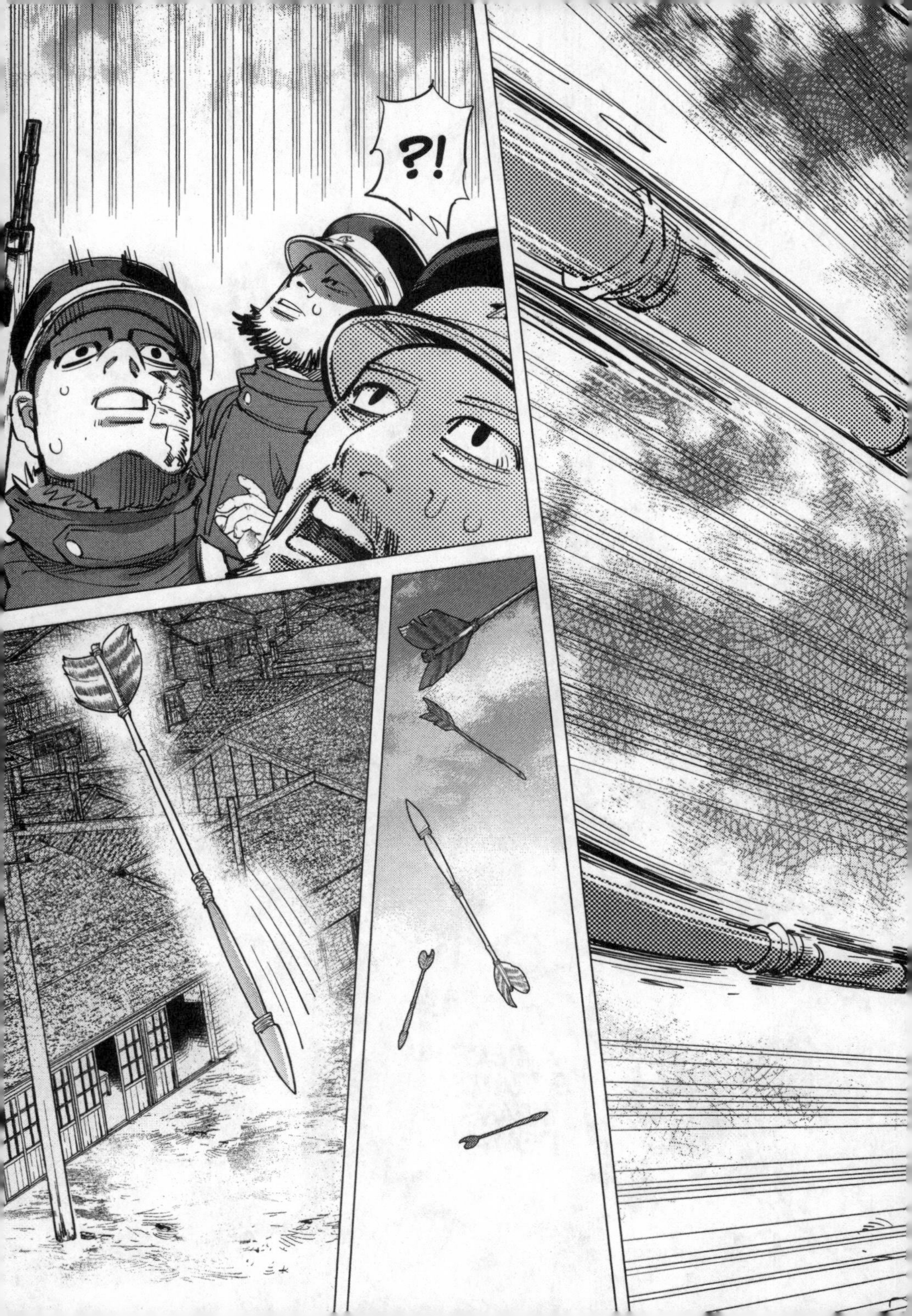
?!

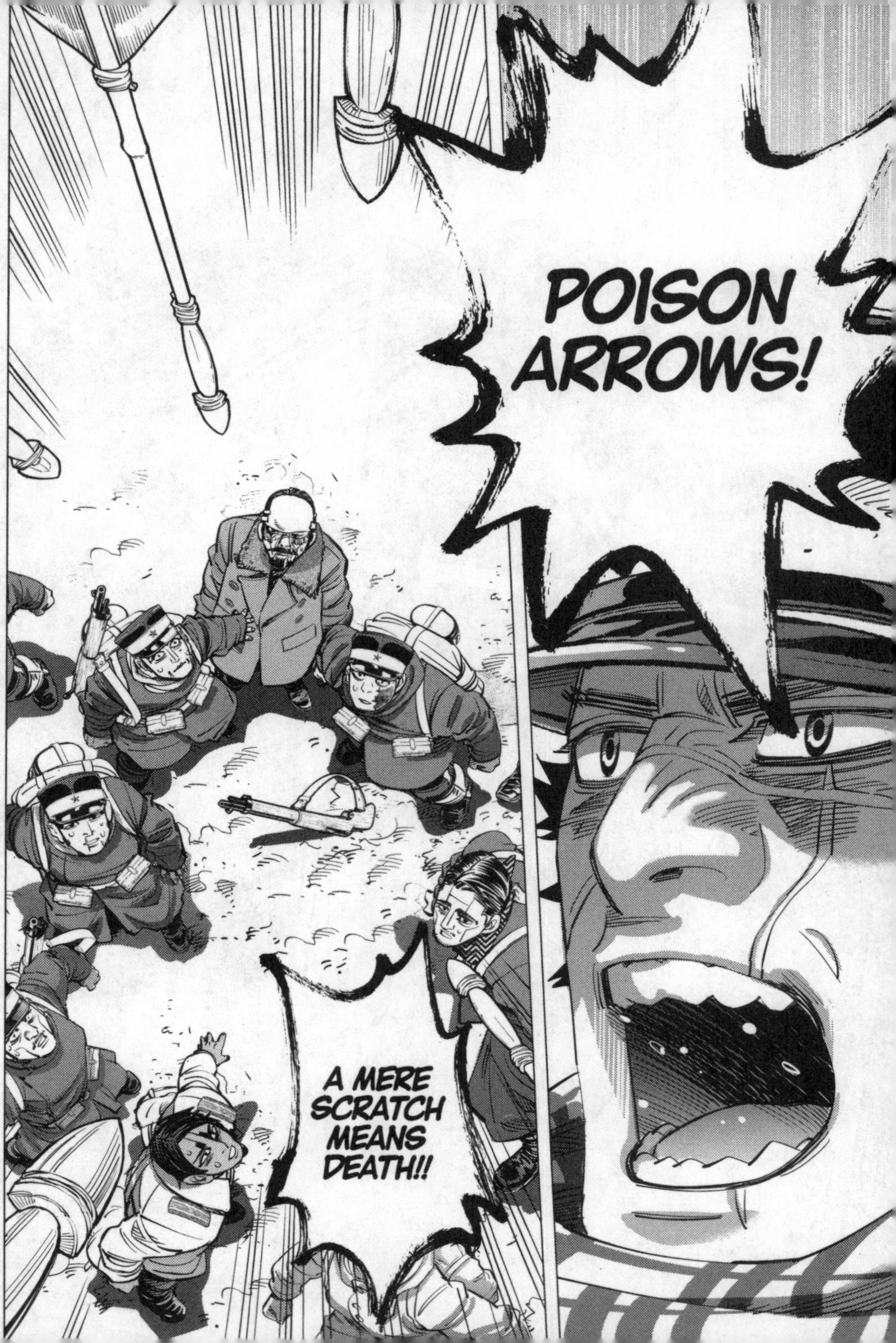
POISON ARROWS!
A MERE SCRATCH MEANS DEATH!!

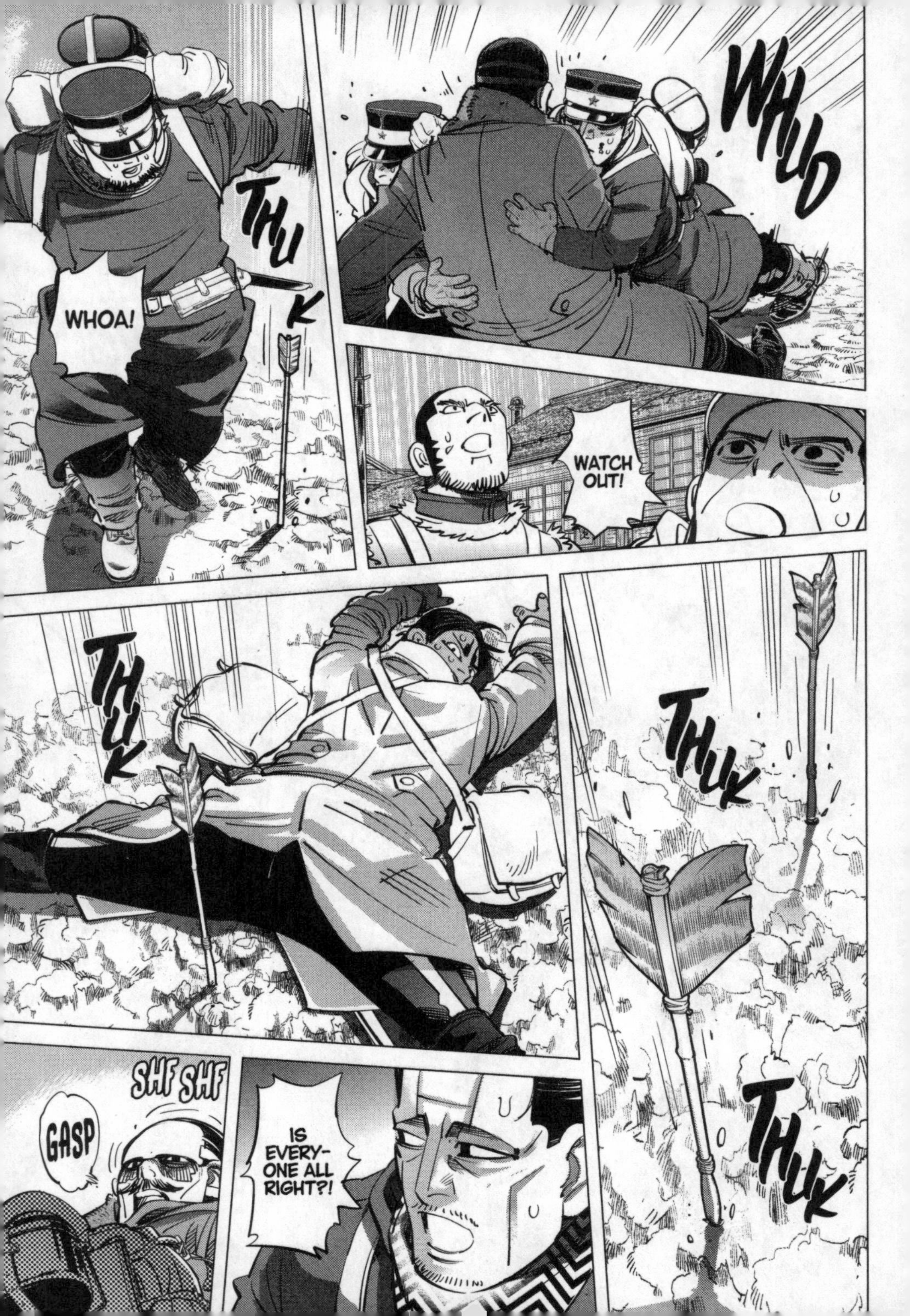
WHUD
WATCH OUT!
THUK
WHOA!
THUK
THUK
THUK
IS EVERY-ONE ALL RIGHT?!
SHF SHF
GASP

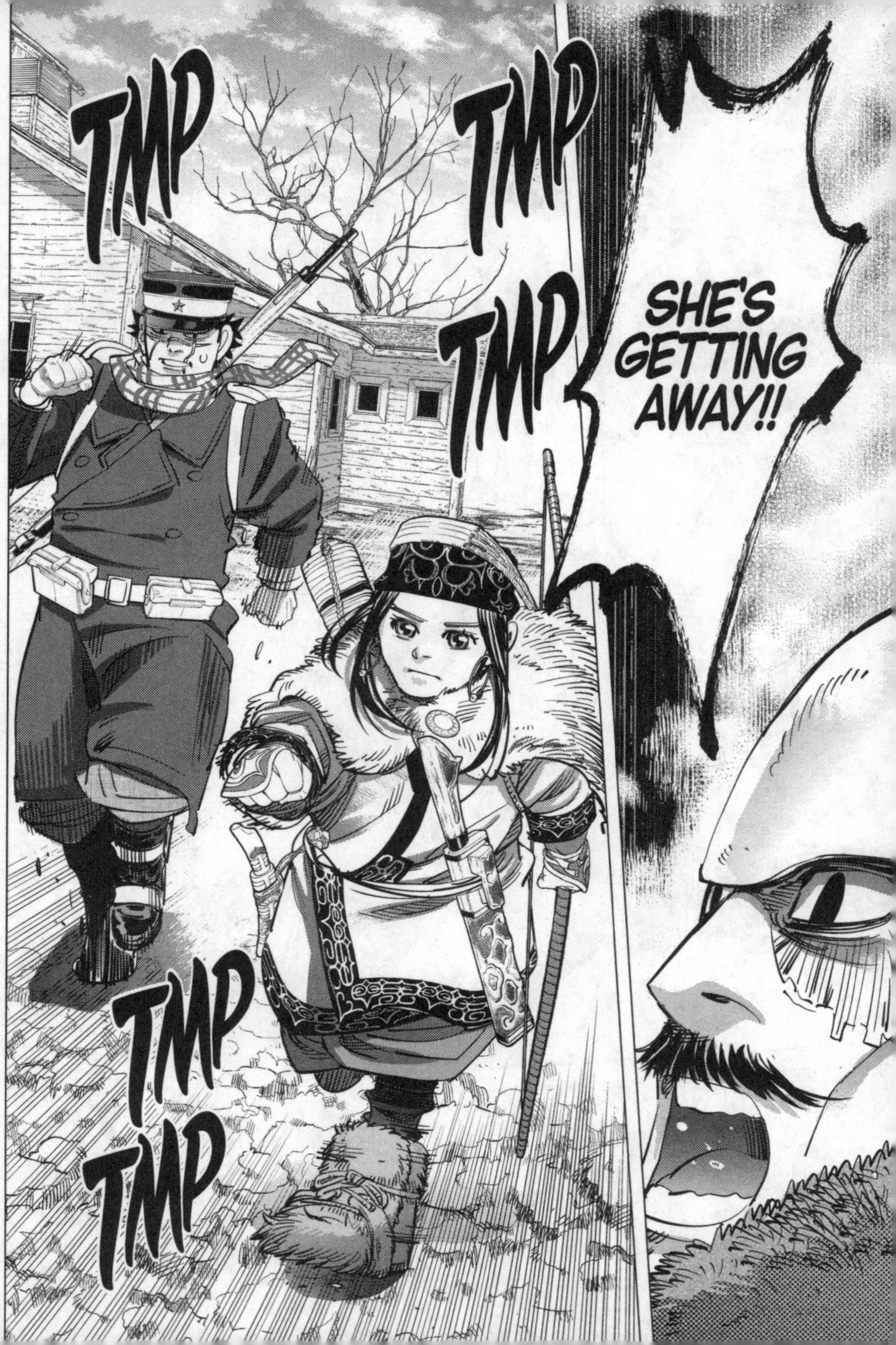
SHE'S GETTING AWAY!!
TMP TMP TMP
TMP
TMP TMP

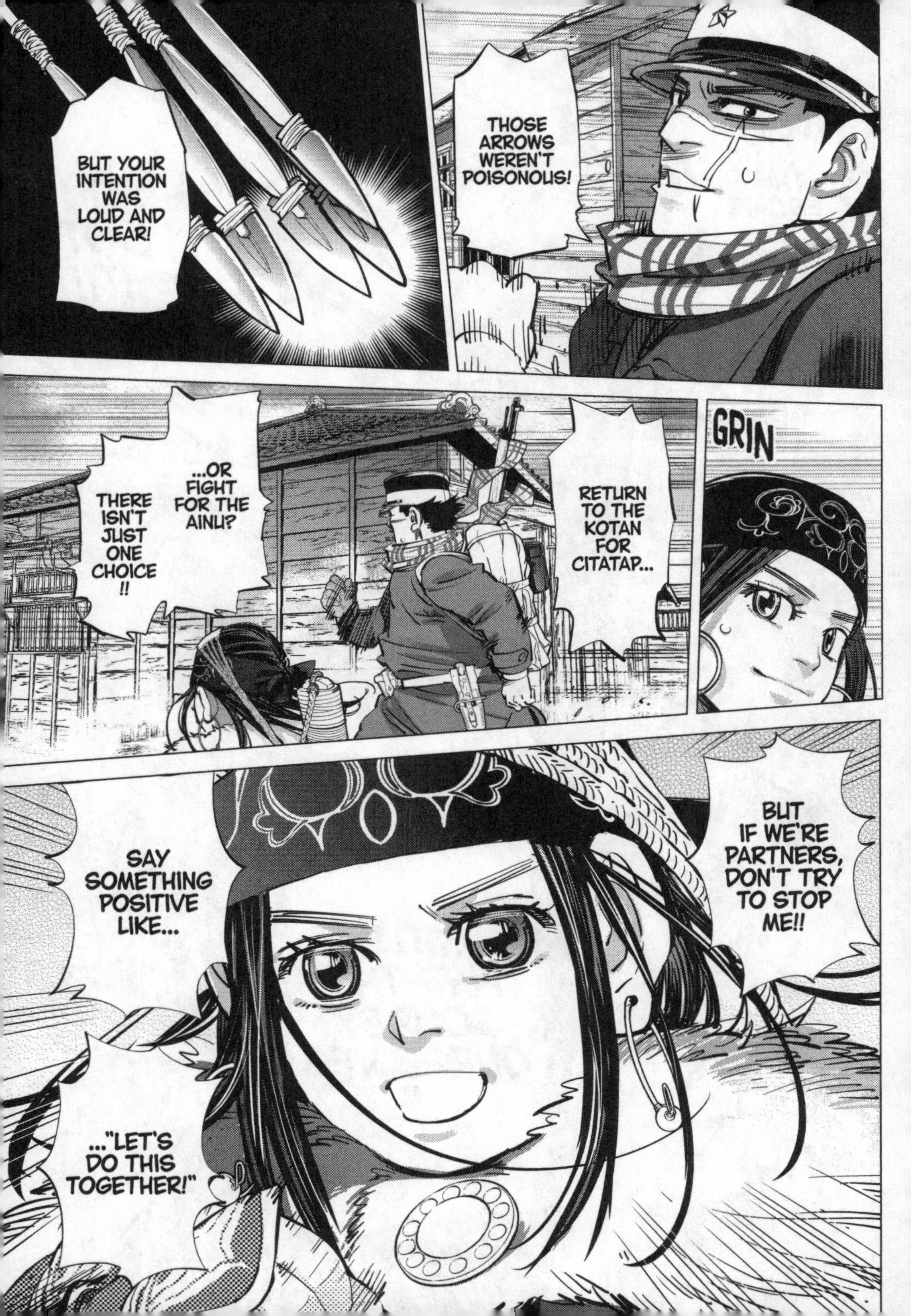
THOSE ARROWS WEREN'T POISONOUS!
BUT YOUR INTENTION WAS LOUD AND CLEAR!
GRIN
RETURN TO THE KOTAN FOR CITATAP...
...OR FIGHT FOR THE AINU?
THERE ISN'T JUST ONE CHOICE!!
BUT IF WE'RE PARTNERS, DON'T TRY TO STOP ME!!
SAY SOMETHING POSITIVE LIKE...
..."LET'S DO THIS TOGETHER!"

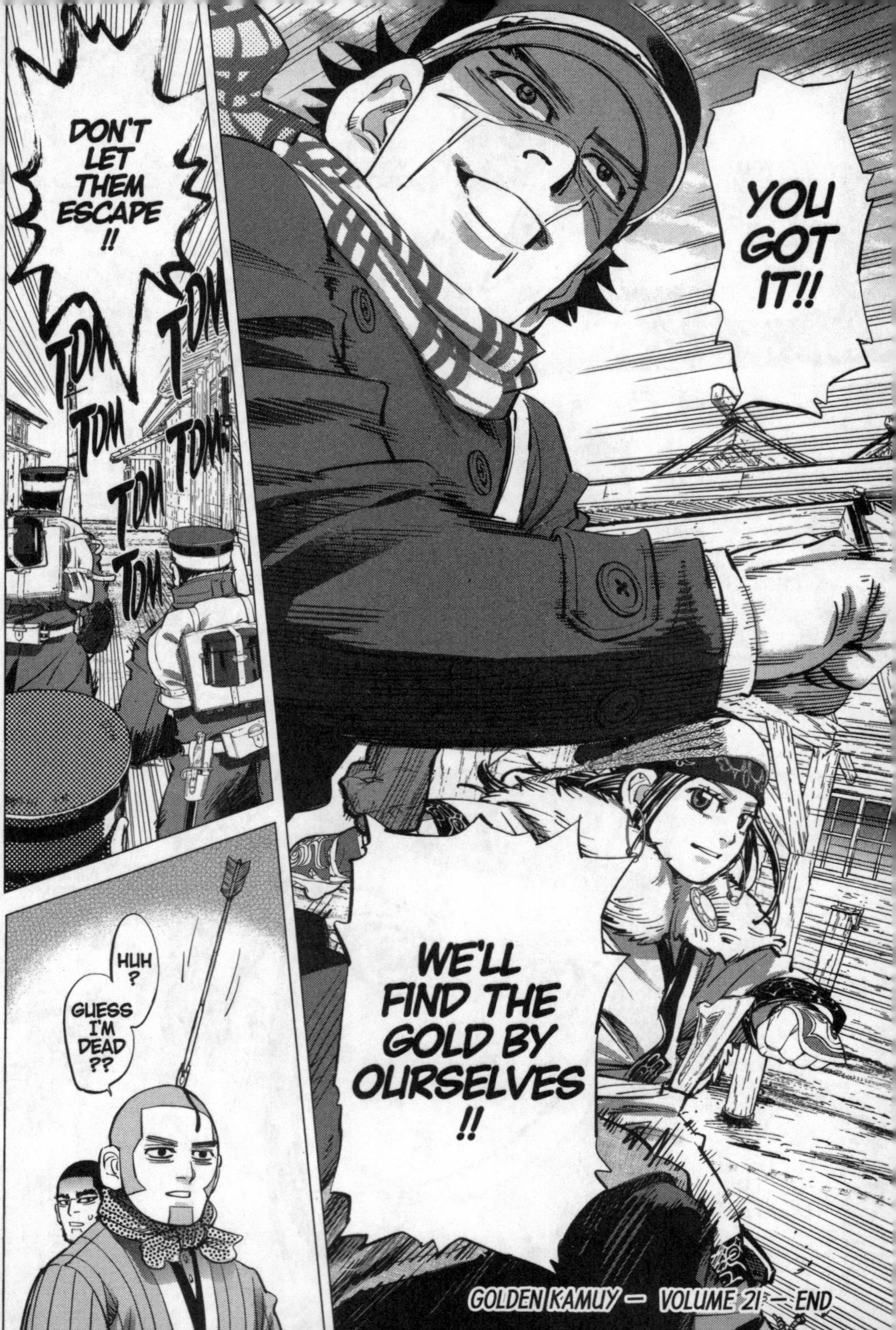
YOU GOT IT!!
WE'LL FIND THE GOLD BY OURSELVES!!
DON'T LET THEM ESCAPE!!
TOM TOM TOM TOM TOM TOM
HUH? GUESS I'M DEAD??
GOLDEN KAMUY — VOLUME 21 — END

Ainu Language Supervision • Hiroshi Nakagawa •
Russian Language Supervision • Eugenio Uzhinin •
Uilta Language Supervision • Yoshiko Yamada •
Satsuma Dialect Supervision • Shogo Nakamura

Cooperation from • Hokkaido Ainu Association and the Abashiri Prison Museum • Otaru City General Museum • Waseda University Aizu Museum • Kazunobu Goto, • Botanic Garden and Museum, Hokkaido University • National Museum of Ethnology • Nibutani Ainu Culture Museum • The Ainu Museum • Moon Kabato Museum • Kushiro City Museum • Atsuyo Hisai • Tatsuhiro Tokuda • Shigeharu Terui • All Japan Federation of Karafuto • Tokyo National Museum • Sakhalin Regional Museum • Shiraishi Hidetoshi • Masato Tamura • Historical Village of Hokkaido • Asahikawa City Museum • Hokuchin Museum

Photo Credits • Takayuki Monma Takanori Matsuda Kozo Ishikawa

Ainu Culture References

Chiri, Takanaka and Yokoyama, Takao. *Ainugo Eiri Jiten* (Ainu Language Illustrated Dictionary). Tokyo: Kagyusha, 1994

Kayano, Shigeru. *Ainu no Mingu* (Ainu Folkcrafts). Kawagoe: Suzusawa Book Store, 1978

Kayano, Shigeru. *Kayano Shigeru no Ainugo Jiten* (Kayano Shigeru's Ainu Language Dictionary). Tokyo: Sanseido, 1996

Musashino Art University – The Research Institute for Culture and Cultural History. *Ainu no Mingu Jissoku Zushu* (Ainu Folkcrafts – Collection of Drawing and Figures). Biratori: Biratori-cho Council for Promoting Ainu Culture, 2014

Satouchi, Ai. *Ainu-shiki ekoroji-seikatsu: Haruzo Ekashi ni manabu shizen no chie* (Ainu Style Ecological Living: Haruzo Ekashi Teaches the Wisdom of Nature). Tokyo: Kabushiki gaisha Shogakukan, 2008

Chiri, Yukie. *Ainu Shin'yoshu* (Chiri Yukie's Ainu Epic Tales). Tokyo: Iwanami Shoten, 1978

Namikawa, Kenji. *Ainu Minzoku no Kiseki* (The Path of the Ainu People). Tokyo: Yamakawa Publishing, 2004

Mook. *Senjuumin Ainu Minzoku* (Bessatsu Taiyo) (The Ainu People (Extra Issue Taiyo). Tokyo: Heibonsha, 2004

Kinoshita, Seizo. *Shiraoikotan Kinoshita Seizo Isaku Shashin Shu* (Shiraoikotan: Kinoshita Seizo's Posthumous Photography Collection). Hokkaido Shiraoi-gun Shiraoi-cho: Shiraoi Heritage Conservation Foundation, 1988

The Ainu Museum. *Ainu no Ifuku Bunka* (The Culture of Ainu Clothing). Hokkaido Shiraoi-gun Shiraoi-cho: Shiraoi Ainu Museum, 1991

Keira, Tomoko and Kaji, Sayaka. *Ainu no Shiki* (Ainu's Four Seasons). Tokyo: Akashi Shoten, 1995

Fukuoka, Itoko and Sato, Kazuko. *Ainu Shokubutsushi* (Ainu Botanical Journal). Chiba Urayasu-Shi: Sofukan, 1995

Hayakawa, Noboru. *Ainu no Minzoku* (Ainu Folklore). Iwasaki Bijutsusha, 1983

Sunazawa, Kura. *Ku Sukuppu Orushibe* (The Memories of My Generation). Hokkaido, Sapporo-shi: Miyama Shobo, 1983

Haginaka, Miki et al. *Kikigaki Ainu no Shokuji* (Oral History of Ainu Diet). Tokyo: Rural Culture Association Japan, 1992

Nakagawa, Hiroshi. *New Express Ainu Go.* Tokyo: Hakusuisha, 2013

Nakagawa, Hiroshi. *Ainugo Chitose Hogen Jiten* (The Ainu-Japanese dictionary). Chiba Urayasu-Shi: Sofukan, 1995

Nakagawa, Hiroshi and Nakamoto, Mutsuko. *Kamuy Yukara de Ainu Go wo Manabu* (Learning Ainu with Kamuy Yukar). Tokyo: Hakusuisha, 2007

Nakagawa, Hiroshi. *Katari au Kotoba no Chikara – Kamuy tachi to Ikiru Sekai* (The Power of Spoken Words – Living in a World with Kamuy). Tokyo: Iwanami Shoten, 2010

Sarashina, Genzo and Sarashina, Hikari. *Kotan Seibutsu Ki <1 Juki / Zassou hen>* (Kotan Wildlife Vol. 1 – Trees and Weeds). Hosei University Publishing, 1992/2007

Sarashina, Genzo and Sarashina, Hikari. *Kotan Seibutsu Ki <2 Yacho / Kaijuu / Gyozoku hen>* (Kotan Wildlife Vol. 2 – Birds, Sea Creatures, and Fish). Hosei University Publishing, 1992/2007

Sarashina, Genzo and Sarashina, Hikari. *Kotan Seibutsu Ki <3 Yachou / Mizudori / Konchu hen>* (Kotan Wildlife Vol. 3 – Shorebirds, Seabirds, and Insects). Hosei University Publishing, 1992/2007

Sarashina, Genzo. *Ainu Minwashu* (Collection of Ainu Folktales). Kita Shobou, 1963

Sarashina, Genzo. *Ainu Rekishi to Minzoku* (Ainu History and Folklore). Shakai Shisousha, 1968

Kawakami Yuji. *Sarunkur Ainu Monogatari* (The Tale of Sarunkur Ainu). Kawagoe: Suzusawa Book Store, 2003/2005

Kawakami, Yuji. *Ekashi to Fuchi wo Tazunete* (Visiting Ekashi and Fuchi). Kawagoe: Suzusawa Book Store, 1991

Council for the Conservation of Ainu Culture. *Ainu Minzokushi* (Ainu People Magazine). Dai-ichi Hoki, 1970

Okamura, Kichiemon and Clancy, Judith A. *Ainu no Ishou* (The Clothes of the Ainu People). Kyoto Shoin, 1993

Hokkaido Cultural Property Protection Association. *Ainu Ifuku Chousa Houkokusho <1 Ainu Josei ga Denshou Suru Ibunka>* (The Ainu Clothing Research Report Vol. 1 – Traditional Clothing Passed Down Through Generations of Ainu Women). 1986

Yotsuji, Ichiro. Photos by Mizutani, Morio. *Ainu no Monyo* (Decorative Arts of the Ainu). Kasakura Publishing, 1981

Yoshida, Iwao. *Ainushi Shiryoshu* (Collection of Ainu Historical Documents). Hokkaido Publication Project Center, 1983

Kubodera, Itsuhiko. *Ainu no Mukashibanashi* (Old Stories of the Ainu). Miyaishoten, 1972

Kubodera, Itsuhiko (trans.). *Ainu Minzokushi* (Ainu People Magazine). Dai-ichi Hoki

Inoue, Koichi and Latyshev, Vladislav M. (coed.). *Karafuto Ainu no Mingu* (Karafuto Ainu Folkcraft). Hokkaido Publication Project Center, 2002

Russia ga Mita Ainu Bunka (Ainu Culture as Seen by Russia). The Foundation for Research and Promotion of Ainu Culture, 2013

Russia Minzokugaku Hakubutsukan Ainu Shiryoten—Russia ga Mita Shimaguni no Hitobito (Russia Museum of Ethnology Ainu Materials Exhibition—Island Peoples as Seen by Russia). The Foundation for Research and Promotion of Ainu Culture, 2005

The Foundation for Research and Promotion of Ainu Culture (ed.). *Senjima, Karafuto, Hokkaido—Ainu no Kurashi* (Ainu Life on the Kuril Islands, Karafuto and Hokkaido). The Senri Foundation, 2011

SPb-Ainu Project Group (ed.). *Russia Kagaku Academy Jinruigaku Minzokugaku Hakubutsukan Shozo Ainu Shiryo Mokuroku* (Ainu Collections of Peter the Great Museum of Anthropology and Ethnography Russian Academy of Sciences Catalogue). Sofukan, 1998

Yamamoto, Yuko. *Karafuto Ainu—Jukyo to Mingu* (Residences and Folkcraft of the Karafuto Ainu). Sagami Shobo, 1970

Yamamoto, Yuko (author and ed.). Chiri, Mashiho and Onuki, Emiko co-authors). *Karafuto Shizen Minzoku no Seikatsu* (Lifestyles of Karafuto Natural Peoples). Sagami Shobo, 1979

Chiri, Mashiho. *Chiri Mashiho Chosakushu 3 Seikatsu-shi / Minzokugaku-hen* (Mashiho Chiri Collected Works, Vol. 3: Lifestyles and Ethnology). Heibonsha, 1973

Yamamoto, Yuko. *Hoppo Shizen Minzoku Minwa Shusei* (Northern Natural Peoples Folk Tales Compilation). Sagami Shobo, 1968

Yamamoto, Yuko. *Karafuto Genshi Minzoku no Seikatsu* (Lifestyles of Karafuto Primitive Peoples). ARS, 1943

Nishitsuru, Sadaka. *Karafuto Ainu.* Miyama Shobo, 1974

Kasai, Takechiyo. *Karafuto Ainu no Minzoku* (Folklore of the Karafuto Ainu). Miyama Shobo, 1975

Tanigawa, Kenichi. Kita no Minzokushi-Sakhalin / Chishima no Minzoku (Northern Ethnography—Sakhalin / People of the Kuril Islands). San-Ichi Shobo Publishing Inc., 1997

Takabeya, Fukuhei. *Hoppoken no Ie* (Houses of the Northern Regions). Shokokusha Publishing Co., Ltd., 1943

Abashiri City Northern Folkore Cultural Preservation Society. *Uiruta no Kurashi to Mingu* (Uilta Lifestyles and Folkcraft). 1982

The Foundation for Research and Promotion of Ainu Culture (ed.). *Zaidan Hojin Ainu Bunka Fukko / Kenkyu Suishin Kiko Shuzo Mokuroku 7 (Ishida Shuzo Kyuzo Shashin) (The Foundation for* Research and Promotion of Ainu Culture Collection Catalog 7 (Ishida Collection Old Collection Photograph). The Foundation for Research and Promotion of Ainu Culture, 2012

Uilta Society Museum Steering Committee (ed.). *Shiryokan Jakka Duxuni Tenji Sakuhinshu* (Museum Jakka Duxuni Exhibition Works Collection). 2002

Bird, Isabella L. (author), Kobari, Kosai (trans.) *Meiji Shoki no Emishi Tanboki* (Report on Emishi in the Early Meiji Era). Sarorun Shobo, 1977

Munro, N.G. (author), Seligman, B.Z. (ed.), Tetsuro, Komatsu (trans.). *Ainu no Shinko to Sono Gishiki* (Ainu Creed and Cult). Kokushokankokai, 2002

Batchelor, John (author), Tetsuro, Komatsu (trans.). *Ainu no Kurashi to Densho* (Ainu Life and Lore). Hokkaido Publication Project Center, 1999

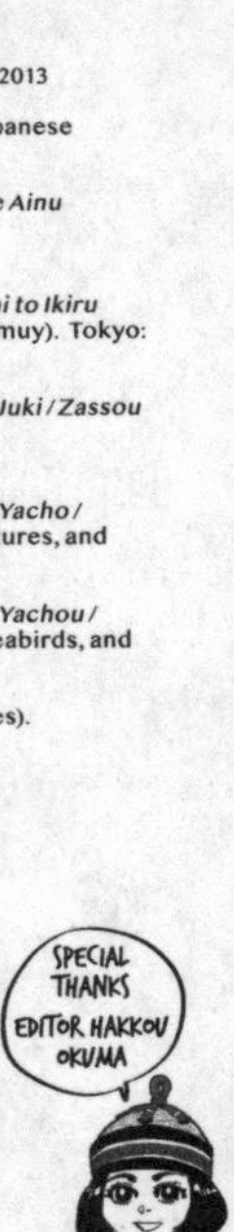
SPECIAL THANKS
EDITOR HAKKOU OKUMA

Kanto or wa yaku sak no arankep sinep ka isam.

Nothing comes from heaven without purpose. —Ainu proverb

TETRAPE (WEED BARK CLOTHING)

KARAFUTO AINU CLOTHES MADE
FROM FIBERS OF NETTLES

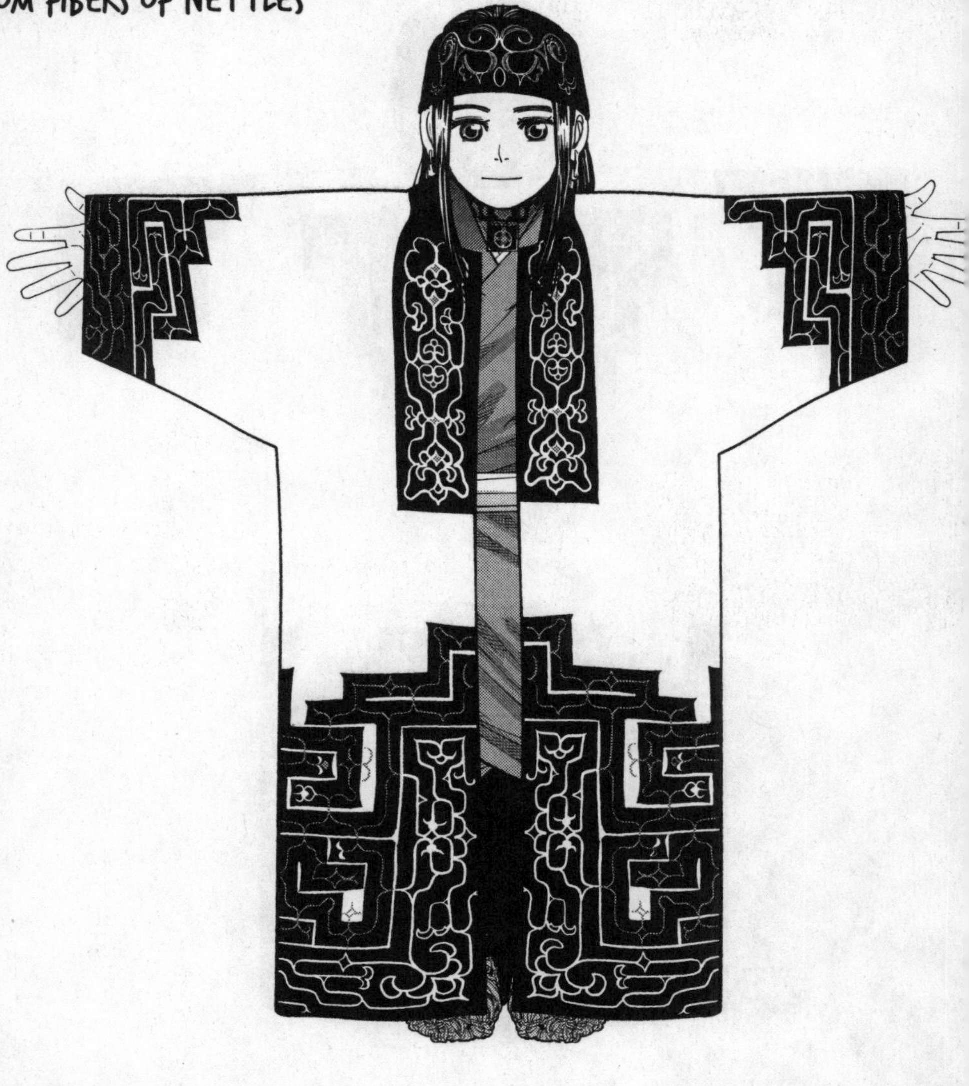

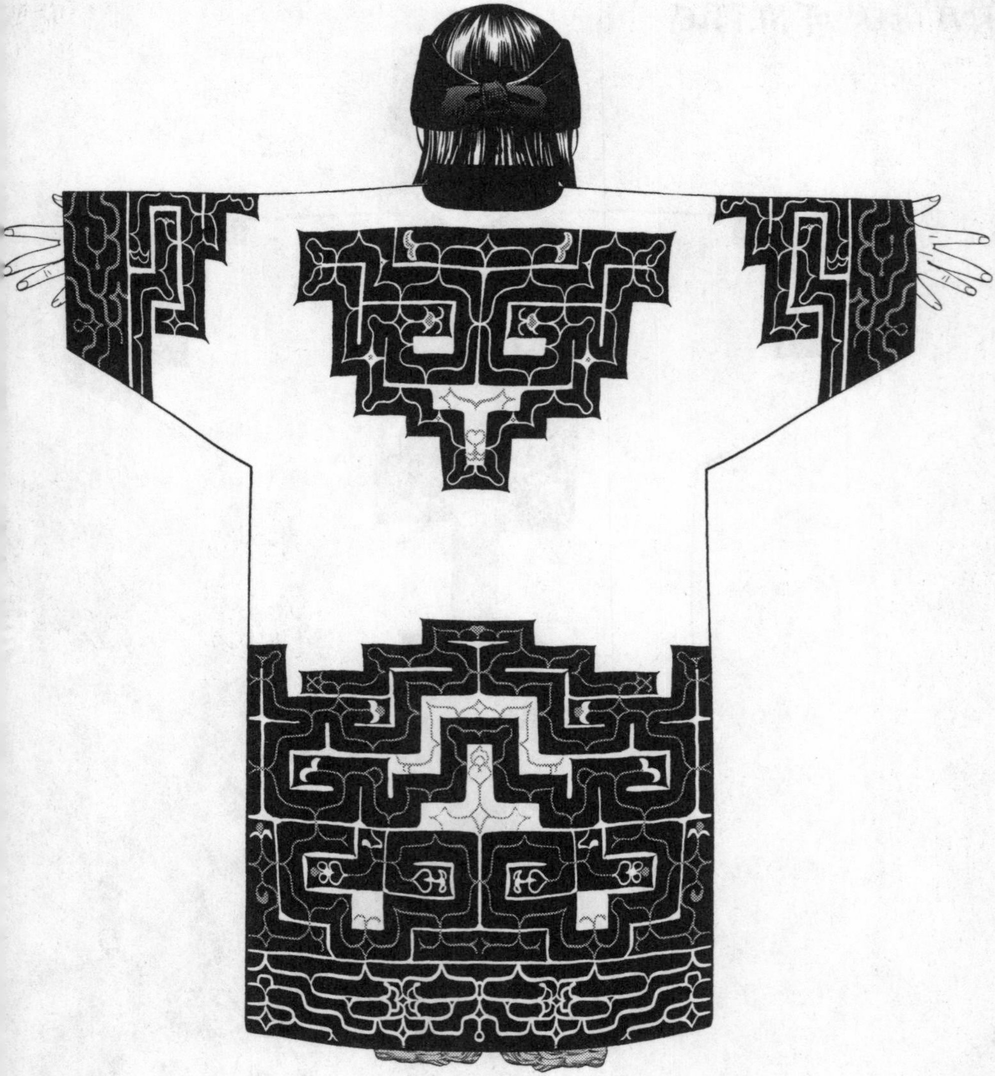

GOLDEN KAMUY

Volume 21
VIZ Signature Edition

Story/Art by Satoru Noda

GOLDEN KAMUY © 2014 by Satoru Noda
All rights reserved.
First published in Japan in 2014 by SHUEISHA Inc., Tokyo.
English translation rights arranged by SHUEISHA Inc.

Translation/John Werry
Touch-Up Art & Lettering/Steve Dutro
Design/Shawn Carrico
Editor/Mike Montesa

Printed in Canada

Published by VIZ Media, LLC
P.O. Box 77010
San Francisco, CA 94107

10 9 8 7 6 5 4 3 2 1
First printing, April 2021

VIZ SIGNATURE

VIZ MEDIA
viz.com

THIS IS THE LAST PAGE.

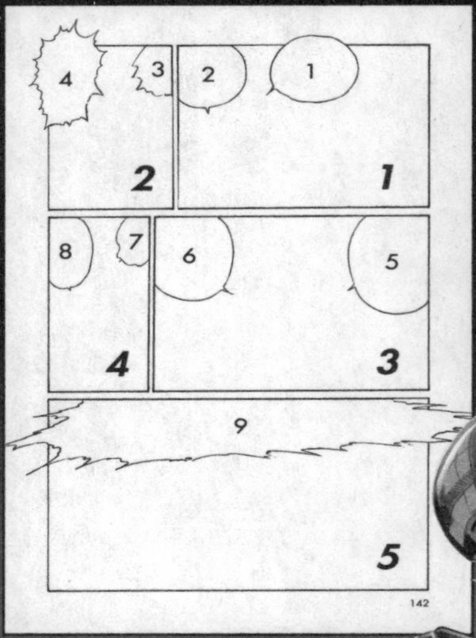

←Follow the action this way.

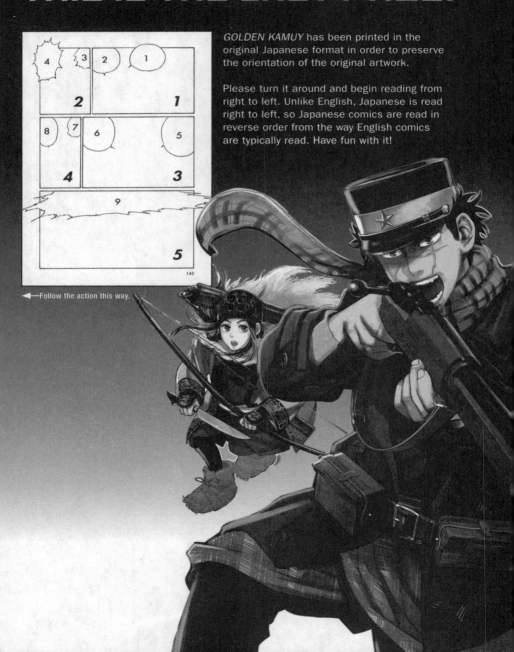

GOLDEN KAMUY has been printed in the original Japanese format in order to preserve the orientation of the original artwork.

Please turn it around and begin reading from right to left. Unlike English, Japanese is read right to left, so Japanese comics are read in reverse order from the way English comics are typically read. Have fun with it!

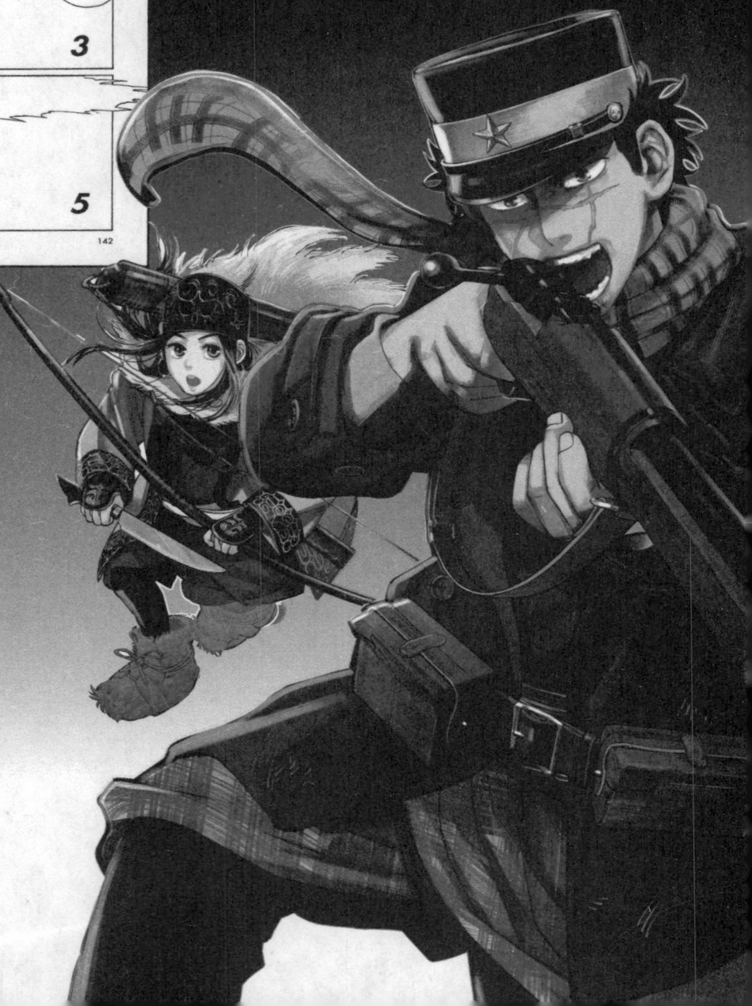